Arab youths

Manchester University Press

Arab youths

Leisure, culture and politics from Morocco to Yemen

Edited by
Laurent Bonnefoy and Myriam Catusse

Originally published in French as

*Jeunesses arabes: Du Maroc au Yémen:
loisirs, cultures et politiques*

MANCHESTER UNIVERSITY PRESS

Copyright © Éditions La Découverte, Paris, France, 2013

While copyright in the volume as a whole is vested in Éditions La Découverte, copyright in individual chapters belongs to their respective authors, and no chapter may be reproduced wholly or in part without the express permission in writing of both author and publisher.

Published by Éditions La Découverte 2013

First English-language edition published in 2023 by
Manchester University Press
Oxford Road, Manchester M13 9PL

www.manchesteruniversitypress.co.uk

British Library Cataloguing-in-Publication Data

A catalogue record for this book is available from the British Library

ISBN 978 1 5261 2745 7 hardback
ISBN 978 1 5261 2747 1 paperback

This edition first published 2023

The publisher has no responsibility for the persistence or accuracy of URLs for any external or third-party internet websites referred to in this book, and does not guarantee that any content on such websites is, or will remain, accurate or appropriate.

Typeset by Deanta Global Publishing Services, Chennai, India

Contents

Contributors		ix
Foreword: Arab youth inside out *François Burgat*		xiv
Note on translation		xvii
General introduction: Deconstructing stereotypes: interwoven trajectories of young Arabs *Laurent Bonnefoy and Myriam Catusse*		1

Part I: Living in the present

Introduction: Living in the present *Laurent Bonnefoy and Myriam Catusse*		19
1	'Go ahead, burn your tyres!': The lust for life of Saudi joyriders *Pascal Menoret*	22
2	'Just watching the time go by': The 'hittists' of Algeria *Loïc Le Pape*	33
3	Coffee shops and youth sociability in Abu Dhabi *Laure Assaf*	43
4	From TV soaps to web dramas: A new platform for young Arabs *Yves Gonzalez-Quijano*	53
5	The *buyat*: Subverting gender norms in Saudi Arabia *Amélie Le Renard*	57

Contents

6 From *jihad* to Sufi ecstasy: Politico-religious trajectories in pre-revolutionary Syria　67
Thomas Pierret

7 The Faculty of Education of Lab'us: Salafism as a student subculture in Yemen　77
Laurent Bonnefoy

8 'A man, a real man!': Halima, a woman rebel in Gafsa (Tunisia)　88
Amin Allal

9 Long-distance supporters: Barca and Real fans in Palestine　93
Abaher El Sakka

10 Commentary in Arabic … or in Tigrinya? Football fans and the search for free television broadcasting　101
Mahfoud Amara and Laurent Bonnefoy

Part II: Rooting the future

Introduction: Rooting the future　109
Laurent Bonnefoy and Myriam Catusse

11 Drinking in Hamra: Youthful nostalgia in Beirut?　112
Nicolas Dot-Pouillard

12 The end of a world? Shifting seasons in Lejnan (Algeria)　121
Mohand Akli Hadibi

13 Finding Baghdad: Young people in search of 'normality'　128
Zahra Ali and Laurent Bonnefoy

14 Two brothers: Family and hospitality in Al-Karak (Jordan)　133
Christine Jungen

15 In Massada Street's coffee shops: The ambiguous social mix of the Palestinians of Israel in Haifa　139
Mariangela Gasparotto

16 In the shade of the *khayma*: Cultural and political resistance of the young Sahrawis at Dakhla　150
Victoria Veguilla Del Moral

Contents

17 Recreation, re-creation, resistance: What roles for *dabke* in Palestine? 160
   Xavier Guignard

18 Taranim and videos: The Egyptian Church stripped bare by its
   children? 170
   Laure Guirguis

19 'My identity is becoming clear like the sun': Theatre in the Shiite
   schools of Lebanon 180
   Catherine Le Thomas

Part III: Constructing oneself

Introduction: Constructing oneself 191
Laurent Bonnefoy and Myriam Catusse

20 'A room of one's own': Young people in search of privacy 194
   Anne-Marie Filaire

21 A different way of being a young woman? Self-defence in Cairo 198
   Perrine Lachenal

22 Chewing alone? The transformations of qat consumption in Yemen 208
   Marine Poirier

23 Gulf holiday-goers in Europe: Five-star family favourites 212
   Claire Beaugrand

24 In SOS Bab-el-Oued: Rappers and rockers between integration
   and transgression 217
   Layla Baamara

25 Leaving the camp: The wanderings of young Palestinian
   refugees in Lebanon 227
   Nicolas Puig

26 'Rainbow Street': The diversity, compartmentalisation and
   assertion of youth in Amman (Jordan) 235
   Cyril Roussel

27 Brahim: Autopsy of a suicide in Kabylia 242
   Kamel Chachoua

Contents

28 '*Bnat lycée dayrin sexy*': From fun to sex work in Tangier (Morocco)   250
    Mériam Cheikh

Part IV: Speaking out

Introduction: Speaking out   263
Laurent Bonnefoy and Myriam Catusse

29 'A bad day for Ammar': When Tunisian bloggers took on Internet censorship   266
    Romain Lecomte

30 A new social world? Young Syrian activists and online social networks   276
    Enrico De Angelis

31 Stand up: Saudi youth take the floor … on YouTube!   285
    Yves Gonzalez-Quijano

32 The café in Jadu: A place for 'revolutionary' emancipation in Libya   289
    Arthur Quesnay

33 From consumerism to political engagement: Young Sunnis in Bahrain react in 'defence of their country' (2011–2012)   293
    Claire Beaugrand

34 When walls speak: Revolutionary street art in Yemen   300
    Anahi Alviso-Marino

35 Art under occupation: The Young Artist of the Year (Palestine)   308
    Marion Slitine

36 'The instinct of rap': Palestinian rap, political contents and artistic explorations   318
    Nicolas Puig

37 Rocking in Morocco: The new urban scene in Casablanca   323
    Dominique Caubet and Catherine Miller

38 Alexandrians in fusion: Trajectories of Egyptian musicians from alternative milieux to the revolution   336
    Youssef El Chazli

Index   347

Contributors

Zahra Ali is a sociologist and assistant professor of sociology at Rutgers University. She is the author of *Women and Gender in Iraq. Between Nation-building and Fragmentation* (Cambridge University Press, 2018).

Amin Allal is a researcher in political sociology at the French Center for Scientific Research (CNRS). He has recently published and co-edited (with L. Baamara, L. Dakhli and G. Fabbiano) *Cheminements révolutionnaires. Un an de mobilisations en Algérie (2019–2020)* (CNRS éditions, 2021) and (with V. Geisser) *Tunisie. Une démocratisation au-dessus de tout soupçon* (CNRS éditions, 2018). His research explores the politics of popular classes, focusing on various scenes of social interactions such as labour mobilisations or 'development' programmes oriented towards the 'poor'.

Anahi Alviso-Marino is a political scientist and scholar-researcher specialising in the political sociology of visual arts in the Arabian Peninsula. She is currently a co-coordinator and postdoctoral fellow at the collective 'Penser l'urbain par l'image', Ecole des Ponts ParisTech/ University Gustave Eiffel.

Mahfoud Amara is currently an associate professor in sport management and social sciences in the Physical Education Department of the College of Education of Qatar University. His publications on sport, business, culture, politics and society in the Arab region include *Sport, Politics and Society in the Arab World* (Palgrave Macmillan, 2012). He recently co-edited with John Nauright *Sport in the African World* (Routledge, 2018) and edited *The Olympic Movement and the Middle East and North Africa Region* (Routledge, 2020).

Contributors

Laure Assaf is an assistant professor of Arab crossroads studies and anthropology at New York University in Abu Dhabi. Her research interests focus on youth, urbanity and migration in contemporary Emirati society and the broader Gulf region.

Layla Baamara is a politicist, postdoctoral researcher (FRS-FNRS, UCLouvain) and specialist in activism, collective action and protest mobilisations in Algeria.

Claire Beaugrand is a CNRS researcher, IRISSO, Université Paris-Dauphine-PSL. She is the author of *Stateless in the Gulf. Migration, Nationality and Society in Kuwait* (IB Tauris, 2018).

Laurent Bonnefoy is a CNRS researcher in political sociology at Sciences Po, Centre de Recherches Internationales in Paris. He is the author of *Salafism in Yemen. Transnationalism and Religious Identity* (Hurst/Columbia University Press, 2011) and more recently of *Yemen and the World. Beyond Insecurity* (Hurst/Oxford University Press, 2018).

François Burgat is a CNRS emeritus researcher. He has recently published *Understanding Political Islam* (Manchester University Press, 2019).

Myriam Catusse is a CNRS research director in political sociology. She currently heads the Institut Français du Proche-Orient in Beirut and is the author of various publications on youth, entrepreneurship and mobilisations, in particular in Lebanon and Morocco.

Dominique Caubet is an emeritus professor in Arabic language at the Institut National des Langues et Civilisations Orientales (Inalco) in Paris. She has published widely on North African dialects.

Kamel Chachoua is an anthropologist and research fellow at the CNRS/IREMAM, Aix-Marseille Université (AMU).

Mériam Cheikh is a lecturer in anthropology at the Department of Arabic Studies of the Institut National des Langues et Civilisations Orientales (Inalco). Her work focuses on sexuality, intimacy and gender relations among working-class youth in Morocco.

Contributors

Enrico De Angelis is an independent researcher focusing on media and journalism in the MENA region. He holds a PhD in media studies and works as a consultant for different organisations such as Free Press Unlimited, International Media Support, Deutsche Welle and others. He is a co-founder of the Syrian independent platform SyriaUntold.

Nicolas Dot-Pouillard is a political advisor at the Center for Humanitarian Dialogue (HD, Genève, Beirut) and Associate Researcher with the French Institute for the Near-East (Ifpo, Beirut).

Youssef El Chazli is an associate professor (MCF) of sociology at the Paris 8 University (Vincennes, Saint-Denis) and an associate researcher at the CEDEJ (Cairo, Egypt).

Abaher El Sakka is an associate professor at the Department of Social and Behavioral Science of Birzeit University in Palestine. His previous research has focused on artistic modes of expression, urban studies and political practices. He is currently working on a social history of Gaza City. The first results were published in a monograph entitled *Gaza. A Social History under British Colonisation, 1917–1947* (The Institute for Palestine Studies, 2018).

Anne-Marie Filaire is a photographer and teacher at the Institut d'Études Politiques de Paris. She has published *Zone de sécurité temporaire* (Textuel/Mucem, 2017), and *Terres, sols profonds du Grand Paris* (La Découverte, 2020).

Mariangela Gasparotto holds a PhD in anthropology and ethnology from the École des Hautes Études en Sciences Sociales, Paris.

Yves Gonzalez-Quijano has taught modern and contemporary Arabic literature at Lyon 2 University. His latest research focuses on digital media and culture and the making of a 'new' Arabness.

Xavier Guignard is a political scientist at Noria Research and a non-resident fellow at CESSP (Paris 1/CNRS).

Laure Guirguis is currently a fellow at the Aarhus Institute of Advanced Studies (October 2019–October 2022) and an associate researcher at the IREMAM-AMU. She has published *Copts and the Security State. Violence, Coercion*

Contributors

and Sectarianism in Contemporary Egypt (Stanford University Press, 2016) and edited *The Arab Lefts. Histories and Legacies, 1950s–1970s* (Edinburgh University Press, 2020). She is now engaged in a new project on culture and politics in Arab–Latin American spaces.

Mohand Akli Hadibi, a graduate of the EHESS in Paris, is currently a professor of anthropology of Islamized Berber societies at the University Mouloud Mammeri of Tizi Ouzou (Algeria). His research focuses on cognitive and religious anthropology, the sociology of the family, youth and civic practices.

Christine Jungen is a research fellow at the CNRS, Laboratoire d'Ethnologie et de Sociologie Comparative (LESC), France.

Perrine Lachenal is a French social anthropologist specialising in gender studies. She works as a CNRS researcher at the CNE (Centre Norbert Elias) in Marseille.

Romain Lecomte is a researcher at the University of Liège. He focuses on the effects of information technologies on mobilisations in North Africa.

Loïc Le Pape is a lecturer/assistant professor in political science at the University Paris 1 Panthéon-Sorbonne. He is a member of the CESSP (European Center for Sociology and Political Science, UMR8209, CNRS-EHESS-Univ Paris 1).

Amélie Le Renard is a permanent research fellow at CNRS, Paris. In English, she has published *A Society of Young Women. Opportunities of Place, Power and Reform in Saudi Arabia* (Stanford University Press, 2014) and *Western Privilege. Work, Intimacy and Postcolonial Hierarchies In Dubai* (Stanford University Press, 2021).

Catherine Le Thomas holds a PhD in political sociology. She has published *Les Écoles chiites au Liban. Construction communautaire et mobilisation politique* (Karthala, 2012).

Pascal Menoret is the Renée and Lester Crown Professor of Modern Middle East Studies at Brandeis University, United States.

Catherine Miller is a CNRS research director at the IREMAM in Aix-en-Provence. She works on the politics of dialects and nationalism in North Africa.

Contributors

Thomas Pierret is a senior researcher at Aix Marseille University, CNRS, IREMAM, Aix-en-Provence, France. He focuses on politics and religion in modern Syria. His publications include *Religion and State in Syria. The Sunni Ulama from Coup to Revolution* (Cambridge University Press, 2013) and *Ethnographies of Islam. Ritual Performances and Everyday Practices* (Edinburgh University Press, 2012).

Marine Poirier is a CNRS research fellow in political science, affiliated to the IREMAM at Aix-Marseille University in France. She studies political elites in contexts of crisis, armed conflict and regime change, mainly in the Yemeni case. Among her latest publications is 'This charming sheikh. Constructing and defending notability in Yemen (2009–2019)', *Critique internationale*, 2020.

Nicolas Puig is a researcher in anthropology at Unité de Recherche Migrations et Sociétés (IRD, CNRS, University of Paris). In Egypt and Lebanon, he studies the fabric of urban environments and the relationships between music, sound practices, urban cultures and politics.

Arthur Quesnay holds a PhD in political science from Panthéon-Sorbonne University. He has published *La guerre civile irakienne. Ordres partisans et politiques identitaires à Kirkouk* (Karthala, 2021) and co-authored with Adam Baczko and Gilles Dorronsoro *Civil War in Syria. Mobilization and Competing Social Orders* (Cambridge University Press, 2017).

Cyril Roussel is a CNRS researcher in geography, currently based in Erbil at the Institut Français du Proche-Orient. Since 1997, he has been working on the relationship between identity and territory, on migration dynamics and on the effects of boundaries and discontinuities (economical, social, cultural borders) in Syria and Iraq.

Marion Slitine is an anthropologist and a postdoctoral fellow at EHESS (School of Advanced Studies in Social Sciences, Centre Norbert Elias), in association with the MUCEM (Museum of Europe and European Civilisation) in Marseille (France).

Victoria Veguilla Del Moral is a professor in political science at Pablo D'Olavide University in Sevilla.

Foreword: Arab youth inside out

François Burgat

In 2013, the authors of this book gave voice to young people of both sexes living in seventeen countries in a predominantly Arabic-speaking but multicultural and geographically diverse area. The blasé tourist from the Persian Gulf visiting Europe, the Palestinian refugee dreaming only of getting out of his camp, the Baghdadi out for a stroll knocking against the confessional walls of his urban confinement, the Libyan militiaman discovering the charms of socialisation not connected with war in cafés that were long out of bounds, Algerian '*hittists*' exorcising their discontent through rigorist religiosity, artists and athletes – all have expectations and trajectories whose differences are hard to summarise.

The foreword writer must consequently refrain from doing what Laurent Bonnefoy and Myriam Catusse have so carefully avoided. Without oversimplifying, there is no way to define the limits of the infinite diversity of mindsets and practices of 'Arab youth' in this century, nor to conclude from it some trends hastily labelled as 'dominant', a designation that would enable us to predict the 'Arab world of tomorrow', preferably in a reassuring way.

The value nonetheless remains in learning about this fine sample of humanity. The novel choice of pastimes as a prism, rather than that of political socialisation or modes of potential involvement in a rebellion, updates classical politological approaches. But the primary value of these pages, written in a highly accessible style, lies perhaps elsewhere. What were the 'Arab youth' of 2013 trying to say to the world? Nothing – or not much in any case – of what we so often want them to say or think we have heard them say!

That is the first benefit of the patient gathering of information and enlightening construction by Laurent Bonnefoy, Myriam Catusse and their co-authors, who bring us closer to the actors' experience and their astonishing diversity. The book is enriched

Foreword: Arab youth inside out

above all through overcoming reductive biases and other widespread fallacies that have flourished since 2011, whenever 'Arab youth' has been invoked to lend meaning to the 'spring' of the same name and to the whole spectrum of transformations initiated by the protests. Many observers have given in to an old reflex of oversimplification, even more damaging than the 'cult of youth' that Régis Debray tackled with humour, claiming the right to maturity, and passion in recalling the Vichy[1] regime's fascination with that 'cult of youth' during Second World War France.

Western man's relationship with the Muslim 'other', especially its disconcerting male component – 'Rachid and his mates', the disturbing throng of adult Muslim males – has always been difficult. But we might be able to get along with his wife Rachida, or better yet, his daughter, and more generally with the young Muslim women only waiting for our support (disinterested, naturally) to free themselves from the violence and machismo of their fathers, brothers and husbands! The fascination in the West with religious minorities, Christian or otherwise, who share our anxiety faced with the 'overly robust' demographics of the Muslim majority, undoubtedly comes from that same paradigm.

As with 'gender', the generational variable all too often fosters wishful thinking by observers. With 'Arab youth', the hope springs up insidiously of seeing the dissolution of these cultural – and even more, religious – 'atavisms', which have long made the coexistence problematic between the northern shore and the southern and eastern shores of the 'Arab' Mediterranean.

This study conducted 'as closely as possible to the actors' experience' vividly confirms that Arab youths from one country and social category to another are not monolithic. Their leisure activities can be transgressive, such as the Saudis' *tafhit* car races, the tomboyishness of their '*buya*' sisters, the virile courage of a Tunisian woman or the outspokenness about morality of certain female students in Morocco. They can also be mundanely artistic or playful – from rock and rap to *dabke* (folk dancing) – or, less mundanely, religious.

But there's more. These youths cannot be reduced to any cultural or ideological atavism, especially not to those that serve to construct dichotomies (Islamist/secular even more so than working class/bourgeois) which often seem to be a foregone conclusion to the media. The authors fortunately remind us that 'leisure activities gravitating around religion distance us […] from a simplistic approach counter-posing "two classes of youth" – the one student and bourgeois, the other labouring and popular' (see page 9). As Pierre Bourdieu reminded us, 'youth is only a word'.

'Youths' – in the plural here – often prefer to reinterpret, reconstruct or recompose their social and cultural heritage rather than bury it. The vectors

Foreword: Arab youth inside out

and modalities of socialisation change more surely than their inescapable centrality in the passage to adulthood. In Yemen, people are seen chewing *qat* here and there alone – the better to stare at a tablet connecting them to a world whose horizons are much broader than the *maqiyal* where their fathers withdrew to consume it. The new technologies, from cars and cell phones to the whole range of cybercommunications – including the magical Bluetooth that allows you in a confined space to contact a thrillingly unknown neighbour while feasting your eyes on them – drive us rather unsurprisingly towards more individualised forms of behaviours, the better to join these barely released atoms in networks as structuring as those jeopardised by technology.

How then can we find out what these young people 'hold in store for us'? First, by 'avoiding viewing them through platitudes', then by going out to discover their everyday lives, learn their languages, decode their old and new rituals and understand their impatience – and also, by analysing our own fears and, through that, convincing ourselves that the sometimes joyful and sometimes anxious, sometimes familiar and sometimes distant humanity of these 'Arab youths' cannot be restricted by often misleading analytical perspectives – from observers neither Arab nor young – generated by the destabilising upheavals of globalisation and the passage of time.

That is why this book is a must-read for all who wish to better understand the reality of societies that have experienced unprecedented upheavals since 2011. Beyond their diverse approaches, the authors, brought together here thanks to the remarkable coordination of Laurent Bonnefoy and Myriam Catusse, share precisely these concerns. Their number, as well as the quality, of their contributions testifies to another important generational renewal – of young researchers who are highly knowledgeable about the countries where they live (or have lived), who speak the language fluently, and are now far more numerous than their elders. I hope this is proof that 'a different outlook' can finally be posited in the face of detrimental oversimplification by proponents of the 'clash of civilisations'.

Note

1 Régis Debray, *Le Bel Âge*, Flammarion, Paris, 2013.

Note on translation

The completion of the translation of this edited volume owes much to the tenacity of three people who, despite numerous mishaps, have kept faith with the project until the end. Together with Miriam Périer, who is in charge of English publications at the Centre for International Studies at Sciences Po (CERI), Laurent Bonnefoy and Myriam Catusse embody the most essential aspects of the role of book editors: conviction of the scientific interest of the project and tenacity. The book has been translated by several people, over several years: Malcolm Imrie and Martina Dervis (Part I introduction, Chapters 2–8, 10–18, 20–21, 23, 30–32, 34–36), Gregory Elliott (General introduction, Chapter 9), Andrew Withaker (Chapters 28, 29), William Snow (Foreword, Parts II–IV introductions, Chapters 19, 22, 24–27) and Laurent Bonnefoy (Chapters 33, 37, 38). Chapter 1 was provided by the author, Pascal Menoret. For their patience, we thank Manchester University Press, and for their funding, we thank the Centre for International Studies (CERI Sciences Po-CNRS) and IREMAM (Aix).

General introduction

Deconstructing stereotypes: interwoven trajectories of young Arabs

Laurent Bonnefoy and Myriam Catusse[1]

During the 2011 overthrow of four aged autocrats, 'young Arabs' became the modern heroes of 'malcontents' the world over. To a large extent, a decade later, their figure has also come to symbolise the failed promises of political uprisings and also, to some extent, of the path to democracy. Occupying the squares of Tunis, Cairo, Sana'a or Manama, they were then to be seen demonstrating under colourful banners, becoming Internet activists and, in some instances, taking up arms. Their mobilisation became a structuring generational moment, highlighting social trends and fault lines that still bear meaning now. These young men and women embodied the revolt of 'peoples' on the move behind the ideals of freedom and justice.

At the time, some became spokespersons of this historical moment. The Yemeni Tawakkul Karman, born in 1979, was joint winner of the Nobel Peace Prize in 2011. Born in 1983, the Tunisian blogger Lina Ben Mhenni, author of the publishing success *Tunisian Girl*, became the muse of a revolution for a while. She died in 2020 of chronic kidney failure. In 2011, Egyptian Google employee and cyber dissident Wael Ghonim, born in 1980, came top of *Time* magazine's list of the 100 most influential people in the world, only to recover anonymity in exile. As for the militant Egyptian feminist Alia Magda al-Mahdi, born in 1991, she posted herself *au naturel* on the Internet to protest against religious puritanism and male domination. This daring publication forced her to relocate to Sweden.

Other young people were inadvertent heralds of the revolution. Anonymous for the most part, the martyrs of these uprisings were mourned in their families, districts, towns and villages. Some, however, became icons of revolutionaries throughout the Arab world and beyond: Mohammed Bouazizi, born in 1984, whose immolation in Sidi Bouzid in Tunisia was the spark that ignited things; Khaled Said, born in 1982, who died at the hands of the Egyptian police in

General introduction

Alexandria; or Hamza al-Khatib, born in 1997, who was tortured by the Syrian forces of law and order.

Before these uprisings, people were often to be heard deploring the fact that the Arab world resisted the waves of democratisation observed elsewhere – Latin America or Eastern Europe – and seemed impervious to the 'positive globalisation' articulated by the liberal vulgate. Using and abusing clichés that have been deconstructed many times,[2] certain media and experts, Arab or otherwise, thus doomed the region to a quagmire of 'misfortunes'. The 11 September 2001 events and the 'war on terrorism' launched by George W. Bush did not resolve things. Other images were diffused and took hold in collective imaginaries, especially Western ones: those of any 'Arab youth' as a potential terrorist. 'Educated', 'urban' and 'modern', but 'indoctrinated' or 'frustrated' by economic, political and social crises, the new Arab generations appeared to be an inexhaustible breeding ground of budding criminals.[3]

Contradicting Orientalist stereotypes, the 'Arab uprisings', elevated into models of democratic mobilisation since 2011, thus brought new figures to the fore, who were for a period of time celebrated even in the suburbs of Tel Aviv and in central Manhattan and Istanbul. Far from being isolated and well beyond the pessimism linked to the development of the so-called 'Islamic State', young Arabs demonstrated a remarkable capacity for influencing the world. Challenging in conjunction with their elders the autocrats who ruled – or still do rule – their countries, some of them suddenly found themselves projected into the vanguard of global cultural phenomena. Indicative of this is the way 'Leave!' (*irhal*) became the slogan of the year in 2011, well beyond the borders of the 'Arab world'. This dynamic lived on. Political contestation continued in Algeria, Sudan, Iraq, Morocco, Lebanon, Oman and Palestine well into the new 2020 decade. The diagnosed failure of the 'Arab Spring' is more ambivalent than it is frequently assessed.

Faced with this waltz of images, mixing the metaphor of 'awakening'[4] with reference to a radical and violent habitus, the idea for this book germinated out of a desire to speak of young Arabs differently from conventional discourses. Ten years after the project was first imagined, this ambition remains more relevant than ever. This publication produced a series of snapshots, well ordered and meaningful, that continue to help us understand contemporary societies in the Middle East and North Africa. They could be completed with portraits of the new generation. To do this, thirty researchers agreed to share their appetite for observation and intimate knowledge of the field to help people see and understand, 'from the inside' and on the basis of their concrete experience,

General introduction

what the youths in Arab countries have been living through before, during and right after the revolutionary uprisings.

Shaking up clichés about 'Arabs'

But who precisely are we talking about when we refer to 'young Arabs'? It would be hard to paint an objective portrait of this generation, given that the predicates 'young' and 'Arab' refer to disparate realities and involve common fallacies.

Let us consider 'Arabs', first of all. Politically speaking, the Arab world is traditionally defined by twenty or so states (the Arab League contains twenty-two), representing a population of 350 million inhabitants and a surface area of thirteen million square kilometres, extending from the Atlantic shores of Mauritania to the Arab-Persian Gulf, from the Syrian Mediterranean coast to the coasts of Somalia or even the Comoros. Four major entities are often distinguished geographically, ecologically and by their common history: the Maghreb (literally the 'west'), the Nile Valley, the Middle East and the Arabian Peninsula. Their economic destinies are sometimes diametrically opposed, with Qatar and the United Arab Emirates among the richest countries in the world, thanks to the godsend of oil or gas, while Yemen and Sudan are among the poorest.

Urbanisation of the region exploded in the course of the twentieth century, to the point where nearly half of its population now lives in massive metropolises (Cairo officially has more than twenty million inhabitants, Baghdad eight million and Casablanca four million) or in small and medium-sized towns. This situation creates new divides: while gaps between urban districts are growing, rural and agrarian societies are marginalised. In a way, it's time to talk to Arab Youth as a new kind of precariat.[5] Another arresting feature is that contemporary Arab societies are experiencing significant flows of migrants – a phenomenon involving younger generations in particular. Added to internal displacement, attributable to rural exodus and the conflicts tearing some countries apart, is emigration to Europe or America, but also – especially in the case of the Lebanese – to Africa or Australia and, in many cases, other countries in the Arab world, where the rentier economies of some attract the workforce of others.

Although often described in terms of its Islamic-Arabness, the region is pluralistic culturally. Islam is the principal religion, in its various schisms (Sunni and Shiite, essentially). But the many Christian Churches also count believers,

General introduction

as does Judaism – even if Arab Jews have emigrated *en masse* to Israel or elsewhere during the twentieth century – and other minorities. While Arabic, the language of revelation of the Koran, has nurtured a shared sense of identity, particularly since the nineteenth century and the region's cultural renaissance (*nahda*), it has numerous dialects and, along with the penetration of foreign languages such as English or French, there are multiple instances of diglossia – that is, the co-existence of a written language and local dialects on the same territory. 'Ethnic' or community identities are just as varied, with, for example, the Berber or Tuareg worlds in the Maghreb, the Kurdish populations in the Middle East and, in many cases, 'tribal', community or confessional solidarities that continue to be vigorously expressed.

'Being Arab'[6] is therefore defined unequivocally in the plural. That is why we have opted to follow 'youths' in eighteen countries, from Morocco to Yemen, who live in the city or the countryside, in different social conditions – and, depending on the case, in situations of violent conflict or relative peace.

Shaking up clichés about 'youth'

Defining the 'young' (in Arab, *shabab* in the plural and *shab* in the singular) is not easy either. The diagnosis of young Arabs is generally far from optimistic: they embody as much as they are the victims of several generations of political failure.[7] While the demographic transition began several decades ago in most Arab countries,[8] it has occurred at very different speeds. The fertility rate among Tunisian women has fallen by 70 per cent in sixty years (from 7.18 children per woman in 1960 to 2.17 in 2020), but by only 40 per cent in Yemen (from 7.29 in 1960 to 3.5 in 2020). Arab societies, which come just behind those of sub-Saharan Africa in this domain, remain characterised by their youthfulness: nearly half the Yemeni population is under sixteen years of age, while the same proportion of the population of Qatar – the 'oldest' Arab society – is under thirty. By way of comparison, the median age in France and Japan is respectively 39.7 and 44.6. Through these figures, we get a glimpse in these countries of the pressure on the job and housing markets, as in the health or education sectors – areas that now appear to be in a 'critical' situation as shown during the COVID-19 pandemic. Thus governments since 2011 have been claiming to act in favour of youth, developing public policies that directly target this group, often suppressing political rights to supposedly favour economic development.[9] Their international partners are fine with that.[10] More often than not, they are empty shells, heavily politicised but with little means. In practice, they obscure the 'problems of the youth' by highlighting 'youth as a problem'. The most brutal example is the Saudi Crown Prince, Muhammad bin Salman, whose vision claims to transform society, in particular through a leisure-based economy, for the benefit of the younger generations he claims to represent, being born in 1985.

Different, less heroic images of young Arabs than those evoked here and which were in connection with the '2011 revolutions' continue structurally to prevail. Even if the statistics need to be qualified, with employment often being informal and the absence of 'unemployment' benefits complicating measurement, the region is the lowest ranked in the world in terms of youth employment. On average, 25 per cent of fifteen- to twenty-five-year-olds are without work, with marked disparities in terms of both geography and gender. The failure of employment and education policies has thus become embodied over the last decade in the emblematic figure of the 'unemployed graduate'.

Employment is not the only source of anxiety. The entrenchment of the status of 'single person' attests to a crisis of marriage associated not so much with disaffection with the institution as with the material difficulties encountered by young couples in setting up homes, with all the frustrations this can create. In the 1960s, the average age of first marriage ranged from eighteen to twenty-one in most countries. Today, with the exception of Yemen, where it remains low, it has risen, exceeding twenty-seven in Algeria, Tunisia, Egypt, Libya and Qatar. The crisis of confidence experienced by the new generations, frequently dramatised by literature, cinema and the arts, has led to the emergence of numerous neologisms, such as '*hittists*', who literally 'lean against walls' in Algeria waiting for time to pass, or the '*harraga*' in the Maghreb, who burn (*harraq*) their identity papers so as to cross the Mediterranean in search of a better future, becoming stateless so as to not be sent back 'home'.

Going beyond the figures and stereotypical images that often underpin discourse on young Arabs, we therefore need new words and new viewpoints to 'shake up' the clichés and to speak differently about those who, from Morocco to the Arabian Peninsula, from Syria to Sudan, are living through this doubly singular era from day to day. It is first of all singular as regards the personal trajectory of every young Arab – their progressive entry into the adult world and the interactions they generate with older and younger individuals – but singular also from a collective and generational standpoint, on account of the upheavals that they triggered in a wide range of the societies studied, which made this youth unique.

General introduction

Attending to a generation

Make no mistake about it. Behind the sudden subversion of clichés generated by political events (which was temporary, as attested by the resurgence of talk about Islamist 'winters' or the success of reactionary projects such as those supported by the Gulf monarchies in countries which experienced uprisings), more muted, more gradual, more uncertain processes should hold our attention. The year 2011's blast of air had the great virtue of contradicting the voices that interminably describe Arab societies as sleeping beauties on the margins of history. But it would be equally absurd to examine the region exclusively through the optic of the 'cult of youth', 'modernity', 'innovation' or permanent 'revolt'.

Rather than focus arbitrarily on a cohort of individuals of the same biological age, this book seeks to arrive at a better appreciation of the diversity of the condition of 'youth' via practices, habits and forms of behaviour – banal and everyday for some, exceptional and disconcerting for others – observable in the Arab world. Obviously, common bounds impart a framework to such observation. But these demarcations remain fluid because they are anchored in social relations. While sexual awakening can, for example, embody youth's 'entry' into the world – in different ways for girls and boys – the horizon of marriage, becoming established in a job and the prospect of autonomy represent 'role switches' or modes of 'exit'. These milestones at once indicate a term – the end of childhood, the transition to the adult world – and a projection towards a future that is desired or feared. If, more than any other stage of life, 'youth' appears to be a transition, the duration of the transition is all the more variable as starting a family is deferred, time spent studying increases and the experience of unemployment and waiting becomes the norm.[11] Often marked by changes in circumstances, with (for some social classes) entry into university and (in some countries still) military conscription, the time of 'youth' tends to stretch out and, ultimately, can encompass those approaching forty. This is a development that tacitly calls into question traditional rites of passage.

In order to disrupt ready-made ideas, particularly those of an Arab youth in the singular, which is by turns apathetic, unemployed and émigré or, conversely, revolutionary, modern, democratic and enterprising, we have therefore explored the varied universes in which Arab youth have evolved. The last decades have been profoundly marked, on the one hand, by rising tensions inworld in general, and the region in particular, represented by the attacks on the United States of 11 September 2001 and the ensuing war in Iraq; and, on the other, by the uprisings and revolutionary processes initiated in 2011, which overthrew some

General introduction

regimes and destabilised others. During this era of changes, which sounded the knell signalling the end of the regimes issuing from nationalist movements and then the resilience and reinvention of authoritarian systems, we have explored what has changed and what persists, superficially but also more profoundly, by focusing on the new generations.

To understand what has been being played out since the start of the 2000s, the authors who have participated in this project have got as close as possible to the realities experienced by young Arabs. Their sources vary: some have long been engaged in research of which they offer us a glimpse here; others, familiar with these countries, their languages and customs, have embarked on new investigations with undisguised enthusiasm. Some share their insider knowledge with us, mobilising their own experience as children, adolescents and young adults, who 'grew up' *in situ* and are returning as observers. Others are fellow travellers with those of whom they speak and with whom they have lived, demonstrated or played music. Yet others adopt the perspective of the ethnographer surprised or intrigued by the behaviour he or she is observing. The wonderful discoveries that have emerged from this work evince, if need be, the extreme creativity not only of Arab youth but also of research on the Arab world.

We are not the first – far from it – to take an interest in 'Arab youth'. In addition to employment, most recent research work on the theme has studied their relationship to identity and political commitment.[12] The last decade has also been a time of increased reflection on the varied effects of national and international youth policies in the region.

In the early 1990s, Mounia Bennani-Chraïbi's detailed work brought out the 'mutant' character of young Moroccans, who were experiencing profound changes in terms of identity and religion.[13] This lead was followed in numerous other publications, including some which were published after the original, French, version of our book hit the market.[14] Several showed how religious practices in the region were becoming personalised.[15] Others focused on everyday practices and the emergence of specific youth cultures, often in connection with global trends and networks.[16] In the same vein, rationales for migration, relations to other horizons and the experience of deracination (lived and imaginary) were carefully explored, both by the research community and by the arts, cinema and music. In the case of those who do not travel, their 'imagined communities' often transcend national boundaries, as attested by their identification with international causes or heroes, like Osama Bin Laden in sometimes equivocal fashion or the Argentinian footballer Lionel Messi.

General introduction

As for the relationship to politics, it yields ambivalent perspectives. While some have long deplored young Arabs' low degree of mobilisation, others have carefully examined new forms of commitment, not without questioning their singular, even sensational, forms – particularly when they have taken a religious form. In any event, the voices of politics are not monopolised by ageing leaders but make themselves heard, on lower or higher frequency, in numerous sites given over to youth, whether universities, campuses, music groups, sports clubs and so on.[17]

Observing social changes on an ongoing basis

For our part, in order to appreciate what young Arabs are experiencing outside worksites and places of political engagement, we have opted to turn our gaze towards free time, the time of 'leisure'. In French and English, the term derives from the Latin *licere* (to be permitted). In Arabic, it might be translated by *tasliya* which, etymologically, refers to consolation and diversion. In other words, 'leisure' is to be considered in its broadest, most commonplace sense, going beyond the study of cultivated forms of distraction *stricto sensu* (reading, music, cinema, the arts).[18] In fact, what we wish to understand is what is going on in interstices rarely put under the spotlight – those moments of youth which are not only 'moratory'[19] but also 'probationary'.[20] Far from being suspended, free time, more readily rendered in Arabic by the phrase *waqt faragh* (empty time), is the opportunity for individual and collective experiences which, in conjunction, go to make a 'generation'. Despite major cleavages – of gender, geographical provenance, social or 'ethnic' origin – certain common features attest to the social changes being experienced by young Arabs in the aftermath of the supposedly foundational moment of the 'Arab springs' that ten years later continue to resonate.

The everyday existence of many of them is divided between schooling or professional training and 'time left over'. Because of mass unemployment, the latter, far from being residual, plays a key role in the lives of youth. With schools and universities going online due to the COVID-19 pandemic for over a year, the centrality of these moments was only reinforced.[21] But they use, perceive, endure or invest this 'free time' in their own fashion, disclosing often different but sometimes common ways of constructing themselves as individuals, grasping gender relations and integrating into social relations. The authors of this book invite us to this interplay of differences and similarities when they describe

General introduction

the exhilarating speed of the Saudi joyrider, the enforced, endured waiting of the Algerian 'hittist', the nocturnal drifting of a Moroccan secondary schoolgirl, the acting classes of Lebanese Shiite pupils, the dance steps of Palestinian adolescents and so on. In some cases, 'pure pleasure', recreation, is hedonistic and ludic. Alternatively liberating or alienating, it can border on high-risk behaviour, flirt with suicidal tendencies and involve temporary liberation from social norms. In other cases, 'good leisure' is supervised, even 'disciplined', and then assumes a more 'pedagogical' significance.

Studying the leisure activities of the young makes it possible to observe the sometimes well-nigh imperceptible social changes affecting Arab societies on an ongoing basis. The various kinds of relationships to 'free time' do not always pertain to a straightforward opposition between 'mass culture' and 'elite culture'. We shall see that the different ways in which the new generations fill this 'empty time' correspond to more or less conscious logics of social distinction, which are not restricted to a class dichotomy. Individualist consumerism, traditionally associated with 'leisure', is first and foremost a characteristic of wealthy societies like the Gulf rentier states. But 'mass' culture, which is too often opposed to 'traditional culture', and whose standardisation supposedly betrays a 'Westernisation of the world' (e.g. with the proliferation of international restaurant or café chains), is not confined to the middle and upper classes.

Similarly, leisure activities gravitating around religion distance us, as enjoined by Pierre Bourdieu, from a simplistic approach counter-posing 'two classes of youth' – the one student and bourgeois, the other labouring and popular.[22] The same is true of the significant development of 'religious' tourism and 'pious' forms of entertainment. For Lebanon's Shiites, new restaurants and leisure centres eclectically combining religious references, Arab and Lebanese, or museums and popular exhibitions devoted to commemorating Hezbollah's anti-Israeli 'resistance' – these are intended for all social classes.[23] In the case of Sunni Muslims, the same applies to controversial plans for a theme park near Mecca devoted to the Prophet Muhammad.

If class relations manifest themselves in the way that the new generations fill their 'free time', it would be a pity to restrict ourselves to this interpretative grid and set aside other cleavages, which are sometimes subtly intertwined. This is what we shall find throughout the book, in the ways the young in the Arab world move in urban space, appropriate digital devices, mobilise for international sporting competitions or engage in artistic work (plastic arts, rap, street art, dancing, etc.).

General introduction

Leisure between discipline and dissidence

To speak of 'free' time is not to imply that individuals are left to themselves. Various institutions – schools, churches, mosques, clubs, etc. – seek to supervise leisure time, either in order to escort personal fulfilment or, on the contrary, to curb it.[24] A detour via the history of the advent of leisure in Europe affords some interesting perspectives.[25] The 'institutionalisation' of leisure activities played a leading role, making it possible for different social structures – state, religious, associational, partisan – to 'discipline' youth and free time: such institutionalisation 'counter-posed arranged time in monitored spaces to a time given over to the happenstance of encounters and neighbourhood'.[26] In the Arab world, by contrast, the institutionalisation of leisure remains comparatively weak. Given the authoritarian nature of these regimes, this might seem surprising. The social history of leisure in the region is still in its infancy, but it seems that the public authorities have, with a few exceptions such as the experiment of the youth centres set up by the Nasser regime in Egypt or the Lion Cubs of Saddam (*Ashbal Saddam*) in Iraq, only invested the field of childhood and youth to a modest extent. When they have done so, such experiments in 'supervision' have been failures, giving rise to '"mass" movements with feet of clay'.[27]

School and university play an ambivalent role in their relationship with 'free time'. They limit its scope via the education they provide, but at the same time 'supervise' and escort leisure via extra-curricular activities. According to UNESCO data, the Maghreb currently educates its children more (91 per cent) than the Middle East (84 per cent) and the Arabian Peninsula (65 per cent). Tunisia is the only Arab country to ensure universal primary school education, but Algeria, Egypt, Bahrain, Iraq, Jordan and Syria also post encouraging figures (from 93 to 98 per cent of children). It remains the case that this schooling is often erratic: public education systems are undergoing profound crises,[28] private education is expensive and, in some countries, like Yemen, political and social instability leads to 'lost years'. For that matter, the effects of the COVID-19 pandemic are yet to be measured. Such difficulties extend the duration of studies when they do not result in their pure and simple abandonment.

If the institutionalisation of leisure is relatively weak in Arab countries, this is also because the associational fabric (youth clubs, etc.) is lacking in density and financial resources. Obviously, for young boys in particular, sports clubs and scouting remain favoured structures for supervising entertainment, including at very local levels. But the institutionalisation of these structures is ultimately discrete and often down to the private sector or, increasingly, foreign partners.

General introduction

As for the 'churches', the non-centralisation of Sunni Muslim religious authority can impede the institutionalisation of activities, in particular during summer holidays centred on religious instruction. The atomisation of initiatives organised around mosques, as well as intra-religious rivalries, have long limited the effectiveness of such processes, which are sometimes burgeoning, but largely in privatised form, as indicated by the enthusiasm aroused by new forms of Islamic preachers – embodying what the sociologist Patrick Haenni called 'market Islam'[29] – and, more generally, by political and religious associations or, in Christianity, by charismatic movements.

If institutions aimed at 'supervising' youth development (so as to guide personal fulfilment, but also to enrol) prove deficient, opportunities for 'time to oneself' are not plentiful since they are subject to a large number of constraints. The family, which imposes sometimes onerous norms, frequently remains decisive in controlling behaviour, especially in the case of women. Moreover, a lack of money or appropriate venues limits people's ability to experience a certain personal or collective freedom in and through leisure activities. The street, cafés, bars and, increasingly, the Internet consequently represent privileged spaces of potential emancipation. While we must be careful not to conceal the hierarchies that develop and the social struggles that unfold in these spaces, which are sometimes crisscrossed by ennui, their disorganised aspect allows a section of youth to experiment with more or less muffled forms of dissidence. In these interstices, the observer can thus study the emergence of 'sub-cultures' that polarise everyday time and help to define the boundaries of an in-group and, sometimes, to widen the gulf between generations. Artistic creation is a remarkable observation post in this regard,[30] especially in its radical and avant-garde dimension. It has formed the subject of several studies in the region, the most emblematic of which is doubtless *Heavy Metal Islam* by Mark Levine, himself a historian and rock guitarist.[31]

Four lines of tension

Studying the way that young generations in the Arab world fill their leisure time therefore seemed to us an experience rich in lessons for understanding the economic, social and political upheavals affecting these societies or, conversely, the perpetuation of ways of being and acting. They are indubitable social and spatial indicators, but complex ones. The thirty-eight chapters that make up this book are not intended to be exhaustive. To each young person, it might be

General introduction

said, his or her own leisure activity. That is why we have chosen to proceed by switching the spotlight from one country to another, from city to countryside, from popular to privileged milieux. In the texts that make up this book, some terrains are more worked than others. Some forms of leisure remain difficult to apprehend – drug-taking and artificial paradises, for example, or filling 'free' time in war situations. We have also opted not to dwell on the young people, fleeting in every sense of the word, who embark on small boats in search of a better future. This theme, abundantly treated elsewhere, nevertheless crops up more or less explicitly in various of the following texts.

While not all the leisure activities described are destined to receive approval or elicit sympathy, especially when they betray particularly conservative worldviews, none of them is to be criminalised. The contributors to this book are not censors, but observers and analysts who apprehend the social world as it was in a particular historical context. As they succeed one another, the chapters also blur the boundary that is too often imposed separating 'indigenous' practices from putatively 'imported' ones, particularly from the 'West'. Depending on one's viewpoint, the latter are progressive and respectful of individuals and liberties or, on the contrary, illegitimate and destabilising. We are much more concerned with offering a nuanced analysis of societies where local, community, national and global dimensions are constantly intertwined.

Since the original publication of this volume in French in 2013, things have not been at a standstill. The trends that highlighted the tensions between generations and with institutions have only become more explicit, even in Tunisia which was, for a decade, rightly considered as the sole success of the 2011 uprisings.[32] Peaceful uprisings, over a span of more than two years in Algeria, are highlighting how governments have perfected their capacity to counter mobilisations, while authoritarian regimes appear to have grown more and more resilient, mastering methods of surveillance and repression. As for the younger generations, made up of those who were only children in 2011, they may well be considered even more disillusioned and wary of political parties than their elders who participated in the uprisings a decade ago. Region-wide opinion polls carried out year after year by the Arab Barometer are suggesting a profound shift in matters of religious belief, in particular among the youth with yet unknown consequences. Much like elsewhere, leisure practices are now more and more structured around the Internet and could also be seen as even more individual. The variety of formats available to produce content or consume it has grown tremendously. This gave rise to a certain fragmentation of practices and of communities. The sudden frenzy around Clubhouse in 2021, before this

General introduction

social network massively came under the guise of Arab intelligence services, highlighted the impressive pace of fashions, and thus the necessity to contextualise these and not hastily consider as revolutionary things that may well be ephemeral. Overall, over this last decade, the amplification of existing trends only confirms the faultlines and specific dynamics that structure this volume.

Not seeking to stage a graduation towards politicisation and commitment on the part of youth, or to integrate it into a chronological narrative extending from a distant past to an inevitable future, the book's arrangement highlights four lines of tension that, in our opinion, continue to characterise contemporary Arab youth compared with youth in other regions of the world. Thus, Part I presents ten emblematic figures that represent in collective imaginaries, Arab and foreign alike, what young Arabs are like and the way they bring social change. Part II more systematically examines the inscription of forms of leisure in an ambivalent relationship to time, composed of nostalgia, ruptures, the questioning of legacies, the reinvention of traditions and projection towards the future. Part III registers the difficulty of self-construction in and through free time, in societies subject to various evolving constraints, be they poverty, repression, male domination, familial determinants or the weight of political and religious institutions. Part IV concentrates on the links between leisure and political commitment, whether ephemeral, like the insurrectionary and revolutionary moments of 2011, or inscribed in the long term. For, in the final analysis, it is precisely the voice of this generation that we want to make heard in and through this series of cameo portraits.

Notes

1 From the outset, and at every stage of its conception, this work has been the fruit of close, exciting and demanding collaboration between its authors and Thomas Deltombe, editor at La Découverte. We are sincerely grateful to him.
2 See Samir Kassir, *Considérations sur le malheur arabe*, Actes Sud/Sindbad, Paris and Arles, 2004.
3 For a radical deconstruction of such clichés, see François Burgat, *L'islamisme à l'heure d'Al-Qaida*, La Découverte, Paris, 2005.
4 Edward A. Sayre and Tarik Yousef, *Young Generation Awakening. Economics, Society, and Policy on the Eve of the Arab Spring*, Oxford University Press, Oxford, 2016.
5 Linda Herrera, 'It's Time to Talk about Youth in the Middle East as the Precariat', *Middle East. Topics & Arguments*, 9, 2017: pp. 35–44.
6 Élias Sanbar and Farouk Mardam-Bey, *Être arabe*, Actes Sud, Arles, 2005.
7 Emma Murphy, 'Problematizing Arab Youth: Generational Narratives of Systemic Failure', *Mediterranean Politics*, 17, 2012: pp. 5–22; Maria Cristina Paciello and Daniela

General introduction

Pioppi, 'Is Arab Youth the Problem (or the Solution)? Assessing the Arab Human Development Report 2016', *Development and Change*, 49, 2, 2018: pp. 629–664.
8 See Youssef Courbage and Emmanuel Todd, *A Convergence of Civilisations. The Transformation of Muslim Societies around the World*, trans. George Holoch, Columbia University Press, New York and Chichester, 2011.
9 Myriam Catusse and Blandine Destremau, *Governing Youth, Managing Society. A Comparative Overview of Six Country Case Studies (Egypt, Lebanon, Morocco, Occupied Palestinian Territories, Tunisia and Turkey)*, Power2Youth Working Papers, Istituto Affari Internazionali, Rome, 2016.
10 Emma Murphy and Nadine Sika, 'Euro-Mediterranean Partnership and Youth Policies in the MENA: Why Policy Discourse Travels but Implementation Doesn't', *Mediterranean Politics*, 2020: pp. 393–406.
11 See Navtej Dhillon and Tarik Yousef, eds, *Generation in Waiting. The Unfulfilled Promise of Young People in the Middle East*, Brookings Institution, Washington, 2009.
12 See Mai Yamani, *Changed Identities. The Challenge of the New Generation in Saudi Arabia*, Royal Institute of International Affairs, London, 1999; Réda Benkirane, *Le désarroi identitaire. Jeunesse, islamité and arabité contemporaines*, Cerf, coll. 'L'histoire à vif', Paris, 2004.
13 Mounia Bennani-Chraïba, *Soumis et rebelles. Les jeunes au Maroc*, CNRS Éditions, Paris, 1994.
14 Sulaiman Al-Farsi, *Democracy and Youth in the Middle East. Islam, Tribalism and the Rentier State in Oman*, IB Tauris, London, 2013.
15 Several works refer to this from different angles and in various contexts. See Linda Herrera and Asef Bayat, eds, *Being Young and Muslim. New Cultural Politics in the Global South and North*, Oxford University Press, Oxford and New York, 2010; Rahma Bourqia, Mohammed El Ayadi, Mokhtar El Harras and Hassan Rachik, *Les eunes et les valeurs religieuses*, EDDIF, Casablanca, 2000; and Saba Mahmood, *Politics of Piety. The Islamic Revila and the Feminist Subject*, Princeton University Press, Princeton, NJ, 2005.
16 Emanuela Buscemi and Ildiko Kaposi, eds, *Everyday Youth Cultures in the Gulf Peninsula. Changes and Challenges*, Routledge, London, 2021.
17 Ronnie Close, *Cairo's Ultras. Resistance and Revolution in Egypt's Football Culture*, American University of Cairo Press, Cairo, 2019.
18 A collective work has done so in remarkable fashion, paving the way for much more research since 2011: see Maud Stephan Hachem, Azza Charara Baydoun, Nazek Saba Yared and Watfa Hamadi, eds, 'Cultural Practices of Arab Youth', *Bahithat*, Vol. XIV, Beirut, 2009–2010.
19 Mounia Bennani Chraïbi and Iman Farag, eds, *Jeunesses des sociétés arabes. Par-delà les promesses et les menaces*, Aux lieux d'être, Paris, 2007.
20 Marc Breviglieri and Vincenzo Cicchelli, eds, *Adolescences méditerranéennes. L'espace public à petits pas*, L'Harmattan, Paris, 2007.
21 Frédéric Lagrange, 'Covid-19, réseaux sociaux et culture pop dans la péninsule Arabique', *Arabian Humanities*, 14, online, 2020.
22 See Pierre Bourdieu, '"Youth" Is Just a Word', *Sociology in Question*, trans. Richard Nice, Sage, London, 1993, pp. 94–102.
23 Mona Harb and Lara Deeb, 'Les autres pratiques de la résistance: tourisme politique et loisirs pieux', in Sabrina Mervin, ed., *Hezbollah. État des lieux*, Actes Sud/IFPO, Paris and Beirut, 2008, pp. 227–245.
24 See Roel Meijer, ed., *Alienation or Integration of Arab Youth. Between Family, State and Street*, Curzon Press, Richmond, 2000.

25 See Alain Corbin, ed., *L'avènement des loisirs (1850–1960)*, Aubier, Paris, 1995.
26 André Rauch, 'Les vacances et la nature revisitée (1830–1939)', in Corbin, ed., *L'avènement des loisirs*, p. 143.
27 Assia Boutaleb, 'Un lieu, deux acteurs, différentes logiques: les centres de jeunesse en Égypte', in Bennani-Chraïbi and Farag, eds, *Jeunesses des sociétés arabes*, pp. 223–248.
28 See Linda Herrera and Carlos Alberto Torres, eds, *Cultures of Arab Schooling: Critical Ethnographies from Egypt*, State University of New York Press, Albany, NY, 2006.
29 Patrick Haenni, *L'islam de marché. L'autre révolution conservatrice*, Éditions du Seuil, Paris, 2005.
30 See Jocelyne Dakhlia, ed., *Créations artistiques en pays d'Islam. Des arts en tension*, Éditions Kimé, Paris, 2006; Franck Mermier and Nicolas Puig, eds, *Itinéraires esthétiques et scènes culturelles au Proche-Orient*, Presses de l'Ifpo, Beirut, 2007.
31 Mark Levine, *Heavy Metal Islam. Rock, Resistance, and the Struggle for the Soul of Islam*, Three Rivers Press, New York, 2008.
32 Myriam Catusse and Olfa Lamloum, eds, *Jeunes et violences institutionnelles. Enquête dix ans après la révolution tunisienne*, Arabesque, Tunis, 2021.

Part I

Living in the present

Introduction

Living in the present

Laurent Bonnefoy and Myriam Catusse

Neither timeless nor detached from practices that have become increasingly transnational, the leisure activities of young Arabs presented in the first part of this book are firmly anchored in specific social contexts. Influenced by specific fashions and technological developments, they reflect changes in young people's relation to time, space, social norms and body politics.

This part focuses on ten different youth cultures through the lens of their leisure activities. In the collective imagination, these activities encapsulate much of what is specific to the lives and identities of young Arabs who were at the forefront of the revolutionary uprisings of 2011. Through their real or imagined novelty, these cultures reflect ongoing social change. Sometimes stereotyped, yet deeply rooted in contemporary reality, they seem like allegories of social and cultural practices. Some social norms are still evolving, while others have already loosened. And new freedoms are starting to emerge in many places, albeit in different ways.

Fifteen years ago, the joyrider, the 'hittist', the *buya*, the Salafist, the Internet user or 'Generation Y' – to name just a few examples from the following pages – did not exist in their present forms. Almost ten years later, they still appear relevant – although 'Generation Z' might be the current label used in the media. Of course, young people's propensity for risk-taking, their idleness, sexual ambivalence, pursuit of faith and means of communication have always influenced the way they use their free time, but they have recently given rise to forms of leisure that are particular to our era, and this is true as much for Arab countries as for the rest of the world. The growing number of neologisms to describe them, or the reappearance of forgotten names (such as 'Salafism') bear testimony to this.

A good example of this shift in cultural practices can be found in the use of *arabizi* (from the English 'Arab easy'), which first appeared in the 2000s. With digital media in the region developing fast, but technical limitations holding back the use of Arabic on keyboards of phones and computers, this new 'dialect' spread like wildfire through the Arab world. Thanks to a combination of Latin characters and Arabic numerals, this new form of transliteration enabled users to write Arabic from left to right: for example, the famous slogan of the 2011 uprisings, 'dégage!' (get out!) is rendered as '*ir7al*', the word 'Arabic' as '3arabiya'. Introducing some striking innovations, the new chat alphabet has also shaken up written Arabic, which often seems frozen in the past (Arabic is the language of Quranic revelation, and its purity is zealously protected). As Yves Gonzalez-Quijano has shown in his book *Arabités numériques*, this 'youth coup' offers those who use *arabizi* – mainly the young generation – completely new ways of 'being Arab'.[1]

This first part takes a detailed look at practices that are specific to youth and its transitory character, but it also considers developments which affect the whole region: the spread of urbanisation, new concepts of gender identity, the individualisation of religious practice and the projection of the imagination beyond national boundaries. Although the individual or collective practices explored here may be perceived as 'deviant' because they reject traditional norms, or 'marginal' because they do not follow the paths traced by earlier generations, we should not overlook their influence on the societies around them.

Whether it is the joyrider skidding his car in Riyadh, the Palestinian football fan taking over the streets on match nights, the 'hittist' spending his days leaning against a wall in Algiers, the young revolutionary on a protest in Tunisia or the Saudi *buya* showing off her 'masculinity' in a shopping mall, the physical and spatial impact that these subcultures exert on their surroundings is often very concrete. That they are often the subject of heated debates demonstrates just how much youth is still seen as trouble, as a threat to public order or established tradition.

It is this challenge to social conventions that often draws suspicion from the rest of society. This is especially true for gender norms. The practices described here certainly show that gender segregation is still quite deeply entrenched, for leisure activities very often reproduce gender arrangements which are taken for granted. But they also reveal, explicitly or implicitly, new mixed spaces that have sprung up. Traditional cafés are still reserved for men, but those located in shopping malls or owned by international chains also welcome or even prioritise women. Football stadiums remain solidly male, but increasing media consumption of football, especially at home, turns even sisters and girlfriends into 'armchair supporters'. Politics remains an almost exclusively male domain, yet

Introduction

the case study of a young Tunisian woman demonstrates that men who admire a woman's political engagement may only be able to express this by comparing her to a man: 'she is more of a man than the men'.

The ten subcultures in this part of the book belong to very different socio-economic groups and a range of cultural contexts. Evidently, some of these practices, over the years, have somehow gone out of fashion or, as is the case of joyriding in Saudi Arabia, been increasingly repressed by the state. Young Arabs continue to experience free time in very different ways. For some, time is 'freed up' by material comfort; it is offered by universities and not constrained by familial demands. But others have to 'endure' it, as they search in vain for a job or are unable to get into university. The leisure practices of young Arab men and women, in the street, in shopping malls, mosques, universities, cafés or online vary according to each different subculture. This part aims to give them a voice, to listen to what they say about themselves rather than to what others say about them.

The youth cultures presented here are neither inferior nor unworthy and should not necessarily be seen, explicitly or objectively, as countercultures, in direct opposition to a dominant culture informed by traditional values. They are found in the codes, shared references, specific experiences and practices of identity formation that can lead to the establishment of alternative communities, often along generational lines.

These practices follow an increasingly transnational logic. Schemes for descrambling satellite signals, international restaurant chains, Japanese cars, Saudi religious leaders, 'personal development' tips gleaned from British and American self-help books and dreams of emigrating to Europe are codes and reference points which shape the leisure activities analysed by the authors of this part of the book. The paths of the young people presented here are rooted in a globalised culture but, conversely, also show contrasting patterns. Without essentialising these differences, we will try to delineate some of the singularities of contemporary Arab youth and contrast them with those of their counterparts in other regions of the world – from their appropriation of public space to their religious practices and gender relations.

Note

1 Yves Gonzalez-Quijano, *Arabités numériques. Le printemps du Web arabe*, Sindbad, Paris, 2012.

1
'Go ahead, burn your tyres!'
The lust for life of Saudi joyriders

Pascal Menoret

> The class war is fought out in terms of [...] crime, riot and mob action.
> – E. P. Thompson (*The Making of the English Working Class*, 1991, p. 64)

Mish'al-Sharari died in a car accident on Riyadh's Twilight Avenue (Shari' al-Ghurub) on 5 March 2006. His three passengers, two pedestrians and the driver of another vehicle were killed along with him. Sharari shared with hundreds of young Saudis the reprehensible and enviable privilege of being a joyrider,[1] a car breaker, an entertainer of idle youth and an enemy of public morality. Like their Anglo-Saxon counterparts, who coined the concept, Saudi joyriders not only drive at high speeds, but have also developed impressive tricks and virtuoso skids.

Sharari died during an acrobatic skidding session, known in Saudi Arabia as *tafhit* or *hajwala*. Earlier that day, his fans had asked him to 'throw the iron' (*siff al-hadid*) and 'tame the steel' (*ta'dib al-hadid*). He refused, preferring to go on a road trip with another joyrider, 'Shaytani' ('Demonic'). Packed into several dozen vehicles, his fans sped off to catch up with him. Won over by their enthusiasm, he finally performed some skids in front of hundreds of spectators who had come to see him.

After a particularly dangerous trick, his car went off the road before mowing down a group of spectators and catching fire. The four occupants were burnt alive in front of a helpless audience. Deeply moved by Sharari's cries of pain, five joyriders in the audience repented and decided to become devout Muslims.

That night, a local legend was born. From the harrowing details recounted by witnesses to the impersonal comments of the local press, Sharari's death became a story of major importance. The story included his admirers' initial refusal to follow him, the pursuit by his fans, and his death on Twilight Avenue. The only thing missing was a love story, an essential ingredient in any good *tafhit* session, as joyriders are supposed to have feelings for young boys akin to chivalrous friendship or Greek love.

This chapter focuses on the dynamics behind the practice of *tafhit*. It examines Riyadh's politically disenfranchised, urban, male youth and the 'lust for life' of some of these apparent 'rebels without a cause'. But unlike the heroes of Nicholas Ray's 1955 film, these young Saudis who competed in their cars did have a cause. What struck me during fieldwork in Riyadh between January 2005 and July 2007 was that most of the young people were less concerned with Salafism and the Muslim Brotherhood than with a good session of joyriding, with its roar, its risks and its forbidden pleasures.

Becoming a joyrider

In Central Arabian dialects, the verbs *fahhata* and *hajja* mean to run away, to escape. Several words are constructed from *fahhata*: *mufahhat* (joyrider), which literally means fugitive, and *tafhit*, which refers to the screeching of tyres skidding on the asphalt and to the shrill cries of children. From *hajja*, the word *hajwala* used by young Saudis to describe joyriding is for their elders synonymous with disorder and confusion. *Muhajwil*, a term derived from the same verb, means vagrant. The youth of Riyadh have reversed the stigma: for them, a *muhajwil* is a tough guy, a street hero.

The *tafhit* scene in Riyadh mainly attracts young men aged between fifteen and thirty, who have dropped out of school or are looking for a job. They mostly belong to the lower middle and working classes and are part of the Bedouin and rural fringe of the city's population.[2] Sometimes older men take the wheel: Badr 'Awad (nicknamed 'al-King') was well into his thirties when he retired from the streets and embarked on a career as a religious preacher. But the majority of those I interviewed were young men from the countryside, whose families had recently moved to Riyadh, or who had themselves emigrated to study or find work. They generally came from such marginal areas as the southern mountains and the Najd highlands. Their prestigious tribal ancestry clashed with their poor living conditions and housing. The opportunities promised by the big city were often only mirages for them, and many dropped out of school or became long-term job seekers.

At the crossroads of town and country, joyriding is seen by the state media as the latest stage in a deviant career that leads from drinking and smoking to theft, homosexuality, drug abuse, drug trafficking and sometimes violent death. An innocent pastime at its beginning, joyriding is now seen as a 'social problem', and its prevention has become the subject of press articles, mosque preaching and police action. Recycling the repertoire developed by the Saudi state against Islamist groups, the media regularly denounce 'joyriding's sedition' (*fitna al-tafhit*) or 'street terrorism' (*irhab al-shawari'*).

Why do people become joyriders? The answer from *mufahhatin* is unanimous: it is because of what they call *tufush*. Saudi sociologists translate this dialectal term into classical Arabic and use the words *faragh* and *malal* (emptiness, boredom). But there is a linguistic gap here, which is a source of misunderstanding. The fight against delinquency targets idleness without trying to understand what the youth of Riyadh are saying when they speak of *tufush*. Like *tafhit* and *hajwala*, *tufush* originally means 'escape' or 'breakaway'. Young Saudis use it to describe the feeling of social helplessness that overwhelms them when they have realised the incommensurable distance between Riyadh's fabulous economic opportunities and their own situation (unemployment, low income, poor housing, hostility from the middle class, etc.). *Tufush* is the feeling of being deprived of social capital in a city where all opportunities are at hand if you can benefit from the right string-pulling (*wasta*). If boredom is 'emptiness, nothingness', *tufush* is, as my interlocutors explain, 'what makes you want to be out of control, to be an *'arbaji* [a thug]', 'to sell the whole world for the price of a bicycle wheel' or 'to consider the whole world as a cigarette butt and to crush it with your foot'. *Tufush*, then, is not just boredom or emptiness, but the rage that overcomes young Saudis when they understand the violent injustice of social hierarchies.

It is relatively easy to become a member of a joyriding group. A group of students living in a predominantly Bedouin neighbourhood compared their school's Islamic education group (*jama'a al-taw'iya al-islamiyya*), which organised cultural and religious activities and was linked to the Saudi Muslim Brotherhood, to joyriding groups. The Islamic group is very selective, recruiting good students and 'uptight nerds' (*dawafir*), they told me. Joyriding groups, on the other hand, target all young people and use various means of communication – leaflets, articles, the Internet – to attract audiences and organise their shows. Therefore, Islamic groups can hardly compete with the attraction of joyriding: 'We were all obsessed with it, we all wanted to become joyriders', says a high school senior, who adds:

> I feel like one percent of people are destined for the religious group. [...] Joyriding groups are more open. At the beginning of college, joyriding fans hand out master keys to students, the keys you use to steal cars. I remember coming home one day

and seeing two first year students saying they wanted to steal a car and they had a key. That's their way of recruiting: they give keys to the students. And they attract a lot of people.

Another student adds:

> Joining a joyriding group is easier than joining a religious group. I mean, you see them from the window, you go down in the street, and there, in front of your door, there is a guy, you chat with him, and this guy, maybe, he'll let you get in his car the next day. It's easier.

Joyriders use stolen or rented cars and need many fresh recruits to 'borrow' the vehicles and hand them over to the skidding heroes. Unlike lowriders or drag racers, now common in Saudi cities, joyriders do not customise their cars. They prefer basic Japanese sedans and are more interested in tricks and skidding techniques than in transforming their vehicles. At school and on the street, the master key is a trial. If one accepts it, one is soon faced with other challenges to climb the ladder within the group and get closer to the joyrider and his circle of assistants. If one refuses, one remains confined to the subordinate position of follower and fan. From the moment one joins the group, a series of tests leads to the formation of established hierarchies.

A brief history of joyriding in Saudi Arabia

Joyriding developed during a period of considerable change for Saudi Arabia: the economic boom (*tafra*) of the 1970s. It emerged in the new suburbs of Riyadh, Jeddah and Dammam, three cities that were suddenly transformed by the tremendous influx of cash into the economy. As Saudi intellectual 'Abd Allah al-Ghadhdhami explains:

> There was a huge gap between building the place and building the man; spatial development got in the way of human development. The human aspect was so neglected that the inhumanity of the place is striking. Look at our great asphalt streets, with their billboards, signs, lights and skyscrapers, and look for man: all you will find is the noise of cars and the squeal of tyres. Whoever seeks a place of his own in this icy splendour can but feel very lonely.[3]

Joyriding groups were born out of urban explosion, the construction of roads and the massive importation of cars. They developed as a celebration of individual courage in the face of machines, those symbols of modernity and power; in the face of society's changing and threatening body; in the face of police repression; and, finally, in the face of death. A few months before Sharari's death, Abu Kab's fatal accident in Jeddah had led the 'joyriding leaders in Riyadh' to instruct their fans all over the country to avoid their usual meeting places because of an exceptional police presence. Since its inception, joyriding has had several similar crises, but it has always managed to survive what its followers thought were decisive blows. The first star of joyriding, Husayn al-Harbi, was imprisoned in 1985; soon after, Sa'd Marzuq picked up the torch before being arrested in 1990, and handed it over to Sa'ud al-'Ubayd, aka 'al-Jazura', and Badr 'Awad, aka 'al-King'. In the meantime, the technical criteria had evolved, although joyriding was still not considered a speed race or a competition. In a truculent text entitled 'Genesis and Evolution of Thuggery' (al-'arbaja, nash'atuha wa namuha), anonymous author Rakan recalls that in the beginning, 'they were joyriding to enlarge their souls [li-wisa'at as-sadr] [and that] it wasn't about winning – it was always an even game anyway. The important thing was to perform one trick after another and attract as many spectators as possible.'

While in Husayn al-Harbi's time, the skids and tricks were performed in Japanese sedans at 140 km/h, the late 1980s saw the dominance of American cars, which required special skills to control because of the automatic gearbox and rear-wheel drive. After a period of 'tafhit amiriki', of which Sa'd Marzuq was the undisputed champion, the fashion for Japanese sedans resumed, culminating in 1995 with the arrival of the new Toyota Camry, which could reach well over 200 km/h. In the days of al-Jazura and al-King, the slightest mistake in driving could lead to disaster, and fatal accidents were common. Al-Jazura died in 2001 and al-King repented a few years later. Both their journeys illustrate one of the great slogans of joyriding: 'The end of joyriding is either death or repentance' (ia al-mawt, ia at-tawba).

The socio-economic structures of joyriding

After the oil boom of 1973, real estate became the main instrument of rent distribution in Saudi Arabia, through land allocation and public loans. In Riyadh, the urban network with its thousands of kilometres of asphalt was the work of reckless developers, investors and subcontractors who, using their connections (wasta) with the royal family, made a fortune in the massive construction of housing and roads. The distribution of economic opportunity was solidified along networks of clientele that the common man calls 'the six families that own Riyadh'. In 2005, when real estate tycoon Badr Bin Saʿidan ran in the municipal elections on the theme of 'decent housing', voters remembered that his family had contributed to the real estate bubble that made it impossible to find 'decent housing' in the capital. Bin Saʿidan was soundly defeated by a candidate close to the Muslim Brotherhood, himself a property developer. Even the opposition had to go through the real estate market.

According to the Riyadh Development Authority, only 2 per cent of urban journeys were made by public transport and 93 per cent by private vehicles at the turn of the century. Licensed dealers dominate the car market and have a powerful monopoly on sales, credit, parts and maintenance. Perhaps the most famous car dealer in the country is Abdellatif Jameel, who started his career as a small subcontractor for the US oil company Aramco and as a petrol station owner in Jeddah. The only Toyota dealer in Saudi Arabia, he became one of the country's richest commoners.

Joyriders and their fans often refer to these monopolistic structures of rent distribution and denounce the vicious circle of consumption and debt that most families are trapped in. They mock the fact that the average Saudi wants to emulate the royal family's lifestyle, which one joyriding fan once described to me as 'a living ad for Western and Japanese consumer products'. Another lamented, 'All we have are streets and cars. Where do you want us to go?'

In the suburbs of Riyadh, the new real estate developments (*al-mukhattatat*), with their wide, empty avenues lined with streetlights, provide an ideal setting for joyriding, as the tricks and spectacles that joyriding implies would be impossible elsewhere. According to the author of 'Genesis and Evolution of Thuggery', some joyriders actually love the real estate market:

> Besides, [joyriders] don't want to hear about the stock market boom. Why not? Because when stocks go up, the real estate market stops or slows down. And if real estate slows down, real estate developments [*al-mukhattatat*] stop, and so do new avenues … And you know how the story ends.

Speaking about the enormous power of car salesmen, a young joyriding fan confided: 'You make cars with our oil. Then you sell them to us at very high prices. And we destroy them.' And to avoid any ambiguity, he adds: 'It's an American-Zionist plot; they import cars to kill our youth.'

Through the destruction of cars and the mobile occupation of new housing estates, joyriding represents the paroxysm of Saudi consumerist culture. It also expresses a popular revolt against it, through the subversion of private property (car theft), the contestation of public order and space (dangerous figures performed at high speed on the avenues) and the violation of familialist ideology (homo-sociality) and religious prohibitions (drug and alcohol consumption). Joyriders challenge police authority by 'jumping the lights, driving like mad, losing the police, and slaloming between cars'. A popular vernacular song (*kasra*) reveals the relationship to the police of Bubu, a *tafhit* star who liked to organise skidding sessions around his young lover's house:

> Honk! Derail and disturb your lover's neighbourhood, Bubu!
> May the cops die of disgust, may they give up the hunt, come on!

For Muhammad al-Hudhayf, one of the Islamist activists who created the Committee for the Defence of Legitimate Rights in 1993 to protect political prisoners from police repression and to continue the reform movement begun during the Gulf War, joyriding, because of its challenge to public order, its extensive organisation and its revolt against the consumerist utopia of the Saudi middle classes, represents 'a complete lack of politicisation'. Like the 'food riots' in eighteenth-century England described by Edward P. Thompson, joyriding nevertheless has an element of politics in its targeting of the source of economic power and social injustice. This irreverence towards the material symbol of economic monopolies can be read as a contemporary version of the old mob actions and popular indignation: joyriding is a car and property riot.

'Madness is plural'

It would be an exaggeration, however, to politicise too quickly what, in the eyes of most aficionados, is first and foremost a way to have fun. The joyriding revolt is formulated in apolitical terms, mainly because of the limited social and cultural capital of its followers. Some of them confess that they 'fell into joyriding' unintentionally because they were unable to belong to more rewarding social networks. Like the lowriding culture in Los Angeles described by sociologist Mike Davis, *tafhit* in its early days opened up 'the "cool worlds" of urban socialisation to new residents coming from rural areas'. This was particularly the case for young Bedouins who came to find work in a booming metropolis. Joyriding gradually became concentrated in neighbourhoods with a large Bedouin population and came to express an assertion of Bedouin pride in the settled urban society.

'Go ahead, burn your tyres!'

A long anonymous *kasra* shows how, and in what context, the Bedouin reference is used:

> Go ahead, burn your tires! The car makes you the 'Antara of our time
> For your time has betrayed you
> The pretty boys applaud you and testify to your worth
> The cops beat you up
> It's okay if they insult you and humiliate you
> Cause you've failed in everything
> Nothing will improve your situation
> You dropped out of school and you hang out with the thugs
> You didn't obey your father when he was crying over you
> Nor your mother when she shouted at you and encouraged you
> You neglected her, you turned your back on her, you wanted to humiliate her
> Go away, disappear and may God dissolve your crises
> Go ahead, burn your tires until your ears explode.

The popularity of the pre-Islamic Bedouin poet and warrior 'Antara ibn Shaddad (sixth century AD) among young Bedouins is due in part to his legendary hostility towards the Banu Tamim, a sedentary tribe that is now a pillar of the Saudi state. Betrayed by his contemporaries, 'Antara died in a tribal war. Joyriders endlessly replay the tragedy, for the Bedouin tribes, of the creation of the Saudi state by the sedentary inhabitants of the oases.

The joyriders' ventures are launched today for the beautiful eyes of young men. The passive sexual partner (*wir'*, plural: *wir'an*) plays a central role in joyriding: it is to seduce him that death is defied and crowds of people mobilise. The famous joyrider Bubu used to 'throw the iron' for Sultan's eyes (*li-'uyun Sultan*). Badr 'Awad is said to have run a procession of seventy cars around his boyfriend's house. For one fan, it is clear: 'We know that joyriding is bad, but it gives us a sense of time and space. [...] And then there are the boys [*wir'an*].' A famous *kasra* says:

> Hamad said to me and asked: why?
> Why do creatures fall into joyriding?
> I pointed at him and said: look at you!
> A beautiful boy stretching to the rhythm [of the tires].

The love of boys is frequently used by the middle classes to stigmatise joyriders as Bedouins and homosexuals. A young middle-class man I met in Riyadh in 2006, who was passionate about drag racing and customisation, clearly distinguished himself from joyriders:

> They are frightening: they look like shit, as if they had just come out of the ground, with their hair standing up and their big moustaches. I know I'm not very attractive, but I wouldn't want to be alone with one of them. [...] We have a goal, we know what we are doing. They behave like madmen; it's all disorder and accidents.

This apparent disorder should not lead to hasty conclusions: there is art in this madness. The rules of joyriding are explained on websites; its tricks are carefully codified and judged by 'referees' during competitions. Songs are dedicated to it, recorded and sold on the black market, and fans memorise poems praising it. The apparent disorder of a procession of cars is actually the result of a meticulous organisation, managed by a 'navigator' (*muajjih*) who maps out the route, checks for police patrols and is ready to re-direct the procession if need be. The joyriders use disorder and speed against the compartmentalisation and control of a city that has become a disciplinary space. They learn crucial skills in an environment characterised by risk and competition. The best of them do not drink, do not smoke, and avoid, as much as possible, falling in love. This self-control is the reason why Badr 'Awad remained unrivalled for sixteen consecutive years, while other less ascetic pilots ended up seriously or fatally injured. As the testimony of one of my interlocutors indicates, the discipline required to become a tough guy (*sarbut*) is sometimes justified in more practical ways:

> If you work in a company where there is an exceptional employee, you will probably want to be better than him. It's the same in joyriding. There is the love of boys [*al-wir'anjiyya*]. But that's a reward you only get if you're the best employee. If you ride for the eyes of a boy, you will be bad at joyriding, and you will lose the boys. You have to become a joyrider for the sake of joyriding. You have to become the best, because boys love excellence and dedication.

These sentences contain the core idea of joyriding: do not care about yourself to show your self-control; forget about boys to conquer them. There is an ethic of joyriding, but it is an ethic of despair. *Tufush*, as we have seen, means to escape, to flee; the word also evokes the disordered movements of a drowning man. Joyriding can be interpreted as a desperate way to stylise these movements, to speed them up, to magnify them, to make them a popular art and a source of collective enthusiasm. In the end, one is always supposed to drown, through death or prison, through accident or unemployment. Joyriding is the last gasp of the drowning man: a means of expressing his fury before he is submerged and annihilated.

It is not so much Islam that defines the politicisation of young Saudis as the social and economic situation they collectively face. Intensive fieldwork in Riyadh has shown that beyond the expressions of Islamic distrust of the state and its foreign backers, which are the subject of much work, many more behaviours can be considered political. Even practices that at first glance appear self-destructive and pathological can rightly be described as political. More than Islamic defiance, deviance from the norms of a rapidly transforming society expresses the everyday relationships that these joyriders have with various spaces of power, including family, school and police. And the fact that joyriding – comprising multiple violations of Saudi order – neglects the larger systems of power does not detract from its political dimension. Delinquency, rioting and mass action are all ways of conducting class struggle, but when the main political institutions are out of reach, this struggle often ends in self-destruction.

Notes

1 'Originating in the United States, the term "joyriding" arrived in the United Kingdom in 1912 and was defined simply as a "ride at high speed. Esp. in a motorcar" (Beale 1984: 629).' Sean O'Connell, 'From Toad of Toad Hall to the "Death Drivers" of Belfast: An Exploratory History of "Joyriding"', *British Journal of Criminology*, 46, 2006: p. 457; P. Beale, ed., *A Dictionary of Slang and Unconventional Language*, Routledge and Kegan Paul, London, 1984.
2 The Bedouin are the descendants of nomads who made up about 40 per cent of the population of Arabia until the middle of the twentieth century but make up less than 5 per cent today.
3 'Abd Allah Al-Ghadhdhami, *Hikaya Al-Hadatha fi al-Mamlaka al-'Arabiyya al-Su'udiyya* [*The History of Modernity in Saudi Arabia*], Al-Markaz al-Thaqafi al-'Arabi, Beirut, 2004, p. 172.

References

Al-Rasheed, Madawi, *Constesting the Saudi State. Islamic Voices from a New Generation*, Cambridge University Press, Cambridge, 2007.
Bayat, Asef, *Life as Politics. How Ordinary People Change the Middle East*, Stanford University Press, Stanford, CA, 2010.

Living in the present

Bonnenfant, Paul, 'La capitale saoudienne: Riyadh', in Paul Bonnenfant (ed.), *La Péninsule arabique d'aujourd'hui*, vol. 1, Éditions du CNRS, 1982: pp. 655–705.

Borden, Iain, *Skateboarding, Space and the City. Architecture and the Body*, Berg, Oxford, 2001.

Davis, Mike, *City of Quartz. Excavating the Future of Los Angeles*, Verso Books, London, 2006.

Thompson, Edward P., *The Making of the English Working Class*, Vintage Books, New York, 1991.

Vitalis, Robert, *America's Kingdom. Mythmaking on the Saudi Oil Frontier*, Stanford University Press, Stanford, CA, 2007.

2

'Just watching the time go by'

The 'hittists' of Algeria

Loïc Le Pape

> They are standing with their backs against the wall, and from morning to night, they watch life go by ... Sometimes the wall goes home in the evening, and they're still there.
>
> – Fellag (*Djurdjurassique Bled*, 1997)

It was at the start of the 1990s, as a gloomy decade gave way to an even bleaker one, that the term 'hittist' was coined in Algeria. Emblematic of a part of the youth of this period, the hittist became a persistent stereotype. This chapter examines its significance and analyses what it tells us explicitly or implicitly about a shared feeling of emptiness (no stable employment, no prospects, no family, nothing to do).

'All the young unemployed of Algeria are leaning against the wall all day long, and after a while they've taken on the wall's name.' As the Algerian comedian Fellag explained in 1997, in a delightful mixture of Arabic and French, the hittists – named after the Algerian word for wall, *hitt* – are young people, more precisely young men, who spend most of their time leaning against the walls of their neighbourhood since they have nothing else to do. The word, as well as the expression 'being a hittist', became extremely popular over the last two decades, and a whole repertoire of images of this generation spread through literature, film, music, the media and everyday conversations.

Inseparable from its era, the term now seems outdated and is falling out of use, superseded by new puns and jokes, new forms of self-mockery. But it retains the force of the prejudices that affected that generation. And even though it is gradually overtaken by other, more contemporary, images that are linked, for instance, to the *harragas*, North Africans who burn their identity cards to illegally immigrate to Europe, nothing suggests that what it described has disappeared. Far from it.

Living in the present

After briefly examining the main characteristics of Algerian youth encompassed by the term, this chapter will try to approach the question in a different form – by imagining a fictional interior dialogue, that of 'the last of the hittists', in order to explore the different manifestations of 'hittism', the different roles it can include and the chances of 'role exit'. But before handing over to 'the last of the hittists' it may be helpful to return to the context in which the term was born and to ask why its use has declined.

Mass unemployment

According to official statistics, young people under thirty made up 57.7 per cent of the Algerian population in 2011. Although unemployment has been falling over the last decade, this high percentage presents a considerable challenge for urban planning, housing, employment, as well as the provision of social care and benefits. In response, a number of support measures for the unemployed in this age group were put in place in 1988, a year which saw large street protests and the establishment of the first programme offering to provide jobs and training for young people (the Youth Employment Programme). The age of blue-collar factory work is over, and promises of full employment have evaporated: institutions like the National Agency for Supporting Youth Employment (ANSEJ), set up in 1996 and funded by state revenue from Algeria's natural resources, fail to offer the protection once provided by public sector employment and instead encourage young people 'to become entrepreneurs of their own destiny'. By promoting microcredit, a booming part of the economy, these institutions do almost nothing to provide stable career paths for people who are struggling to get by, and merely serve as a fig leaf to conceal poverty, or sometimes even help to foster clientelism and corruption at a local level. In any case, *wasta* (pulling strings), *tchippa* (bribes) or family connections seem to be indispensable for securing a first job, even in the public sector. In this context, hittism (which in some respects overlaps with the situation of the 'unemployed graduate' in Morocco, Tunisia or Egypt) is frequently presented as a 'fate', a destiny hard to reverse, the symptom of a chronic disorder affecting both Algeria's young people and its politicians. Fellag sums it up rather nicely in a sketch about his friend Mohammed:

> Hittism is the new Algerian philosophy. It's all these young people who are ready for the *hitt*. All these young people coming out of universities […] heading for the

walls ... if there's room. But Mohammed was one of the founders of hittism. He had a doctorate in hittism. He was number one in the hitt parade.

Entry into the world of hittism starts as soon as young men finish school or university, when they leave education and cannot find work. There is nothing to do but wait – for a job, for an opportunity. Obtaining an employment contract, a steady job, or even getting married or travelling somewhere are all ways to escape this situation, for good in some cases (e.g. for those who are lucky enough to find permanent employment), but usually just temporarily, because young Algerians often live on odd bits of casual work, taking whatever comes up. So hittism is a kind of waiting room, a passage between childhood and the adult world, between school and professional life, between inactivity and activity – a process which demands as many adjustments as there are life choices in Algerian society.

The official figures speak for themselves: according to the Algerian Office for National Statistics, the unemployment rate for those under twenty-five is around 25 per cent, reaching 39.5 per cent for women aged between twenty and twenty-five. Yet these 'jobless' do participate in national development, sometimes despite themselves, by contributing to the informal economy. Philippe Adair and Youghourta Bellache estimate that around 40 per cent of Algeria's GDP derives from the parallel economy, and those who are described as hittists play a part through casual jobs, undeclared work, petty retail trade, resale of illegally imported goods or various other rackets, notably second-hand trade (mobile phones, computers or games consoles). Such informal trade involving salvage, repair and resale is one of the easiest ways of making ready cash.

The reign of boredom

Lack of work is not the only bane of the hittist's life. Boredom also occupies a prominent place. It is revealing that the use of the term hittist became widespread during the violence of the 'Black Decade' (1992–2002), a time of curfews and constant danger, when any kind of nightlife or other opportunities to go out and have fun were severely limited. The novelist Maïssa Bey describes in her short-story collection *Nouvelles d'Algérie* how hittists while away their time:

> The day is still long. Nothing else to do but hang out with your mates. Too early to share the first joint. You lean against the wall. The same wall since the dawn of time. Everyone has his own patch. That one over there will soon take on the shape

of our backs. Maybe that will be more comfortable. But at least nothing obstructs the view there, in the front row: there's the crossroads, the cars, the police roadblock a bit further up, the shops, the passers-by on the pavements – we don't miss a thing. Of course we know all this by heart, it's always the same people who go by, you end up recognising them, and they do the same, some even say hello, really they do! But there's enough to keep your eyes busy, if not your mind. Just watching the time go by.[1]

There is not a lot going on: few people venture outside their neighbourhoods, and no one is planning to go anywhere. Heated discussions with friends about sport, music or politics are the main activities. While boredom is a universal phenomenon, hittism is very much an urban one, concentrated in the cities and medium-sized towns. In less populated places, unemployed young men will quickly be offered jobs, most commonly in family businesses or helping out with farm work. In urban spaces, hittists are, by definition, standing in strategic spots; they observe all the comings and goings in their neighbourhood or their block of flats. Leaning against the walls, they are also keeping a casual eye on visitors. This 'surveillance' is double-edged. It can become a nuisance for local inhabitants if the youths decide to restrict the movements of young women or encourage dealers to come in. On the other hand, their permanent presence in public spaces can also help to prevent trouble and thus be reassuring for residents.

With the advent of high-speed internet access and mobile data on smartphones, new forms of entertainment developed, from game consoles to online games. Similarly, TV series and films available for streaming now fill the days and nights of young hittists. The paradox is that these activities are pursued indoors, often inside a shop or a garage, thus blurring the definition of a hittist, which may be one reason why this subculture is losing its relevance. The film *Bab el Web* (2005), a social comedy by Merzak Allouache, the Algerian director of *Omar Gatlato* (1976), *Bab El-Oued City* (1994) and *Harragas* (2009), features two such hittists of the cyber generation. Bouzid (Faudel) and Kamel (Samy Naceri), who both still live with their parents, receive a visit from Laurence (Julie Gayet), a young woman they have 'met' in a chatroom. They use various tricks and pretences to make her believe that they have jobs, earn money and live independently – the truth is that they sell cigarettes in the street. One misunderstanding follows another and Laurence, who is no fool, joins in their efforts to build the semblance of a 'normal' and happy life, far from their everyday worries, while their friends look on with knowing smiles. Merzak Allouache offers a humorous view of the resourcefulness of young Algerians, while questioning issues of sexuality and gender, important themes in many of his films.

'Just watching the time go by'

Another noteworthy activity, often neglected by researchers, is the consumption of drugs, notably *zetla* (or *kif*, cannabis). Soft drugs are the most popular ones among young Algerians, but some hittists may also take harder narcotics, like heroin, ecstasy, drug cocktails or the notorious 'Madame Courage' (Artane), a psychotropic probably used by the special forces at the height of the civil war against Islamic militants. Although selling any kind of drug is illegal, and harsh penalties are handed down by the courts, cannabis use is widespread (no statistics are available). People smoke in groups, often in strict secrecy. Hittist smokers may also do some dealing in their neighbourhoods to cover the costs of their personal supplies.

Between Islam and secularisation

One of the other social issues connected to hittism is this generation's relation to religion. The term became more widespread during a decade marked (and ravaged) by religious questions, or more precisely politico-religious questions: the confrontation between the Islamic Salvation Front (FIS) and public authorities in the 1990s, the growth of jihadist groups during the civil war and the repression used against those suspected of Islamism, the Civil Concord amnesty after the war and the place of former 'terrorists' in society today. These questions are still burning issues in Algerian society, and the hittists were partly defined in relation to religion and by the fact that, throughout this period, they were a special target or 'easy prey' for recruitment by 'armed groups'.

Hittism shows the ambiguous relationship that a particular segment of Algerian youth has with religion. Despite their personal beliefs and a relatively strong identification with religious models, these young men display a certain degree of opposition to the social power of religion, which is 'controlling' their lives and above all defining their futures. Religion certainly offers some very convenient arguments for representing hittism in a negative light: those young men leaning against the wall were first seen as lost souls, even unbelievers, who spent their time judging others, swapping jokes and blasphemous remarks. Later on, during the worst moments of the civil war, they were accused of joining terrorist groups in large numbers, of 'going underground'. It is thought that today hittists constitute a large proportion of a Salafist movement in Algeria that has returned to a purely individual and religious commitment.

As Maïssa Bey reminds us, religious life determines the hittists' pattern of daily life:

Living in the present

> On the street corner you bump into your mates coming back from the mosque. They're your reference point. Handy for knowing the time, almost to the minute. No need for a watch. The same goes for meetings. It's always before or after one prayer or another. Especially since there's nothing else to wait for. At the call to prayer, we rise as one, we go to the mosque and join in worship. It's the prayer, the same gestures, the same words, a few minutes of great fraternity, and then, back at our observation posts, we wait for the next time.[2]

But it is also among these same groups of young men that we see direct challenges to the traditional religious order: chasing out a local imam who is too radical, confrontations with Salafist groups who try to take over a building, sometimes even open rejection of the Ramadan fast by eating and smoking in public.

Providing social order, shared reference points and endless debates about the theological position on particular acts, religion is also criticised for having too much social power and for being used for political ends.

Why have hittists disappeared?

Being a hittist is neither a profession nor a destiny, and still less a choice; it is just a point in time. And beyond that, it is also the melting pot for all the different representations of young Arabs. Hittism is just a waiting room, a period between youth and integration into conventional social life (marriage, a permanent job), or between youth and social breakdown. Many young men who once were hittists are now employees, bosses, fathers of families, emigrants, drug addicts, suicides, *harragas*, delinquents or company directors. Their hittist period was a moment in their lives when, without a steady job, they hung out with their mates in their neighbourhood, getting by and getting bored.

From early on, hittists were hostile to the *tchitchi*, the favoured youth of Algeria, sons and daughters of the privileged elite. Frequenting the nightclubs and bars of grand hotels, they are not in any danger of remaining stuck at the foot of a wall. Hittists and *tchitchis* are at the opposite ends of a spectrum, not just of a geographical space where mobility in the city is experienced differently, but above all a mental space where hopes and perspectives for the future unfurl unequally.

Hittism is a process, a moment between childhood and adult life, but it is also the intimate exploration of boredom, poverty, precariousness and despair. These social experiences are lived through in groups to make them more bearable, but perhaps also to find a way out of them more easily. Every 'exit' from *hittism* promises a life that will be 'normalised' and hard (work, marriage, children, etc.), a life with an aim and at least some prospects, which gives hope for a better future, however tenuous it may be.

The last of the *hittists* of Algeria

And here, finally, are the fictional memories of 'the last of the *hittists*'. Choosing fiction as a form of writing about this experience leaves room for different ways of expressing a social phenomenon that I hope may convey more than any overview, however detailed. Any resemblance to true stories is therefore entirely normal.

> My name is Mohammed, I'm thirty-one and I live in El Harrach, in the suburbs of Algiers. I am the last of the hittists. All my mates have gone. They have left their previous lives. Sometimes literally. There are lots of other young guys who hang out with me, but it's not the same: they're younger, lost in video games and endless online 'chats' with strangers. They get radicalised more easily and they're already pissed off with everything. This generation worries me, they're not like us. We didn't react much when we were treated with *hogra* [contempt, scorn], but they are already full of *samm* [rage (literally poison)]. But OK, if they decide to rise up one day, like in Tunisia, I'll obviously support them. We were true hittists: out on the street all day long, sometimes going for a wander, with no work, no spaces of our own. Our life was just the entrance to the housing estate where our families still live. Let me introduce my friends.
>
> My best mate is Farid. He's the same age as me, he's been married for five years and is already a father. We were always hanging out together, here or downtown. We were inseparable, people used to say we were twins. Nowadays, his life is more difficult: he looks after his two kids while his wife goes to work. Can you believe it? An Algerian man who looks after his children – that's revolutionary! He was always a bit like that, a nonconformist. He's great with them, takes them out for walks, keeps a close eye on them while they are playing outside the block. But he and his family are still living in his parents' flat, and he could leave the children with his mother. His wife works only two days a week because she does stocktaking in some of the big stores. It doesn't seem to pay much, but more and more young women are doing jobs like this, two or three days a week. They really want proper jobs but all they get is contracts for a couple of days a week. Actually this suits Farid quite well, since he can't look after the kids all the time. Because he's working too, about two days a week, a bit here, a bit there, always local. In short, nothing stable and all very precarious. It's a struggling family! But with kids and a job, even if it's casual work, you're not a hittist any more. You haven't got the

time. Ah, sometimes he loses it completely, works himself up into a fury, shouts that his kids, his wife, his parents, the whole lot of them, can all go to hell. Some say he's violent, but I've never seen that and I've witnessed these fits more than once. He told me that it happens all of a sudden, when he's listening to the news, hearing about some injustice or simply feeling bad, and once he was in a rage he couldn't calm down. He turns red in the face and shouts at the top of his voice. I think these attacks are like a symptom – it's because he can't bear being poor in a rich country, having children and not having the means to take them on holiday, to be married and not have his own home. All the things you imagine when you realise you're never going to make it. He's stayed in the neighbourhood, so we meet from time to time. I hang around outside his block and if he has time he'll come down and join me. We smoke a little joint and remember the things we used to talk about.

My other mate, Sélim, has also found work. He's employed by a security firm at the airport. He got this job thanks to one of his brothers-in-law who works in some ministry. There's some link between this ministry and the security firm, I don't know how but from what I've understood people can get hired if they are recommended by somebody 'high up' in the ministry. That's called pulling strings, a bit like favouritism. You can call it corruption. Sélim says it's just being resourceful. It all depends on your perspective. Sélim is lucky because he's been making enough to buy a car. A very small one, on credit, and it is Korean. But he's got air-conditioning and a radio in his car, and he's got freedom. Since he still lives with his parents, he prefers to spend his life in the car. Well, he's already spent half of his life in traffic jams! But in the other half he lives like a king. He has his freedom, and he can pick up girls, take them for drives along the Corniche, or to Tipaza, or he can go and see his friends and maybe take them on a day out together. He prefers girls, though. He's always on the pull, Sélim, a seducer at heart. He should make it his profession! And now with the car as well … No need anymore to meet downtown, in the zoological gardens or wherever. He doesn't have a regular girl-friend, he has several. Sélim is a bit crazy with girls – sometimes he goes too far and nearly gets a kicking from their angry brothers. But he also knows how to talk his way out of trouble, and that's always saved him. He says he will never get married because there's no hope for a better life in this country and he doesn't want to be part of a couple under these conditions, let alone have children. He thinks our great asset in Algeria isn't natural gas or Sonatrach, the state-owned oil company, but girls, and he intends to exploit this asset! He drops by to see me now and then when he's not working. He turns the car radio up as loud as it will go and we drive off to look down at the sea and the port of Algiers from the hills. We share a little joint up there, between brothers.

Another mate, whom I don't see any more, is Mousse. Mousse, as in Mustafa. He left, and that's just as well, really. He was somewhat in disgrace locally, in fact close to being on the run … You see, he's a hittist who became a *harraga*. He burned his papers. And jumped across borders. He set off for Spain, via Morocco. It's a long story, his departure. We went with him as far as Oran, in Sélim's car.

'Just watching the time go by'

There we found him some people, rather shady characters, who were willing to take him as far as the Moroccan border. He only had to pay for the petrol. But did you know this border is closed? Actually, it isn't closed to traffickers – that makes you wonder whether it is kept closed to justify the existence of traffickers! To keep it short, Oran was where we said goodbye to Mousse. He was heading on to Saïdia, a Moroccan town on the border. Apparently his plan was to set off in a high-speed boat, a BGV (bateau à grande vitesse) from somewhere round there – we all had a good laugh about that. It must be one and a half years now since he left and I still haven't had any first-hand news. I've no idea whether he sank or swam, so to speak, is putting his feet up or feeding the fishes. At least he tried. But to do this he first had to get enough cash. He needed money to pay the smugglers, to get through several days' wait in Morocco and several more days after arriving in Spain – in cash, obviously. He worked out his plan in secret before he told us about it. Mousse was the neighbourhood dealer. He mostly sold hash, but sometimes he had more serious things (ecstasy or heroin). It was because he made a fair bit of money from dealing that he thought eventually that he could leave. Still, it was quite risky, because he was doing business with big shots from the *tchitchi* who sold drugs in bulk. He never talked about it – to protect us, he said. He wasn't a big dealer, never travelled beyond the neighbourhood, and anyway, it's a gang from Belcourt who now sell drugs round here, they control a large territory and small franchises. Mousse was a bit of an amateur, really, a bit reckless. In the end he set off with 250 grams of hash which he hadn't paid for ... Frankly, he left in a great hurry, and he had to borrow money from everyone – friends, parents, brothers and sisters. It was quite a sum, around 1,500 euros. I don't even know if his parents have had any news. Some say he preferred to forget where he came from once he'd found a new life.

The last member of our dream team was Hicham. No mystery in his case. He's dead. Suicide. He came to a bad end, but I still can't understand when and how he went over the edge. Because there were five of us, we lived on the same estate, we hung out together, grew up together. That's all it was, being a hittist: growing up with your mates and being bored all the time. Anyway, Hicham went off the rails and I don't know how it happened. But I wonder whether maybe it had something to do with the mosque. Because back in the years between 1990 and 1995, the mosques were controlled by Islamists, but sometimes there were also a few terrorists passing through ... For a couple of years, between the age of 18 and 20, he went to the mosque, but he never joined the underground, never talked of getting involved, never said anything about our little schemes reselling SIM cards. He called himself a Muslim but for me he was more like a mystic. Sometimes he'd vanish for a couple of days but he'd always come back looking good, and he said he'd been with his family. We were never really convinced, but since we had no proof of the opposite we thought that he'd just been chilling out at his parent's place. In fact he was messing around in criminal circles. And he was drinking more than was good for him. But when he was with us he was the same as always, warm and friendly, a nice guy. I only found out later, through Sélim, that in 1995, when the curfew was lifted, he spent his nights in smoke-filled back rooms, and he'd often emerge at dawn a lot poorer. He was slowly destroying himself but we had no idea. We finally found out one day when he came back bleeding, drunk and frozen. He'd been beaten up by thugs working for some crime boss from Algiers to whom he owed a lot of money. Instead of trying to pull himself together, he hit the bottle, hard and fast. From then on we only saw him occasionally, and he was always in a bad state. He didn't go back to his parents' place any more, we didn't know how he got by. Then one day he was found hanging in a garage in a housing estate nearby, where he had friends. It was a sad end, because Hicham had a very noble idea of friendship, the future, and Algeria. He found superhuman strength in carrying out that last, despairing act.

As you will have understood, the last of the hittists is a fiction. Although the term has had its day, there are still scores and scores of young people leaning against walls in every part of Algiers and the rest of Algeria. They are people without hope who try as best they can to earn a living, or sometimes just to stay alive. We were five mates, and now there's just me, standing at the entrance to our estate. I think about them when I smoke a joint, every now and then.

Notes

1 Maïssa Bey, *Nouvelles d'Algérie*, Grasset, Paris, 2011, p. 51.
2 Bey, *Nouvelles d'Algérie*, p. 61.

References

Adair, Philippe and Youghourta Bellache, 'Emploi et secteur informels en Algérie: Déterminants, segmentation et mobilité de la main-d'œuvre', *Régions et développement*, 35, 2012: pp. 121–149.
'Algérie, 50 ans après' (special issue), *Confluences Méditerranée*, 81, 2012.
Cellier, Hervé and Abla Rouag-Djenidi, eds, *Algérie-France. Jeunesse, ville et marginalité*, L'Harmattan, Paris, 2009.
Chouaki, Aziz and Bruno Hadjih, *Avoir 20 ans à Alger*, Alternatives, Paris, 2001.
Fellag, *Djurdjurassique Bled*, 1997.
Martinez, Luis, *The Algerian Civil War, 1990–1998*, trans. Jonathan Derrick, Hurst, London, in association with the Centre d'Etudes et de Recherches International, Paris, 2000.
Talahite, Fatiha, ed., 'Vingt-cinq ans de transformation post-socialiste en Algérie' (special issue), *Revue Tiers Monde*, 210, 2012.
Vergès, Myriam, 'La Casbah d'Alger: Chronique de la survie dans un quartier en sursis', *Naqd*, 6, 1993: pp. 36–43.

3

Coffee shops and youth sociability in Abu Dhabi

Laure Assaf

October 2011, Thursday morning, 8 a.m. Zaynab, an Emirati student whom I got to know a year earlier, has arranged to meet me at a Starbucks near her university. Like many such cafés in Abu Dhabi, it is part of a bigger structure: a commercial centre whose shops are still closed at this hour, within a hotel complex. Inside, a few customers are in line, placing an order – most of them are men, perhaps hotel guests. Zaynab is waiting for me nearby, sitting in one of the leather armchairs, her *shayla* (a light, black headscarf worn by women in the Gulf region) wrapped tightly around her face. We order two lattes and go sit down on the balcony, where the few tables are not directly visible from the inside. Thus hidden from view, Zaynab lets her *shayla* slip back, and we begin to chat.

Zaynab is twenty-three years old. She is completing an engineering degree at a university that recently opened a female campus: she will soon be one of the first women to graduate in her sector in the Emirates. She often comes to this café, about five minutes' drive from her campus. 'If you come at lunchtime, you'll see everybody', she says. 'All the girls come here, but they don't tell their family. […] Their parents won't approve because it's a hotel; there are men.' Zaynab leaves home at the same time every morning, no matter when her first class starts. Whenever she has a gap in her schedule, she takes advantage of this free time, away from family supervision, to come to Starbucks.

This chapter explores the social and leisure practices of young adults in and around coffee shops in Abu Dhabi in the early 2010s. In the multilingual context of the United Arab Emirates (UAE), the English name 'coffee shop' refers to upmarket cafés – often franchises of international brands like Starbucks, Costa and others – with cosmopolitan menus. A part of the urban landscape of the UAE since the turn of the millennium, they offer a new kind of sociability to the generations who have grown up alongside these urban transformations.

Living in the present

The ethnographic study from which this text is drawn focused on young adults, Emiratis and Arab expatriates, who grew up in Abu Dhabi and came of age in the first decades of the twenty-first century. They are mostly students and young professionals and belong to what could be considered the middle class. The various ways in which these young adults appropriate the space of the coffee shop reflect their lifestyles, aspirations and contradictions. Halfway between leisure activity and youth subculture, visiting coffee shops offers a degree of emancipation from the family and opens up a space of relative autonomy for the youth. Simultaneously, the consumerist space of the coffee shop fosters the emergence of new sets of norms and practices specific to this generation.

Urban mobility and independence

Zaynab's ability to enjoy Starbucks is the result of her persistent efforts towards negotiating more independence. An orphan, she lives with her brothers and sisters on the outskirts of Abu Dhabi, in one of the 'popular houses' (*al-buyut al sha'biyya*) built by the government in the 1970s in order to sedentarise Bedouin populations. Her family is far from wealthy, but they have benefited from the free public education guaranteed to Emirati citizens. Zaynab was awarded a university scholarship and uses this money to maintain her car and finance any necessary repairs to the family house. Although women are still in the minority in her engineering curriculum, they comprise the majority of the student population at public universities, on a national level. Higher education offers a route for young Emirati women to find a well-respected, highly skilled job, thus legitimising their presence in the workforce.

As she lives more than forty-five minutes away from the university, Zaynab managed – not without difficulty – to obtain from her siblings permission to drive her own car. She had to negotiate with her brother, now the head of the family, and her older sisters, most of whom are already working. In a city like Abu Dhabi, where public transport is rare – with the exception of public buses mainly used by low-income populations – going for a coffee with friends indeed raises the question of mobility. Having access to a car is an important concern for the youth, especially for young women, whose families often regard taking taxis or buses as inappropriate, both in terms of personal safety and reputation. Among my interlocutors, gender hierarchies were marked by different timelines in terms of access to mobility. Young men typically started driving as soon as they had a licence, while their female siblings depended on a family member

Coffee shops and youth sociability in Abu Dhabi

(or a private driver for those of wealthier backgrounds) to move around the city throughout their student years. Having their own car tended to happen later in life: it often coincided with their entry into the professional world. Zaynab, however, illustrates how these boundaries are flexible: she grew tired of being late for class because her brother would not wake up on time to drive her. With a laugh, she explains how she finally wore her family's resistance out: 'I cried! I cried and cried a lot, many times, until I convinced them to [let me] have a car.'

For many young people, having access to a car depends on their ability to pay for at least part of its upkeep, or maybe even its purchase. Driving therefore reflects twofold independence: it means being both mobile and, to a certain extent, financially independent. The car marks a stage in the life of young adults which also corresponds to the moment when they start meeting in cafés and paying for their food and drinks with money they have earned themselves. My interlocutors often described sociality in the coffee shops by contrast with their childhood and teenage years, spent wandering about in shopping malls (often without much money), stopping at fast-food joints after school or buying cheap snacks from neighbourhood grocery shops and sharing them on the street. The coffee shop is associated with a more adult form of sociability, while still being closely tied to college years.

Gendered spaces and new sociabilities

I meet Samir for the first time in late 2011. He comes to pick me up in a car which he says belongs to his mother, though he has been driving it since he was eighteen. Now that he is going to university, he has almost exclusive use of it. Samir does not like staying at home. A twenty-two-year-old Lebanese student, he is pursuing a master's in information technology at a private college. Before his classes, which begin towards the end of the afternoon, he typically joins his friends in a café. They chat, eat lunch together and sometimes do their homework. After class, he goes straight back. 'The good thing is that I don't need to call anyone', he says. 'I can just go and I know they'll be there.' Each group of friends he hangs out with has its favourite café, and Samir chooses which place to go based on whom he wants to meet. He makes a clear distinction between the 'men's cafés', small streetside places where the drink of choice is cheap *ahwé turkiyyé* (Turkish coffee) in a smoke-filled room, and the 'coffee shops', the more upscale, 'international' category of cafés, where he can meet his female friends.

Living in the present

He takes me to one of these coffee shops, the Tche Tche, located not far from the Corniche. The menu is a mix of shawarma and Caesar Salad, lattes and shishas. The prices are three to four times higher than those in streetside cafés, but the ambience here is more comfortable: leather seating and wooden tables, walls painted red and yellow, soft lighting and air-conditioning. Samir introduces me to his group of friends: Nawal, also twenty-two, the daughter of a Lebanese father and a British mother, and her best friend Maryam, a nineteen-year-old Palestinian accompanied by Saleh, whom she introduces to me as her fiancé. Maryam is dressed in a fitted top and black pants; her nails are painted the same bright yellow as her t-shirt. Nawal is wearing a red and black *hijab*, and a matching tunic and long skirt. Samir and Saleh are in jeans. We share a shisha, and from time to time Nawal lights a cigarette. A television screen is showing trendy Lebanese pop music clips: Nancy Ajram, Nawal al-Zoghbi, Mohamed Skandar. 'Basically, we live here', Nawal tells me.

Nawal, Samir and the others are representatives of a generation of Arab expatriates born in Abu Dhabi. Their fathers came to work in the Gulf in the 1970s and ended up staying and bringing their families. Regardless of how long they have been in the UAE, however, they are considered by the Emirati government as 'temporary workers': they can neither obtain permanent resident visas nor acquire Emirati citizenship. Under the *kafala* system, which governs foreigners' residence in the UAE, parents can act as sponsors (*kafil*) for their children until they turn eighteen for young men, and until marriage for young women. Samir's current course of study is partly a consequence of this rule. Extending his student visa by pursuing a master's degree was a convenient way to maintain his residence in the country while looking for a more permanent job. While these foreign youths, born and raised in Abu Dhabi, are more or less invisible in official discourses, they constitute an important part of its urban society. They appropriate the city notably by inhabiting cosmopolitan spaces like the coffee shops – spaces whose emergence itself is concomitant to their coming of age.

The considerable presence of young women in the coffee shops is certainly one of their most striking features, distinguishing them from other mostly male-dominated cafés. The coffee shop is not only a place where young men and women can mix, but also one of the main spaces in Abu Dhabi where it is possible for women to socialise among themselves. While access to public space for the youth varies considerably depending on one's family norms, it is generally difficult to invite new acquaintances to one's home. The domestic sphere is only open to longstanding friends, whom the family has gotten to know and trust.

Coffee shops and youth sociability in Abu Dhabi

Meeting at a café thus allows them to build a wider social circle, which includes acquaintances met at the university, at work or during outings in town. Zaynab almost exclusively meets other students at Starbucks and on campus, occasionally at birthday or graduation parties. When she occasionally has them over, it is typically during official holidays, like the Eid al-Fitr – moments when hospitality can be extended beyond the regular circles. Samir and Nawal met when they were both doing the same temporary job, helping with the organisation of Abu Dhabi's Formula One Grand Prix (their student visa only allows them to work part-time). They got along, stayed in touch, and Nawal then introduced Samir to the rest of the group. While Nawal's parents know that her group of friends includes young men, Maryam is the only one who has been to her home: mixed-gender friendships are reserved for the Tche Tche. In this sense, coffee shops act as an extension of other young adults' spaces, like the university campus; they are a place where the relationships fostered in these spaces can develop, and where new ones can emerge.

Friendships, intimacy and anonymity

Appropriations of the coffee shop exist along a continuum of which these two scenes probably constitute the two poles: the pursuit of familiarity on the one hand, and anonymity on the other. Nawal, Samir and their friends, who spend most of their time at the Tche Tche, know the waiters very well. They are all Arabic speakers (the waiters are Lebanese and Syrian), call each other by their first names and sometimes sit together around a table to chat. The group occupies the space of the café with a casual familiarity: even though they leave their bags beside a table, they come and go as they like, popping out in small groups for a chat, or moving the tables around to accommodate newcomers, whenever other friends decide to join them. The café, which is at once public and enclosed, is for them an intimate space outside the home. Few young adults indeed live alone: the constraints of the housing market in Abu Dhabi make it difficult even for financially independent young people to leave the family home. Studios and small apartments are in short supply, and rents are very high. The coffee shop is thus a place of collective intimacy for the group of peers.

For Zaynab and many of her classmates, the Starbucks near their campus also represents an intimate space away from home. But here, intimacy is achieved through a certain degree of anonymity. Indeed, being in a public space – and in particular, being seen by a member of their extended family in a public space – constitutes a risk to the reputation (*sum'a*) of young women. How these rules are verbalised and enforced varies widely according to the family, but most young women I met mentioned the need to be careful when navigating the city. As Shamma, another Emirati student I met through Zaynab, puts it: 'My family knows that I don't do anything bad. But you know, it's very important to take precautions.' Shamma distinguishes between her immediate family – parents, brothers and sisters, with whom she has a relationship of trust – and the extended family, whose intentions and judgements are less predictable. Taking precautions can mean, for example, bringing along family members when going out. 'There are exceptions. If you go to a public place with a certain objective, and you're part of a big group, for example five people … and if one of them is your mother, or your older sister, that's good; people know you are not there to have fun or to do something bad', continues Shamma. Young women often go out with their sisters and their female cousins. Sometimes, the elder ones make the younger sit at another table, so that they can chat freely. Female friends can then occasionally be integrated into these groups. By contrast, the coffee shop across from their campus is relatively safe: used mainly by foreigners and tourists, there is little risk there to meet someone they know, beyond other students. Even if they were to be seen, they consider Starbucks to be respectable enough for their presence not to truly damage their reputations.

At times, however, the desired form of sociability runs directly against social norms – like in the case of romantic relationships. Since relationships before marriage are socially transgressive, flirting or meeting someone of the opposite sex supposes to circumvent the usual codes of behaviour in public spaces. In the mid-2000s, the use of Bluetooth-enabled mobile phones, which can send messages to other phones located within a certain distance without knowing their number, became a popular mode of communication in the Arabian Peninsula. Since the phone's owner is only identified by a pseudonym, it made it possible to communicate with members of the opposite sex under a veil of anonymity, without breaking the norms of decency. The space of the coffee shop, both intimate and public, is ideal for this type of interaction. In the 2010s, Blackberry Messenger fulfils a similar function. Swapping BBM pins with other users has replaced the exchange of telephone numbers: as the pin is neither associated with a name nor a phone number, it greatly facilitates interaction, while also making it easier to withdraw. The conversations thus engaged may eventually lead to a meeting or a serious relationship, but they most often come to nothing, and are mainly sought after for the temporary transgressions they allow. Just like the coffee shop or the car, mobile phones have opened up a sphere of intimacy and confidentiality for young adults: conversations and photos exchanged via instant messaging escape family control more easily than, for example, a phone conversation.

Navigating class, cosmopolitanism and belonging

The emergence of coffee shops in Abu Dhabi is yet another instance of a process of constant urban change which has characterised the Emirati capital since the beginning of oil exploitation in 1962. The young people described in this chapter grew up along with the development of skyscrapers and shopping malls, with and within an ever-transforming urban space. In this sense, recently built public spaces lend themselves to the invention of new ways to interact in, share and occupy these urban territories. While young people are not the only users of coffee shops, they appropriate this space in ways that are specific to their generation.

At the same time, coffee shops participate in the production of social hierarchies within Abu Dhabi's urban society. Indeed, if coffee shops are available for youth sociality, it is in part because they are exclusive spaces: their prices, very high compared to streetside cafés and restaurants, make them the preserve of Abu Dhabi's middle and upper classes. The capital's population is indeed characterised both by its impressive diversity – 88 per cent of its inhabitants are foreign residents – and by strong hierarchies which tend to superpose nationality, ethnicity and class. Coffee shops' prices and location (they are often found in upscale shopping malls) make them in practice inaccessible to the poorer categories of the population – mostly male South Asian expatriates occupying low-skilled jobs. These social barriers are at the heart of the success of these establishments: they ensure that coffee shops are considered by their clientele as safe, socially homogeneous spaces. In addition, the presence of staff members and, in locations like shopping malls, security personnel, guarantees respectability: although some of the groups are mixed-gender, staff and other visitors ensure the social control necessary to limit any close physical contact. The perceived comfort and safety of coffee shops are what allow youth sociality. Families can be reassured that nothing wrong will happen and, even when they are kept in the dark, like in the case of Zaynab, the risk posed to young people's reputations is limited. The fact that many customers are part of the same group of peers thus facilitates frequentation.

If the comfortable, upscale atmosphere of coffee shops makes them particularly available to young users, their cosmopolitan dimension also plays an important part in their appropriation by young people. Orders are often placed in English, and the food is international: even regional dishes like *mezze* tend to be standardised. Linguistic code-switching between English and Arabic constitutes a characteristic of the generations who grew up in the Gulf. English is the dominant language of education: even within Emirati public school curricula, all subjects are taught in English, with the exception of Arabic language and civilisation and religious education, which are taught in standard Arabic. Parents and grandparents regularly complain about young people's lack of proficiency in classical Arabic. As for my young interlocutors, they distinguished between the dialectal Arabic they spoke at home – related to their family's country of origin – and the language they used with their peers. The latter borrows from both colloquial and standard Arabic, thus blurring regional differences in order to be understood by all, in a context where groups of friends include members from all across the Arab world.

Finally, the cosmopolitan dimension of these cafés takes on an emancipatory character by enabling young adults to expand their horizons beyond the local and to assert their belonging to a more global community. Zaynab and her friends are familiar with the codes of behaviour expected in places like coffee shops. Therefore, they feel at ease at Starbucks, even though their families might not entirely approve of their presence. Indeed, Zaynab makes a direct connection between going to the coffee shop and her choice of studies. When I meet her at Starbucks, she has just finished an internship with a government company. She eagerly recounts how she asserted her status as an engineer by refusing to sit with the secretaries (the only other female employees) during a collective meal, even though this meant that she was the only woman at her table – and thus felt very uncomfortable. For her, bypassing family norms by sneaking into Starbucks in-between classes and disrupting gender hierarchies at work are part of the same quest for more autonomy.

This emancipatory dimension is perhaps even more pronounced for the second group described earlier. Like numerous young people of their generation, Nawal, Samir and Maryam were born, grew up and studied in Abu Dhabi. Although their status as foreign residents means they might have to leave the country if they cannot find a job or if their visa is not renewed, they feel a strong sense of attachment to the city: 'I love Abu Dhabi. If I had to leave I would die', Nawal tells me, after mentioning the holidays spent with her paternal family in Lebanon. In this context, the coffee shop thus offers a means of appropriating Abu Dhabi in its global and cosmopolitan dimension, beyond the (exclusive) national scale. It becomes, in short, a site of belonging.

It is precisely their international formula, together with the fact that they emerged recently, that turns coffee shops into spaces where new forms of sociability can be experienced. Highlighting a tension between social constraints and the individual and collective tactics devised by the youth to bypass them, the coffee shop also redefines gender relations, at least to a certain extent, as well as modes of belonging. Indeed, the collective practices at play in these spaces draw the contours of a group defined in terms of age and generation, rather than through the binary between citizens and noncitizens. As such, the forms of sociability invented in this space correspond both to a moment in the lives of these young adults and in the transformations of Emirati society.

Post-script (2021)

Since this chapter was first written, almost nine years ago, the landscape of coffee shops in Abu Dhabi – and, alongside it, youth sociability – has largely transformed. In recent years, locally owned 'speciality cafés', with hipster decors and sourced coffee beans, have become especially popular among Emirati youth, and have led to more differentiated and spatialised youth practices, along the lines of nationality, gender and class. Instagram, Snapchat and TikTok have relegated the BBM Messenger of the early 2010s to a fleeting fashion and a thing of the past that most of today's young adults probably do not recall.

If many of the social dynamics described in this chapter remain accurate, one aspect has also undergone an important shift. The 'invisibility' of foreign youths, which I discuss here at length, has been called into question in the past decade – both in academic literature and, importantly, by these UAE-born generations themselves. In a sense, youth practices have become more self-reflective, with many young artists and writers tackling the question of belonging. Their work notably highlights how many commercial urban spaces like international coffee shops – often discarded as a uniformised non-place – were instrumental in the shaping of their identities.

References

Deeb, Lara and Mona Harb, *Leisurely Islam. Negotiating Geography and Morality in Shi'ite South Beirut*, Princeton University Press, Princeton, NJ, 2013.

Living in the present

Le Renard, Amélie, *A Society of Young Women. Opportunities of Place, Power and Reform in Saudi Arabia*, Stanford University Press, Stanford, CA, 2014.
Peterson, Mark A., *Connected in Cairo. Growing up Cosmopolitan in the Modern Middle East*, Indiana University Press, Bloomington, IN, 2011.
Vora, Neha, *Impossible Citizens. Dubai's Indian Diaspora*, Duke University Press, Durham, NC, 2013.

4
From TV soaps to web dramas

A new platform for young Arabs

Yves Gonzalez-Quijano

After reigning supreme over the cultural practices of the majority of the population for half a century, the TV screen is now being supplanted by increasingly powerful new rivals in the Arab world – computer screens and smartphones. The decline in viewing figures is driven largely by the youngest segments of the population who have been abandoning television for audio-visual online offerings. Studies on consumption and cultural practices suggest that from Morocco to Saudi Arabia, watching satellite channels is still the main leisure activity for large parts of the population, but it is the web, with its multiple uses and infinite possibilities, that has become the first choice for young people.

Around the year 2005, the quiet revolution of Web 2.0 exponentially accelerated the growth of the Arab Internet, so that social networks – which originally were anything but political tools – are now bringing about another turning point in the cultural habits of the region. Gone is the era of watching TV soaps and series, a quasi-religious ritual, which had become closely linked to the social rhythm of the month of Ramadan: after breaking the daily fast, families and neighbours spent the long evenings together, watching and discussing TV series that had been written and filmed long in advance for this peak-time audience. But now is the age of the online series.

The astonishing success of *Shankaboot*

Fed on a diet of satellite channels and video clips, Arab youth – at least urban middle-class Arab youth – are increasingly turning to the Internet. Unlike previous generations who watched TV at home with their families and grew up with the same soaps and series, the most famous of which were broadcast all over the region, the millennial generation is abandoning domestic screens,

Living in the present

even high-tech plasma ones, to log into their own programmes whenever they want, following their own rhythms and their own choices of social networks and nomadic applications that now determine the pattern of their everyday life.

The spirit of this small cultural revolution is encapsulated in the astonishing success of *Shankaboot*, the first drama series in Arabic to be exclusively broadcast on the Internet. With peaks of more than 3,000 viewings a day, mostly from Lebanon, where it is set, but also from other Middle Eastern countries, *Shankaboot*, launched in 2010, has been watched more than 600,000 times on YouTube, while its Facebook page has 40,000 members. This success was crowned by a prestigious Emmy Award (the only previous Arabic winner, in 2008, was *Al Ijtiyah*, a Jordanian production). Its title, a neologism that cannot be found in any dictionary, is quite a story in itself. A portmanteau word combining two different Arabic terms for the web – *shabaka* (web) and *'ankabut* (spider) – *Shankaboot* is the name which the teenage hero of the series, Suleiman, has given to his scooter. Suleiman, who is fifteen but tells everybody he is twenty, has left school and is earning a living as a delivery boy in his neighbourhood, fetching the shopping for the old lady upstairs, bringing the spare parts for the workshop on the corner, or flowers and gifts for happy occasions. Presented in episodes that are just a few minutes long (a format adapted to the slow download speeds in Lebanon but also to the ways young people navigate the web), Suleiman's local encounters offer a pretext for talking about topics that are rarely tackled by classic TV productions: drugs, confessionalism, prostitution and sex, the treatment of immigrant workers, and foreign domestic staff in particular, and the social realities of a society preoccupied with money and appearances. Although reflecting Lebanese experience, these subjects are relevant to a greater or lesser extent in many of the societies of the region. Young Arabs can readily identify with the characters in *Shankaboot*, all the more so because the series neither moralises nor preaches. It explores issues that mainstream media would not normally touch, approaching them through the eyes of young people today, with their own way of questioning things, their own cultural codes and their own language.

The series' production company, Batoota Films, headed by Katia Saleh, whose previous experience includes a stint at Channel 4 in the UK, certainly did not invent the concept of online drama, but it did give it a local identity by working with a team of young writers like Bassem Breish, who researched the script carefully – for example by meeting the real people involved in the various events that inspired their writing. *Shankaboot* is much more than just a series: the site where episodes can be viewed (in addition to Facebook, YouTube

From TV soaps to web dramas

and Twitter) has been devised to encourage as much interactivity as possible. The audience is invited to discuss the various topics raised in the series and even to intervene in the storyline, for example, by voting on an ending deliberately left open in the original screenplay or 'correcting' one proposed by the scriptwriters. There are also presentations in schools and at festivals and other events aimed at local youth. Workshops in neighbouring countries attempt to spread the '*Shankaboot* spirit' throughout the region (a third of users, mostly aged between fifteen and twenty-five come from neighbouring countries like Jordan, Egypt and Saudi Arabia). A section of the site called 'Shankactive' offers a platform where tomorrow's talents can showcase their work by uploading short videos they have shot on their mobile phones.

A generation conquers the screens

With funding from the BBC World Service Trust and other high-profile commercial sponsors, including the Finnish mobile phone manufacturer Nokia, *Shankaboot* is not really a commercial project. Its main aim is to use the universe of modern communication to encourage a public debate about social questions among young people. From the start, the concept drew on the full range of dialogical possibilities of social networks, rather than just the monological structure of the TV channel: *Shankaboot* wanted to help fifteen- to twenty-five-year-olds to escape their 'digital lethargy' by offering them something other than bland soap operas like those made in Turkey or Latin America.

Its mission has certainly been accomplished, judging from the impact the series has had, and also from subsequent events in the Arab world! Of course, *Shankaboot* does not claim to do anything more than to entertain, albeit intelligently, but it is still hard not to draw a link between its concerns and the uprisings that shook the Arab world a little less than a year after the first episodes were shown. In both cases, it has been young Arabs who through a multitude of social network platforms have conquered the screens and thus expressed a political demand that had remained silent until then. These fictional stories about young Arabs may not be part of a political discourse in the traditional sense, but it is easy to see, beyond each specific story, echoes of the wider questioning that has inspired the youngest and most active fringes of popular protests. Among many other examples, a particularly striking video was produced as part of a workshop in Syria organised by Batoota Films for Shankaboot followers recruited through their site. Aired in May 2011 on the 'Shankactive' section of the website, this short tale of only a few minutes, filmed with a Nokia N8 phone as specified by the site, tells the story of a young Syrian travelling up and down his country 'looking for the cheapest possible grave'. A succession of brief interviews with ordinary people intercut with speeded-up shots of Syrian streets, it foreshadowed the many dramatic videos that the opposition would post on social media just a few months or even weeks later.

Despite considerable success both in international professional circles and with the local audience, plans for a sixth season that would have seen *Shankaboot* expand to new horizons have been slow to get off the ground. More recent online series, like *Fasateen* (the story of three young Lebanese women whose paths cross) or *Mamnou3* (which pokes fun at censorship), have shown that the market for online drama in the Arab world is still too narrow to attract investors. Broadcasters still prefer traditional series, especially foreign productions, which are rapidly dubbed into Arabic and are available at prices that are difficult to beat. Despite its success – or rather because of it – *Shankaboot*'s boldness and its commitment to freedom of expression scare off potential backers in the region, especially in the Gulf States. Paradoxically, it might be its internationalisation that could give the Arab adventure of *Shankaboot* the chance of a longer life. One of the future projects that Katia Saleh's team is pitching is a sequel in which Suleiman travels around the world, perhaps still on his scooter, meeting other young people (especially distant descendants of Lebanese immigrants to Latin America). This could be one way to amplify the voice of young Arabs, first heard on social networks, and then, after the uprisings of 2011, in the street.

References

Facebook page: www.facebook.com/shankaboot
Wikipedia entry: https://en.wikipedia.org/wiki/Shankaboot
YouTube channel: www.youtube.com/user/Shankaboot

5

The *buyat*

Subverting gender norms in Saudi Arabia

Amélie Le Renard

> It is strictly forbidden to wear large chains with pendants that have motifs contrary to correct practice, such as skulls, indecent expressions, or photographs of famous people. It is also forbidden to have piercings in unusual places such as the mouth or chin, or the upper part of the ears, near the eyebrows, etc.

This was the message from the Bureau of the Supervision and Guidance Unit displayed in 2008 on wall posters at the women-only campus of King Saud University in Riyadh.[1] These prohibitions, ignored by quite a number of students, were aimed at various minority 'styles' that have sprung up there, particularly those of 'goths' and 'emos' ('emo', from the word 'emotion', originally referred to a particular genre of rock music; the term now designates a subculture that is characterised by dark clothes and make-up), as well as the *buyat*. This last neologism comes from the English 'boy', to which the Arabic suffix of feminisation -a (plural -at) has been added. In many countries of the Arabian Peninsula, and notably Saudi Arabia, the Emirates and Kuwait, the term is applied to people assigned female who wear clothes considered 'masculine'. They may avoid figure-hugging outfits, replacing them with men's shirts, football jerseys and other loose-fitting tops, and occasionally a band or binder to flatten their chest. This is markedly different from the 'Islamic' form of dress intended to conceal what are considered to be female physical attributes, but without casting doubt on gender classifications. Those who define themselves or are regarded as *buyat* usually have short hair and sometimes piercings in the upper part of the ear or on the eyebrow ridge. Some of them wear masculine scents, and a few choose to be called by a male first name. The ones I talked to used their (female) given names and the corresponding pronouns. In the course of conversation, without me asking the question, they defined themselves as *buyat*, an identity around which various online forums and open pages or closed Facebook groups have been created, which allow users to meet and exchange personal stories, photos, videos, etc. Whereas some press articles and debates on Gulf TV channels treat the 'phenomenon' as pathological, using the term 'masculinisation' (*istirjal*), and often associate it with 'affective relationships between girls', the Saudi students I met more often describe it as a 'style' – using the English word with Saudi pronunciation. It is thus interpreted as a fashion or subculture.

It was in the course of extensive sociological fieldwork researching young Saudi women's access to public space in Riyadh (carried out between 2005 and 2009) that I was given permission to visit the women's university campus. As men are forbidden to enter, female-assigned students do not wear a veil or an *abaya* (a long black overgarment) as they would in mixed spaces; long skirts are obligatory and trousers forbidden. This is a public university and students pay no fees. Almost all the students are Saudi nationals but they come from very different social backgrounds. The campus is the most accessible social space they have: there they form different friendship groups, which would not necessarily meet elsewhere, given the restrictions on women's freedom of movement in the city.

The public performances of *buyat*, and their interpretation in terms of 'style', reveal the struggles and negotiations around gender norms that are played out in the spaces shared by young urban Saudi women. Following an ethnographic approach based on observation of the campus and discussions with students, I will analyse the meanings attached to the *buya* style within the Saudi context and its characterisation by those who adopt it – as well as by others. Even though transgressive styles and sexual categories circulate transnationally, globally and regionally, they are charged with local values and meanings.

It would be important to explore other examples of subcultures beyond the *buyat* – academic research has often amplified the invisibilisation of minorities in a number of contexts. Many publications on Arab societies have made generalisations about 'youth' even when they have only been talking about 'young men': these are then often described as dangerous, unemployed, Islamists or rebels. 'Women' on the other hand have been treated as a single, homogeneous group, without age, class or convictions, oppressed and in danger. It is time to abandon such binary clichés. The choices made by young Saudi women – some might define themselves in other ways, as we shall see – are actually diverse and complex and do not necessarily correspond to the most common stereotypes.

The *buyat*

Challenging dominant norms of femininity

It is certainly nothing new for persons categorised as female to adopt self-presentations more commonly associated with men. Yet the word *buya* is relatively new, just like the 'style' it refers to and the occasional media interest in this 'social phenomenon'. While it was probably still marginal at the beginning of the 2000s,[2] the *buya* style had become highly visible and widespread on campus by 2008.

When I began to discuss the subject with students, whether *buyat* or not, several of them told me about the American/Canadian TV series *The L Word*, which was viewable on the internet (with Arabic subtitles). Launched in 2004, it follows the lives and loves of a group of lesbians in Los Angeles. Several young Saudi women told me that many of their peers were infatuated with one of the characters, Shane, who, with her short shaggy hairstyle, was often described as the most androgynous character in the series and became a model for them. But despite this repeated reference, the *buya* style is more than just an import from the United States. Characters who transgress dominant gender norms have also been created for local TV series and broadcast throughout the Arabian Peninsula. In the Kuwaiti series *'Adil ruh*, for example, shown for the first time during Ramadan in 2005 (hence soon after the first showing of *The L Word*), the female comedian Shujun al-Hajiri plays a *buya*. Popular among young Saudi women, this series stages the ups and downs of a wealthy Kuwaiti family. One of the adult children of the household is a *buya*, and she is treated just like all the other characters.

Several *buyat* affirm that these series had an impact on them, not just in terms of the content they presented but also because they were the starting point for online forums that brought women together. The kind of self-presentation popularised by programmes like these involves meanings and practices that are specific to the Saudi context. During our conversations, several women justified their self-presentation as *buyat* by saying that they would have preferred to be men, which would have allowed them to move around freely ('I want to be able to drive, not wear an *abaya*, to breathe'). They said that they were tired of always having to tell their parents where they had been and where they were going, and having to ask for permission to go out ('My parents are always saying, "You're a girl! When are you leaving? When are you coming back?" etc.'). Some of them refused to cover their hair in mixed spaces and complained about having to wear an *abaya*, which directly puts them in a gender category, whereas without the *abaya*, they could sow a seed of doubt in people's minds or be categorised as male. One of them deplored the fact that Saudi women consider themselves to be physically weak and in need of help and support from male family members. Some affirmed that they would not hesitate to fight and that female students sometimes came to blows on campus – something I witnessed myself. Some told me that they had been 'tomboys' since their early childhood, whilst others said that they had become *buyat* a little later in life, often when they went to secondary school or to university. The views expressed here do not constitute the reasons for assuming such a self-presentation but rather show how the persons I met justify their choice *a posteriori* and make sense of the difficulties they face in everyday life. The 'style' is also often accompanied by challenges to the dominant model of femininity, which does not necessarily mean that those who adopt it pursue a conscious strategy.

Fluidity of sexual categories

If a character like Shane in *The L Word* is simultaneously identified as both 'androgynous' and a 'lesbian', this link between self-presentation (in terms of gender) and 'sexual orientation' (which constitutes in itself a situated discourse) is obviously not inevitable. What is more, in the Saudi context, having emotional, loving or sexual relationships with members of the same sex is not necessarily considered the basis for an individual identity that has to be lived in public (for men, this could lead to very harsh punishment). The majority of *buyat* with whom I discussed this issue confided that they had different types of relationships with other young women, but that nobody apart from their closest friends was privy to the fact. Suzan, a nineteen-year-old interviewee, explained it like this:

> My parents know I am a *buya* and they give me a hard time because of it. I tell my parents that I am normal, that I am the same inside as outside. My mother knows about it because of my appearance but [she does] not [know that I am a] lesbian. She says that I am pretending, that I am playing, and I tell her that if I tried to be a girl that would be playing.

Students, whether *buyat* or not, use different words to describe their practices and relationships, as is shown by a discussion I had with a group of them. After we had talked about the university and the campus, Shaykha, the most welcoming towards me, who did not identify as *buya*, asked me straight out if I was surprised by the presence of *lesbians* on campus. A little later we discussed how others see *buyat*:

The *buyat*

Shaykha: For me it's a matter of personal freedom, I'm with everyone, I'll sit down with anyone. I don't have relationships, either with boys or girls.
Badriyya: I used to have relationships with girls, but I don't any more. I stopped because Islam forbids it (*haram fi-l-islam*).
Nura: I went out with boys, then with girls, then with boys again.
Badriyya: No one else knows what we're telling you, otherwise we'd be in trouble.
Shaykha: But actually very few girls love neither boys nor girls, they are *straight*, and they feel fine without any love relationships.
Nura: Sorry to tell you this, Shaykha! 'Straight' means girls who love boys [laughter].

In this conversation, we can observe constant slippages between questions of 'masculinisation' and 'sexual orientation'. We see how different meanings can be given to terms that are borrowed from English and then become part of Saudi language. The informants quoted here have travelled very little, if at all, and their English is very basic. Talking to me, Shaykha defines herself as 'straight' because she does not have secret relationships with either boys or girls and does not feel the need for them. She uses the word in a specific Saudi context, in which relationships outside marriage are banned. Nura uses it in a different normative framework, to classify different forms of 'sexual orientation'. Words such as these, which are mostly borrowed from English, are only used by the younger generation, those who watch TV series that can be viewed on the Internet. But a little later in the conversation, Nura and Badriyya explain to me that they also use an old, obsolete dialect word for 'female friend' (*khawiyya*), to designate an intimate relationship. According to another interviewee, this is a continuation of older forms of relationships between women that go beyond friendship – and here she was speaking of her grandmother's generation.

Some of those who do not self-define as *buya* automatically associate 'masculinisation' with 'loving girls', or 'homosexuality', as does this non-*buya* during an interview:

> The proportion of homosexuality is very high in our schools. My sister, who's a bit younger than me, says 'there are lots of *buyat*'. These are masculinised girls. They don't remove their body hair, they cut their hair short, like boys, and they love girls.

But this was not the case with all of them. Fuz, a student who did not self-define as *buya*, explained it this way:

Living in the present

> There are masculinised girls who behave like men, or who would like to be men, and who have friends who are really chic, cute and feminine [*na'uma, bannuta*], I'm the boy, you're the girl, that's part of it. Those are lesbians [*lesbian*]. But not always, sometimes they're not lesbians, sometimes you realise that the girl is just happy for someone to take care of her, and that's all, she's not a lesbian. But sometimes not.

Fuz's vocabulary here reflects the classification of gender performances which exist today in the 'society of young women'. She uses not only the adjective 'masculinised' but also terms describing the partner's 'hyperfemininity'. The first dialectal term (*na'uma*) is formed from the adjective for 'feminine' with an added amplification ('hyperfeminine'); the second (*bannuta*) is the diminutive of 'girl' and usually refers to a cute little girl. On campus, some students walk along as couples, hand in hand, or arm in arm, one being, according to the terms used by the informants, a *buya* (short hair, baggy sweatshirt, men's trainers) the other, 'feminine' or 'cute' (blow-dried long hair, waisted, figure-hugging clothing). These categorisations and classifications take us back to the adoption of words from English, which acquire a particular meaning in the Saudi context. The *buya–cute* couple might be close to the *butch–femme* couple, marking the opposition in the US context between two kinds of gender performance (one being characterised as 'masculine', butch, and the other as 'feminine', femme). However, the *buya–cute* 'couple' is inscribed in an urban context where gender segregation means that the married heterosexual couple has no real public existence. In Riyadh, it is very rare to see a Saudi husband and wife strolling hand in hand together in a park, along a promenade or in a shopping mall. They may walk together but need to keep some distance apart, and the woman wears an *abaya*, generally with her face covered. *Buya–cute* couples perform a public image of the couple which in fact does not exist in Saudi Arabia except on advertising posters. Their performance makes visible emotional, loving and/or sexual relationships between girls even when these are more often stigmatised and hidden: in certain situations some of them, but by no means all, define themselves as 'lesbians'. Moreover, as Fuz's remarks show, they are not necessarily categorised as such by those around them.

Multiple interpretations

The dominant interpretation of *buya* self-presentation as a 'style' – at least among young Saudi women – has ambivalent effects. In a number of societies, the first decade of the twenty-first century, especially after the Queen Boat affair (the arrest and trial of some fifty men in a Cairo gay club in 2001), was marked by both an increasing public assertion of LGBT demands and a radicalisation of anti-gay statements and actions, which were often justified by a supposed cultural or religious 'authenticity' that sets itself against 'Western interference'. This discursive register of threatened 'authenticity', together with that of a denunciation supported by references to Islam, of 'sexual deviance' (*shudhudh*) and '(gender) confusion' (*tashabbuh*), was used in relation to the *buyat* in *An Hour of Frank Speaking*, a broadcast (in Arabic) by a preacher on the Kuwaiti channel Al-Ra'i. But this is only one of the possible registers in the many broadcasts devoted to 'masculinisation' on Emirati or Kuwaiti channels.

In Saudi Arabia, where no one is making public demands for the rights of lesbian, gay, or trans people, the few press commentaries on 'masculinised women' or 'affective relationships between girls' most often borrow from a transnational psychological register of pathology. The tone is rarely one of indignation. For example, in a readers' letters column published in August 2008 in the Islamic women's magazine *Hayat*, aimed at fifteen- to twenty-five-year-olds, a reader who specifies that she is pious and practising (*multazima*, literally 'committed to religion') asks for advice on the subject of the 'love' and 'affection' she feels for her (female) friend. The reply first identifies this attraction as a form of 'deviance', a breaking of religious rules, then recommends looking look for causes in childhood (sexual abuse, etc.) and undergoing psychotherapy. This is also the register that certain female preachers adopt at campus conferences on 'masculinisation'. A poster for this type of event in 2008 states 'Be proud of your femininity; masculinisation is not for you: we are making a stand against whatever confuses your feminine nature'. Moreover, some preachers work directly with women psychologists and other specialists in the education of 'young women'.

The non-*buyat* I spoke to often adopted this psychological register when they explained the phenomenon by invoking a 'psychological problem', an 'emotional lack' or a 'family break-up'. But most often they insisted on the fact that many of those who adopt the *buya* style do so because of 'fashion'. More precisely, they went beyond the diversity of appearances (from a simple short haircut to the adoption of a masculine first name) to set up a binary distinction between 'real' *buyat*, that is, those who had wanted to dress or behave like men since childhood, whose desire came from 'inside', and those who adopted short hair and an ambiguous appearance simply because that was the fashion, to 'attract attention'. It is this latter attitude that Fuz (quoted above) talked about:

Living in the present

There are girls who wear men's football jerseys etc., like American rappers, they wear clothes like this and walk like boys, but inside, no, you talk to her and she's a girl, but that's her style. […] There are places where you can see this, but these are not places where I go very often. You find it for example in the *mamlakat al mar'ah* shopping mall [she refers to the women-only floor at the Mall Kingdom Centre in Riyadh]. You sometimes find that style there, the girls who cut their hair short, don't wear the veil and walk like this [she tries to imitate a walk that she considers 'masculine'].

Consumerism and the ambivalences of a 'style'

Although self-presentation as *buya* transgresses the dominant norms of femininity found among young Saudi women, it is nevertheless inscribed in the context of fully developed consumerism. In the 2000s, shopping malls, offering all the big international brands, spread throughout Riyadh, from the wealthiest districts to lower-middle-class areas – everywhere apart from the poorest neighbourhoods. In the spaces where they meet – campuses, workplaces, commercial centres, private parties – young Saudi women see it as very important to have a 'style', to follow fashion, yet be original at the same time. The most common version of femininity performed by young, urban Saudi women in the spaces from which men are excluded seems to be inspired by Lebanese singers on the Rotana TV channel – figure-hugging clothing, high heels, blow-dried long hair and make-up. Conforming to this pervasive 'style', just like conforming to *buya* style, requires students to buy fashionable accessories, go to the hairdressers regularly and get their hair cut and dyed according to the latest trend. These two 'styles' are not just reserved for the wealthiest but adopted by students from all classes, even if not all of them can afford to buy the 'top brands' or go to the trendiest hairdressing salons.

On campus, the *buyat* do not constitute a separate group from those categorised as 'feminine'. Some groups, like Shaykha's, do include them but others do not. Some students judge *buyat* very harshly (calling them 'dirty', 'common', 'deviant'), but the fact that this self-presentation is partly considered as a 'style' and adopted by so many youths is probably one of the reasons why, despite its subversive charge, it escapes outright condemnation. This, in turn, favours its spread on campus, where breaking rules about public behaviour (rules which are particularly strict in relation to clothing) can enhance status, at least up to a point. This subversive model can thus be partially adopted even by students who do not necessarily identify as *buyat* or for whom this is not linked to other practices that transgress dominant norms of gender and sexuality. This leads to an ambivalence between the resistance to dominant gender norms and consumerist practice, an ambivalence that can be found not just among the *buyat* but also among many young Saudi women.

Even though *buya* 'style', like other fashion 'styles' adopted in Saudi Arabia, means buying European or American fashion brands, it is not widely discredited as a 'Western import'. This is despite supposed 'Western influence' constituting one of the arguments frequently used in Saudi Arabia and in other Arab societies to oppose claims for women's rights. That public institutions such as the university are trying to ban the *buya* style has much more to do with the fact that it does not conform to a model of 'respectable' femininity. Due to the strict gender segregation in the capital, divergences from the dominant norms of femininity are probably less severely punished than they would be in mixed social spaces, but on campus, in the absence of men, institutional regulations aim at compelling students to conform to 'feminine' self-presentation. Yet these students seem to pay little attention to the prohibition quoted at the beginning of this chapter. The *buyat* I interviewed had received frequent warnings from the 'supervision and guidance unit', had signed 'promises not to do it again' and sometimes lost marks from their end-of-semester grade; yet even so, they said that this would not make them change their behaviour in the slightest. Nonetheless, in spite of this casual defiance, this self-presentation seemed relatively less visible on campus in 2012 than it had been in 2008. We might suppose, then, that its subversive possibilities do not prevent it from 'going out of fashion', that is, becoming less popular, precisely because many saw it as a 'style'. But it has certainly not disappeared.

Post-script

This chapter was written before the development of academic queer studies in the Middle East. My intention when writing was to respect my interviewees' use of words and categories. As I read the text ten years after its initial writing, however, I had the feeling that it did not leave enough space for female-assigned persons who did not define themselves as women. I chose to insert more gender-neutral terms in the present translated version, while still avoiding the use of categories (such as *trans*) that the people I met did not use at the time, at least in my presence. To my knowledge, there has been no study of *buyat*, or of other gender and sexual minorities in Saudi Arabia since then, but the global and regional circulations of categories and cultural products through the Internet have tremendously intensified, and it would be interesting to update this modest study.

Notes

1 My thanks to Cha Prieur and Alexandre Jaunait for re-reading this chapter and for their suggestions. All the ideas expressed here are of course the author's own.
2 It was also described as such in the 2005 bestseller *The Girls of Riyadh*. Using the device of (fictional) emails that a female narrator sends to a listserv, the book tells the story of the trials of four young Saudi women (their studies, everyday life, friendships, family conflicts, early careers, marriages and divorces, etc.).

References

Alsanea, Rajaa, *The Girls of Riyadh*, trans. by the author with Marilyn Booth, Penguin, New York, 2008.
al-Harez, Siba, *The Others*, Telegram Books, London, 2009.
Broqua, Christophe and Fred Eboko, eds, *Autrepart*, 49, 2009: *La fabrique des identités sexuelles*.
Butler, Judith, *Gender Trouble. Feminism and the Subversion of Identity*, Routledge, London and New York, 1990.
Kunstman, Adi, and Noor al-Qasimi, 'Queering Middle Eastern Cyberscapes', *Journal of Middle East Women's Studies*, 8, 3, 2012: pp. 1–13.
Le Renard, Amélie, *A Society of Young Women. Opportunities of Place, Power and Reform in Saudi Arabia*, Stanford University Press, Stanford, CA, 2014.
McRobbie, Angela, *Feminism and Youth Culture*, Routledge, New York, 2000.

6

From *jihad* to Sufi ecstasy

Politico-religious trajectories in pre-revolutionary Syria

Thomas Pierret

Young people's participation in religious activities in a Muslim context is often seen as a potential antechamber to political engagement. Such a view is not necessarily mistaken, as can be seen, for example, from the recruitment strategy of the Muslim Brotherhood. But nor is it always accurate, and the relationship can in fact sometimes be the exact opposite: the desire for social and political engagement ultimately leads to a new form of religious practice. Following the trajectory of young Syrian Muslims seeking a religious discourse with a political purchase, or one at least capable of coming to grips with contemporary realities, I will show how this quest led them to join a religious congregation whose real nature as a Sufi brotherhood they only gradually came to discover. Without disregarding the religious nature of this experience, I will also consider its more worldly incidental benefits, that is, access to relatively elite social networks.

The case study discussed in this chapter concerns a group of some hundred young men and women who were followers of Dr Mahmud Abu al-Huda al-Husseini. A general practitioner, born in 1960, Dr al-Husseini was also the preacher at the 'Adiliyya mosque, an Ottoman edifice in Aleppo's old souk. Between 2006 and 2008, I regularly spent time with this group, and in particular, took part in a ten-day retreat at the mosque during the month of Ramadan. I also established and maintained friendly relations with some of the followers.[1]

Rather than gradually narrowing the focus by beginning with the context, that is, the group, and then concentrating on each member's trajectory, I have chosen the opposite approach, taking the paths followed by individuals as a starting point before examining the features of the group as they become clearer to followers over time.

Living in the present

A preacher 'in tune with the realities of our time'

It was by chance, or through the recommendation of a friend, but never at the instigation of their parents, that these young people first came to attend the Friday sermons or the theology classes given by Sheikh Mahmud Abu al-Huda al-Husseini. Already observant Muslims at the time of the encounter, they were attracted by his distinctive approach to Islam. Many of them travelled several kilometres to attend the mosque, whose congregation was thus not drawn from one particular area, as is often the case in Syria. Salima,[2] a young maths teacher who lived in al-Hamdaniyya, a middle-class neighbourhood in western Aleppo, confirmed that 'none of the sisters [i.e. group members] comes from the neighbourhood of the mosque; Sheikh Mahmud's sermons aren't suited to the merchants of the souk'.

The sheikh's sermons were addressed to a public that, like the circle of his close disciples, was made up of students and graduates from the secular faculties of the university, especially the most prestigious ones, namely medicine, pharmacy and engineering. Al-Husseini was relatively young for a preacher (aged forty-six in 2006) and stood out among Aleppo's religious elite by combining a religious career with having a profession. Medical student Abd al-Rahman told me why he thought he had become so popular:

> It was perhaps the first time that I had listened to a preacher whose discourse met the intellectual expectations of a student public. The discourse you normally hear in the mosques is addressed to ordinary people: it's emotional, it's all about the lives of the Companions (of the Prophet) or the basic commandments of religion. Dr Mahmud spoke a different language. It was sophisticated, his arguments were rational. His sermons were in tune with the realities of our time.

Salwa, a social science student, summed up what was special about the sheikh's sermons in terms that refer to a notion of a balance between worldly and non-worldly concerns: 'He doesn't just talk about spiritual matters, he deals with contemporary problems, he's interested in concrete things, and he encourages action.' To understand what an exceptional figure al-Husseini was we need to remember the context in which he was active during the first decade of the new millennium: the city's clergy had been decimated during the repression of the Islamist insurgency[3] between 1979 and 1982 and thus deprived in particular of its most highly politicised members, who were often those closest, intellectually speaking, to the student youth. This crackdown had created an environment that was more favourable to popular preachers and reclusive ascetics than to clerics interested in 'the realities of our time'.

From *jihad* to Sufi ecstasy

The 'contemporaneity' (*mu'asara*) of al-Husseini's ideas (his disciples never spoke of 'modernity', *hadatha*, a term with secularist connotations) soon became apparent in the structure of his sermons, which resembled that of lectures. On a Friday in June 2006, for example, he proclaimed:

> The war that is being waged against Islam takes two forms. The first is armed warfare; the second ideological warfare.
> At a time when armed warfare is intensifying, Muslims are perhaps forgetting this other war that is being waged against them. [...] [The media of East and West] do not wish to present Islam under its true aspect [...] The method adopted today in this ideological war against Islam is to depict an Islam whose role is no more than the inculcation of moral standards.
> Our religion is distinguished by three very important features:
> 1. The universally comprehensive scope of its juridical pillar: our religion is worship and social practice, society and economy, a legal system and experimental research, government and politics;
> 2. Its awareness of invisible divine realities through its theological pillar;
> 3. The specificity of its spiritual pillar.

The systematic structure of his sermons was underpinned by a PowerPoint presentation on a screen that had been hung on an archway of the Ottoman mosque. His use of such a tool for a sermon was a 'world first', al-Husseini proudly claimed. This innovation was part of the managerialist culture promoted by the sheikh – and it was welcomed by his followers, who shared the new craze for 'how to succeed in …' books and courses with a great many Muslims around the world. His lectures included such typically managerialist topics as 'The Importance of Teamwork in Islam' or 'Discovering Leadership Potential in Children'. On the penultimate day of the Ramadan retreat that I attended in 2006, participants were given evaluation forms so that they could indicate how satisfied they were with the organisation of the event. The next day the results were displayed as graphics on the screen used for the Friday sermons.

'Taking control of society'

As already shown, the most obviously original feature of al-Husseini's religious activity came from his interest in topics which strictly speaking fell outside the ambit of religion: science and technology, management, economics and also politics. When it came to politics, the sheikh's language was unusually frank, even in contexts where the mixing of politics and religion remained taboo. In June 2005, for example, he openly expressed his dissatisfaction when the Tenth Regional Congress of the Ba'th (President Bashar al-Assad's party) dashed the hopes of those who, like him, had expected the introduction of a multi-party system open to religious parties:

> Today, throughout the Muslim world, we hear promises of democracy. Subject to one limitation, it has to be said: democracy is reserved for secularists who publicly proclaim that their spirits are untouched by the divine word!

It was no secret that al-Husseini's hopes of political liberalisation reflected personal ambition. But when the political field remained closed to him, he changed his plans, and in 2010 the government appointed him as director of Aleppo's Directorate of Religious Endowments. What matters here is that he included his young followers in his dreams of political participation, addressing them not just as a religious congregation but as members of a movement, an idea that found expression in his frequent use of the term *jama'a* to describe the group. In a contemporary Islamic context, *jama'a* denotes an informal religious group formed for the purpose of social or political action. Al-Husseini's followers thus did not join the group just to acquire the goods of salvation but were invited to actively participate in a common project of social transformation. The sheikh usually presented this project in relatively consensual terms, referring to *da'wa* (the preaching of religion). Abd al-Rahman, the medical student already quoted, explained how this task gradually became the group's collective responsibility:

> When I started attending the mosque, *da'wa* was the responsibility of the sheikh and his assistants. But the sheikh became very busy with his social duties, and we came to understand that *da'wa* was a collective responsibility. For example, at the beginning he ran his website himself; today there are ten to fifteen people who work on it.

Bakri, a literature student, reported that it was the invitation to participate in this collective endeavour that convinced him to abandon his plans to go and fight the Americans in Iraq:

> I met the sheikh just after the invasion of Iraq [in 2003]. I was very angry, and had even started talking with friends about the idea of going there to fight the occupation. But we first wanted to hear the opinion of a scholar. I followed no particular sheikh at that time and it was more or less by accident that I met Dr Mahmud.

From *jihad* to Sufi ecstasy

He said to me: 'You're a student at the university, you speak English. You would be more useful here helping us reveal the true face of Islam to the world. That too is a noble jihad.'

When the sheikh addressed his disciples in a more intimate setting than that of the Friday sermon, for instance during a day spent beside the pool at his house in the country, he spoke in terms that suggested that the role of his *jama'a* was not limited to preaching. Its destiny, he said, was no less than 'taking control of society'.

The political dimension of this ambitious undertaking did not escape his young listeners. Mahmud, an architecture student who had only recently joined the group when I met him, said, eyes sparkling, that he was 'reminded of Hassan al-Banna', Egyptian founder of the Muslim Brotherhood. The enthusiasm did not last, though, and a few months later Mahmud complained that 'the sheikh talks a lot about his plans for the group but nothing happens'. This was hardly surprising; at a time when no political reform was on the horizon, any organised form of politico-religious activism remained entirely out of the question. However, Mahmud went on to say, he did not plan to leave the group, for in the meantime he had discovered 'other reasons' to stay.

Social distinction and occupational integration

Attendance at the 'Adiliyya mosque did not just answer to the desire for a religious discourse in tune with contemporary realities or the hope of participation in an Islamic project of social and political transformation. For the young people who spent much if not all of their free time there, the mosque was a space where they could construct their individuality. There was of course a religious, spiritual dimension to this process, to which we shall return. Yet it also had more prosaic aspects, since the mosque was the centre of a social network whose logic of social distinction could potentially boost students' career prospects or even help them to find a job.

The 'Adiliyya mosque functioned as a kind of exclusive club, and we have already discussed how the discourse employed by its leader helped to draw in the members he wanted. Full of carefully chosen words and sophisticated ideas, his language mainly attracted university students from secular faculties and deterred less cultivated listeners. A second selection was made directly by al-Husseini himself, whose explicit policy was to recruit only the brightest. When Mahmud took part in the Ramadan retreat at the mosque, he was not yet on close terms with the sheikh. In the course of the retreat, however, the latter found out from followers that Mahmud had graduated first in his class at university and was impressively well-versed in general culture and religion. One evening, as al-Husseini was addressing some hundred participants in the retreat, he invited the young man to come and sit beside him, without giving any particular explanation. Delighted by such flattery, Mahmud was keener than ever to carry on coming to the group after the end of Ramadan.

At the mosque, Mahmud would meet young men like himself, pious and well-educated. Encouraging the sense of belonging to an elite, al-Husseini frequently reminded his followers that he wanted to bring together those with 'exceptional profiles', for 'five light bulbs give more light than fifty candles'. It should be noted that the logic of distinction at work in the group was cultural rather than socio-economic since members were not generally from wealthy families but from the lower middle class – (very) small-scale self-employed, office workers and civil servants. The future prospects of these young people would be guaranteed neither by family connections nor by a state that was busily slimming down in a time of deregulation and privatisation.[4]

The social networks formed around the 'Adiliyya mosque were thus of considerable interest to the sheikh's young followers, for they brought them into contact with the heads of a number of SMEs who also gravitated around him. One of these, a manufacturer of electric clocks showing the times of the five prayers, recruited most of his staff from among the congregation. Furthermore, some months before the revolution of 2011 a group of young disciples set up a small consultancy company, using offices and computers made available by the sheikh. These opportunities were, however, far from sufficient to meet the needs of all his followers. Like many other young Syrians, they had to look for work abroad, mostly in the Gulf monarchies: two of those mentioned above (Bakri and Mahmud) moved to Saudi Arabia not long after my visit to Syria. Others continued their studies in Europe or North America, a departure meant to be temporary but which, even before the 2011 revolution, was often the first step towards long-term emigration.

Initiation into Sufism: exaltation and resistance

The fact that the congregation offered its members benefits such as social contacts and career opportunities certainly does not mean that its only raison d'être was the 'interests' pursued by its members. The group was first and foremost a social and spiritual community united by the religious practice of the Shadhili order of Sufism. Named after its founder, the Moroccan saint Abu al-Hassan al-Shadhili (1196–1258), and introduced into Syria in the early twentieth century, this tradition is particularly popular with the country's ulama and urban middle classes.

The mystical dimension of the congregation's practice was not immediately apparent to those joining it. The more advanced followers who acted as recruiters would initially encourage neophytes to come and hear the sheikh's sermons and lessons. Only after several weeks or even months would newcomers be invited to take part in the *hadra*, the Sufi ritual involving the collective repetition of the name of God (*dhikr*). In the Shadhili tradition, the *hadra*, which can last up to an hour, includes chanting, accompanied by swaying and jumping. As the chanting grows louder and the movements get faster, devotees often fall into a trance-like state, which may be followed by weeping as they emerge from it at the end of the ritual.

Repeated every Wednesday evening, this extremely powerful spiritual and emotional experience created strong affective bonds between the members but also between them and the sheikh who guided them on the path of spiritual purification. At the appropriate moment, the master formalised his spiritual bond with the disciple through a pledge of allegiance (*bay'a*), in which the disciple undertook to recite every day a litany (*wird*) from the Sufi tradition of his master. The disciples' descriptions of the affective dimension of their relationship to the sheikh suggest that the Sufi doctrines he imparted to them, which revolve around the love the disciple feels for the master who holds the key to the secrets of the divine, constituted a framework for channelling adolescent passions. Al-Husseini's personal charisma was of course an essential factor, and it is also worth noting that it was not just the sheikh's ideas and oratory skills that attracted followers but also the self-assurance that this tall and well-built man exuded. Bakri felt that the sheikh had exerted a 'mysterious power' on him:

> Even if I talked all day I wouldn't be able to express the relationship I had with Dr Mahmoud in the early years. After a few months, I started to be attached to him, to love him, without really knowing why. I loved him more than my family or friends, I no longer saw anyone but him. Behind this attraction there was a sort of mysterious power. He inspired me by his deeds, his ideas.

This phase of passionate attachment to the master was often accompanied by very regular attendance; some students even made the mosque their permanent base. For a whole year, Bakri devoted all his free time to congregational activities, individual meditation or personal service to the sheikh. Without having gone quite so far, his fellow disciple Mouaz remembered how his parents complained about his poor results at university during the time when he spent all his evenings at the mosque, 'often till one o'clock in the morning'.

For many followers, Sufism gradually became the primary reason for belonging to the group, to such an extent that they began to neglect the mosque's exoteric teachings (theology, *hadith*, *fiqh*). On at least one occasion during my time there, the sheikh threatened to expel those who lacked commitment to religious scholarship.

Given the key role that mysticism played in the cohesion of the group, why was its practice so very discreet? During the Ramadan retreat, for example, which was open to all, the *hadra* was performed during the night and the organisers made sure that they only invited those who were confirmed disciples. This caution can be explained by the fact that Sufism, despite being the dominant strand of Islam in Aleppo, still faced much criticism from rationalist and Salafi camps, both of which had particularly strong support among university students, especially those in the sciences.

When they first came to the mosque, newcomers often had to overcome prejudices against the Sufi ritual. Bakri reported that his approach to Islam had been 'Wahhabi' and thus anti-Sufi until he met al-Husseini. Adil, a medical student, explained that despite the influence of his grandfather, a Sufi cleric, he had gone through several months of 'inner turmoil and self-questioning' between his encounter with the sheikh and his 'acceptance' of Sufi practice. On the other hand, Mouaz, one of his fellow students, had left the congregation because he had come to the conclusion that they were 'contradictory to reason and revelation'.

Such polemics aside, followers whose youthful enthusiasm had waned often went through a phase in which they maintained a relative distance. This usually coincided with the end of their studies and their entry into adulthood and marked the beginning of a more rational relationship with the master and the congregation. After speaking of his years of fusional relationship with the sheikh, Bakri concluded:

> Now I have to make a living, I have to pay my bills, but the inspiration I gained from those moments is still with me. That period when I was always close to him was a time of preparation, of training: a temporary escape from society to give me an idea of what a true Muslim ought to be, before returning into society.

From *jihad* to Sufi ecstasy

Epilogue

In December 2010, al-Husseini was dismissed as head of the Directorate of Religious Endowments in Aleppo, a post he had held for less than a year. Given this fall from grace, which was engineered by a rival cleric, the master of the 'Adiliyya mosque was hardly well-disposed to the regime when the revolution broke out in March 2011. After publicly denouncing the violent attacks on protesters, al-Husseini came under a variety of pressures, and one of his right-hand men was held in custody for several weeks. In the summer, he took refuge in Turkey, where he was followed by several of his disciples. Of those who remained in Aleppo, some joined the opposition, armed or civilian, while others simply tried to save themselves and their families in a city that from July 2012 would be ravaged by war. At least two members of the brotherhood were killed in the months that followed: Said Sino, a young engineer, was shot dead by a sniper on his way to work; Muhammad al-Khalid, the mosque's official cameraman, was arrested and tortured by the regime for having filmed demonstrations, freed again but subsequently executed by the leader of a rebel group whom he had filmed looting. I dedicate these pages to Said and Muhammad.

Notes

1 I was only able to make contact with female disciples on one occasion, during an interview authorised by the sheikh. The women listen to the sermons and lectures in an adjoining room, through loudspeakers.
2 All names of interviewees have been changed.
3 Initiated by the Fighting Vanguard, a radical split-off from the Muslim Brotherhood, this armed insurrection sparked a popular uprising in some cities of northern Syria. The uprising was brutally crushed, and many thousands of people were killed in the Hama massacre in February 1982.
4 The year 2004, for example, saw the end of the public sector's legal obligation to offer employment to all engineering graduates.

References

Ardito, Aurelia, 'Les cercles féminins de la Qubaysiyya à Damas', *Le Mouvement social*, 231, 2010: pp. 77–88.
Chih, Rachida, *Le Soufisme au quotidien. Confréries d'Égypte au xxe siècle*, Sindbad, Paris, 2000.
Geoffroy, Éric, *Une voie soufie dans le monde. La Shâdhiliyya*, Maisonneuve et Larose, Paris, 2005.

Haenni, Patrick, *L'Islam de marché. L'autre révolution conservatrice*, Seuil, Paris, 2005.

Pierret, Thomas (ed.), 'L'Islam en Syrie: Analyses et témoignages', *Maghreb Machrek*, special issue, 198, 2008.

Pierret, Thomas, *Religion and State in Syria: The Sunni Ulama from Coup to Revolution*, Cambridge University Press, Cambridge and New York, 2013.

Pinto, Paulo, 'Religion et religiosité en Syrie', in Youssef Courbage, Baudouin Dupret, Zouhair Ghazal and Mohammed al-Dbiyat, eds, *La Syrie au présent. Reflets d'une société*, Actes Sud/Sindbad, Arles, 2007.

Pinto, Paulo, 'Sufism and the Political Economy of Morality in Syria', *Interdisciplinary Journal of Middle Eastern Studies*, 15, 2006: pp. 103–136.

Pinto, Paulo, 'Sufism, Moral Performance and the Public Sphere in Syria', *Revue des mondes musulmans et de la Méditerranée*, 115–116, 2006: pp. 155–171 (available at http://remmm.revues.org).

7

The Faculty of Education of Lab'us

Salafism as a student subculture in Yemen

Laurent Bonnefoy

In the last few years, the term 'Salafism' has enjoyed remarkable popularity in the media. Yet its widespread use, especially in the aftermath of the 'Arab Spring' of 2011 and the emergence of the so-called Islamic State in the context of the wars in Iraq and Syria, often seems inversely proportional to the collective ability to grasp the complexity of this emerging fringe of Sunni Islam. Nowadays the label serves less to describe a social reality than to lend legitimacy to the knowledge or analysis of whoever is using it, be they journalists, academics or researchers. In the dominant media imaginary, the word 'Salafism' is invariably synonymous with radicalism, violence, terrorism and jihadism, whether in Tunisia or the Paris suburbs.

We therefore need to demystify Salafism, recontextualise it and understand its development and diversity by looking at concrete practices, the interactions and leisure activities of those who claim to be Salafis, rather than at texts written by great 'scholars' and theologians. Broadly speaking, Salafism can be defined by the desire to return to the original practice of Islam, to purify it by eliminating all those elements that its followers consider to be human innovations which corrupt its original perfection. There are a number of different currents, some more marginal than others, with a range of attitudes to political engagement and violence.

This chapter explores the daily lives of male Salafi students in Yemen, the ways in which they relate to their surroundings as well as their relationships with others who do not necessarily share their beliefs. Yemen, by virtue of its particular history and because of the image it holds in the Muslim imaginary, offers a fascinating case study. In what follows, I seek to explain how these students, in the heart of a circumscribed group of young Yemenis (belonging to the apolitical, so-called 'quietist' branch of Salafism, distinct from jihadism and the 'political' current), shaped their own distinct identity and created a subculture

Living in the present

that does not represent a political or social threat but, prior to the 2011 uprisings embodied much of the questions that erupted with the Yemeni Spring and still bear meaning after this experience failed, leading to war.

The Faculty of Lab'us

Surrounded by high mountains, Lab'us is a small town of some five thousand inhabitants in the region of Yafi' of former South Yemen (People's Democratic Republic of Yemen). In the late 2000s, one of the first things that strikes visitors, and not just those from abroad, is the large number of young men who define themselves as 'Salafis'. The proportion of Salafis is even greater at the small public Faculty of Education, a local branch of the University of Aden mainly dedicated to teacher training. Founded with Kuwaiti support in 1998, the faculty initially only offered one course, a two-year 'cut-price' diploma training teachers for the rural primary schools which are scattered across the surrounding mountains and valleys (teachers in cities and secondary schools have to study for four years). As student numbers rose, a four-year degree course was added in autumn 2004. But the two-year course, the only one of its kind in the region, remains popular with students from low-income families who cannot afford to pay for long periods of study. Other attractions include the (somewhat dilapidated) dormitory accommodation and, above all, the daily bursary of 200 Yemeni riyals (less than one euro then), which is funded by 'Umar Qasim al-'Isa'i, a wealthy Saudi merchant born in Yafi', who supports many charitable causes in the region as well as Yafi'i immigrants in Saudi Arabia. Unlike in other faculties in the region or the University of Aden, women and men hardly ever mix in Lab'us (there are rarely more than just one or two female students per year, and all the teachers are male), something that the more conservative students value highly.

Admission is highly selective, and applicants are drawn from a very wide area. The transport infrastructure is poor and travel costs are high, so students are often compelled to stay on campus for months, unable to go back to their villages to see their families. Cut off from the rest of the world, this small, self-contained university is an ideal place to examine social interactions and processes, especially relating to religious emulation and the roles played by charismatic figures.

About a third of the four hundred students, some of whom come from far away, claim to be Salafis and are seen as such by the others. Their full beards and trimmed moustaches, traditional skirts (*ma'waz*) or tunics (*thawb*) reaching to mid-calf and keffiyehs on their heads make them instantly identifiable as a group as well as recognisable to each other. In this respect, there is nothing exceptional about this particular region, town or faculty. What has developed here almost spontaneously is a very specific Salafi culture which rarely corresponds to the clichés and has no obvious connection with violence. For many students, Salafism seems to consist of a number of relatively volatile and flexible practices which 'wear out over time'. It is a politico-religious identity whose doctrinal intransigence and numerous prohibitions, especially in relation to leisure activities, often lead to religious burn-out or gradual role exit. Liminal moments such as entering the adult world, looking for a job or starting a family shape young people's trajectories and encourage them to reassess the strength of their commitment to the doctrine and the movement. These life changes also lead Salafis to adapt, even to abandon Salafism, when the pressures or temptations of their immediate familial or professional environment become so big that they feel the need to compromise. Salafism is essentially a generational phenomenon, a demonstration of the desire to reject (usually at the least cost) what some young people see as the concessions and compromises, both religious and political, that their parents have made. The great majority of Salafis are rebels created by contemporary Yemeni society.

To avoid reification, it is important to take into account the fluidity of trajectories of students and teachers labelled as 'Salafis'. In the specific case of the Lab'us faculty, being a practising Salafi implies neither a particular allegiance nor the possession of any kind of 'party card', and it certainly does not entail any fixed religious or political stance. The doctrines laid down by Yemeni or foreign religious leaders do provide some guidance points but these can be applied in many different ways, and we should not underestimate the polyphony of sources, influences and practices. Although the label 'Salafi' is used both by researchers and the actors themselves, identities are complex and many seemingly contradictory meanings can be attached to them.

In Lab'us, Salafism manifests itself less in violence and intolerance than in rituals and codes, especially dress codes, as well as in particular leisure activities which set Salafi students apart from others. Here, Salafism has evolved outside the strict religious framework of the *madrasas* (literally, schools) found elsewhere, without externally funded proselytism and even without a charismatic leader. A relatively recent phenomenon at the faculty, it has been able to develop mainly thanks to the enclosed environment of the student residences, the generational and political balances in Lab'us, and the fact that the region of Yafi', and Yemen in general, has close links with Saudi Arabia and the other Gulf nations through a shared history and a network of migration.

Political connections: a mode of distinction

The branch of Salafism that has become the dominant one in Yemen since the early 1980s – among students and elsewhere – is marked by an aversion to political involvement. This opposition to any allegiance to a political party or faction (*hizbiyya*) is a distinctive feature of Salafism and sets it apart from other religious movements, most notably the Muslim Brotherhood. Politics, seen as competitive struggle to manage public affairs, is widely accused of spreading division among believers. That political parties are displaying allegiance to something other than God is regarded as sinful. Open expression of opposition to the government in power, even when that government is corrupt or authoritarian, is thus proscribed, following the doctrine formulated by leading contemporary *ulama* (scholars) like Muqbil al-Wadiʻi, ʻAbd al-ʻAziz Bin Baz, Muhammad al-Albani or Rabiʻ al-Madkhali. Demonstrations, sit-ins, uprisings or bomb attacks are all considered illegitimate – as is voting. Established or self-proclaimed Salafi leaders advise 'citizens' to be patient, and see themselves as the only ones authorised to give secret counsel to political rulers. In theory, this quietist approach demands automatic loyalty to the existing regime as soon as it calls itself Muslim, and explains why leading figures of 'apolitical' Salafism were strongly critical of the revolutionary uprisings in the Arab world in 2011.

Election campaigns in Labʻus, especially those for student representatives in which candidates are almost always supported by one of the major national parties, offer a good opportunity to assert political and religious identity. One such campaign was enlivened by calls for a boycott by students claiming allegiance to Salafism. The ensuing debate over the legitimacy of the election and, by extension, of democracy, polarised the faculty, including the teachers. This led to verbal jousting between Salafis opposed to *hizbiyya* and supporters of political engagement ranging from sympathisers of the Muslim Brotherhood to socialists or members of the current ruling party, the *Muʼtammar*, which had been founded by the former president ʻAli ʻAbdullah Saleh, who resigned in 2012. A clash like this between seemingly irreconcilable positions has created tension, but so far the situation has never got out of hand. In this micro-environment, everyone plays their own role, takes their own position and finds reasons to break with others or to unite around shared values and references. Audio

The Faculty of Education of Lab'us

recordings of lectures by great Salafist sheikhs – Yemeni like Muqbil al-Wadi'i, Yahya al-Hajuri or Muhammad al-Imam, or Saudi like Rabi' al-Madkhali or Salih al-Fawzan – are often regarded as authoritative. Although Internet connections are scarce because of a lack of hardware and electricity in the village, students can find and buy the latest publications or cassettes at relatively modest prices from the two small bookshops defining themselves as Salafi, which are situated about five kilometres from the centre of Lab'us. During the campaign, students informed visitors and the occasional foreign researcher about the issues, took them to impromptu gatherings and urged them to express their opinions or weigh up the pros and cons of different positions. Breaking the monotony of the university year, the election campaign thus turns into a leisure activity, a way of spending one's free time and asserting oneself.

Before the popular uprisings in 2011 which eventually led to the resignation of President Saleh, the local head of *Mu'tammar* in the faculty claimed that half the students were card-carrying members of his party. Although this figure is probably exaggerated, it does show the influence of clientelism. Rightly or wrongly, a number of students believe that membership of the party in power is essential for a successful completion of their studies and might help to secure a job in the public sector. At the micro-local level, the polarisation between members of *Mu'tammar* and Salafi students has slowly exhausted students' ability to mobilise for the Al-Islah party, which represents the Muslim Brotherhood in Yemen and the main opposition to Saleh. As a result, there now seem to be fewer politico-religious alternatives than before.

Stigmatisation and segmentation

Apart from some heckling during the election campaign, partisanship in the faculty is usually fairly harmless and manifests itself in different ways. Since the students all know each other and spend a lot of time together, confrontations are contained and violence is rare. More serious clashes do occur very occasionally but everybody seems to get distracted by particular regional issues. In former South Yemen, where the secessionist movement has been on the ascendant since the moment when it became clear that the unification with North Yemen enacted in 1990 had its limitations,[1] the 'Northerner' has become the bogeyman for many. It is significant that the spread of armed Islamist movements claiming to be close to an Al-Qaida base in Abyan, less than 100 kilometres from Lab'us, has not brought more violence. Everyone seems to belong to the same camps in Lab'us: the South, youth or morality – a diagnosis that has only been confirmed by the war, which started in 2015. Salafis, some of whom were students in Lab'us, were integrated into groups that were fighting the Huthi militias from the North. Identities are thus constructed in complex ways around meanings that largely transcend Salafi subculture, which flourishes in the special context of the university but more often than not ends up running out of steam in the outside world.

Yet the jibes and the mutual stigmatisation give the two 'camps' a means to set themselves apart and to demonstrate their creativity, and indeed their sense of humour, by poking fun at various stereotypes with more or less explicit references. The Salafis are often called *abu lihiya* (literally 'bearded fathers'), terrorists (*irhabi*) or *wahhabî* (a reference to their real or imagined links with Saudi Arabia and its 'Wahhabi' dogma). For their part, the Salafis take their 'opponents' to task for their consumption of qat or the socialist legacy of former South Yemen, which they consider to be outdated.

The polarisation of the faculty also has an effect on the way space is used. Students are housed in groups of eight, often according to the regions they come from and their religious adherence. In the dormitories occupied by Salafis a bench or wooden board is placed across the door, just as in mosques, to mark the boundary and remind people to take off their shoes before entering. In the middle of the interior courtyard of the dormitory building, a volleyball court and ping-pong table provide a space for physical activity that transcends partisanship and stigmatisation.

The consumption of qat, a plant whose leaves are chewed by the majority of Yemenis from all social and geographical backgrounds for their stimulating and euphoriant effects, fills much of the afternoons and evenings for many students. Some even believe they cannot concentrate on their studies without it. For Salafis, qat consumption is forbidden. They thus cut themselves off from the common form of socialising and must find other things to do during their spare time: they read, listen to sermons and attend nearby mosques, or, if they can afford it, undertake proselytising trips or training in religious institutions outside the region. The following scene illustrates well how the consumption of qat separates the two camps. One evening, as the sunset call to prayer (*maghrib*) echoed out, some students were relaxing in their bedrooms chewing qat and chatting, when two young Salafis asked if they would like to accompany them to the mosque, saying 'Let's go, it is time for prayer!' Smiling and brandishing their stalks of qat, the students answered in unison: 'For us it is time for *takhzina* [i.e. time to chew a ball of qat]!' Such a brazen refusal to attend prayer can constitute a very serious insult, but in this instance, it was merely seen as a bit of teasing. In an indirect response to the religious shortcomings of his fellow students, one Salafi even transcribed a *fatwa* by the Saudi *alim* Bin Baz on the wall above his bed, explaining that those who miss the *fajr* prayer (at about 5 a.m.) because they went to bed late, commit an act of impiety (*kufr*) without themselves being impious (*kafir*). He explained:

> This text is for those who visit our dormitory, who skip prayers because of qat or because they are lazy. When they read it, they know they are doing something wrong. [...] There are different levels of *kufr*. The devil can make you commit an act of impiety, but since you had no desire to leave your religion, you are not a *kafir*!

A moral exhortation like this, not without a touch of humour, follows from the Islamic principle that all must 'enjoy what is good and forbid what is evil'. It was even supported by some of the teachers in the faculty. In a class on the *tafsir* (interpretation of the *Qur'an*), one professor mocked those who postpone the time of prayer, asking them: 'Why pray the *'asha* [the 'night prayer' recited around 8 p.m.] even though this is exactly when the effects of qat are at their strongest?' He told his students:

> Even when you're chewing qat, you still have to pray! Take the qat out of your mouth and put it aside. The prayer only takes a quarter of an hour, including five minutes for ablution and ten minutes at the most for the prayer itself [...] Prayer is the foundation of religion. How can someone who does not pray claim to be a Muslim?

Watching television (along with all representations of human beings, and anthropomorphism) is another leisure activity proscribed by the quietist current of Salafism. This, too, shapes social relations in Yemen and creates spatial boundaries in the faculty. The two cafeterias on campus where students go for lunch or buy notebooks, pens, soap and food are a tangible example of these divisions of affiliations and space. One is run by a young man who studied for two years in the main Salafi teaching institute in Yemen, Dar al-hadith, more than 600 kilometres from Lab'us. Ensuring that Salafi doctrine is respected in his cafeteria, he may provide guidance to some students through an attitude that has become more prevalent over recent years and that is based on a set of rules which are becoming increasingly well defined. The second cafeteria is more 'liberal', and on evenings when the electricity is working, its television offers students football matches and American or Egyptian films. One of the dishes on offer for lunch consists of rice and frozen, battery-farmed chicken, known as 'French chicken' since it is imported from France. The Salafis, backed by a *fatwa*, reject it because it is not *halal*, they claim. Consequently, food also becomes a source of dispute and distinction. The Salafis sometimes replace the imported chickens with locally reared, far more expensive poultry, or with tinned tuna or vegetables. Along with the ban on qat and television, the rejection of 'French chicken' is thus a powerful concrete symbol of adherence to Salafism. It becomes a marker of distinction and group adherence, even an element of social integration which the students are careful to respect. Through these practices, they symbolically choose their camp even though for most of them the attachment to it is relatively superficial.

Rather surprisingly, the choice of mosque was of no great importance to the students. Whatever their particular religious adherence, most students went to the nearest mosque, even though some accuse it of supporting *hizbiyya*. For Friday prayers, students and teachers attended a mosque built in 2004 with funds raised by Saudis from Yafi', which is larger but further away (*masjid al-'Abadi*). Despite the mutual stigmatisation among students and teachers (some of whom, educated in Moscow or Havana and close to the Socialist Party, can scarcely be suspected of Islamist sympathies), Salafis are generally in charge of organising collective prayers. They thus enjoy at least a formal monopoly on the means of salvation and are able to set the rules that guide worshippers, once the prayer or sermon is over, to find their own compromise with everyday life, and reconcile apparent contradictions.

Divisions and compromises

Even though this Salafi subculture owes much to the specific environment of the faculty, it cannot be detached from the wider context, which is marked by the resurgence of religion and generational divisions. In Yafi', as elsewhere in former South Yemen, the fall of the socialist regime in 1990 brought about a revival of religious movements. The socialist government in Aden had fostered a certain degree of 'deculturation' (for example, by nationalising religious property and banning headscarves from universities), which contemporary re-Islamisation is seeking to correct. In Lab'us, the grand mausoleum celebrating the glory of the martyrs in the anti-colonial guerrilla wars of the 1960s has been abandoned, and a new mosque now faces it across the recently asphalted road. In a conference talk available as a recording, in which the Salafi scholar

The Faculty of Education of Lab'us

Muqbil al-Wadi'i (who died in 2001) talks about his observations in Yafi' in the mid-1990s, he implies that the rise of Salafism is a reaction against socialism. Having visited the region and spoken to local inhabitants about the evils of Marxism, politics and democracy, he had encountered 'young people, free from all *hizbiyya*' who had said to him, 'there's no need at all to tell us about communism, we already know it!'

The socialist experience also led to a particularly marked generation gap, which is inscribed in the global process of the individualisation of religious practices. Offered more and more choices by television, politico-religious movements or experiences of alterity (facilitated by significant migratory flows of Yafi'is to Saudi Arabia and the Gulf states), many young people believe that they can construct their own hybrid religious identities, even though life in the faculty leads to strong polarisation.

In this context, Salafism, while claiming to belong to the heritage of the first Muslims, is undergoing a twofold division. It distinguishes itself not only from popular Islam but also – for young people in Yafi' – from the lax religious practices of their fathers, who were educated under the regime of the People's Democratic Republic of Yemen.

Because of the weak structure of the local Salafi camp and the absence of any training institute in Yafi', students were only superficially socialised into the doctrine they claimed to follow. In many respects, they treated their adherence to Salafism as a mere formality and something that can be reduced to a few 'minor behaviours'. Even though a few students and teachers had spent some time in Dammaj or another Salafi institute, the majority only had a vague notion of Salafism. In a recording made during a visit to Yafi' in 1997, Muqbil al-Wadi'i expressed annoyance at the questions from his audience. He expected to be asked about profound theological issues but people only wanted to hear about internal and transnational Salafi disputes, and seemed to focus on matters which he considered trivial.

Although the students enjoy following the many debates and controversies within Salafism, they do not always consider their deeper implications at a local level. They may listen to and share recordings and texts that deal with internal divisions, refer to eminent Yemeni or Saudi Salafi clerics and criticise the Muslim Brotherhood and the Sufis, but they only partially adhere to Salafi doctrine. At the individual level, Salafi practice is guided not just by the rules, guidance and prohibitions set down in the sermons, books and teachings of eminent clerics, but it is marked above all by a (sometimes unconscious) desire to adapt to local contexts and issues. A flexible practice thus often coexists with rigid theoretical views. One Salafi student, for example, staved off the boredom of a life far from home by watching television, even though this is forbidden by the doctrine he claims to espouse. When this inconsistency was pointed out to him, he admitted that he was aware of bending the rules but he only watched 'football matches and some American action films!'

Another anecdote indirectly reveals how Salafism is not always easy to reconcile with the demands of the outside world. The faculty received a visit from 'Abd al-Wahhab Rawah, the former Minister of Higher Education, who had just been appointed President of the University of Aden. This was a rare opportunity for the teachers and students to draw their guest's attention to the dilapidated state of their dormitories, their lack of funds and the delay in payment of support from their donor 'Umar Qasim al-'Isa'i. Both teachers and students were keen to show themselves and their community in the best light. The whole campus was cleaned up and a large banquet was planned. On the day of the visit, teaching went on as normal while the President visited the classrooms accompanied by the Dean of the faculty and various local dignitaries. But one third-year student attending his Islamic law class seemed ill at ease. Probably shy, and nervous at the thought of encountering such an important figure, he tried to cover his legs by draping his *keffiyeh* headscarf over his thighs. Like other practising Salafis, he was not wearing trousers but a *ma'waz*, a wraparound short skirt which only reaches down to mid-calf. Aware that this item of clothing might not be appreciated by the visitors, he covered his legs to hide what would normally have been a conscious mark of distinction. He seemed almost ashamed of his religious adherence and did not want to reveal it by being seen wearing a conspicuous garment. This was probably not the last time that he and his fellow students would feel the need to adapt or deny certain practices, and it illustrates how adherence to Salafism can easily fluctuate.

Such self-conscious, even childish reactions indicate that not all Salafis are the threatening figures that they are too often presented to be. Just like other forms of teenage rebellion in European and American societies (hippy, punk, grunge, goth, etc.), Salafism can be understood as a fashion or subculture, a social and generational marker whose meaning depends on its context. It does not always fulfil a political function that can be determined *a priori*. The Salafi subculture expresses itself through the adoption of signs (the beard, clothing, 'minor behaviours') and leisure activities which lead adherents to dissociate themselves from the rest of society and symbolically reject it, but in fact, to use the terms Dick Hebdige applied to punk subculture in the 1970s, its members may be either 'harmless buffoons', who isolate themselves from society, or 'threats to public order'.

An approach like this challenges the dominant image of Salafis as potential criminals who are inevitably linked to international terrorist groups and networks. The adaptation and appropriation of clothing and other 'minor behaviours' demonstrate that Salafism can take on very different meanings depending on whether it is practised in Toulouse, Detroit or Timbuktu, or in Lab'us or Riyadh.

Note

1 North and South Yemen followed different historical paths. The former, home to three-quarters of the population, never experienced Western colonisation while the latter, with Aden as its capital, was a British protectorate until 1967. The struggle for independence in the South, mostly led by left-wing movements, gave birth to the only socialist regime in the Arab world. It lasted until the unification of the North and the South in 1990, which was largely a result of economic and ideological exhaustion of the South. Unification was not always peaceful; a short war in 1994 pitted supporters of unity against secessionists in the South. In former South Yemen, this graudually led to resentment and the feeling of having been colonised by the North, leading the way to deeper fragmentation in the context of the armed conflict which began in 2015.

References

Bonnefoy, Laurent, *Salafism in Yemen. Transnationalism and Religious Identity*, Hurst/Columbia University Press, London/New York, 2011.

Burgat, François and Mohamed Sbitli, 'Les salafis au Yémen ou … la modernisation malgré tout', *Chroniques Yéménites*, 10, 2003: pp. 123–152.

Fuchs Ebaugh, Helen Rose, *Becoming an Ex. The Process of Role Exit*, Chicago University Press, Chicago, IL, 1988.

Mahmood, Saba, *Politique de la piété. Le féminisme à l'épreuve du renouveau islamique*, La Découverte, Paris, 2009.

Rougier, Bernard, ed., *Qu'est ce que le salafisme?*, Presses Universitaires de France, Paris, 2008.

8

'A man, a real man!'

Halima, a woman rebel in Gafsa (Tunisia)

Amin Allal

'*Rajjala 'alihum*': the expression seems paradoxical. The literal meaning is 'she is more of a man than the men', or more precisely, 'she has more masculine qualities than them'. In the Tunisian dialect, *rajjal* means someone who has courage, but also honour and integrity. The expression, which refers to exclusively 'masculine' qualities, those of the trustworthy man, proves to be ambivalent since it is applied to Halima, a courageous young woman from a working-class area of Gafsa, the capital of the eponymous region, located some 350 kilometres southwest of Tunis, and home to about a hundred thousand inhabitants.

I met Halima one evening in the spring of 2008. An illegal gathering had taken place in downtown Gafsa. That evening, the demonstrators were protesting against the arrest the previous day of the leaders of the revolt in the Gafsa mining basin. For several weeks, a protest movement, unparalleled under the Ben Ali regime, had been shaking the region. Workers, activists and young people in the region, mostly unemployed, were rebelling against the corrupt hiring practices of the Compagnie des Phosphates de Gafsa (CPG). The public company, which operates eight open-pit mines in the region and is the country's main source of wealth, became the focal point of discontent in the region where it provided fewer and fewer jobs. The uprising, hardly mentioned in the media, lasted six months and was violently suppressed.

During yet another day of protests, clashes with police had intensified; angry high-school students who had turned out in force seemed edgy and unpredictable. In the evening, when the group of seasoned activists (unemployed graduates, militants from the Tunisian Workers' Communist Party or the General Union of Tunisian Students) gathered not far from the regional headquarters of the national trade union federation (the Tunisian General Labour Union, UGTT), there were not many protestors left on the streets. Those few who were still outside protesting against the prohibitions of the authoritarian regime were the most defiant. I was surprised to see a young woman there, the only one among a score of men involved in confrontations with the police. I asked who she was. 'Halima, *Rajjala 'alihum*', one of the far-left activists who was with me replied, admiringly.

'No one is going to tell us what to do'

Described with admiration by most young men and women in her neighbourhood, which has few places where men and women mix, thirty-five-year-old Halima is seen as a heroine, a fair and selfless woman who commands respect. She attended school until the age of fifteen before training as a typist, which, she says, had been 'a waste of time'. Now she works on and off as a sales assistant in a clothing shop but is otherwise unemployed. She spends a good part of her afternoons and evenings with local boys: '*el-awled*', as she calls them, the 'neighbourhood kids'. Whenever she has the time, she goes further afield to chat with people in cafés. Her favourite spot is a terrace behind the Kasbah wall (*borj al-kasbah*). 'Among the trees, you feel protected', explains Halima, 'I like the calm, slightly secret atmosphere.' She will sometimes sit on the terrace till late into the evening, sipping a lemonade. There, too, she is often one of the few women. 'Sometimes a girlfriend will come with me', she says, 'but most of the time I take my little ten-year-old nephew along. It reassures my family, and it avoids misunderstandings.'

In her neighbourhood and in the cafés, discussions among young Tunisians are usually about unemployment, the high cost of living and their desire to leave and go to Europe or the United States. But in Gafsa, during the revolt, talk focuses on the economic marginalisation and the neglect of the region by the Ben Ali regime. Halima is the linchpin of the debates. 'We can't let them push us around', she declares, 'we must keep fighting'. She sounds like an opposition militant, although she is not. She is even rather critical of the opposition:

> They talk all the time ... I've never been to university. I like clarity. And when we are demonstrating to free activists who are in jail, things are clear, they are right, and no one is going to tell us what to do.

Halima is not a member of any party, and nobody in her family circle is an activist or trade unionist. Her first experience of political action came in 1991 while she was still at school: she took part in a demonstration at the start of the

Living in the present

first Gulf Wa, and became an accidental leader of the protests. Visibly moved, she tells me how her father, who has since passed away, was summoned to the police station to explain his daughter's 'riotous behaviour'. Having worked as a *chaouch* (factotum) at the Labour Ministry until his retirement, he was not the protesting sort. 'He was illiterate, he kept out of politics, but his silence was a kind of pride', she explains. 'He kept a low profile, but you could see the anger in his eyes.' Behind his strict paternal gaze, Halima sensed that he secretly approved of her rebellion:

> Once, when I got home after being expelled from school for throwing stones through the windows, I thought I was going to get a good beating. But he put his hand on my shoulder and said to me: 'Just be careful, my daughter.' It was not the same with my mother, she spent her time following me around to make sure I stayed at home. She was more afraid, and she didn't understand why I always had to get involved in things like that.

Between 'transgression' and 'normalisation'

Surrounded by men, Halima seems to be a figure of transgression. Her forthright manner and strong views do not fit the largely conservative norms of femininity in Gafsa. The few women who can be found mingling with young men in this kind of neighbourhood late in the evening are sex workers. Reduced to their role as providers of sex for cash, they could not be more different from Halima. She is not, however, a 'tomboy': always impeccably dressed and stylish, she conforms to the dominant aesthetic norms of femininity. She often wears make-up, her hair is carefully coiffed and she likes earrings, bracelets and necklaces. She usually wears jeans with flat shoes. 'They're more practical for running', she confides. The two packs of cigarettes she smokes per day – taking liberties with the social convention that 'good' girls should not openly smoke – do not alter her clear, sharp voice. She speaks only when necessary, and does not mince her words. Halima has absolutely no desire to be seen as one of the men. When asked if she feels 'like the men', her answer is unambiguous:

> No, everyone has their place! But I don't see why I shouldn't be here … I am a bit braver than most women … it's been like that ever since [I was] a little girl. But I am not the only one. There are other girls like me.

During the revolutionary uprising of the winter of 2010–2011, Halima was once again in the thick of it. She joined the demonstrations, braved the evening curfew with the boys from her neighbourhood and was involved in clashes with the police, throwing stones and dodging gunfire. She still suffers from pain in her shoulder which was dislocated during one of those clashes. Gradually, she has become a central figure of public life in her neighbourhood.

But Halima now seems to want to draw a line under it all. Having recently got engaged, she appears to be taking on the role of the model daughter. And although she agrees somewhat nostalgically to talk about her rebel adventures, she now places more emphasis on her new responsibilities: 'Finding a steady job and keeping it, taking care of my fiancé.' When she talks about him, we can sense a potential return to traditional gender roles:

> He is a man, a real man. He has never given up in the face of tyranny and oppression. He completed his studies and is on the priority lists to be hired as an engineer at Sonede [Tunisia's national water company]. Then we can get married and live in a good neighbourhood, in a separate part of my future sister-in-law's house; she's a widow and has no children.

Having been unmarried and unemployed for so long, Halima was confined to the 'waiting-room' of youth. Now that she is making the transition to the 'adult' world, she seems to see her outings with the boys and her long evenings spent in cafés as a thing of the past. And as if to close this chapter, she even attributes her political engagement to her fiancé, even though he was not active during the 2008 protests or the uprising – they just met in a café one evening during one of the political debates. He admires her because 'she is a role model, a strong character, but she's not an *aicha rajel*, a tomboy'.

Forms of female protest

Although she is finally 'settling down' to lead a life that conforms to the local 'arrangement between the sexes', Halima's rebellious path challenges the clichés too often peddled about the Arab Spring in recent years. In the public imagination, women frequently appear as mere 'companions', sitting on the shoulders of a man (their brother?), their hair blowing in the wind or sporting a tidy headscarf. It is an image that reinforces a binary conception of political engagement: one where men lead the struggle, do the fighting and make all the strategic decisions, while women only take part in peaceful, playful protests, their roles confined to providing emotional and logistical support. Halima's trajectory defies this binary opposition, which permeates representations of revolt.

Living in the present

Although atypical in the specific context of Gafsa, her story confirms that there are gender-specific ways and moments to appropriate the spaces that surround us. It shows that norms are not fixed and that women, when they negotiate or transgress those norms, are not necessarily met with contempt, condemnation or condescension, but can actually arouse genuine admiration.

While women in the Gafsa region do not generally turn out to protest, careful examination of the circumstances that led them to become politically active during the uprisings in 2008 and 2011 helps us to understand women's political engagement: hardened protestors like Halima, mothers and wives of imprisoned activists, women showing up in solidarity, etc. When they mobilised in 2008 and the violence peaked, protest action reached new heights. This was the case, for example, during the women's demonstration for the release of prisoners, which took place in the middle of the weekly market on 27 July 2008 in Redeyef, a mining village located to the west of Gafsa, and which turned into a confrontation with police. The female protestors then conspicuously assumed the mantle of the repertoires of contention usually attributed to men.

Ultimately, Halima's trajectory, which is exceptional for how long her radical involvement lasted, illustrates the importance of female participation, which is often invisible in the dominant representations of protests. Through the contrast between her long-standing experience of protest action and her recent decision to settle down, it also shows the transient, ever-changing nature of political protest, how it can switch from militant direct action – often costly – to being something entertaining, even playful, for both men and women.

References

Allal, Amin, 'Réformes néolibérales, clientélismes et protestations en situation autoritaire. Les mouvements contestataires dans le bassin minier de Gafsa en Tunisie (2008)', *Politique africaine*, 117, 2010: pp. 107–125.

Geisser, Vincent and Larbi Chouikha, 'Gros Plan: Retour sur la révolte du bassin minier. Les cinq leçons politiques d'un conflit social inédit', *L'Année du Maghreb 2010*, vol. VI, CNRS Editions, Paris, 2010: pp. 415–426.

Latte Abdallah, Stéphanie, 'Les femmes dans les révolutions arabes', http://printempsarabe.regionpaca.fr, March 2012.

9

Long-distance supporters

Barca and Real fans in Palestine

Abaher El Sakka

It is football evening in Ramallah. There are klaxons, yelling, flags and traffic jams. Giant screens are erected in cafés and supporters are coming out, some of them with painted faces and many of them wearing shirts in their favourite team's colours. The match does not pit two Palestinian teams against one another, but Real Madrid and FC Barcelona. Whenever the two Spanish teams meet for league and cup ties, a party is organised. How can one understand the mobilising power of globalised or, at any rate, 'extra-territorial' football among supporters attached to it neither by birthplace nor by residence? While the two clubs' 'capacity to mobilise and symbolise collective affiliations' (in the words of sociologist Ludovic Lestrelin) has been studied in other contexts, in what ways is the phenomenon now visible in Palestinian society, which confronts a colonial situation? This chapter seeks to understand the rationale for the syndrome of 'long-distance support', which is structured around sporting contests but also political and even ideological issues, in the 'café-stadiums' of the West Bank and Gaza.

A recent phenomenon

Football is often legitimately regarded as a 'total social phenomenon', to adopt Marcel Mauss's terms. Considered the sport of popular mobilisation *par excellence*, it arouses passion among those who watch it, including in Palestine, amid the internationalisation of the entertainment industry and the commodification of sport. In this respect, the rivalry between 'Barca' and 'Real' that developed outside Spain during the 2000s is remarkable. Matches between the two teams are characterised as '*clasicos*' (the Spanish term has established itself, including in Arabic) and are one of the encounters most eagerly awaited by fans

Living in the present

– '*socios*' in Spanish – in Europe as in the Arab world or Africa. To nurture this enthusiasm internationally, the two teams, as veritable multi-nationals, have had a policy towards the '*socios*' for several years now: official recognition of supporters' clubs abroad, organisation of training courses and even financing of small training centres, but also a strong presence on Internet sites. For many Palestinian supporters – especially youth – the virtual world has rapidly developed as their preferred space for expressing passion for their 'long-distance team'. Via Twitter, Facebook or blogs, they exchange points of view and relay news or rumours. The commercial Arabic Internet site kooora.com (meaning 'balloon') has been particularly invested by Palestinian supporters, while other sites bringing together photos and information, like the Facebook page *Barshaluna ila-l-abad* ('Barcelona forever'), have been launched locally – for example, in Gaza or Nablus.

'Long-distance support' has had particular resonance in Palestinian society and, more generally, the Arab world. Mahmoud, a twenty-four-year-old student at Birzeit University, a few kilometres from Ramallah, explains:

Mahmoud: I know perfectly who I do and don't support. It's true that Barca is a European football club, that these guys earn a lot of money. I'm aware of all that, but I just watch the football.
Interviewer: In that case, why don't you watch Palestinian football?
Mahmoud: Well, there's no football in Palestine, it's 'taking the piss'. They can't play, they're useless, they're not up to it. I really love my country, I haven't got a complex about the Europeans, but it's true that Palestinians can't play. You've got to admit that showing matches on TV screens is nothing like going to stadiums. But us, all our stadiums are small.

Cafés openly supporting one club or the other thus serve as stadiums, transforming each match into an event. In Palestinian towns and cities, including Jerusalem, privatised social spaces and socialising sites devoted to the Spanish *clasico* delineate an urban geography of the rivalry between the two teams. What also emerges from this footballing geography, however, is other issues and cleavages. Some popular, traditional cafés have an exclusively male clientele, whereas the more chic ones, which serve alcohol, are frequented by a mixed clientele on match evenings. To avoid polarisation and serve more effectively as a 'stadium', others display the flags of both rival teams on their facade and try to attract a wider clientele. Material issues are important for the cafés (which offer their customers access to subscription sports channels).[1] In addition, they sustain a not insignificant local economy. *Clasicos* have developed as a local advertising medium and are used by a growing number of entrepreneurs, who know that by invoking these clubs' stars (frequently contravening their copyright in images) they will succeed in capturing the attention of the youth audience.

Enthusiasm for the two Spanish clubs (and, to a lesser extent, other European championships) is accompanied by a certain disaffection with the Palestinian football championship. As we can appreciate from listening to Mahmoud, local teams are no longer the stuff dreams are made of and are incapable of mobilising beyond the micro-level of districts, villages or refugee camps. The difference in sporting level between local and international competitions, and the significant mediatisation of foreign championships, doubtless explain the magnetic power exercised by Barca and Real. In the Palestinian context, however, there is another explanation for this fascination. In fact, the phenomenon became conspicuous at the time of the second *intifada*, during the first half of the 2000s. In these years, marked by violence and Israeli repression, much of the youth was confined, being subjected to extended curfews when not imprisoned in Israeli jails. While the local championship could not be held, youth, to kill time, turned to European matches and developed ways of getting around the encryption of the subscription channels broadcasting the matches.

In particular, the Qatari satellite channel Al Jazeera, which developed rapidly in these years as a result of its programming and the aura of its commentators, played a key role in the development of the two clubs in Palestine and the Arab world. Its star commentator 'Issam al-Shawali, Tunisian by nationality, has become famous for the emotional register he employs for his digressions on the history of the Arab world or 'international relations'. In addition to the 'pleasure of hearing classical Arabic spoken', the commentator's comic register, as well as his political one, 'takes people out of themselves via football', stresses Akram, a twenty-three-year-old from the Jalazone camp on the outskirts of Ramallah. In wartime, faced with occupation, the two clubs provided an escape that Palestinian political debate could no longer offer. Thus, despite their numerous defects and a universally criticised commodity system, high-calibre sportsmen emerge as new heroes.

Moments and sites of sociability

The gradual termination of the *intifada* during the second half of the 2000s did not impede the spread of football as a long-distance leisure activity – on the contrary. For many Palestinians, the pursuit of family time together, a certain carefreeness or a kind of 'normality' after years of violence led to further investment in the rivalry between the two clubs in its ludic, light-hearted aspect. Lamia, a twenty-eight-year-old teacher, explains:

> I'm the eldest in the family, and all my brothers and sisters are football fans. The whole family comes to the house to watch the *clasicos* and I prepare cakes and things to eat. But in truth I don't give a damn about football. I just want to please my brothers and I love it when they're happy to watch the match in my living room. They eat the nice food I've prepared, it's family time for us all. We feel united ... Even if I sometimes feel a bit stupid organizing these evenings, when I'm politically committed to the Palestinian cause and against the occupation, it's just to give my family pleasure.

In fact, while the passion for football seems to evince a kind of de-politicisation, it above all reveals growing distrust of parties and 'politicking'. This distrust is more pronounced than in the past when life was largely structured around partisan loyalties. It derives from a profound crisis of leadership in the Palestinian ruling class. And while it involves Palestinian society as a whole, in the first instance such disenchantment affects the generation under thirty that has grown up with the failure of the 'peace negotiations'.

In this context, football is a tremendous source of sociability for many young people. Football matches are regarded as party time that makes it possible for youth to construct a relatively autonomous culture. Maher, an eighteen-year-old sixth-form student, is an unconditional fan:

> I've bought a Barca flag, tee-shirt, cap and keyring. All that, it's for posing ... but what grabs me is the Thursday evening parties. The next day it's the weekend, so my parents let me go out. I hate it when the matches are on late in the evening [on weekdays] because I'm not allowed to go out and then I watch it on TV. Besides, mama has told me that I've got to stop watching football because I'm wasting time, I'm not studying enough, and I'm getting fat because I snack in front of the TV. But that doesn't bother me. What matters is that now everyone watches the matches. It's fashionable, people rave over it on Facebook, Twitter, we even write the names of the teams we support on our school bags!

The broadcasting of matches is also presented as encouraging exchanges within the family. If enthusiasm for the Real–Barca duel involves young men *en masse*, it does not exclude women. For Nahed, who is twenty-three, several concerns converge in her attraction to Barca:

Long-distance supporters

A few years ago, I became an addict of the Barca team. I was initiated by my brother, who's a fan of the club. It was a moment of real happiness to gather in front of the TV with the whole family! It strengthens the bonds with my brother and I can get more from him in the following days. As well, it's amusing to know about the private life of the players, their partners and their social worlds, and with girlfriends who support Real Madrid we tease each other. And it's a way of killing boredom.

As for Hiba, a twenty-one-year-old student, the pleasure of football is above all one of 'atmosphere':

I never watch the matches at home. I go out with my friends, especially my girlfriends, to a café and we spend the evening smoking the hookah, snacking, telling jokes, having a laugh. And to tell you the truth, I couldn't care less about the football, it's the atmosphere I like, it's a moment of happiness, of peace. Happiness for me is when our team – Real – wins. But I don't know why I support Real, I think it's down to the influence of girlfriends who used to talk about it all the time. In fact, it's become a habit. Everyone's interested in it, it's the fashion, it shows I'm connected [*faya'a*] and not 'out'.

Heroic identification, political projections

Over and above the socialising aspect of enthusiasm for the two Spanish clubs and the clash between them, the phenomenon of 'long-distance support' is apt to produce identification and advance the image of the hero in Palestinian society. Players like Lionel Messi or Cristiano Ronaldo embody social and economic success, not to mention virility. Firas, a nineteen-year-old worker who follows all Real Madrid's matches, owns the team shirts and is part of the Facebook group, says it without false modesty: 'I often give tee-shirts for my nephews' birthdays. I really like the players, I think it's an excellent team. I like Cristiano Ronaldo a lot. I identify with him; he's handsome, athletic, he's my hero.'

Such identification does not supplant other heroes – fighters, activists or martyrs for the Palestinian cause. But the political crisis and the stalemate of what was once called the 'peace process', like the internal Palestinian division between Fatah and Hamas, corruption and the harshness of arbitrary colonial rule, have played a not insignificant role in this search for substitute heroes, even imperfect ones, off the 'battlefield'. The phenomenon is a vector of social transformation in and through integration into globalisation and the consumer society.

Living in the present

The results of matches, along with the internal life of clubs and the transfer of players on astronomical salaries, have become subjects of animated conversation, competing with, or even eclipsing, political discussion. However, this symbolic, 'long-distance' rivalry between Barcelona and Madrid fans is also played out on more mundanely local terrain. Matches are often followed by demonstrations and the main squares of Palestinian towns can be blocked by supporters (and the forces of law and order). *Clasicos* evenings have thus become a time of traffic problems. Sporting oppositions fuel other cleavages. Matches can give rise to brawls and punch-ups between rival gangs, which often oppose the residents of towns and youth from the refugee camps, who are perceived by the former as 'violent', 'frustrated' and 'bad mannered'. While the clashes are often limited, they nevertheless fuel a whole series of 'urban legends', such as the death (fabricated) of a supporter in Nablus in 2012.

Palestinian fans of the two teams employ a multitude of arguments to justify their commitment to one of the clubs – first and foremost, admiration for high-quality sport. The players' physical ability, their playing techniques or the teamwork of a particular player – these are acclaimed by '*socios*'. Five-time winner of the *ballon d'or* for the best player in the world, Lionel Messi, is regarded by many Barca fans as a 'football genius'. Along with his technical skills, some also stress his 'human qualities'. While his salary is unquestionably very high, 'he gives away some of his money to the poor'.

A number of supporters employ a second register of allegiance, which is more ideological and political. Thus they endow their choice of team with political significance. For example, Muhammad, a twenty-nine-year-old civil servant, estimates that Barca is a 'poor people's' team in a region marginalised by Spain's royalist central government. The cogency of such an assertion is of little relevance. Many young Barcelona supporters identify with the supposed commitment of their team to Catalonia and autonomy. Thus, Real Madrid is equated with the monarch, government and centralisation. For many supporters, particularly 'left-wing' ones, Barca is a politicised team defending a 'just' cause – that of the 'oppressed'. Despite their stupendous salaries, Barca's players are sometimes presented by the most fervent as comrades-in-arms.

Faced with this, Real's supporters happily mobilise a third repertoire of identification – religion or ethnicity. They point out the fact that 'their' team includes several Muslim players, whether Arab or hailing from Africa. In the Palestinian context, this is far from insignificant and Barca's logo is a source of much controversy. Thus, the cross on the arms of the Catalan club has been deliberately erased by the manufacturer of some blue and garnet-red flags made in Hebron workshops. However, this subterfuge has not gone unnoticed and has been criticised by supporters who prefer to display the original logo on their t-shirts or in their cars.

Gilad Shalit in the grandstands!

Israel's colonial control of Palestinian society explains the success of a fourth register of mobilisation – the transposition of the situation Palestinians experience into the *clasico* itself. The conflict also colonises leisure activities. The rivalry between the two Spanish clubs is no exception. Some go as far as to say that they have seen Israeli flags in the ranks of Real's supporters in Madrid stadium, allegedly betraying the club's sympathy for the Zionist project. Such forms of stigmatisation are persistent and give rise to plenty of rumours. In reality, through their '*socios*' policy, both clubs help finance teams and training schools in Palestine, like the two that opened in Gaza and Ramallah amid a publicity campaign.

In October 2012, the 'Shalit affair' ended up sowing seeds of doubt in the minds of Barca fans, who are unquestionably in a majority among young Palestinians. Ten days before a new meeting between the two clubs, a news item, relayed by the media, reported that FC Barcelona had invited the former Israeli soldier Gilad Shalit, held prisoner by Hamas in Gaza for more than six years and freed in October 2011, to attend the match against Real in the VIP grandstand. This led to sparring between supporters on the Internet. The media ignited, the debates reverberated on the pages of Facebook, and political parties, with Hamas in the lead, condemned Barca's initiative. An appeal to boycott the match was launched by the highly influential BDS (Boycott, Disinvestment and Sanctions) Committee, rallying numerous actors from civil society. In the face of this revolt, Barcelona denied having invited Shalit and explained that the ex-soldier had himself asked to attend the match. The club explained that it had also invited the former footballer Mahmoud Sursok, a native of the Gaza Strip imprisoned by Israel for three years and released in July 2012 at the end of a long hunger strike. Palestinian activists then brought pressure to bear on him. For some, his presence would make it possible for 'the cause of Palestinian prisoners' to get a hearing on the international stage. For others, particularly the BDS movement, attendance would validate Israel's strategy. Mahmoud Sursok finally chose the second option, stating that he refused to 'play along with symmetry between "colonizer and colonized" and "victim and executioner", the soldier Shalit being a prisoner of war whereas I am a prisoner of colonization, of the colonial system, and there are currently 5,800 prisoners like me'.

To sum up, the enthusiasm felt by this generation of 'long-distance' supporters of the Spanish teams, Barcelona and Real Madrid, has several dimensions. While it fits squarely into a process of globalisation and cultural domination, even into the manifest development of a consumer society, which is far from being confined to the borders of Palestine, it is combined with quite unique experiences in a context of violence and detachment from party politics. While encouraging shared values and activities, by renewing relations of collusion, solidarity or friendship away from the battlefields, it also nurtures identity construction, both personal – around new heroes – and collective – because of the colonial situation and cleavages within Palestinian society.

Note

1 See Mahfoud Amara and Laurent Bonnefoy, Chapter 10 in this volume, 'Commentary in Arabic ... or in Tigrinya? Football fans and the search for free television broadcasting'.

References

El Sakka, Abaher, 'Revendication identitaire et représentations sociales: Émergence d'un nouveau mode d'expression artistique de groupes de jeunes Palestiniens', *Cahiers de recherche sociologique*, 49, 2010: pp. 47–62.

Facebook page of supporters of FC Barcelona: www.facebook.com/#!/Arab.Barcelona.Fans?fref=ts

Facebook page of supporters of Real Madrid: www.facebook.com/#!/REAL.MADRID.AR.C.F?fref=ts

Lestrelin, Ludovic, *L'Autre public des matchs de football. Sociologie du 'supportérisme à distance'*, Éditions de l'EHESS, coll. 'En temps & lieux', Paris, 2010.

Sites of supporters of the Barca and Real in the Arab world: www.clasicooo.com

'Sociologie du sport', *L'Année sociologique*, 52, 2002: pp. 507–532.

10

Commentary in Arabic ... or in Tigrinya?

Football fans and the search for free television broadcasting

Mahfoud Amara and Laurent Bonnefoy

Without a doubt, football is the male leisure activity *par excellence* in the Arab world. Boys play it and young men often watch it – or rather try to watch it, because viewing matches on television sometimes proves quite a challenge. Whereas domestic leagues were the main attraction until the 1990s in many Arab countries, European matches and international competitions have gradually grown in popularity. Interest in the big Arab clubs – including the most renowned, Al Ahly and Zamalek in Cairo, Espérance Sportive in Tunis and Jeunesse Sportive de Kabylie in Algeria – has waned somewhat, although it still survives in some groups of 'ultras' inspired by the European 'hooligans' of the 1980s.[1]

Broadcasting rights and a feeling of exclusion

With the liberalisation of the Arab satellite space in the first decade of the twenty-first century and the emergence of a number of pay TV channels, the majority of viewers in Arab countries lost access to their favourite football leagues, particularly those in Spain, England and Italy. In the competition for broadcasting rights for major events, free national channels lost out to pan-Arab channels, primarily Al Jazeera Sport and the Saudi private capital consortia MBC and ART. This liberalisation of media space tipped the balance of sources of information and televised entertainment in favour of the Gulf countries and introduced fierce competition between channels. The sports sector has become one of the main battlefields, as the popular appetite for competitions is intense, transcending as well as reproducing a number of social, ethnic and geographical divisions. Al Jazeera offers sixteen paid TV channels to its subscribers, while Abu Dhabi Sport has eighteen. The launch of three Al Jazeera beIN Sports channels catering for French and American audiences has expanded media coverage from the Gulf capitals even beyond the Arab world.

The feeling of exclusion that the rise in power of paid TV channels engenders among football fans varies from country to country and depends on household income. But it is still very real in many countries, including Algeria, Egypt, Jordan, Syria and Yemen, and causes heated debates before every major sporting event – the FIFA World Cup, the European Championship or even the Olympic Games – but also, and more regularly, before every domestic league game. Fans have responded by developing new practices – with repercussions not only for the young but for society as a whole – that illustrate a number of contemporary social dynamics. Sport and television lie at a crossroads of issues linked to the construction of identities against a backdrop of globalisation and social inequality.

As early as 2002, when the issue of football broadcasting rights was only starting to emerge, many Yemenis who were short of money but did have satellite receivers turned to the Eritrean national channel to watch matches in the FIFA World Cup, which that year was hosted jointly by South Korea and Japan. Viewers may not have understood the commentary in Tigrinya, which railed against the exclusion suffered by Arabic speakers, and they may have been rather bemused by the ads or the half-time entertainment provided by female folk dancers, but they adjusted to the situation. Nonetheless, frequent loss of reception or untimely interruptions by news programmes singing the praises of the Eritrean president Isaias Afwerki eventually led them to ask friends (this was before the era of the mobile phone or Internet forums) about alternatives and to look for other, more exotic or restricted channels.

Since the 2006 World Cup in Germany, this lockout has become institutionalised. Exclusive broadcasting rights for Arab countries for that year's event, as well as the following two tournaments, were acquired for more than 100 million dollars by the ART consortium (which had already broadcast the 2002 tournament, but encryption had improved in the meantime), owned by the Saudi businessman Salih Kamil. Accused in numerous newspapers, such as the Jordanian daily *Al Ra'i*, of having deprived the poor of the Arab world of the competition, Kamil defended himself in a long interview with the pan-Arab magazine *Al Watan Al Arabi* and went back on the decision by announcing the free broadcast of certain matches, including the final.

The debate became so heated in the Arab countries affected that the religious authorities stepped into the fray. In the same year, clerics at the Al-Azhar

Commentary in Arabic ... or in Tigrinya?

University in Cairo, including Abdel Muti al Bayyumi, who some years later would endorse the French law prohibiting the wearing of the niqab, were invited into television studios or wrote columns voicing their opinion on popular enthusiasm for football and the practices of illegally accessing ART package subscriptions. These religious authorities, close to the ruling regimes, condemned all descrambling attempts, declaring them to be a form of theft.

Just before the 2010 World Cup, Salih Kamil sold his channel and broadcasting rights to Al Jazeera for a sum estimated by the media at three billion dollars, evidence of the inflation that broadcasting rights had undergone in just a few years.

Bypassing subscription services

In response to this institutionalisation of exclusion, methods of circumventing payment have proliferated, particularly among young men. This has led to a thriving underground economy and a virtual community, to which public authorities often turn a blind eye, no doubt happy to see their young men seemingly forgetting political issues (and overlooking the fact that football often accompanies explicitly political mobilisation). Feeling pressure mount at street level, some governments intervened in 2006 to guarantee a minimum of access to the FIFA World Cup. This was the case in Jordan, where the king had giant screens set up in all the big cities. In Algeria, pre-paid ART cards were subsidised by the authorities and sold in post offices. But the gradual appropriation of leisure by private companies was ultimately a further sign of the failure of governments, who tried as best they could to react to their waning influence on public media, which they had once controlled so easily.

At an individual level, cheaper and sometimes even free substitutes have sprung up in Arab countries, allowing access to matches over the Internet or, more often, through sophisticated schemes to access channels by means of fake cards or other subterfuges. For some, these actions are legitimate and even constitute a form of resistance to the hegemony of the market.

In the Maghreb countries, French channels holding broadcasting rights can be received thanks to a simple technical trick. Viewers who live near the border with Israel merely need to redirect their terrestrial antenna if they want to watch games broadcast on Israeli channels. Until 2012, the Eritrean channel remained a must for some fans of English football as it was the only free-to-air channel to broadcast matches from the English league. The Eritrean folk dance interludes had probably lost their exoticism by then, and viewers might even have learned a few words of Tigrinya! However, in 2013, the Algerian public channel, accessible throughout the region on the Nilesat satellite, began broadcasting some English league games thanks to a sponsorship deal with Mobilis, a mobile telephone operator.

But it is over the Internet that such strategies are most effectively deployed. Forums created on a territorial basis or around the fans of a particular club offer advice on how to unscramble encrypted channels. They spread not only a particular kind of technical jargon, feeding into a universal, yet more or less Arabised geek culture, but also an ethic that embraces an ideal of sharing and freedom, as well as a national, Arab or even Islamic solidarity. The desire to watch matches without paying is not only driven by financial necessity but is also a game that is part of the football experience. Forums help to create a sense of community through which new generational codes emerge. Religious, moralising interventions are common in the forums, and while it is deemed acceptable to resort to illegal decoding for watching football, the sharing of information for accessing pornographic channels is condemned. Far from being deterritorialised, these seemingly insignificant strategies are interconnected with the major debates that are shaping Arab societies and the often difficult relationships between generations.

Note

1 The capacity for the mobilisation of these 'ultras' played a significant role in the revolutionary movement in Egypt in 2011. Following the fall of Mubarak, these supporters continued to spearhead opposition to the new power of the Muslim Brotherhood and suffered considerable repression. As illustrated by events in Port Said in February 2012 – when seventy-four Al Ahly supporters were killed by those of a rival club without any intervention by the police – the stadium remains an outlet for antagonism and the symbol of a dysfunctional state and of social tensions.

References

Amara, Mahfoud, 'Football Sub-Culture and Youth Politics in Algeria', *Mediterranean Politics*, 17, 1, 2012: pp. 41–58.
Amara, Mahfoud, 'When the Arab World was Mobilised around the FIFA 2006 World Cup', *The Journal of North African Studies*, 12, 4, 2007: pp. 417–438.
Bashir, Muhammad Jamal, *Kitab al-Ultras*, Dawn, Cairo, 2011.

Commentary in Arabic ... or in Tigrinya?

Gonzalez-Quijano, Yves and Tourya Guaaybess, eds, *Les Arabes parlent aux Arabes. La révolution de l'information dans le monde arabe*, Sindbad, Paris, 2009.

Lamloum, Olfa, *Al-Jazira, miroir rebelle et ambigu du monde arabe*, La Découverte, Paris, 2004.

Lamloum, Olfa, Anne-Françoise Weber and Arnim Heinemann, eds, *The Middle East in the Media. Conflicts, Censorship and Public Opinion*, Saqi Books, London/Beirut, 2009.

Talon, Claire-Gabrielle, *Al-Jazeera. Liberté d'expression et pétromonarchie*, Presses Universitaires de France, Paris, 2011.

Part II

Rooting the future

Introduction

Rooting the future

Laurent Bonnefoy and Myriam Catusse

As shown in Part I, the leisure activities of Arab youth are rooted in their times, yet also have an ambivalent relationship with the past. The younger generation has been shaped by nostalgia, a desire to make a break, question their heritage and reinvent traditions.

While youth is commonly perceived as a time conducive to building one's future (through studies, the quest to 'marry well', build capital, etc.), the texts in this second part also remind us that the future does not come out of nowhere. Inherited conflicts, wounded identities and 'lost paradises' have affected the leisure time of young Arabs across social, geographical and cultural differences. From the revival of Coptic religious songs in Egypt to the political nostalgia of some leftists in Lebanon and the remarkable success of 'traditional' dance companies in Palestine, young Arabs remain deeply influenced by previous generations.

How young people perceive the past is a fascinating subject. As we saw in the previous part, the leisure practices of young Arabs attest to the development of particular subcultures. They also reveal the paradigms through which younger generations reproduce family customs and appropriate the norms that have been transmitted to them, even when these are reshaped by cutting-edge technologies or changing contexts. As many observers have pointed out, the 2011 revolutions cannot be seen as an 'immaculate contestation'[1] without a past or premise. Similarly, leisure activities must be understood within historical trajectories, made of breaking with the past and passing it on. The shaping of social, 'ethnic', political, gender-based and generational 'echo chambers' reproduces identities, inequalities and forms of domination and submission that are often internalised and sometimes co-opted. Beyond the need to be entertained, to keep busy, or even to 'fill the void' while waiting for 'youth to pass', the leisure activities of young Arabs reflect the social divisions and many other fault lines that run through Arab societies.

The feeling of nostalgia holds a special place in the stories collected by the authors who have contributed to this second part of the book. Nostalgia contains different facets and finds a distinct means of expression in leisure activities. In many cases, it reflects the at times distressing uncertainties characteristic of transition periods. Faced with the economic crisis, unemployment and a precarious job market, many young Arabs wonder what the future will bring. That anxiety is even greater for those who are directly confronted with political unrest, civil strife or protracted wars, like Algerians and Lebanese in the past, Libyans, Syrians, Yemenis and Iraqis today, and Palestinians for several generations. From Kabylia to Baghdad and Beirut, youths in Arab societies are sometimes tempted to reject the present in the name of a fantasised golden age.

Then, faced with what are perceived as attacks on the identity of the group (and not just of young people), other more collective forms of 'nostalgia' are sustained and even invented. In the previous part, we saw how contemporary forms of Salafism and Sufism could be fuelled by references to an often imaginary 'golden age'. The texts that follow invite us to meet young Sahrawis, Iraqis, Palestinians and Lebanese who are also reflecting on a 'heritage' they wish to preserve or regain (literally for the Iraqis after the closure and looting of museums during the conflict following the American invasion in 2003), in order to politically defend their homeland or community and to engage in civil resistance against powers whose authority they contest.

Whether implicitly or explicitly formulated, this 'nostalgia' is not always articulated within an institutional framework such as a school, an association, a club or a summer camp. In cafés in the Israeli city of Haifa, for instance, one may witness the dismay of a Palestinian community eroded by 'social diversity' that is full of ambiguity. But it is likely the family circle that remains the place of choice for expressing respect for, and sometimes rejection of, customs, as we found out in a town in southern Jordan at a reception held by a Christian family.

While young people may be interested in the past, this does not imply any passivity on their part. Their heritage is constantly reinvented, to the point that fathers and mothers find it hard at times to recognise what they have passed on. This is the case for Coptic religious songs taken up by charismatic movements, for tents set up in the summer by young Sahrawi city-dwellers, for plays staged

Introduction

in schools linked to the Lebanese Hezbollah or for *dabke* dance steps performed in Palestinian clubs. The past is reinvented everywhere, the better to put down roots for the future.

Note

1 Amin Allal and Thomas Pierret, eds, *Au cœur des révoltes arabes. Devenir révolutionnaires*, Armand Colin-Iremam, Paris, 2013.

11

Drinking in Hamra

Youthful nostalgia in Beirut?

Nicolas Dot-Pouillard

The history of Hamra Street in west Beirut is marked by daytime *flânerie*, which is linked to the distinctive sociability of its cafés, especially their outdoor terraces. The idle drifting of Hamra's *flâneurs* is also synonymous with consumerism: the street's public space is dominated by banks, fashion houses and ready-to-wear clothes stores. During the evenings, Hamra Street has supplanted the legendary Rue Monnot in the eastern part of the city, which was the centre of Lebanese nightlife in the 1990s but is now deserted. It competes with Gouraud Street and the Gemmayzeh and Mar Mikhaël neighbourhoods, yet the liveliness of the street and the surrounding 'Hamra quarter' owes more to pubs, bars and cafés than to upmarket nightclubs. English-language names are particularly popular: Rabbit Hole, Captain's Cabin, Main Street, Butter Mint, etc. This was already the case in the 1960s, when pubs and bars were called Horseshoe, Duke of Wellington or Jack's Hideaway, despite the avowed anti-imperialism of some of the youth of that time.

Hamra also has its own cultural capital: theatres and cinemas (al-Medina, Metro), small venues catering to a new, alternative Lebanese music scene (Democratic Republic of Music), bookshops (Orientale, Antoine), publishing houses and daily papers (*as-Safir*) link back to the pre-civil war period, when Hamra was one of the epicentres of the city's political and cultural life. Empty and abandoned, its neon sign long extinguished, the Piccadilly Theatre stands as the last witness to that time gone by. Attracting visitors from all over, the neighbourhood also brings together very different social groups. Business people and office workers rub shoulders with the 'wretched of the earth'. There are beggars and day labourers of all ages, from shoe shiners to hawkers selling pirated DVDs. Some of the older ones are Lebanese, while the youngest, often underage, are Palestinians from the camps, Kurds, 'Gypsies' (*nawar*), stateless or undocumented immigrants (*bidun*) or Syrians. Sex workers, often from Eastern

Drinking in Hamra

Europe, congregate in some of the seedy hotels in Hamra's side streets, as well as in the adjacent neighbourhood of Ain al-Mreisseh.

Past or present: a divided youth

Hamra is a space full of political and social contradictions. The recent success of 78th Street, a little alleyway running between Hamra Street and Maqdissi Street, and the lively atmosphere sparked by the opening of Dany's restaurant in 2008, may deceive inattentive *flâneurs* into believing that they are in a cosmopolitan, 'post-modern' neighbourhood, a transnational Babel. A bilingual crowd, mostly Lebanese middle and upper-class students from the nearby American University of Beirut (AUB) and the Lebanese American University (LAU), mixes with an endless flood of expats: staff of NGOs and international organisations, young journalists and researchers, foreign students.

Within the narrow confines of the Estral Center, establishments like Madame Om, Mezyan, Bobo and Marc's Place – this last a deliberate pun on the author of *Capital* – add a different flavour. The young crowd here seems more political: the close-knit alternative scene of Lebanon's artists exists next to that of young activists of the radical left and of the Lebanese Communist Party, of young Palestinians working for various NGOs and, more recently, certain Syrian oppositionists. Yet these different spaces are not completely isolated from each other: the twenty-four-hour opening of cafés and bars introduced more than eight years ago and ever-changing fashions in leisure culture have created circuits of nocturnal nomadism in which the paths of the different groups can easily cross.

But there is a striking contrast between these two very different crowds, each with their own distinctive practices and cultures. Both ways of appropriating the street's cafés are based on a form of imitation. Some of the young people experience Hamra's nightlife and entertainment as part of a globalised culture, and their nights out are increasingly difficult to distinguish from the latest crazes in Paris, New York or Barcelona. The use of English as lingua franca, the music played in many of the pubs and bars – pop, soul, funk, electro – and clothing fashions which follow the latest global trends all contribute to an increasingly post-modern Hamra, largely detached from time and space. They mostly subscribe to a conception of time that could be described as a self-sufficient 'presentism', as defined by the historian François Hartog: Hamra's own history is completely absent from it. Partying becomes a way of forgetting the past and not worrying about the future. Another group of young people, however, the more politicised ones, still hope to find 'under the tarmac, the paving stones', as the philosopher Daniel Bensaïd put it so pithily. They experience the street as a nostalgic appropriation of a buried past. In Hamra, *flânerie* and hedonism do not reflect a single and homogeneous youth culture.

A lost golden age?

Hamra remains the symbolic centre for those young people who see themselves as the political heirs of earlier generations. They may be members of one of the many left-wing organisations, or intellectuals involved in the voluntary sector or the media – such as the dailies *al-Akhbar* and *as-Safir* – or simply the sons and daughters of a previous generation of activists. The café space facilitates unusual networks in which the familial and the partisan can easily coexist. Antiglobalist and far-left Europeans and North Americans, who either visit the city or live there, are also drawn to Hamra.

The language and references of these young people show continuities with the Hamra of the 1960s and 1970s when the cafés were the meeting places for a generation characterised by a globalised left-wing radicalism and solidarity with the Palestinian national movement. From today's perspective, the student Hamra of those days is perceived as a golden age, with all its foundational events and emblematic figures. The strikes and occupations at the AUB between 1967 and 1975, the prominence of Mohammed Dajani of the General Union of Palestinian Students (GUPS), and the strong presence of the Fatah movement within the student councils at AUB lent Hamra and its surrounding quarter an air of Third-Worldism. Young militants and intellectuals exalted the 'Palestinian Revolution', yet they met in a neighbourhood whose architecture and social makeup were worlds apart from the Palestinian refugee camps of Sabra, Shatila, Mar Elias or Tall al-Zaʻtar.

The outbreak of the Lebanese Civil War in April 1975 and the subsequent militarisation of politics contributed to the slow and gradual decline of Hamra's cafés as the intellectual repositories of the left and of the Lebanese nationalist movements. The PLO's withdrawal from Lebanon, the Israeli occupation of Beirut in September 1982, and the rise of a Lebanese anti-Israeli resistance, which became increasingly Islamic, marked the end of an era. With the decline of the left and of secular nationalism, the hopes of a political generation had been crushed. In this time of political and economic crisis, many of the most popular cafés of the 1960s and 1970s left, including Moka and L'Express, closed.

Drinking in Hamra

In the course of the 1990s and the first decade of the new millennium, their place was taken by banks, ready-to-wear clothing stores and new chain cafés and burger restaurants. A certain form of global neoliberal consumerism seemed to have wiped out the leftist and Third-Worldist utopias of the 1960s and 1970s for good.

The end of the Civil War in the early 1990s did however allow a partial revival of the old tradition, a timid attempt to recover the militant heritage. Abou Elie, Chez André (since renamed Regusto), the Baromètre, Walimat Wardeh and Zico's House gave young people who had escaped the military conflict the opportunity to meet older generations who had been shaped by the leftism and Third Worldism of the past. But the belief in a better future soon gave way to disenchantment and melancholy.

A politics of nostalgia

The younger generation of leftists clearly lacks a recent foundational event. The softly lit interior of the Baromètre illustrates this rather well: a front page from the daily *as-Safir* from May 2000 is proudly displayed on the wall, celebrating the withdrawal of Israeli troops from Southern Lebanon with the headline *al-janub yuhariru al-watan* ('The south liberates the homeland'). But the Hezbollah that had brought about the departure of the Israelis was one that had long since eclipsed left-wing and Arab nationalist organisations both politically and militarily to such an extent that they now play no more than a marginal role.

The legacy of the nationalist 'anti-imperialism' of the past seems more often aesthetic than political. If 'progressive', 'secularist' and 'Arab nationalist' ideals survive in the cafés, they are less linked to the present than to a mythical past, which is celebrated in a purely hedonistic way. The politicised youth of today listens to music from the glory years of the left and the Lebanese National Movement, when Zyad Rahbani, Marcel Khalifé and Cheikh Imam sang of a free Palestine and a coming Arab revolution. Drinking, dancing and smoking seem a natural accompaniment, now that the Marxist-Leninist austerity of the 1960s and 1970s has partly given way to a world revolution limited to lifestyle. The re-appropriation of a leftist and 'progressive' legacy can also be exclusively visual: the little Abou Elie café in the Caracas quarter, between the end of Hamra Street and the coast, displays photos of Mao, Trotsky, Guevara and Castro on its walls, in a strange reconciliation of Marxist currents once opposed to each other, as if to suggest that these political differences no longer really matter.

Rooting the future

Listening to their conversations, one may gain the impression that the young activists of the Lebanese Communist Party or the Socialist Forum – a small Trotskyist organisation formed after the war – seem less concerned with changing the world than with defending a heritage. They may discuss the French government's refusal to release Georges Ibrahim Abdallah, the last Lebanese 'communist' prisoner in France, in January 2013. Commenting on the most recent ups and downs of the Syrian crisis, or what they judge to be the disastrous record of Egypt's Muslim Brotherhood and Tunisia's En-Nahda, they express disenchantment about the paradox of Arab revolutions, which have failed to bring the left to power. An echo of the 1960s and 1970s can also be found in the clothes they wear: the Palestinian *keffiyeh*, literally nowhere to be seen in the bars of east Beirut and Gemmayzé Street, is omnipresent here. This not only evokes the radical imaginary of the past but also forms a link with the far left and anti-globalisation youth in Europe. Where new, alternative practices do emerge, they are not always associated with the universe of meaning shared by the Lebanese left: the Bardo, for example, a gay bar and restaurant, carefully avoids any suggestion of the political. Venues that are explicitly associated with particular political parties often do not survive for very long: the Red, set up by members of the Union of Lebanese Democratic Youth (UJDL), close to the Lebanese Communist Party, shut its doors in 2012, only two years after opening.

The politics of nostalgia sometimes does give way to attempts to bring about intellectual and political renewal. Zico House, in Spears Street, not far from Hamra, houses the offices of the LGBTIQ organisation Helem and regularly provides a platform for Arab left-wing intellectuals. In November 2012, for example, the Palestinian-Syrian Marxist Salamah Kaileh was invited to give a talk on the Syrian crisis. Zico House thus tries to bring together people of all ages, who may have very different experiences but share the same frame of reference. In the winter of 2012, the launch of *Bidayyat* ('Beginnings') – a left-wing journal edited by Fawwaz Traboulsi, then a professor at LAU and one of the leading figures of Lebanon's progressive scene – at Walimat Wardeh brought together, at least for the duration of the event, older intellectuals from the 1960s and young Lebanese activists supporting feminism, anti-racism or solidarity with the Palestinians. Established in 2006, the café T-Marbouta sees itself as an integral part of the avant-garde, and its progressive ideal goes beyond a melancholy gesture. During the war between Hezbollah and Israel (*Harb Tamuz*) in July and August 2006, it was the meeting place for groups supporting the 'Lebanese resistance': young left-wingers, third-sector volunteers, militant environmentalists and LGBT activists, known collectively as *Samidun* ('those who resist'). Events organised at T-Marbouta highlight issues that do in fact link past and present: concerts by rap groups from the Palestinian refugee camps (Katibeh Khamseh – 'Batallion Five' – from Burj al-Barajneh[1]), evenings in solidarity with migrant workers in Lebanon, regular sociological discussion groups informed by recent critical theory, and poetry and literature echoing the Arab insurrections – such as the evening with Tunisian poet Mohamed Saghir Ouled Ahmed in October 2012.

The street and its paving stones: an impossible appropriation?

The young militants who congregate in Hamra seem to find it difficult to escape the hedonistic space of the café. Occasions to politicise this space are rare. Only the Palestinian question is capable of drawing people out into the streets in a unity transcending party-political or religious affiliation which does not exist in other neighbourhoods of Beirut or other regions of Lebanon. In December 2008 and January 2009, during Israel's 'Cast Lead' operation against Gaza, a number of peaceful demonstrations set off from the Al-Medina theatre, at the heart of Hamra. In a symbolic act, several hundred demonstrators carried homemade coffins to the Egyptian embassy, to denounce a government that they accused of closing its frontier and abandoning Gaza's population to the Israeli bombs. Since then, young activists involved in the boycott campaign against Israel have been assembling in front of the Hamra Street Starbucks, to demand the closure of the chain which the nationalist left in Lebanon suspects of giving financial support to the Israeli state.

These diverse movements and organisations present less of a united front on other issues. In the spring of 2011, the movement for the abolition of the confessional political system – organised in part by sections of the Communist Party youth, the far left and the Syrian Social Nationalist Party (SSNP) – wanted to harness the revolutionary momentum that had unfolded in Egypt and Tunisia. But internal divisions over the Syrian crisis made this impossible: some activists displayed an evident sympathy for the Syrian regime while others supported the insurrection. In the summer of 2011, a demonstration in solidarity with the uprising was organised in front of the Syrian embassy in Maqdissi Street by young people of the far left, only to be violently attacked by defenders of the Syrian government. Just a few months earlier, both sides had been demonstrating side by side for the abolition of confessionalism. In July

2012, a supporter of the Syrian government was stabbed to death outside Café Younes by an opponent of the regime. Relations between 'leftists' and young members of the SSNP, many of whom worked as waiters in Hamra bars and cafés, were equally tense. Other causes failed to generate any significant mobilisations. The rare demonstrations by migrant workers were unequivocally supported by the young Lebanese Anti-Racism Movement, without garnering any more widespread support. In the summer of 2012, demonstrations by graffiti artists against censorship in Lebanon took place in Hamra Street but received only lukewarm support from the young activists of the Lebanese left, some of whom even dismissed the cause as trivial.

The uncertain future of a left-wing romanticism

What young people who identify with the founding paradigms of the Lebanese and Arab left do share with the older generations of the 1960s and 1970s is Hamra Street and its history. But unlike previous generations, today's youth does not have any contemporary founding myths. Too young to remember Billancourt or Gandour,[2] which galvanised the struggle for Lebanese workers' rights in the 1970s, they have failed to make real contact with the working class. This deep disaffection felt by many set in after the structural crisis of the Arab left in the late 1980s. The politics of nostalgia displayed in certain Hamra bars and cafés by politicised young people, who replay the divisions of the 1960s and 1970s in a melancholic mode that is more aesthetic than political – a repetition without any true re-appropriation – thus seems to be one of their last means of keeping a tradition alive at a time of acute political divisions. It reveals the historic structural failure of the left, of Lebanon's nationalists and 'progressives', and of a generation that is struggling to find its own political temporality and whose only foundational utopia is rooted in political or artistic mythologies of the past. Yet paradoxically, this politics of melancholy may also be their last available means of surmounting the crisis of left utopias, a form of intergenerational legacy passed on against all odds.

Rescuing the tradition, however, seems all the more difficult when the competition comes from bars and cafés which, having abandoned politics long ago, are pinning their hopes on a commercial revival of Hamra Street with an aesthetic and with styles and forms of musical expression that cater for a young, Lebanese and foreign student crowd, which is largely apolitical. Hamra could therefore also be described as the place of a silent confrontation between two kinds of youth whose outcome is still uncertain. One group is redrawing the face of Hamra in a post-modern fashion, having abandoned any search for a political or ideological 'grand narrative'. The other thinks it has found one, but it is one that lies in the past and is still far removed from the present.

These two kinds of youth and the aesthetic and symbolic conflict between the bars and cafés of 78th Street and the leftist venues of the Estral Center are themselves representative of developments in a neighbourhood and a street whose cultural, political and even architectural heritage is precarious. The British geographer David Harvey notes that the 'irresistible lure' of monopoly rents offered by urban locations with 'special marks of distinction' brings with it a 'homogenizing multinational commodification' that threatens to destroy them: 'The dilemma – veering so close into pure commercialisation as to lose the marks of distinction that underlie monopoly rents or constructing marks of distinction that are so special as to be very hard to trade upon – is perpetually present.' The success and unique atmosphere of Hamra Street was partly built on a distinctive cultural capital which – unlike that of other Beirut neighbourhoods – melded daytime *flânerie* and night-time partying with an identity that was simultaneously political, artistic and intellectual, and capable of defining its own utopias. Paradoxically yet logically, this capital that defined the character of Hamra past and present is today under threat, even if it is still championed by some politicised young people. In this politics of nostalgia that is played out in some of the bars and cafés, it is sometimes difficult to distinguish between an 'end game' whose romanticism has no illusions about the future and a hesitant attempt to free the street of its bewitchment by the commodity. But there are some who still believe that 'beneath the tarmac, the paving stones', and perhaps even 'beneath the paving stones, the beach'.

Post-script

Since the first publication of this paper in French (2013), much has changed on Hamra Street: pubs, restaurants and collective public spaces have suffered severely from the 2019 Lebanese economic collapse, and many of them had to close their doors. In the meantime, Hamra Street and its surrounding neighbourhoods have returned to their protest tradition and street politics: for two years now, leftist protestors face police and security services in front of the Central Bank of Lebanon and Interior Ministry, which form a few tens of metres of Hamra Street.

Notes

1 See Nicolas Puig's chapter in this collection, Chapter 36, p. 318.
2 On 16 May 1968, workers spontaneously occupied the Renault car plant in Boulogne-Billancourt on the outskirts of Paris and issued a series of radical demands. The occupation lasted for thirty-three days. In November 1972, the 1,200 non-unionised workers at the Gandour biscuits factory in Chiyah just outside Beirut went on strike, demanding higher wages, equal pay for men and women and the right to trade union organisation. During a demonstration at the factory gates on 11 November, police shot dead two of the strikers.

References

Bardawil, Fadi A., *When All This Revolution Melts into Air. The Disenchantment of Levantine Marxist Intellectuals*, Columbia University Press, New York, 2010.
Bensaïd, Daniel, 'En flânant sur les macadams: La ville insurgée de Blanqui et de Benjamin', in *La discordance des temps. Essais sur les crises, les classes, l'histoire*, Éditions de la passion, Paris, 1995, pp. 221–231.
Douaihy, Chawqi, 'Être hors de la ville dans la ville: Les cafés de Hamra', *Du privé au public, espaces et valeurs du politique au Proche-Orient*, Les Cahiers du CERMOC, 8, 1994: pp. 71–76.
Hartog, François, 'Présentisme et émancipation: Entretien avec Sophie Wahnich et Pierre Zaoui', *Vacarme*, 53, autumn 2010 (available at www.vacarme.org).
Harvey, David, 'The Art of Rent: Globalization, Monopoly and the Commodification of Culture', *Socialist Register*, 38, 2002: pp. 93–110.
Mermier, Franck, 'Commémorer la résistance à Beyrouth ouest', in Franck Mermier and Christophe Varin, eds, *Mémoires de guerres au Liban (1975–1990)*, Actes Sud/Sindbad/Ifpo, Arles, 2010, pp. 185–204.
Sawalha, Assel, *Reconstructing Beirut. Memory and Space in a Postwar Arab City*, University of Texas Press, Austin, TX, 2010.
Trabulsi, Fawwaz, *Surat al-fata bi-l-ahmar. Ayam fi-l-silm wa-l-harb* (Portrait of the Young Man in Red: Chronicles of War and Peace), Riad El-Rayyes Books, Beirut and London, 1997.

12

The end of a world?

Shifting seasons in Lejnan (Algeria)

Mohand Akli Hadibi

Lejnan, one of the villages of the AthWaghli tribe, lies a mile and a quarter from Chemini, the administrative centre of the district. In the heart of Kabylia (Algeria), it is some thirty-five miles to the south-west of the coastal city of Béjaïa. Anthropologists and sociologists might describe its population as being organised into nine broad lineages, each descending from a common ancestor. Three of these mainly occupy the lower part of the village. Claiming descent from a local holy marabout, these *mrabtin* rather unusually share their mosque, fountain and assembly in the village. Their entwined histories have cemented the links between the different lineages, religious or otherwise, almost irreversibly: marriage alliances formed and re-formed between them render the social fabric particularly dense and interlinked.

The village is built on a verdant little plateau. Its name, *lejnan (al-jnan)*, means 'garden' in the Algerian dialect. Stretching out behind a ridge of hills that tower over the Soummam valley, it is bordered on either side by two streams, which create a natural boundary between the inhabited space – *le'mara* in Kabyle, the principal tongue of the local people – and uninhabited open spaces known as *lexla*. To the west lies *azaghar*, the wild space, and to the east the main administrative centre. At the bottom of the village runs an old 'discrete' road that was once used exclusively by women. The villagers get drinking water from two fountains throughout the year. The village assembly is generally held in the courtyard of the mosque when the weather is clement, while gatherings of the religious lineages take place inside the mosque.

Despite its various extensions, Lejnan still has physical boundaries along family and lineage lines, and each part remains accessible solely to the members of the family and their allies. Those who are not part of that structure have no reason to be there, except for particular events, such as a death or a celebration. In 2013, the village consisted of around 200 houses for a population of 1,800 inhabitants. It had a religious school (*zawiyya*, generally linked to a marabout) and a state school dating back to colonial times. These two institutions trained an elite that was important both in the nationalist movement and in the staffing of the administrative, healthcare and economic institutions of independent Algeria. Electricity reached the village in 1979, and with it, televisions and refrigerators started to appear. Nowadays, all the houses have individual satellite dishes and telephones, and some even have Internet access.

The remains of the peasant universe

The peasant world of Kabylia described by the sociologists Pierre Bourdieu and Abdelmalek Sayad in the 1960s survives only in nostalgic retrospect in Lejnan, as a mental reconstruction buried in the memory of the living. It is a world that endured in part until the 1980s. Life in the village followed the rhythm of agriculture, with each season fitting into a pattern of ritual practices observed by everyone. Activities, roles, positions and spaces seemed to be divided up immutably, according to whether a person was male or female, child or adult, single, married, widowed or divorced and also sane or mad – in short, depending on who was inside or outside 'the order of things'. Uncertain situations usually adjusted over time, with a degree of tolerance so that 'anomalies' could eventually be corrected and 'social norms' reproduced. Various mechanisms of socialisation and control thus enabled the reproduction of the social order.

Games and leisure activities, as well as the spaces allotted to them all fit into these structures. In collective and individual memories of Lejnan, those activities were deeply gendered. Girls played hopscotch as well as 'house' and weddings, games that prepared them for life as wives, mothers and housewives. The boys' games were more strenuous, involving hunting and fighting, and thus taught them how to defend and attack, and how to protect the weaker members of their community, such as children and women. Leisure activities changed in nature and location as children grew up. The youngest children played in their own area of residence. As they grew older, they moved to the *djema'a* (gathering place). During the autumn, the central square thus provided the setting for a game known as *sumen*, which is not unlike the British game of leapfrog. One of the boys bends over at a ninety-degree angle and keeps still as the others jump over his back. Whoever touches his head has to take his place, while the others carry on jumping under the watchful eyes of the elders, who ensure that the rules are properly observed.

The end of a world?

Once they had reached puberty, adolescents were left to themselves, outside the village, to work with others of similar age in the fields and in the forest. Direct social and family control decreased. Looking after sheep and goats made them useful to the family economy and gave them a certain amount of individual freedom. In the pasture lands, far from prying eyes, these young men could try out their creative talents, for example by playing the flute (*tajewwaqt*), something that tradition did not allow them to do within the confines of the village. This 'wild world' was also considered favourable to poetry – it was a place where a young man could compose his first verses on the subject of girls and love.

As winter approached, the hunt for starlings and other birds preoccupied men of all ages almost entirely for a whole month. Hunting afforded them a sense of freedom. In his novel *The Poor Man's Son*, set in Kabylia in the first decades of the twentieth century, the Kabyle writer Mouloud Feraoun describes the role that young people play during the hunt:

> Huge areas are strung with snares. Each of them has two, three or even five hundred of them. They head off in the morning under a frosty chill to change the bait – luscious, shiny olives – then gather in groups under the big olive trees, on a high hill from which they can watch their traps. They light a fire to warm their feet and fingers and wait anxiously for the moment to make their rounds. […] The kids forget to eat and feel neither cold nor rain nor thorns. When they see a starling arched against the flexible rod buried in the ground, to which it is held by the end of a string, all their efforts have paid off. They slit the birds' throats, pluck their feathers, and fill their hoods. The last visitors of the evening are taken home alive.[1]

During the depths of winter, young men also met to play *tiqqar*, a game in which participants aim kicks at each other. Each player tries to score the most points by striking blows with his feet while avoiding blows himself. *Tiqqar* contests usually involved two or three boys. A precise code of honour controls the phases of attack and riposte, and reputations were made and unmade, with fighters emerging either as outstanding or unworthy. If the rules were observed, the game could go on for hours, but it could also degenerate into pitched battles.

The rhythm of the seasons in Lejnan was marked by religious festivals, breaking up the monotony of village life with a few special days. During these festivals, young people could mix and enjoy themselves, learn certain customs and, most importantly, gain recognition. 'Greater Eid' (*'Īd el-Kebīr*), a Muslim festival celebrating Abraham's (*Ibrahim*'s) sacrifice, provided another opportunity for the various lineages and families to compete with each other. A unique spectacle unfolded every year on Tijnanin, the main square, the widest and flattest spot in the village. From six in the morning, every father would be there, accompanied by his family and a ram chosen for the occasion. The whole village would gather to watch a battle between rams. Pairs of animals would fight it out, with the stronger one staying in the ring until he too was defeated, and eventually a winner was declared. The spectators followed these battles as if they were the ones doing the fighting; when their own animal lost the duel, they were upset, whereas the owners of victorious rams made a great show of their pride. For children and teenagers, these contests offered a carnivalesque introduction to how honour was staged and put to the test. A source of pride and family solidarity, they also taught young people about the norms of social confrontation, using animals as stand-ins. Ashura (literally the tenth day of the month of *muharram*), the second religious festival, is very popular with the youngest children, boys and girls alike. It takes place at the nearby *zawiyya* (mausoleum) of Sidi Yahia, with thousands of pilgrims from the various tribes gathering to pay their respects to this popular local marabout.

Summer, the hottest season, was the time of weddings, a period of abundance and rest during which everybody in Lejnan seemed more light-hearted. There would be huge get-togethers, much to the delight of the younger members of the community, who could sing and dance till morning for three days. For a brief spell, the elders stepped back from their roles as moral guardians, and girls in particular could parade more than usual: relationships were renewed or strengthened, while others started to form and young people of both sexes became objects of mutual desire.

In search of another world

Since the 1980s, the traditional games that accompany the changing seasons and the different stages of life in Lejnan have changed irrevocably. Everyday life in the village has also been transformed. One important reason for this is that working life now starts much later because of changes in the labour market, along with emigration to towns or to Europe, as well as the decline of the village's agrarian economy. This has left a gap which so far has not been filled by any new collective practices. And while flight from the land is putting an end to peasant life, the spaces that were once used for many different leisure activities are gradually disappearing, along with the rituals that gave rise to them. The old road used by women, for example, no longer exists. It has been abandoned

The end of a world?

along with the fountain where women once met; water comes from the tap now. The fields have been deserted by the peasant farmer, the shepherd and the starling. The festive spirit of former days has waned; religious events have ceased to invigorate daily life as once they did.

The same is true for the *buma'ad*, the village's public space used for threshing cereal and herding cattle and goats before they are led to their mountain pastures. The flat, grassy area and particularly the threshing floor (Kabyle *annar*) occupying part of this space were ideal for endless ball games or other pursuits, such as *sumen* or games of marbles. Young people used to hold football tournaments there during the summer. But from the 1980s onwards, more and more cars were imported, paid for with emigrants' wages and their French pensions, and now garages have been built on that land. They have been bought mostly by the most powerful families in the village, who are turning this space into a private area, sometimes covertly, sometimes quite brazenly. On the pretext of restoring the old fountains and clearing away village rubbish, and with financial pressure from emigrants who live on the outskirts, they had a tarmacked road built which runs right across most of the open ground. Having turned from a space used for sporting contests into an object of local political contention, it reveals divisions of a new kind between families and lineages. For a while, the local authorities considered building social housing there, but this plan met with opposition from people living nearby. The idea to build a sports ground proved equally unpopular with some of the residents and was also dropped.

The young men of the village have been trying to find a new space for their leisure activities. They now gather on a tarmacked road which crosses the upper part of the village and links the local administrative centre to Lejnan. The road connects the two sides of the village, with the lycée at one end and the vocational college at the other, two institutions with male and female students. This results in twice-daily processions of small groups of girls on their way to or from school, followed by boys, with a certain 'required' distance separating the two. Whenever the boys and girls come out of the lycée or the college, young people not fortunate enough to attend one of these establishments line up outside, standing or squatting down under the gaze of seemingly indifferent adults. None of this replaces the bonds or competitions between families that young people experienced in the past. On the contrary, young people are increasingly frustrated. They meet in new places such as cafés or clandestine bars on the outskirts of the village, or they squat in public buildings, which sometimes results in widespread violence, as in 2001, when in many parts of Kabylia young people clashed with paramilitary police, seeing themselves as defenders of their villages in their own right, rather than leaving this role to their elders.[2]

Instead of playing public games in pairs, youths now go off together in groups of three or four to isolated spots, which are well-known hideaways, to drink, smoke cannabis or sing all night.

In autumn and winter, when the holiday-makers have returned to the cities or to Europe, the village feels empty and soulless. With the weather turning, monotony sets in. Groups of young people, the 'regulars' who are always there, hang around idly in the most remote parts of the village during the day, as if they are hiding; they observe what is going on, but keep their heads down. At night, when the cold starts to bite, they give free rein to their thoughts and expose the hidden face of the village and the intrigues involving various people, especially those who think that they embody the social and moral order. They discuss the latest robberies and describe 'shocking' scenes. Those who have access to the Internet chat online in their homes or in the village's only cybercafé, often in the hope of some important chance encounter that might help them to escape abroad.

The daily rhythms of secondary school students are determined by the time they spend at school. Their education includes what is commonly called 'physical education', activities that the students regard to a large extent as an imposition of the school system. But school sport does provide the opportunity – sometimes the only one – for boys and girls to mix and come into relatively close contact with each other outside the home. Boys and girls share a classroom but do not sit at the same desks or even in the same rows. But as Essaid Allem has pointed out, sports competitions are often governed by a code of honour: students competing against each other have to be equal in size; if one is smaller or weaker, or if a girl is up against a boy, the student declines the challenge. Young people are also members of sports clubs run by the local public authorities. Less strictly supervised, these clubs mainly offer combat sports such as judo and karate and are open to both girls and boys.

The eagerly awaited return of summer brings holidaymakers, festivals and fun. The DJ of the moment plays deafening music which drives away all the adults, to the great delight of the young. The nights grow longer, the groups larger, strolls in the dark seem to last forever, and young men and women talk till dawn.

Yet the leisure activities of children and young people in Lejnan have definitely changed over time: the distant melodies of *tajewwaqt* are no longer heard in the village; hunting birds has lost its appeal, and games of marbles, football

The end of a world?

or *tiqqar* seem old-fashioned or difficult to organise. Some people still feel nostalgic and mourn their own lost youth, while others welcome the present and hope for a future life somewhere else or at least one that is different from that of their parents. Yet whatever their views, the village of Lejnan today seems suspended between many different eras and many different worlds.

Notes

1 Mouloud Feraoun, *Poor Man's Son. Menrad, Kabyle Schoolteacher*, University of Virginia Press, Charlottesville, VA, 2005, pp. 90–91 (translation modified).
2 April 2001 saw the outbreak of what was called in Kabylia the 'Black Spring'. After a number of high school students were arrested and one young student died in police custody, an uprising spread across the region and continued throughout the year. The rebellion was finally crushed by troops. More than a hundred protesters were killed and many more injured.

References

Akli Hadibi, Mohand, 'Conquérir l'espace public par la force', in Marc Breviglier and Vincenzo Cichelli, eds, *Adolescences méditerranéennes. L'espace public à petit pas*, L'Harmattan, Paris, 2007, pp. 187–203.

Akli Hadibi, Mohand, 'Projets en fragments et avenir de jeunes de Kabylie', *Insaniyat*, 49, July–September 2010: pp. 41–53.

Akli Hadibi, Mohand, *Wedris, une totale plénitude. Approche socio-anthropologie d'un lieu saint en Kabylie*, Éditions Ziryab, Algiers, 2003.

Allem, Essaid, *Essai d'analyse du phénomène ludique en Kabylie*, MA thesis, University of Bejaïa, 2006.

Ben Adi, Hocine, *Pratiques et représentations des jeux traditionnels depuis l'indépendance à nos jours au village: Tagnitt At Yahia (Grande Kabylie)*, master's thesis, Université Mouloud Mammeri de Tizi-Ouzou, 2019.

Bourdieu, Pierre and Abdelmalek Sayad, *Le Déracinement. La crise de l'agriculture traditionnelle en Algérie*, Éditions de Minuit, Paris, 1964.

Feraoun, Mouloud, *Poor Man's Son. Menrad, Kabyle Schoolteacher*, University of Virginia Press, Charlottesville, VA, 2005. (French original published as *Le Fils du pauvre*, Seuil, Paris, 1954.)

13

Finding Baghdad

Young people in search of 'normality'

Zahra Ali and Laurent Bonnefoy

More than fifteen years after the invasion of Iraq by US forces and their allies in March 2003, Baghdad is unrecognisable to its inhabitants. Following significant displacement linked to the violence that reached its peak in 2006, the population is now essentially divided along denominational (Shiites, Sunnis or Christians – since 2003 scarcely a dozen Jews remain in Iraq) or ethnic lines (Kurdish, Arab) in neighbourhoods separated by endless concrete walls, psychological barriers and institutional boundaries that have become entrenched in everyday life.

Life for the seven million Baghdadis (the majority of whom are Shiite) is punctuated by checkpoints, identity controls and searches carried out by the army and police, but also and especially by militias attached to ethno-community political groups. The ascension to power of Shiite political parties and the ongoing security issues have profoundly transformed the city, in which a strong conservatism now prevails. The feeling of suffocation constantly expressed by its inhabitants especially affects the city's women, who are also subjected to norms of dress and behaviour from which men are spared. The fact that mobility is still restricted or even prohibited for everyone further destroys social bonds and the sense of sharing a city and an identity.

The simple idea of going for a stroll, of lingering a while in a public space, today seems unrealistic for many people, women in particular. As a result, leisure activities are mostly confined to the closed worlds of family or community, and this encourages the revival of certain religious practices, particularly those linked to specific forms of worship, for example at the Shiite mausoleum of the seventh imam, Mūsá ibn Ja'far al-Kāzim, in one of Baghdad's northern suburbs. Since the fall of Saddam Hussein's regime in 2003, pilgrimages have become more frequent and widespread.

Religion goes hand in hand with commercialism. Consequently, the majority of places for 'relaxation' are food and drink outlets: cafés, ice cream parlours,

Finding Baghdad

fruit juice stalls and restaurants, one after another along the same street or near small shopping malls. Most restaurants, which are guarded and strictly monitored, have set up a system of segregation, with one side reserved for 'families' – in other words, for women – and another for 'men'. Many cafés are reserved for male customers from 5 p.m.

The breakdown of social bonds in the city and the militarisation of Baghdad are compounded by the destruction caused by aerial bombardment during the war and local bomb attacks, as well as the collapse of street cleaning and waste disposal. The capital looks both chaotic and neglected. Despite this, young people in Baghdad, just like those in neighbouring Arab countries, enjoy squares and green spaces, as well as an extremely rich historical and architectural heritage. The city's youth make the most of the few existing places, like the main streets in the Al Mansour and Karada districts – where cafés are still open to all denominations but are only accessible to the very wealthy – to cope as best they can with the situation and enjoy a few moments of respite. Since 2011, echoing the upsurge of resistance elsewhere in the Arab world, a number of initiatives led by young Baghdadis have sought to escape political and community divisions by taking to the streets to fight for a unified city. Through campaigns organised in public spaces, students, artists and activists have expressed their desire for unity and their resistance to the violence that marks everyday life in a city they often equate to a 'paradise lost'.

A nostalgic return

The disintegration of Baghdad did not just happen in the last decade; it is anchored in an older and more complex history. The Iran–Iraq war of the 1980s, the choice of an all-out militarisation of society and the blind repression carried out by Saddam Hussein's brutal regime, the Gulf War of 1991 and the UN embargo that lasted until 2003 have all contributed to the withdrawal of people into their own communities, the disintegration of national feeling and the metamorphosis of a city that was the pride of its inhabitants. Dynamic and open to the world, Baghdad was once the cultural capital of the Arab world.

Young Baghdadis born between 1980 and 2000 have never really known anything but war. They live (probably with an overdose of nostalgia to mask the difficulties of the present) with a sense of social *déclassement*; they feel that there has been a general breakdown of their country's education and health systems, which once performed so well that Iraq was the envy of the Arab world and

Rooting the future

Asia. They point to the disappearance of intellectual life and the inhabitants' ability to make the city their own. Everyone remembers that the banks of the Tigris were once dotted with restaurants serving the famous *masgouf*, a traditional fish dish – even during the embargo, when only a tiny minority of the population, often those with connections to the Baathist regime, could afford to eat in them. The less affluent could still enjoy the riverfront, strolling with their families or sweethearts along Abu Nawas Street – named after the great Baghdadi poet of the eighth century. The opportunity to wander down the streets of Karada with its clothing stores, or to idly browse in the bookshops of Al Mutanabbi Street (named after another Iraqi poet) helped lay the roots for an urban identity that now only survives as a memory. The Iraqis' love of literature has been steadily undermined over the last three decades. During the 1990s, while the country was in the grips of the embargo, inhabitants would sell off the treasures of their family libraries every Friday on the dusty pavements of Al Mutanabbi Street – a harrowing symbol of the loss of status experienced by the middle class and intellectual elite.

Reclaiming Baghdad

Encouraged by the protest movements which have had such a huge impact on the Arab world since January 2011, but also by the relative stabilisation of the security situation in Iraq, some young Iraqis of both sexes now seem ready to move on from the violence and fragmentation of the city and its population. Organised in conspicuous fashion in the urban space, sometimes in symbolic locations, cultural events seek to promote another form of urban life in Baghdad.

The roots of the '*Ana Iraqi wa ana aqra*' ('I am Iraqi and I Read') campaign, launched in September 2012, can be traced to the booksellers' street, Al Mutanabbi. It was aimed explicitly at encouraging the population, young people in particular, to reconnect with the cultural heritage of a country known for its 'love of reading and science'. The campaign's nationalist message and its festive dimension were significant: in a sense, the organisers were trying to sweep away decades of cultural decay. For several days, young students and social activists describing themselves as 'independents' (*mustaqil*) – in other words, those who refuse to be associated with any political party – distributed books of all kinds around Al Mutanabbi Street, leaving hundreds of them along Abu Nuwas Street to be read by passers-by. The books had been collected in previous weeks following an appeal for donations launched on a Facebook page announcing the project. This initiative, run by affluent and liberal young people, including Muhammad 'Abd al-Zahra, a student and human rights activist, and Athil Fawzi, an engineer and popular science blogger, concluded with a rally in Abu Nuwas that brought together several hundred people, most of them young, at a gathering of artists and intellectuals reciting poetry, singing and dancing. This celebration of reading was repeated in several places outside the capital, even in the holy Shiite city of Najaf, where the Communist Party and local authorities did everything they could to 'hijack' the event.

Reclaiming Baghdad and reinventing the Iraqi nation was also one of the objectives of the small independent *Yum al-thaqafa al-iraqi* (Iraqi Culture Day) association, which counted a few dozen members. In 2013 they launched an initiative that was part of the programme celebrating Baghdad as the Arab Capital of Culture. Coinciding with the tenth anniversary of the looting of the National Museum of Iraq in April 2003 (against the backdrop of the fall of Saddam Hussein's regime), the association, particularly active on Facebook, organised the first public tour of the museum since the war. The members, mostly students from different parts of the capital, sought to promote the 'unity' of their country by exploring its ancient history not just in the museum collections but also through specific local customs, like the Kurdish New Year celebrations, Nowruz, or public talks by leaders of religious minorities, such as the small Mandaean sect. Described throughout as independent and apolitical, the group's aims are not neutral, however, since they revived the idea of a mosaic nation. They received support from the Ministry of Culture, which opened the doors of the museum, showing the wish to rebuild the nation through culture, from the bottom up and across the divides.

In January 2013, the youth section of the National Symphonic Orchestra decided to hold an outdoor public concert in Uqbah bin Nafi Square, in front of the National Theatre and near the Karada shopping district. The organisers, who aimed to make music a 'vehicle for unity and togetherness', initially had their project stopped by the police but were eventually allowed to go ahead under tight security. Six months earlier, a car bomb on the same square had killed seven people.

Since it is still difficult to move across the city, projects of this kind in public spaces, launched by comparatively affluent young people, remain quite tentative. But more and more people are coming out in support of making Baghdad a more beautiful city, creating more green spaces and preserving the Abu Nuwas river walk, threatened in 2013 by a government plan to privatise spaces and cut down trees. All these campaigns illustrate the importance of leisure and free time for people starting to reclaim an identity that has been damaged by the war and to find ways of resisting social and urban fragmentation through ordinary, everyday acts of resistance.

The uprising was the culmination of all of these initiatives in one space, Tahrir Square in central Baghdad. One of its features is the re-appropriation of public space by protesters, who set up their miniature utopian society in Tahrir Square, central Baghdad. In and around the square, young people established a cinema and a theatre, listened to music, danced together, displayed paintings and gathered around books in the street libraries they built. For months, people from diverse backgrounds met and celebrated life itself, showing that they are not defeated by the various forces of death that have structured Baghdadi inhabitants' everyday lives for decades.

References

Ali, Zahra, *Women and Gender in Iraq. Between Nation-Building and Fragmentation*, Cambridge University Press, Cambridge, 2018.
Al-Rasheed, Louloua and Édouard Méténier, 'À propos de la violence "irakienne". Quelques éléments de réflexion sur un lieu commun', *A Contrario*, 5, 1, 2008: pp. 114–133.
Dawod, Hosham, 'Usages politiques des cartes ethniques "minoritaires"', *Confluences Méditerranée*, 73, 2010: pp. 129–138.
Harling, Peter, 'Dix ans après, que devient l'Irak?', *Le Monde diplomatique*, March 2013.
Pieri, Caecilia, 'Reflections on a Reconstruction-to-Be: Of History as a "Strategy of Vigilance", the Case of Baghdad', *Bulletin of Royal Institute for Inter-Faith Studies*, 8, 1–2, 2006: pp. 69–93.
Facebook page for the 'I am Iraqi and I Read' campaign: www.facebook.com/aqraanaaqra
Facebook page for the Iraqi Culture Day organisation: www.facebook.com/iraqi.culture.day

14

Two brothers

Family and hospitality in Al-Karak (Jordan)

Christine Jungen

'*Ahlan wa sahlan*', welcome!' Abu Nabil settles back comfortably on the sofa. Silence has fallen since the noisy arrival of his guests, with all the embraces and greetings. While he mechanically fingers his prayer beads with a meditative air, before restarting the conversation, his son Jamal has grabbed the coffee pot that stands proudly on the low table. Quietly and with sure and precise movements, the young man serves the coffee in little cups without handles for the members of the gathering seated in the living room armchairs.

Jamal and Karim

Jamal spent the morning in the kitchen, preparing this lunch for which the members of the extended family group – uncles and aunts, cousins, young nieces and nephews – have travelled a hundred kilometres, all the way from the capital Amman to Al-Karak, a little town in the south of Jordan. Jamal, who is around thirty years old and the second eldest of four brothers, grew up in this rural region, home to Muslim and Christian tribes, like the one to which his family belongs. An engineer by training, he has found work in the Jordan Valley. During the week he sleeps at the home of his eldest brother Nabil, who, like their sister, is married and lives now in Amman. Jamal is still a bachelor, just like the youngest brother, the only one who still lives in the family home. It isn't unusual for him to take advantage of the weekend to go back to Al-Karak to see his parents, visit his childhood friends or, as is the way of it this Friday – the weekly day of rest – to take part with all his siblings in hosting relatives.

While his father and Nabil looked after the cooking of the *mansaf* – that essential dish in Karaki hospitality, composed of rice and lamb cooked in a sauce of fermented dried yoghurt – Jamal took care of the *mezze*, the appetisers that would be served with the aperitif. He chopped the parsley that would be mixed with the sesame paste, broke the cones of dried yoghurt into little pieces, sliced carrots and cucumbers, and laid out slices of mortadella on plates. In a nice little touch, he sprinkled the *mutabbal* – the aubergine dip – with sumac, the dark colour of the spice highlighting the creaminess of the purée. As part of the final preparations, he laid out in the living room, with stacks of little cups all around it, the thermos of so-called 'Arabic' coffee, a very dark, slightly bitter beverage, flavoured with nutmeg, which his father put on to boil early in the morning.

It is this coffee, emblematic of tribal hospitality and ritually presented to guests as a mark of welcome, that Jamal is now serving: he pours the beverage into the little cups, holding them in his left hand as he does so, filling them one-third full – more than that would be bad manners – and hands them to the guests. With their attention monopolised by the general conversation that has now resumed, they take them without a word and swallow little sips of the coffee before handing the cup back to Jamal who immediately pours out more, unless they have shaken the cup as they hand it back which indicates that they have had enough. In this way, Jamal goes around all the adults until all the cups have been handed back. He then puts the coffee pot down with the stack of cups on a corner of the low central table and sits down in one of the still unoccupied armchairs at the outer end of the gathering. His eye remains vigilant, his body alert, ready to get up and fill a guest's cup again.

It is at this point that Karim, the youngest boy, five years younger than Jamal, a little distracted, emerges from the basement in which he has fashioned a sort of bachelor pad for himself. It is there he spends most of his time, surrounded by his books, between his television and his computer. Unlike Jamal, who has been very much involved in family life since his return from Russia where, like many young Karakis, he studied with the help of the local Communist party, Karim has chosen to keep himself to himself. He is, in fact, taking a correspondence course as part of a programme offered by a Sudanese university. Jamal, when he is there, likes to keep his father company on the terrace that overlooks the street. Together they silently gaze out at the desert on the horizon as the sun's last rays fade, hailing passers-by from time to time. Karim, for his part, prefers to spend his evenings in his den, one eye on his computer screen, the other on the latest American films which are broadcast by the Gulf TV stations. The group of friends he has made come there sometimes – the basement has its own separate entrance – in the evening to keep him company around a shisha or a pack of cards. He only goes upstairs sporadically, usually to fetch

Two brothers

something to nibble or a bottle of water, then quickly slips away again. He gets a regular dressing-down over this from Jamal, who takes the view that his young brother doesn't help his parents enough or involve himself sufficiently in family tasks, particularly those associated with the duty of hospitality.

Beneath his brother's gaze, Karim greets everyone, grabs a chair, sits down by the door and readies himself to take part in the discussion. He jumps up when his father says, 'Karim, go and see if your mother needs help!'

Between dining room and kitchen

Abu Nabil, seated in the 'highest-ranking' position – the one beneath the portrait of the Virgin Mary and facing both the entrance and the television – directs the conversation with authority: his body solidly propped up in his seat, raising his hand from time to time to give greater weight to his words, he asks everyone's news, tells jokes and comments on current family matters. The gathering hangs on his every word, with laughter and exclamations accompanying the conclusion to each anecdote. Most of them – apart perhaps from the very youngest – already know most of Abu Nadil's stories. But they still appreciate the way he tells them, the comical punchlines with which they are studded, and, quite naturally, the opportunity to laugh at some local notable or some member of the tribe.

From time to time, the tone becomes more serious. Abu Nabil is telling now of the *sheikhs*, the tribe's great leaders in days of yore – their wars, their raids, the hospitality they dispensed, their capacity for 'greatness' and for risking their honour in competition with rival tribes. A young nephew accompanies the end of the tale with an appreciative, admiring, 'God, I didn't know that story!' A delighted Abu Nabil ends his tale with an '*Aywa!*' ('Yes indeed!') and takes a brief pause before continuing.

Abu Nabil will remain in his seat, while around him his two youngest sons pass to and fro, serving drinks and hors-d'oeuvres, making sure no guest wants for anything, at the same time adding the last touches to the *mansaf*. Ignoring the restrained chatter and bustle around him, he steers the conversation imperturbably. At the same time, he keeps a discreet check on the smooth functioning of the hospitality being afforded to his guests and interrupts himself from time to time to signal to one of his sons that he should serve another *arak* – an aniseed-flavoured spirit – or more *mezze* to one of the guests.

In the kitchen, Umm Nabil, the mother, has laid out fine wheat flour flat-breads on the two platters to be used for the meal. Assisted by his wife, Nabil serves out the rice on to them and then arranges the chunks of meat. At the top of the little pile, he places the sheep's head, the brains being a particularly prized delicacy. Jamal and Karim busy themselves now with making space around the table in the *diwan*, the reception room. They put out the chairs and Nabil is already there, bearing the first platter of *mansaf*. He puts the dish down at one end of the table, while Jamal arrives with a second platter which he sets down at the other end. Umm Nabil follows with the pan containing the yoghurt in which the meat was cooked.

Around the table

At the solemn invitation of their hosts, the guests get up and take their places around the table, the women around one of the two platters, the men on the other side. Without waiting, they begin to eat, each taking a portion for themselves from the platter. Abu Nabil and Umm Nabil see to it that their guests are properly served in each group: they tear up the pieces of meat by hand and put them onto the portions of the platter of the guests who are most worthy of respect, and regularly pour yoghurt on the rice. They are too absorbed in their task to be able to share in the meal at this point; it is only when the first guests begin to leave the table that they themselves begin to eat. The gathering is silent, concentrated on the meal; at most, the silence is interrupted by the master of the house urging his guests to eat their fill.

Except for the oldest of them, the women eat with a spoon; some have even transferred their 'portion' from the platter to an individual plate. That is more *sympathique*, says Jamal, using the French word, while he takes pride in eating – as all the men do – in the traditional manner. Thus he and his brothers break the meat up into small pieces with their right hands, rolling these up into little balls with the rice, then they lift the balls to their mouths, throwing them skilfully, with the aid of a turn of the thumb, into their throats, taking care that their fingers do not touch any part of their body in the process.

Whereas Karim lingers around the platter, Jamal is quickly done. He washes his hands, then disappears for a while – perhaps to go and smoke a cigarette discreetly, out of sight of his father (it would show a lack of respect to smoke in front of him). He then busies himself serving more Arabic coffee to those who, having finished their portion, have settled down once again in the living room. Now that they are full, the guests slump back in their chairs. Jamal and Karim,

Two brothers

the latter having now also returned to the living room, are more relaxed; they take time to participate more actively in the conversations, even if each of them continues to jump up from time to time to attend to a guest.

It is getting late in the afternoon and the children are falling asleep. Those who want to get back to Amman before nightfall get up and make signs that they are leaving. 'Already? But it's too early!', exclaims Abu Nabil. The following quarter of an hour is filled with never-ending discussions between hosts and guests, the former pointing out how early it is, how intense the heat still is and how the children are settled down for their naps, etc. The arguments deployed, however, are just polite rhetoric, and in the end, after the guests have responded to each and every reason why they should stay, they will not linger much longer. Everyone gets up and, from the doorstep, Abu Nabil wishes goodbye to all his guests as they get into their cars. He has all his family around him, except for Karim who has already slipped away to the basement some time ago and hasn't reappeared since.

Learning

'There's nothing to do in al-Karak!' You hear this litany time and again from young people who dream enviously of the bright lights of the capital, with its high-tech cafés and chic restaurants. Here, far from Amman, in the villages and housing developments worn away by the dust of the bordering desert, entertainment consists primarily of watching TV – it is switched off only when guests are received – and in interminable visiting, from house to house, between neighbours, relatives and friends. It is on these occasions that the learning of a subtle knowledge takes place, of the sort Jamal is keen to pursue, or relative rebellion against that knowledge as in the case of Karim. It is a knowledge that is both knowing a skill (*savoir-faire*) and knowing how to be (*savoir-être*): it means listening, to the point where one knows them by heart, to the *sawalif*, the anecdotes about particular persons that mark out the network of associates and relatives as allies, Christian and Muslim, among the Karaki tribes; conforming properly to obligations to provide hospitality; and learning, along the way, how to 'hold yourself' and speak well. In short, it means learning to be a *shabb mu'addab*, a 'well-brought-up' young man, but also learning to become, with marriage in mind, a master of the house (*sahib bayt*), a man who is *mutharam* – worthy of respect – and *karim* – honourable (literally 'generous').

References

Jungen, Christine, *Politique de l'hospitalité dans le Sud jordanien*, Ifpo/Karthala, Paris/Beirut, 2009.

Rivoal, Isabelle, ed., 'Les jeunes dans le Sud de la Méditerranée', *Ateliers d'anthropologie*, 42, 2015.

15

In Massada Street's coffee shops

The ambiguous social mix of the Palestinians of Israel in Haifa

Mariangela Gasparotto

The population of the port town of Haifa in the north of Israel is approximately 86 per cent Jewish and 14 per cent Palestinian.[1] While Palestinians in Israel are often referred to as 'Israeli Arabs', they generally self-identify as '1948 Palestinians'. Indeed, 1948 marks both the creation of the State of Israel and the *nakba*, the Palestinian 'catastrophe' which led to the exodus of a large proportion of the local population, as well as massive destruction of the social and urban fabric. In Haifa, Jewish and Palestinian communities live in spatially distinct areas, which reflects a social, cultural and economic hierarchy. Such a division is deeply embedded in their everyday lives. It can be considered a direct consequence of the policies conducted between 1948 and 1966 by the military government regarding the Palestinians who remained in the land. During that period, their political rights and the right to freedom of assembly were seriously restricted. The military authority used to ban certain zones to Palestinians and they also used to force them to leave their homes. Long curfews were imposed, and the police arbitrarily arrested people. Throughout this period, the three thousand Palestinians who used to live in Haifa were not allowed to leave the Wadi Nisnas neighbourhood without permission. While the 'downtown' (Wadi Nisnas), which is located near the port, at the foot of the slopes of Mount Carmel, was until now inhabited by the Palestinian population, the summit of the Mount is home to the majority of the Jewish population. As Rashid, a twenty-eight-year-old Palestinian explains, 'they [Jewish Israeli] may no longer formally forbid us from visiting Carmel, or from living there, but we still don't do it. You know, sometimes people's attitudes can have as big an effect on you as any law.' In his opinion, Palestinians avoid going to some parts of the city: for him, this is due both to the history of the city and to people's current attitudes.

However, Haifa has the reputation of being the most important 'mixed town' in Israel. Indeed, it is sometimes referred to as the *madina mukhtalata*, in Arabic, or as *ir me'urevet*, in everyday Hebrew. Some sociologists and anthropologists even describe the city as a model for the tolerance shown between its Jewish, Muslim, Christian, Druze and Bahai inhabitants, since Haifa is also the site of the main mausoleum of the Bahai faith, whose prophet, who died in 1892, was Iranian. This vision is contested by most of the Palestinians living in Haifa, however, who see it as expressing a double violence exerted by the dominant Jewish population. First, this image divides Palestinians themselves along religious lines, while most of them consider themselves to be members of a Palestinian community. Secondly, it fails to recognise the pressures, discriminations and acts of bullying which they feel are parts of their daily lives.

In this chapter, I consider the idea of the 'mixed' town through the lens of some coffee shops located on Massada Street, in the Hadar HaCarmel zone. This neighbourhood is the principal point at which 'downtown' and 'uptown' meet and mingle. As a result, it might seem at first sight to confirm the reality of the city's cultural, religious and ethnic social mix. Here, Palestinians make up 22 per cent of the population according to official statistics. In some cases, Palestinians live in the same buildings as Mizrahim (Oriental Jews) or Russian immigrants, most of whom arrived in the late 1980s.

'Palestinian', 'mixed', 'Jewish'

Massada Street is partly a residential area and partly a shopping street. Here, families, students and artists of various origins live alongside one another. There are eight café-bars, several restaurants and clothes shops, two grocery stores, a bookshop and a cultural centre. The street has an ambiguous reputation. Most of the inhabitants of Haifa do not consider it to be 'respectable', due both to the fact that it is close to the city's psychiatric hospital and to the ethnic origins of the majority of the residents and people who frequent it. In particular, racist stereotypes promote the idea that Russians are given to drinking, doing drugs and fighting. These stereotypes are further reinforced by the very tight control of the police over the neighbourhood. For others, Massada Street has a different image: for them, it is above all a focal point of alternative politics and what some describe as a 'miracle' of social integration. Then, one can also hear it referred to as a 'bubble of hypocrisy'.

In Massada Street's coffee shops

Life in the coffee shops in the Hadar HaCarmel neighbourhood is somewhat different than in the bars in the 'uptown'. Customers of the cafés on Massada Street are quite different from those who frequent the cafés and restaurants on Ben Gurion Street, another lively Haifa neighbourhood. There, the clientele, whether Palestinian or Jewish, tends to be older and – perhaps for that reason – better off economically. Ben Gurion Street cafés, such as Fatoush (named after a well-known Arab salad dish), are thus more expensive and chicer. And as they are also close to Bahai Gardens, they attract tourists, who go there to enjoy Palestinian cuisine in a comfortable setting and to savour a moment of peaceful coexistence between Jews and Arabs, as described in their guidebooks.

For many clients of Massada Street coffee shops, they function effectively as a 'second home', a refuge where they can escape from difficult family contexts or from the solitude of a cramped one-person apartment. Some consider Massada Street's coffee shops as a workplace: customers receive colleagues and clients, and they use the Internet to stay in touch with their professional networks. Regular customers tend to perceive these spaces as 'friendly' and 'homely'. They usually spend hours at the bar, chatting with the waiting staff and the other clients. While some travel a considerable distance to enjoy this ambience, most of the clients live nearby. At the café, they spend their time either reading, studying, writing or talking. Whenever they pass by, they will tend to drop in to have a chat, drink a coffee or, if they are in a hurry, just greet their acquaintances.

This familiarity is partly a result of the distinctive ambiences of each of these establishments. Each one has a more or less pronounced characteristic that singles it out. Some are known as the haunts of 'leftists', 'alternative types' or 'anarchists'. One of them is referred to as a 'gay bar' by some and as a 'right-wing bar' by others, even though its owner describes himself as straight and apolitical. None of these cafés highlights the identification with a particular religious community. This unusual feature is a consequence of the history of the street and the sociological composition of its population. In the 1970s, Massada Street became a favourite haunt of Haifa's intellectuals and artists, thanks in part to its location within easy reach not only of the Israeli Technological Institute – which at that time had its main campus in Hadar HaCarmel – but also of two theatres and two municipal cultural centres, as well as the offices of many NGOs. Café Katan opened first. In its early days, it was managed by Elias, the son of a mixed Israeli-Palestinian couple. In the opinion of the café's older clients, Elias succeeded in embodying his 'double identity' in his 'little café' (*katan* is the Hebrew word for 'small'). Since Elias' death, the business has changed hands several times, and it is now known as the Zoom Café.

Today, the cafés along Massada Street are often labelled as 'Palestinian', 'Jewish' or (more rarely) mixed. They attract these labels on the basis of their names, the food they serve, the origins of the owners and their staff or the political opinions (real or imagined) of their habitués. This is the case with, for example, the Elika, the Massada Café and the Puzzle. The first of these is a Palestinian café. Managed by a Druze, it employs Palestinian staff, who themselves may be Christians, Muslims or Druze. According to those who work there, this mixture is evidence of their having put their religious differences behind them. According to them, religious boundaries only 'play into the hands of the Israelis'. Although some of the café's clients are Jewish, most of them are Palestinian, and they include a large number of artists and students. The green-painted walls are covered with posters for Arab films and photographs of Arab writers. Amongst them can be seen photos of the images graffitied by the English artist Banksy on the Separation Wall, as well as a portrait of Ernesto Che Guevara. The Elika serves Taybeh beer, which is brewed in a village close to Ramallah, along with typical Palestinian dishes. On the bar, next to the glass for tips for the staff, there is also a box used to collect donations for the residents of Gaza.

The Massada Café, on the other hand, is generally perceived as 'mixed'. Its owner is a Jew of Hungarian origin who employs both Palestinian and Jewish staff. His clients are equally diverse. The walls are decorated with small images of palm trees, and the main room is filled with photographs of Lebanese and Egyptian actors and singers. A framed drawing explains that people carrying weapons will not be served, and countless stickers in many different languages proclaim slogans against sexism and the embargo on Gaza. Other bills support the cultural, academic and economic boycott of Israel. Just beside the door, on the cork board used to display small ads, a text pinned up declares that 'Zionism is fascism'.

The Puzzle has a different style. It is seen as a 'Jewish' café, because its manager, its waiters and its clients are Jewish. It is also considered a 'gay' café, in particular because of the multi-coloured LGBT flag displayed at the entrance and the rainbow mobiles hanging from the ceiling. Only a few Palestinian residents of the neighbourhood come to the concerts and film screenings that are regularly organised on the Puzzle's terrace. They feel excluded from these events and criticise the atmosphere of the place, which they find too 'trendy'. They also complain about the racist remarks made by the regulars.

In Massada Street's coffee shops

Each of these establishments has its own faithful clients, and these different groups largely tend to keep to themselves. Religious and ethnic identity, economic capital and gender all contribute to keeping them apart, in a city where ethnic boundaries are very clearly marked. Nevertheless, some of these cafés take a strong political stance that has enabled them to break down these 'ethnic' or 'religious' boundaries, at least in part. Thus, regular clients at both the Elika and the Massada Café declare that they try to invent a society that would not only oppose the Zionist ideology of the state, but other dominant practices too, which they see as reactionary and sexist. For them, all these political struggles are part of the same larger struggle against capitalism and imperialism. On Massada Street, taking such a political stand is not simply an abstract theoretical gesture. Some years ago, the Luna bar was obliged to close when its Palestinian manager refused to serve a group of soldiers. Her decision provoked an outcry across the neighbourhood. During the following night, the windows of her café were broken and the walls outside were daubed with insults. A legal case was brought against her, and the court found against the woman. She subsequently moved to Ramallah. A little later, a waiter at the Massada Café also refused to serve a soldier. But although he was denounced to the police, the café was neither closed down nor physically attacked.

Real mixed, stated mixed

For the last ten years, Massada Street has been the subject of an 'urban renovation' plan. Concretely, this project provides financial aid for Jewish students who wish to settle in the neighbourhood during their studies. Presenting it as a form of 'integration' and renewal, a number of policies explicitly aimed at gentrifying the street have been launched. Thus, rents have shot up, to the point where they are now beyond the means of the poorer residents. Artists have been brought in to decorate the walls of several buildings with graffiti, and several new cafés, restaurants and bars have opened. One vacant lot left where a building was demolished has been turned into an open-air museum showcasing local artists. But these policies are, in fact, in contradiction with the ideal of 'peaceful coexistence' that is so central to the city's public image. On the one hand, the city council claims it wishes to protect the special nature of the street and organises events where the ethnically and socially 'mixed' characteristics of the neighbourhood are celebrated. On the other hand, it implements discriminatory policies, in particular against some of the cafés and shops, which are threatened with closure if they do not conform to the council's self-image. As a result, only certain cafés are able to get the authorisations required in order to hold concerts or show films. Meanwhile, the police control the area in a way which is itself discriminatory. Young Palestinians feel they are the main victims of these policies. According to them, it is the places they hang out at that are under threat, and it is their political opinions that are stigmatised.

In these conditions, can integration still be considered a reality? The spatial fragmentation of the city of Haifa along ethnic lines is certainly very real. Outside of the Hadar HaCarmel neighbourhood, most of the Palestinian population has long been concentrated in the Wadi Nisnas and Wadi Salib areas, which are effectively mono-ethnic. Looking at the city through the lens of its neighbourhoods also reveals how these ethnic divisions intersect with socio-economic differences. Together with Jews of Russian and Oriental origin, Palestinians are mainly to be found in the 'lower' town, where rents and rates are less expensive. Meanwhile, Ashkenazi Jews tend to live in the pricier neighbourhoods, higher up on Mount Carmel.

Palestinian children, for their part, go to schools (whether public or private) where they are taught in Arabic and where they have almost no opportunity to interact with the Jewish majority. The same is true of their spare-time activities, both those organised by religious institutions and those connected to the scouting movement. The only part of life in which some of the young people I interviewed felt able to escape from the boundaries of their community was amateur sport. The occasions on which young Palestinians can meet and interact with Jewish children and teenagers are thus very rare. An exception exists for Palestinians who attend those public schools which are mixed to a certain degree. Others have to wait until they go to university to find themselves in a mixed environment. And these encounters, when they do happen, do not always leave good memories. Many people described with real bitterness their experience of 'mixed schooling'. In the schools where they meet Jews, Palestinians are always in a very small minority. They have to put up with both hypocrisy and open insults, directed at them by their teachers no less than by their peers. Some feel that their grades suffered significantly because of the way they were treated.

These experiences point to the essentially fictitious nature of a form of social mix which rarely enables people to move outside the real ethnic boundaries that are defined both by the city and by society at large. Ahmed, a twenty-seven-year-old photographer, describes just this kind of segregation as omnipresent in daily life, in Haifa as much as in the rest of Israel:

In Massada Street's coffee shops

> People's origins are always an issue. It's crazy. Here, when you meet someone, the first thing you ask yourself is whether they're a Jew or an Arab. You go close to listen to the language they are speaking, before you decide whether to talk to them or not. […] And you know the other guy is asking himself the same question: you are categorized, the same way you categorize others. It's not healthy, all that … This sickness can't go on forever. The body looks healthy from outside, but inside, it's all rotten.

Despite its reputation, the same ethnic question hangs heavily over the cafés of Massada Street. In appearance, the street is able to transcend the divisions and mistrust that are so prominent in daily life elsewhere. Young people from all communities rub shoulders here, and it is not unusual to see Palestinians and Jews talking together over a coffee or a beer. However, real friendships remain circumscribed by the limits of one's own community, for it is only within those limits that one can share one's most personal projects and dreams. 'Everyone lives their own life here', in the words of Malik, a thirty-year-old graphic designer who works in advertising. 'Drinking beers together doesn't mean we're friends.' For this young Palestinian, the interpersonal relationships they have in the local cafés remain shallow. Real friendships can only exist between people who suffer the same injustices and share the same history.

Nevertheless, most of the young Palestinians who hang out in the cafés of this neighbourhood recognise the limits of a binary reasoning that would construct too radical an opposition between Jews and Palestinians. Although they themselves have to live with discrimination every day, they agree that there are exceptions – people who, even though they are of Jewish origin, do not behave 'like Jews', who are 'decent', and for whom, '*like for us*, it isn't easy living here'. Among the most frequently cited examples, it is not surprising that those young Jews who have refused to do their military service – the *refuseniks* – figure prominently. Their decision creates a bond between them and the Arabs living in Israel, who (with the exception of the Druze and the Bedouin communities) do not have to do military service. Another example that often comes up is those Jews who have taken the trouble to learn Arabic. Those I interviewed frequently told me that such Jews 'could be' Palestinians, and indeed that is how they themselves identify – as 'Jewish Palestinians', or 'post-1948 Palestinians'. Although they may make up only a tiny minority of Israelis, the positions they take on the conflict – refusing military service and recognising the trauma of the *nakba* – make it possible to at least imagine an end to ethnoreligious hierarchies and the creation of a truly horizontal relationship between all the inhabitants of the land.

Rooting the future

'An apparent normality'

While social mix continues to be presented as a possible horizon, for customers of Massada Street's coffee shops and bars, this remains more an idea than a reality. The more sceptical even describe this apparently generous vision as ultimately motivated by a form of perversion and hypocrisy. According to this argument, the image of Massada Street as a unique place where people would be able to talk politics, express their criticism of the Israeli government, invent alternative solutions for the coexistence of their peoples and engage in highly politicised artistic collaborations is above all intended to serve the Israeli government and to promote its social system.

For many Palestinians in Haifa, the fiction of social mix not only does not help but also constitutes a tangible obstacle to real exchange and understanding between communities. For Muhammad, a twenty-seven-year-old Palestinian filmmaker, Massada Street is an example of the false 'normality' that characterises the Israeli society. In his opinion, its apparent 'openness' conceals a pathological relationship to reality and otherness:

> The normality of this street is just an appearance. Everyone seems to be happy and carefree, but in reality here you can feel the violence and the depression, all the time, and everywhere. Israel is completely upside-down: what is normal here would be abnormal anywhere else. We don't pay attention to it any more. It's become our second skin. It's only when we leave the country that we notice the difference.

Behind the apparent integration of Massada Street, people are still looking for places where they can be alone together, where they can get away from the stifling atmosphere of Israeli society, especially young Arabs. In particular, many Palestinians say they are made to feel awkward by the attitudes they meet when they enter the Jewish cafés. So they internalise this distance and stop going to those places. 'They don't like us, and they do nothing to conceal it', explains Rima, a twenty-five-year-old Palestinian. 'Why should I have to feel sick to my gut whenever I want a coffee or a beer?' The atmosphere is even less welcoming in the nightclubs. There, the bouncers often prevent Arabs from entering. And as a result, Palestinians give up even trying to gain admission.

An outside observer might point to a kind of harmony in the daily life of the neighbourhood. But even there, the segmentation of space is constantly raising its ugly head – especially during certain religious feasts, at neighbourhood festivals or at moments of political tension. If one decides to drive around Hadar

In Massada Street's coffee shops

HaCarmel on Yom Kippur, when it is forbidden under Jewish law to use a car, he would provoke some of the locals to anger. At such moments, the latent tension between the communities at the national level feeds directly into more local fears and projections.

Though he himself has never been attacked or insulted, Noam, a twenty-eight-year-old Jewish actor, got into the habit of changing his usual route every Friday to avoid passing in front of the Elika. Friday is the first day of the weekend, and it is also the day when there are more Arabs in the café than on the other days of the week. It is widely believed that Friday prayers at the mosque can have a potentially electric effect on the crowd that gathers there:

> It's not that I don't like them, on the contrary ... Some of them are friends, I know them, I work with them too ... But I feel judged, you see? On Friday, they are all together ... I have red hair and light skin, you see? I am not like them.

Latent divisions can become even more visible during the neighbourhood celebrations that are organised regularly by the town council. On these occasions, the street is closed to cars, musical groups play outside every café, and traders set up stalls to sell their craftwork. In 2010, a Palestinian group gave a concert on Massada Street. Someone was asked to translate the Arabic texts of their songs into Hebrew. Unfortunately, the interpreter made a mistake when translating one of the songs, and the sense of the original text was distorted into a threat against Jews. Those present on that occasion remember how the concert was brought to a violent halt, as the police made arrests and fights broke out up and down the street. For months afterwards, the inhabitants of the neighbourhood continued to talk passionately about this incident.

In 2011, another event was organised just one week after the murder of the actor Juliano Mer-Khamis, the son of a Jewish mother and a Palestinian father. Khamis was a pillar of the Massada Street 'community', and the director of the Freedom Theatre in Jenin, in the northern West Bank. In the wake of his death, some of the locals who were still mourning were unwilling to take part in the planned festivities. They were promptly accused of being 'opponents of peace' and of attacking an event that was supposed to constitute 'a celebration of coexistence'.

During moments of political tension or clashes, the symbolic appropriation of space becomes even more obvious. In recent years, there have been several events that led the communities to withdraw into themselves. During the Lebanon War of 2006, or Operation Cast Lead against Gaza in 2008–2009, for example, residents and regulars all sought to visibly mark out *their own* spaces. Thus, in 2008–2009, the regulars of the Massada Café were forced by the police to take down a banner which compared the attack on Gaza to the Jewish Holocaust. They subsequently replaced it with a black flag. Meanwhile, the regulars at the Puzzle Café put up an Israeli flag, while the café Elika closed for a day as a sign of mourning. When it reopened, the owner and waiters turned the premises into a platform for permanent debate. A huge screen showed non-stop news reports on the war from Al-Jazeera, while the regulars organised a series of informal meetings during which they read the newspapers together and discussed the political situation. Since this time, relationships on the street have been more difficult. The Jewish owner of the 'House of the Artists', which is located just next to the Massada Café, made a point of prominently displaying his Israeli flag. As Karim, a thirty-year-old lawyer, told me, this decision was greeted with contempt by several Palestinians:

> Before the attacks against Gaza, there were Palestinians who would spend a lot of time at the House of the Artists, playing the guitar and singing … He would give them hashish and beer … During the attack, with his flag on display for everyone to see, he gave them even more hash, to try and make them even more apathetic. Some of the young people continued to go there, but many of them stopped.

These tensions reveal the flaws in the claim that Haifa is the living embodiment of 'social integration'. If there are indeed places on Massada Street where people can meet beyond communities' boundaries, they are relatively few and far between. And despite the contacts that take place there, the polarisation produced by the Israeli–Palestinian conflict automatically re-emerges during moments of crisis. In daily life, this polarisation is deeply embedded in stereotypical practices and discourses generated by the physical and symbolic violence that is exerted by politicians at both city and national levels. This ongoing violence makes the creation of a shared, non-antagonistic outlook impossible. As many of the people to whom I spoke told me, the tensions inherent in the Israeli State prevent residents from the different communities from looking at each other in a 'relaxed' manner.

Yet, despite this atmosphere of reciprocal fear, mistrust and even contempt, and the many real political constraints that accompany it, in certain spaces that are marked out by their commitment to active and radical politics, I was nevertheless able to observe the everyday reality of practices of mutual aid and assistance. In this respect, it should be noted that, although the younger generations

In Massada Street's coffee shops

of Arabs did not experience the military government that ruled over Galilee and other Palestinian-dominated areas until 1966, they are no less attached to their unique identity than their parents were. To be part of the life of Massada Street and its cafés is not an innocent act for them. Rather, it is a form of political action. For the young people who hang out in these cafés, integration becomes acceptable when it produces political self-consciousness, and makes it possible to foreground a Palestinian identity, rather than allowing it to be dissolved into the dominant identity.

In this way, these cafés, which started out simply as places people went to drink, rest, entertain each other and escape from the pressures of the rest of their lives, are today spaces in which political debate is engaged and where a form of internal dissidence, however weak it may seem, can begin to emerge.

Note

1 This chapter is based on fieldwork conducted in the city in 2010.

References

Depaule, Jean-Charles, 'Les établissements du café du Caire', *Études rurales*, 180, 2007: pp. 245–262.

Desmet-Grégoire, Hélène and François Georgeon, eds, *Cafés d'Orient revisités*, CNRS Éditions, Paris, 1997.

Dumazedier, Joffre and Aline Ripert, *Le loisir et la ville*, Vol. I, 'Loisirs et culture', Seuil, Paris, 1966.

Eleb, Monique and Jean-Charles Depaule, *La société des cafés. Espaces, rituels sociaux et vie quotidienne*. Rapport final du Programme interministériel 'Cultures, villes et dynamiques sociales', Paris/Los Angeles/Cairo, 2004.

Pétonnet, Colette, 'L'anonymat comme pellicule protectrice', in *La ville inquiète*, Series 'Le temps de la réflexion', Vol. VIII, Gallimard, Paris, 1987, pp. 247–261.

Tamari, Salim, *Mountain against the Sea. Essay on Palestinian Society and Culture*, University of California Press, Los Angeles, CA, 2009.

16

In the shade of the *khayma*

Cultural and political resistance of the young Sahrawis at Dakhla

Victoria Veguilla Del Moral

It is summer 2003. We are driving out of the city by the only land route. The view is magnificent. Dakhla is on the Atlantic Ocean, at the heart of a narrow, more than 25 km long peninsula forming a bay where the browns of the desert clash on the horizon with the blues of the sea. A few kilometres past the Moroccan Royal Gendarmerie checkpoint, white shapes are visible. They are *khayyam* (singular: *khayma*), traditional tents used by the Arab nomads. Some tens of these *khayyam*, a hundred perhaps, are strung out along both sides of the road that runs beside the sea. But what are these improvised houses? They are relics of the history of the indigenous population of this Sahrawi region that is currently disputed between Morocco and the Polisario Front. This once nomadic society, structured in tribes of both Arab and Berber origin, has now become settled under the combined effect of armed conflict, repression, droughts and urbanisation. But in the summer, tens of families and a large number of young Sahrawis put up their *khayyam* a few kilometres from Dakhla – a strange juxtaposition that sees an expanding city studded with satellite dishes sitting alongside these villages of apparently age-old tents.

In summer 2012, not a single *khayma* is on the horizon. None at all. At our first stop at the Oum Labouir ('the Woman of the Well') beach, there is a single *khayma*. At our second stop, fourteen kilometres from the city at the Batalha ('Seaweed') beach, there are eight *khayyam* on Sunday and only three the next day. These – discreet – *khayyam* have been erected right beside the sea, behind the rocks, invisible from the road. The ones we visited in 2003 were along the side of the road that ran down to the beaches. What has happened? Have the Sahrawis given up on the summer leisure activities that were so emblematic? Have the young people given up on their 'very own' moments beneath the *khayyam*? M., a twenty-seven-year-old Sahrawi student, explains:

In the shade of the *khayma*

> Camping, as you were familiar with it, is prohibited now. The remaining *khayyam* are authorized, since they belong to people well-known to the police and not suspected of engaging in militant activities ... [As for the others,] the tents are authorized only on Sundays and in the daytime, if there aren't too many of them. At night – no way. Large numbers of them – no way. Young people – no way. If we still go ahead and put them up, the [Moroccan] police ask us to take them down.

It is the events that took place in 2010 at Laayoune, at the Gdeim Izik camp, then in 2011 at Dakhla, that explain the hardening of the Moroccan authorities' position: confrontations between young 'Sahrawis' and young 'Moroccans'. These clashes have upended the urban societies of the Sahara, profoundly modifying the summer landscape of the Bay of Dakhla. If the Moroccan police controls the installation of *khayyam* so drastically, trying quite simply to make them disappear, that is because those tents, apparently leisure-related and inoffensive, have a strong identitary – and hence 'dissident' – dimension in Sahrawi society.

The *khayma* before its prohibition

Dakhla is a recently built city 300 kilometres from the Mauritanian border. It seems very remote, as though it had been set down in the middle of nowhere. The closest towns are Boujdour, 350 km away, and, around 500 km away, Laayoune, the capital of Western Sahara. Agadir, the flagship Moroccan city of the Sous region, is 1,200 km away. There is a single road across the desert, the only way out by land for the adventurers who choose that route. As for air travel, it is expensive: around 1,500 dirhams (135 euros) to Casablanca, when the median monthly income of Moroccan households is 5,300 dirhams (477 euros), according to the official figures (2009). Dakhla, a remote city, is almost cut off. Its inhabitants are too.

However, the city has great political and symbolic importance. Capital of the Oued Ed-Dahab-Lagouira region and known at the time of Spanish rule as Rio de Oro, it stands on the territory that opposes Morocco, which annexed the territory when Spain withdrew in 1976 and has managed it since, to the Popular Front for the Liberation of Saguia el-Hamra and Rio de Oro, better known as the Polisario Front (the government of the Sahrawis in exile). The controversy over the *khayyam* has to be seen in this general context.

During the 2000s, many settled Sahrawi families in Dakhla had formed the habit of spending the summer period in these *khayyam*. Very often, the men carried on working in the city and made the round trip at the weekend, while the – rarely employed – women and children spent their whole time there. For visitors, however various they might be, Sahrawi tea is offered, a tea prepared and consumed in tranquillity – three glasses of a tea brewed over coals, as tradition demands. Concentrated and strong, it is served in little glasses that are half-filled, and covered with a plentiful foam that forms as the tea is poured repeatedly from one glass to another. The tradition is handed down from one generation to the next, and the young are no less faithful to it than their elders. Some of these young people spend their time working for Western tourists who come to do 'kite-surfing'. For some ten years or so, kite-surfers have found a spot here that is almost unique across the world. Some young Sahrawis, taking advantage of the bonanza this represents, cultivate passing foreigners to earn a few pennies. After lunch, they prepare a milder tea with mint for these 'beach tourists' who apparently have no interest either in the city or its population. This 'Moroccan' tea, as the Sahrawis call it, is one that the young people of the region don't even taste. They also share with them the ritual of the *jira* or *gadha*, a wooden bowl filled with camel's milk passed around among the occupants of the *khayma*. The less adventurous tourists can fall back on fruit juice or milk from a carton.

For young Sahrawis, summer isn't just the chance to earn a little money. It gives them an opportunity to leave the city and get away for a few days with friends. They imitate their parents and also put up their *khayyam*. This mobile, ephemeral dwelling offers them a place apart, a space between equals where generational proximity affords a release from proprieties and the respect due to the elders. It has to be said that the norms of coexistence (*cohabitation*) between the generations in Sahrawi society are particularly constraining. In the presence of an older person, there is no smoking or talk of intimate personal matters and television programmes are chosen carefully. These rules also apply to relations between the sexes. Though at a certain point, it becomes obvious, a woman's pregnancy, for example, is only mentioned by the spouses concerned or between women. It is a subject regarded as belonging to the private sphere: 'For us, this subject is part of the universe of sexuality', states Hamid, aged thirty-three. 'To refer to women's pregnancies is like speaking about sex.' Even when confronted with a protruding belly, it is thought improper to comment until the child is born. It is the same with love affairs. There is no question of parents and older brothers or sisters being informed explicitly, even when obvious facts take over from mere rumours. And what can we say of allusions to alcohol or cigarettes? These are all subjects that are only raised among friends.

In the shade of the *khayma*

So, when it comes to spending time with one's own age group, the imagination brims over. Pretence and 'shooting a line' form part of social norms and are not really penalised socially unless certain red lines are crossed. These latter may concern 'over-personal' relations with non-Sahrawis (exogamy) or drug use, hashish being regarded as a product introduced by the Moroccans and hence endogenous to the Sahrawi population. Though the Sahrawis remain vigilant in their relations with 'the outside world', the limits of the group are, nonetheless, a function of context-dependent complex, malleable constructions, the nomadic past of these populations additionally making the notion of a 'border' difficult to grasp. In this context, the degree of assimilation of Sahrawi customs and traditions and the expression of nationalist allegiance play a crucial role in establishing identity.

These social norms are valid for all, at whatever age. For the youth, to escape them briefly, for the duration of a summer, in the shade of the *khayma*, is part of a maturing – if not, indeed, an initiation – process. Such escape routes exist and are themselves part of daily practices. For girls, the undertaking is outwardly more transgressive, since the practice of endogamy is more of a concern for them (their children will be Sahrawi if the fathers are) and they are expected to preserve their virginity. These girls are under closer 'supervision'. There is no question, for example, of allowing camping that involves young people of both sexes unaccompanied. How can these strict norms be circumvented? Sometimes the girls pretend to stay with a female friend or say that the older brother of a friend (a man known and respected by the family) will be accompanying them. In this way, there are always tangential paths that enable them to enjoy a little freedom, while respecting the traditions to which they claim to be particularly attached.

Taking part in the tea ritual in the *khayyam* provides the opportunity for the young Sahrawis to air any subjects of concern and to chat about them: girls or boys, sex, football, music, politics 'here' and 'over there'. In the case of young boys, three overlapping questions receive the greatest attention: first, the difficulty of having sexual relations with girls before marriage (if you love her, you have to preserve her respectability); the 'need' to marry a Sahrawi girl to preserve the group; and, lastly, the difficulty of putting together the requisite amount of money to set up a marriage.

From place of apartness to symbol of identity

Being Sahrawi is no trivial matter for these young people who fear their assimilation into another – much larger – group that seems to have them surrounded and dominate important aspects of their life. In this region, the demographic question remains a substantive issue. The latest census data shows a large rise in the population of the Oued Ed-Dahab-Lagouira region, more than 90 per cent of which lives in the city of Dakhla: 36,751 residents in 1994, almost 100,000 in 2004. There is talk of there being some 150,000 in 2012. The flow of migrants from north to south is not stopping. The 'Moroccan-ness of the Sahara', touted as a national cause since the emblematic 'Green March' of 1975 led by Hassan II to 'reconquer' this territory, has a great deal to do with this process. But this – very political – resolve to promote north–south migration does not alone explain the migratory dynamism here. On the one hand, the city is enjoying a significant economic boom, after a period of crisis due to its dependency on the fishing sector. The reorganisation of the local fisheries sector, begun in 2005, and the diversification of the local economy (tourism, construction, agriculture) have made Dakhla an attractive city for job-seeking migrants (the unemployment rate in Morocco stands officially at 8.9 per cent in 2011). Moreover, the proactive urban policy of the Moroccan state, implemented from 2008 onwards, has offered migrants who have settled at Dakhla since the 1980s the chance to build their own houses. Economically prosperous and with its slums cleared in a manner that is exceptional for Morocco, Dakhla is a city that has 'pull'. As a result, persons 'of Sahrawi stock' are in the distinct minority there. To the recently arrived migrants can be added at least one generation born in the Sahara to parents from the 'north'.

In this context, it remains important for the Sahrawis to differentiate themselves. That distinction is achieved mainly through the practice of endogamy and the preservation – and even reinvention – of their own customs and traditions. The *khayyam* are part of these traditions insofar as these ephemeral dwellings represent one of the elements that make up the configuration of their collective imaginary. However, the use made of them is readapted to the current living conditions of the population. In addition to being a space for rest and apartness, the *khayyam* are used for marriages and at election times. They have thus gradually become an identity marker that distinguishes the group, in its way of life and traditions, from the populations that came to settle in the Western Sahara after the Spanish decolonisation of the territory.

Music represents another focus for the negotiation around identity, in which novelty mingles with tradition. Like their parents, young Sahrawis remain closely attached to *hassaniyya* traditional song (*hassani* is the dialect of Arabic spoken by the Mauritanians and the Sahrawis). For them, too, the Mauritanian 'diva' Dimi is an important reference. In another style (militant Sahrawi nationalist song), Myriam Hassan is all the rage. Unlike their elders, however, they

In the shade of the *khayma*

are also fans of a new generation of Mauritanian rap musicians in the *hassani* dialect, such as, in recent years, Oulad Leblad ('the Children of the Earth').

This reinvention of traditions shows, in its way, these youths' attachment to politics. In the local context, this is not difficult to understand: at the time of Spanish decolonisation in 1975, a large number of families became divided between those who decided to leave for Algeria – particularly to the Tindouf refugee camp – and those who chose to remain on this disputed territory. Many of these families have not seen each other since, with the result that a lot of young Sahrawis, who have nonetheless a precise knowledge of their history and follow current events closely on television, do not know their grandparents, brothers or cousins.

The *khayyam* as place of protest

As we have seen, attachment to an identity does not exclude innovation. What is new relates particularly to the young Sahrawis' sense of being frontline actors: living out the conflict that sees them opposed to Morocco in its local dimension, they sometimes see their actions picked up by the international media – a situation which enables them to get beyond the sense of impotence a large proportion of them had before the mid-2000s.

As a result of repression, the difficulty of travel and the controls exerted by the Moroccan authorities on information, their elders actually remained isolated for many years. Having no possibility of making themselves heard, either within the disputed territory or beyond borders that were strictly controlled by Morocco, their voices were drowned out by the discourse of the Moroccan authorities who presented them, from the 1991 ceasefire to the turn of the 2000s, as *de facto* defenders of the Moroccan national cause.[1] Being suspected of sharing Moroccan positions with regard to the territory, by contrast with what has happened in Palestine for example, those who had remained in the interior, so to speak, were regarded with a degree of suspicion by the 'Sahrawis of the exterior'. Hence, when it came to discussing the plans for a referendum on self-determination that the UN was going to organise (but which never took place), local and international commentators had formed the habit of distinguishing between how the 'Sahrawis of the interior' and the 'Sahrawis of the exterior' might vote. Yet the Sahrawis 'of the interior' remained committed to their *Sahrawi-ness*, following their own traditions and constructing an identity for themselves in opposition to the new arrivals from the north, with whom they found it difficult to coexist.

Rooting the future

The installation and development of digital networks dealt a blow to such assumptions and gave new political impetus to Sahrawi youth. They now have unprecedented access to information and, most importantly, an opportunity to communicate with the outside world – for example, with international organisations that support the cause of the Polisario Front. They can also provide instantaneous visual evidence, through photographs and videos, of local news events. The idealised collective identity might even be said to be bolstered among the younger generation. It is 'young people' who have established new organisations, such as the Action Committee against Torture at Dakhla, and who launched what they called the Sahrawi *intifada*, brandishing the flag of the Polisario Front in the streets. More and more regularly since 2010, it is also those young people who clash with other Dakhla 'youth' of 'northern' origin.

It is in this context that the *khayyam* became a weapon of political expression and mobilisation. In Western Sahara, tents have long been places of mobilisation: candidates campaigning in the general and local elections have used them as places to host and motivate their supporters and the curious. It was also from their *khayyam* that some of them contested the results of the general elections of 2002. But the phenomenon increased enormously in scope in October and November 2010, with the installation of a camp known as Gdeim Izik some kilometres from Laayoune and the uprising that took place there. This vast, unexpected, spectacular protest movement, which mobilised more than 20,000 people, attracted the attention of the foreign media who were alerted to the protestors' cause. Though initially socio-economic, the demands of the movement took on a distinctly communal dimension: the protestors, of Sahrawi origin, demanded from the authorities land to build on, jobs in the public sector and social welfare for the most deprived. Following the violent dismantling of the camp and the death of a Sahrawi adolescent killed by Moroccan law enforcement forces, the demands assumed an explicit independentist aspect and the protest led to very violent, lethal confrontations between, on the one hand, the forces of law enforcement and hundreds of demonstrators and, on the other, these latter ('Sahrawis') and counter-demonstrators ('northerners'). Tensions have not subsided since.

The Gdeim Izik uprising has had obvious effects on the lives of the Sahrawis of Dakhla, not merely from the political point of view but also in terms of leisure: having become symbols of a reinvestment in identity, the tents are now prohibited except in controlled situations. During the legislative elections of 25 November 2011, a year after the events, no tent was erected. Similarly, in the summer of 2012, the seaside holidays under canvas that were common

In the shade of the *khayma*

throughout the preceding decade have disappeared. They are subject to a prohibition which certainly cannot be explained by Gdeim Izik alone. At Dakhla, confrontations between the youth of the two communities are not uncommon. 2011 was a particularly tense year. Two affrays in particular rocked the town, first on the occasion of a cultural festival (the Sea and Desert Festival, suspended in 2011 after violent brawling), then after a 2011 football match between the city's team Mouloudia Dakhla and Chabab Mohamadia from a town to the north of Casablanca. Whereas the Moroccan media downplayed these clashes, attributing them to the disappointment of the local team's young supporters after 'their' team lost 3–0, witnesses to the incidents stressed the role of a more general resentment. This, for example, is what was explained by S., an eighteen-year-old student:

> Tension was already running high with the 'Moroccans' and it was during the football match that the spark came. It had nothing to do with the result of the match, as Mouloudia Dakhla is no longer a Sahrawi team. In the past, there were a lot of Sahrawis among the players, but today there are only three.

These riots, after the protests at Gdeim Izik led to the prohibition on using *khayyam* for outings and for meeting up in large numbers outside the city in the summer months, which entailed a change in behaviour and in young people's capacity to meet up in privacy.

After the prohibition

Dakhla is no longer the same after these incidents. Today young Sahrawis know the places where their presence may be regarded as provocative. They are in a distinct minority there. It is out of the question for them, for example, to walk around the new district being built in the south of the city (*Madinat al-wahda* – 'Unity Town'). This is where families have been housed that have benefited from the slum clearance policy implemented in Dakhla since 2009. These are mainly groups that were part of the first waves of migrants produced by the 'Green March'. Formerly housed in the '*al wahda* camp', a shanty town inhabited by the migrants of the 1980s, they have since received subsidies for basic provisions distributed by the military authorities. Also involved, though more marginally, are groups from the *Lahraït* (Gardens) camp, the new penniless migrants who settled at Dakhla looking for jobs. Their children, today young Dakhlawi, were born in these slum dwellings.

Both groups know, and are recognisable to, each other. There are, however, exceptions, as S., the eighteen-year-old Sahrawi student, reminds us: 'I've a pal who isn't Sahrawi, but the way I see it, in reality he is one. He acts like us and, when it comes to fighting, he's on our side.' In this context of latent tension, the different groups try to mark out their particular territories, but also, more simply, their sites of apartness. Cafés are an example of this. Some young Sahrawis go to a café near an old district with a majority Sahrawi population, the *El Dorado* having been built by the Spaniards and taken over by the locals when the colonisers left in 1975. Now owned by a Sahrawi, it is a place to meet up and talk. These young people get together there to chat or watch football matches. Young women go only very seldom and, when they do, they keep to their female friends. Their presence in public places such as cafés or restaurants is still frowned upon.

In this context of exacerbated control and prohibition, outings from the city are becoming less common. Of course, young people still go to the beach in summer. But they don't stay as long. The sun is hard to cope with in these latitudes. It poses a particular problem for the Sahrawi women who see the whiteness of their skin as a mark of beauty and prefer to cover their faces with the traditional *melfast* (a multi-coloured veil). The very strong wind is also inconvenient. Though the foreign kite-surfers love it, it prevents the young Sahrawis, who are spending their days by the sea, from lighting the coals that enable them to make the tea which, beneath the protective shade of the *khayyam*, had become a powerful marker of their identity.

Note

1 That ceasefire, promoted by the UN and signed by the Polisario Front and the Kingdom of Morocco, temporarily put an end to more than ten years of armed conflict. By the agreement, Morocco controls and administers around 80 per cent of the territory, while the Polisario Front controls 20 per cent behind a long 'buffer strip'. The parties agreed to hold a referendum on self-determination to put an end to the conflict over sovereignty in Western Sahara, but the referendum has still not taken place.

References

Caratini, Sophie, *Les enfants des nuages*, Seuil, Paris, 1993.
Gómez Martin, Carmen, 'Sahara Occidental: Quel scénario après Gdeim Izik?', in *L'Année du Maghreb 2012*, Vol. VIII, CNRS Éditions, Paris, 2012, pp. 259–276.

Hernando de Larramendi, Miguel and Bernabé López García, 'Nuevo impulso diplomático en el Sáhara', *Afkar/Ideas*, 4, autumn 2004: pp. 22–25.

Longoria, Álvaro (director), *Oulda lemzun* (*Hijos de las nubes* – Sons of the Clouds) (film), 2012.

Mohsen-Finan, Khadija, *Sahara Occidental. Les enjeux d'un conflit régional*, CNRS Éditions, Paris, 1997.

Pointier, Laurent, *Sahara occidental. La controverse devant les Nations unies*, Karthala, Paris, 2004.

Veguilla, Victoria, 'La gestion localisée de conflits "invisibles": les mobilisations socio-économiques des jeunes Sahraouis à Dakhla', in Céline Aufauvre, Karine Bennafla and Montserrat Emperador-Badimon, eds, *Maghreb et sciences sociales 2011. Marges, normes et éthique. Thème I*, IRMC-L'Harmattan, Paris, 2011, pp. 95–104.

Veguilla, Victoria, 'L'articulation du politique dans un espace protestataire en recomposition. Les mobilisations des jeunes Sahraouis à Dakhla', *L'Année du Maghreb 2009*, Vol. V, CNRS Éditions, Paris, 2009, pp. 95–110.

Veguilla, Victoria, 'Le *pourquoi* d'une mobilisation "exceptionnelle": Dakhla', in Mounia Bennani-Chraïbi, Myriam Catusse and Jean-Claude Santucci, eds, *Représentations et mobilisations électorales au Maroc (Les législatives de septembre 2002)*, Karthala, Paris, 2004, pp. 235–264.

17

Recreation, re-creation, resistance

What roles for *dabke* in Palestine?

Xavier Guignard

> I don't really understand this notion of tradition, of folklore. It's just a question of temporality. If I dance like my grandfather, I'm doing folk-dancing and if I move away from that, I'm killing the tradition. But let's look at history the other way round: if people like the moves I do today and my children repeat them, then what I do today will be tomorrow's folk-dancing, won't it?
>
> – Raed, a dancer in his thirties in Jerusalem

A stone's throw from the Mahmoud Darwish Museum at the Palace of Culture in Ramallah, the 'heritage festival' opens on 18 October 2012. Hundreds of relatives, friends and interested individuals have come to sit in this luxurious theatre to watch a two-hour dance show. The cameras of Palestine's TV channels are there too. At the first notes of the Palestinian national anthem, everyone gets to their feet. Then they remain standing for many minutes applauding the dancers on to the stage, as they, aged between eight and twenty, come down the steps smiling and essaying a few dance steps. Among the audience, a group of fifteen or so adolescents accompany them noisily, improvising a round dance, stamping their feet in the customary fashion. The crowd sits back down when the first group comes on stage. For some minutes, these dancers in their magnificent costumes offer a glimpse of what they have learnt in their dance lessons. They are followed then by some twenty other troupes. The evening will have provided an opportunity to showcase the full range of music and choreography known as *dabke*.

From the refugee camps that stud Palestine to the new districts of Ramallah, the default capital of the Palestinian authority, clubs exist to teach this *dabke* to young people and spread it among them. At shows, the term used is 'dance troupe', but few of these have the means to project their fame and style beyond the local space. And even the best-known clubs are, in very large part, run by volunteers as charitable associations. It is these 'troupes' and their young dancers of both sexes that we shall examine here, mainly in the West Bank and Jerusalem. Given that, in other parts of the world, the younger generations are said to be indifferent to 'tradition', how are we to explain the success of *dabke* among young Palestinians? What does this dance represent for young adults of the 2010s and what meanings do they ascribe to it? To discuss this question, we have chosen to concern ourselves here with the *dabke* that is taught, choreographed and performed in shows, not with the more spontaneous form mainly danced at weddings.

As told by its dancers and choreographers, the recent history of the staging, diffusion and learning of *dabke* is characterised by the reinvention of a cultural 'heritage'. The practice of the dance, at the point where professional ambition meets recreational activities, assumes a particular meaning in the social world of a generation of young people constrained by the Israeli occupation. As for the training studio, that turns out also, at another level of observation, to be a space for adolescents to learn gender relations. The political charge of this dance – and its interconnections with other forms of resistance, with which it may combine – provides an opportunity to question these actors on the motivations of their engagement and the place of *dabke* above and beyond the theatrical context.

'Rediscovering one's traditions': conservation or invention?

In the early twentieth century, *dabke* was mainly an uncodified male, village dance in which the roles of the singers and dancers were not strictly defined. It was danced at celebrations throughout the *bilad al-sham* region (Palestine, Lebanon, Syria and Jordan). Punctuated by jumping and foot-stamping, the dance varied from one region to another.

When Israel declared its independence in 1948, the ensuing war forced 800,000 destitute Palestinians into exile (*nakba*). Jordan and Egypt administered the territories the new Jewish state had not appropriated within Mandatory Palestine. This trauma, which de-structured Palestinian social organisation, engendered within the refugee camps a mixing of social origins favourable to the adoption of a common identity reference. That was how this village dance became a 'national' practice, the distinction between village- and town-dwellers tending to fade among the population in exile. Gradually, the entire population came together around the dance, among other cultural references (the wearing of the village *keffieh* being one example). At the same time, the Jordanian regime, which administered the West Bank and East Jerusalem (until 1967), began to promote a pan-Arab culture structured around shared identity markers, *dabke* being one strand of this. Festivals were created throughout the region, particularly at Amman, Beirut and, later, Ramallah, which contributed to the 'folklorisation' of the dance: costumes, dance steps, progressive distinction between dance and singing, the introduction of new accompanying music, etc.

In the 1960s, *dabke* thus became established as part of the regional cultural landscape in a 'modernised' form. Recognised for its mobilising force, both within the national territory and among those in exile, the young Palestinian national movement became increasingly invested in it. While *dabke* was increasingly in evidence at political events, the lyrics of the musical accompaniment to the dance took on more militant connotations. This is the specific feature of contemporary *dabke* as encountered in Palestine, freighted with a nationalist history and heir to a more regional practice of teaching and codification that lends it its artistic dimension.

Among the first teachers who came, in this period, to teach within the informal setting of the festivals was a group of dancers, mainly from Syria and Lebanon, who had spent time in Moscow's ballet schools. This was particularly the case of the couple Wadea Jarrar Haddad and Marwan Jarrar, both of whom were Palestinian refugees in Lebanon. They were chosen in 1956 to follow courses in European folk dance at the Bolshoi, choreographed *dabke* shows in Lebanon, took part on four occasions between 1962 and 1966 in festivals at Ramallah and also participated in the first teaching done in the West Bank. They offered other choreographic options beyond the basic moves of Middle Eastern *dabke*. Whereas this latter depends largely on leg movements and jumps, they integrated arm and upper body movements into it, products of the styles of dance they had learnt in Moscow.

Thus *dabke* has been constantly evolving and 'hybridising' for decades. Today's adolescents, for example, employ the '*harakat jaksun*' ('Jackson move'), bringing steps from Michael Jackson's famous 'moonwalk' into their dances. The themes of *dabke* songs also reflect current affairs: whereas the earliest dances were accompanied by songs about weddings or harvesting olives, you endlessly hear on the radio or in Palestinian markets now the famous '*udrub, udrub, Til Abib*' ('Strike, Strike Tel-Aviv'), composed by young Gazans after the attacks on Gaza in November 2012 and the rockets launched by Hamas and its allies that struck the Israeli capital for the first time. Alongside this development, there is now the possibility of online distribution and sharing of both songs and dance performances, a contrast with the early-century confinement to particular localities. *Udrub, udrub Til Abib*, for example, had more than a million hits on YouTube in a matter of a few weeks.

Closeness between the sexes

Chatting up girls, travelling, finding a job – the opportunities offered by learning *dabke* are not confined to the acquisition of dance techniques. The rehearsal room becomes a little closed world where the norms in force in the other – external – world are discussed.

For many teachers, male and female, the reinvention of *dabke* means taking into account the freedom and equality of the sexes. As a forty-eight-year-old teacher we meet at Ramallah named Huda explains, dance involves a process of social learning:

> My role as a dance teacher is to teach my students to embody their characters, to make them credible on stage. My hope as a Palestinian woman is that the values enacted in our classes or on stage – equality of the sexes, freedom – will influence their behaviour outside.

Though originally a male dance, *dabke* as practised and performed in Palestine today grants significant space to women. They may be choreographers, frontline dancers or even *lawih* (leaders). For some years now, women have been challenging men for this role of leader of the dance, symbolised by the stick the dancer holds, replacing the sabre that was carried in the Mandate period.

It can't be taken for granted that men and women should share the same rehearsal space or the same stage, as a nineteen-year-old female dancer reminds us: her aunt, who lives in Hebron, has not spoken to her since she saw her dancing with a man in a television broadcast of a *dabke* performance. What is negotiated within the space of the dance class – the place of women, the interactions between dancers – is not confined to the rehearsal room. As several female dancers explained, it is easier for them to negotiate intimacy with the – male – other when that is associated with an art that is experienced, by those around them too, as a nationalist activity, as the vehicle of an 'authentically' Palestinian identity. The 'folk' dimension of the dance thus enables physical proximity to occur, together with light contact and the opening-up of masculine roles to women in a manner not necessarily encountered in other manifestations of popular culture.

The proximity between males and females produced by the dancing is, moreover, one of the motives for some young dancers' participation in the lessons. Rehearsing together, observing, touching and even "using their charms" on each other are all facilitated by belonging to the group and may be done to meet the needs of the choreography. Several times a week, sometimes over years, these dancers, who begin as young adolescents, meet in the closed, intimate space of the rehearsal room. Eighteen-year-old Fadi, who lives at Kafr 'Aqab (a suburb of East Jerusalem cut off today by the Wall), explains that he joined *dabke* classes to 'get to know girls of [his] age who were not at the same school or friends of [his] sister'.

A visa for 'the outside world'

Dancing doesn't just afford an opportunity for a different take on the relation to the opposite sex. For many dancers, male and female, it is a gateway to an 'elsewhere'. For twenty-two-year-old Amal, to look back on her path to becoming a dancer is to see herself taking a different route from the one marked out for her and getting away from the territory to which many Palestinians feel confined:

> I was never very good at school work, and from childhood I wanted to be in the arts, though not necessarily as a dancer. My parents forced me to go on with my studies to qualify as an accountant, rejecting the idea that their daughter could be a professional dancer. But after years of *dabke*, I began contemporary dance and they can see that I'm good at that, getting invitations to travel abroad.

Many dancers have memories of trips abroad, responding to invitations from across the globe. Dance offers an opening, then, to travel in the outside world. Though some smaller associations have managed to perform abroad, it is mostly city-based troupes that take part in international events. In the former case, it is largely to take part in events organised around 'support for Palestine'. In the latter case, we are talking more often of artistic events whose goal is to promote 'traditional cultures'. The context and the audience differ, but these are all opportunities to promote Palestinian *dabke* throughout the world: in South America, the Gulf, Europe and even Asia.

These invitations are sometimes addressed directly to one of the associations that offer dance classes, but most often it is the Palestinian Authority's Ministry of Culture that receives the invitations and hands them out to the various troupes. There are few complaints of favouritism so far, though performing in the Gulf is not so exciting and exotic for these young people as flying off to South America, for example.

The dancers find pleasure here not so much in what they do on stage as in their meetings, on these trips with other young people who have also come to represent their country. For Mohammad, a choreographer in his thirties whom we met in his home in Jerusalem, it is an opportunity to talk with others, discover different cultures and enrich his artistic knowledge, so as to vary the classes he offers in Palestine. Having already travelled a great deal, he no longer feels the same excitement as the young fifteen- or twenty-year-old dancers when they leave Palestine for the first time. But the mere fact of 'travelling', of 'getting out of Palestine' nonetheless enables everyone to leave behind them the reality of school, family obligations and the pressure of the occupation, if only for a few days.

It was, indeed, this possibility of travel that induced Shadi, a twenty-one-year-old Palestinian from Nazareth, to take *dabke* lessons in Jerusalem and then in al-Bireh near Ramallah:

> I began playing football at school, but I heard our friends who were doing *dabke* talk about the possibility of travel. We were still very young, but I thought to myself that it was worth a try, I'd never been outside Palestine. Today I've seen more than 15 countries and speak English much better than I did.

Though he is the holder of an Israeli passport, having been born in Nazareth in Israel, which makes it easier to obtain a visa than the document issued by the Palestinian Authority, Shadi shares this vision with his friends: dance can open up unsuspected gateways to the outside world. This is an opportunity that isn't so common: leaving Palestinian territory through Egypt or Jordan (since citizens of the Palestinian Authority are not permitted to use the Israeli airport) is an ordeal. And obtaining a visa with the 'travel document' that serves as a Palestinian passport, even for a country as near as Syria or Lebanon, requires a sheaf of documents and personal guarantees that prevent many candidates from travelling.

Beginning to learn dance by the *dabke* route may therefore offer a range of resources. Like Amal, Majd, who is twenty-five years old, also took contemporary dance lessons after beginning in *dabke*. She is taking her third trip to the USA this year to take part in dance workshops that could bring the prospect of shows and tours. Majd, who began *dabke* as a way of having fun with her school friends, never imagined she might leave her little West Bank town to go and live

Rooting the future

abroad. With her years of dance as her passport, it is, however, quite possible that she will soon do that. Though something exceptional for these dancers, the possibility of joining an international dance troupe is indeed an option for the most brilliant among them. Others choose to become teachers: dance schools are opening regularly and have need of teachers. Even if the teaching is often on a voluntary basis, the most famous schools, such as Wishah, al-Funun or Sariyyat Ramallah, employ permanent staff to give classes in *dabke* and contemporary dance. Teaching *dabke* is a good way of reinvesting years of study and can be transformed, when it is a paid activity, into an opportunity in a Palestine severely hit by unemployment. It is also an excellent conduit to jobs that arise as part of the educational support services provided by the many NGOs present in the West Bank.

Not forgetting the occupation

Whether it be the case of a dancer injured at a demonstration against Israeli occupation, a trip made impossible by an Israeli checkpoint or the choice of texts for a particular show, the practice of *dabke* can never disregard the political situation. If the occupation of the West Bank makes its way into the dance, then the resistance does too. Dancing isn't just mere escapism: *dabke* overspills its entertainment framework and is interwoven with other forms of resistance. In the actors' careers, as in the symbolic burden of their art, there is a marked dimension of political protest.

Going on the road and confronting Israeli soldiers is already a form of political protest: refusing confinement in the micro-territories marked out by the growing presence of settlements. For example, Ahmad, who is twenty-seven years old and lives in Birzeit, remembers the day when, setting out from Ramallah to do a show near Bethlehem around twenty kilometres away, he spent four hours waiting for soldiers to finish inspecting the load on his lorry. That is how it is with travel between two cities in the West Bank. Yasmine, who grew up in England before settling in Ramallah, also attests – not without humour – to the constraints on the dancers:

> Less than a month ago, we were invited to China for a few days to take part in a traditional dance festival. The whole troupe went, going through Jordan to catch the plane. On our return, we had to cancel the show we had planned at Jerusalem, since the Israeli authorities refused to issue permits to some of our number. You can see that it's easier for a Palestinian to dance in Beijing than in her own capital.

Recreation, re-creation, resistance

The training room itself isn't a 'protected' space, as there are no places in Palestine where the occupation doesn't make itself felt. And another experience can be added to travel difficulties: being arrested. Here again, the daily life of dancers is incredibly banal in a context where almost a third of Palestinians from the West Bank and Gaza have seen the inside of an Israeli prison. But when this 'banality' runs up against an apparently 'playful' world, 'leisure activities' take on a particular connotation. That is the impression we get the day we watch a rehearsal at the Ibdaa Cultural Centre in the Daheisheh camp near Bethlehem. That day, Ghazi, the 'leader' of the group, is missing: the young man, twenty-two years of age, was arrested the previous day and placed in 'administrative detention', an arrangement for circumventing the normal judicial process that allows the Israeli authorities to imprison anyone without charge or sentence for a – multiply renewable – six-month period. So no one knows when Ghazi will be back. In the dance studio, suddenly transformed into a political arena, the dancers are in a quandary. What should they do? Cancel the show? Begin rehearsals again? Give one of the characters the prisoner's name? If unity is strength when it comes to facing up to these daily dramas, the close-knit character of a group that is sufficiently small for everyone to express their opinion also enables the right words to be found, views to be weighed against each other and reactions to be controlled with respect to the humiliations inflicted by the occupation.

Though the dancers suffer the violence of colonisation individually, as all other Palestinians do, it is sometimes dance itself that is targeted. Khaled, director of one of the troupes at Ramallah, was arrested in 1989 during the first *intifada* with some fifty other dancers for the very reason that they were dancing. For the Israeli authorities, it was about prohibiting an unlawful gathering, as they might have done a demonstration or a political meeting. However, the dancers, male and female, that we met saw Palestinian identity as the thing the occupation was attempting to crush, to wipe out. Political consciousness also emerged from these relations with the authority they opposed and combatted, and this re-defined the dancer's relation to their environment. From the experience of domination, the dancers become aware that they can, through their work, mount a resistance that goes beyond a mere claim to identity. It is not unusual, for example, to see young protesters, marching in a number of villages along the Separation Wall every Friday, perform a few dance steps only yards from the Israeli soldiers.

Political consciousness is particularly highly developed in some dancers, as is attested to by the way, when we meet him in his office at the headquarters of the al-Funun troupe, Youssef, a forty-two-year-old choreographer, comes straight out with the following question:

> Before we start our interview, I have a question. Are you working with Israeli institutions or on Israeli dance troupes? I don't know if you're familiar with Palestinian reality, but I wouldn't agree to this discussion if that were the case. And I don't care if that were to make you think I was too rigid, or racist.

The question being asked is, in fact, about the 'normalisation' (*tatbi'*), that is to say, the 'neutralisation' of an art that some regard as intrinsically political and inseparable from the occupation. It is this rejection of normalisation that lies behind Youssef's desire to probe the intentions of those who claim to be interested in *dabke* and, in the event that the posters of Yasser Arafat and of commemorations of the *nakba* (exodus) had passed them by, to remind them that the place isn't devoid of all critical thinking. With this preliminary out of the way, the conversation continues around the choice of a poem by Hussein Barghouti (*sahit al-ward*, 'The Valley of the Roses'), set to music for one of al-Funun's latest shows. The poem is a love story between two ghosts of the war of 1948 separated forever and roaming around until they can find a place for their love.

This same rejection of normalisation underlies a polemic between young people from a troupe at Bethlehem and the organisers of the International Heritage Festival organised in Switzerland in August 2012. The latter, taking the view that these 'traditional cultures' resonated with universal values of peace and tolerance had invited a Palestinian dance troupe and an Israeli one to perform on the same evening. When they saw the schedule, the *Judhur* group's sixty or so Palestinian dancers (*Judhur* means roots in Arabic) preferred to miss an opportunity for travel rather than share the stage with Israelis and encourage a European audience to think that the Israeli–Palestinian conflict was a clash between two equal parties that could be overcome merely by youth activities. The adolescents who experience the Israeli occupation on a daily basis do not want to endorse such a notion – however much they might enjoy the trip or putting on the show.

Taking *dabke* classes in Palestine today may seem like a banal leisure activity, part of a timeless folkloric world. Yet it is the product of an appropriation – a reconquest – of identity that has occurred only in recent times. That history and the contemporary Palestinian context make it a commitment that runs up, sometimes dramatically, against the occupation. *Dabke* is both a prop for memory and itself the site of a collective memory, of an exploration of the past in which the younger generation remains an inventive driving force.

References

Al-Ghabdan, Yara, 'Palestines imaginaires: La scénographie comme ethnographie', *Anthropologie et sociétés*, 28, 3, 2004: pp. 15–37.
Kaschl, Elke, *Dance and Authenticity in Israel and Palestine. Performing the Nation*, Brill, Leiden, 2003.
Rowe, Nicholas, *Raising Dust. A Cultural History of Dance in Palestine*, I.B. Tauris, London, 2010.

As an example of contemporary *dabke* performances available on video, see Ramallah, Sariyyat, '*al-hajiz* (At the Checkpoint), 2010; and Al-Funun, *suar wa-dhakirah* (Images and Memory), 2009.

18

Taranim and videos

The Egyptian Church stripped bare by its children?

Laure Guirguis

Rasha loves to sing. Her passion for the *taranim*, those Christian devotional songs that are distinct from Coptic liturgical music, carries her away from the beaten track of Orthodoxy.[1] Coptic communal space admittedly grants a large place to *taranim*. However, it is the Protestant churches and some rare Coptic Orthodox churches led by priests under the influence of charismatic currents that give a home to the most recent products of this type.[2] Moreover, *taranim* are associated in these churches with new forms of piety. As she sings these songs and makes such excursions outside Orthodoxy, this very pious young Egyptian woman is unwittingly participating in one of the most striking transformations of her Church: its 'charismatization' to use an expression coined by the historian Febe Armanios.

The contemporary renewal of *taranim* (singular: *tarnima*) and the production of videos inspired by these songs are a product of the development of a Coptic 'mass culture'. Regarded by most Copts as the current expression of a centuries-old culture, *taranim* give concrete expression to the sense of belonging to the community. But these songs – and the videos that have been associated with them for around a decade – intersect with, or are stimulating, a diversity of social, religious and cultural practices that deviate at times from the code of behaviour prescribed by the Church. Combined with the attraction that charismatic currents and the 'born again' Christians have exerted over Christian youth in Egypt over the last twenty years or so, *taranim* as renewed show up Coptic dissatisfaction with clerical dogmatism. It also brings into play a vision of the individual and faith opposing that of the Mother Church.

In this sense, the youth's infatuation with *taranim* is one expression of the rejection of the highly hierarchical authoritarian structures of both a Church that saw unprecedented development – and an administrative and institutional overhaul – during the forty-year patriarchate of Shenouda III (born in 1923, consecrated patriarch in 1971, died in 2012) and the political despotism of the Hosni Mubarak regime. Embodied in the figure of young Khaled Said, beaten to death by a detested police force, that rejection momentarily and apparently unified the sectoral demands of the Egyptian population and led to the revolutionary uprising of 25 January 2011. On a deadlocked political scene, the destruction of the underpinnings of political and religious authoritarianism is also occurring thanks to a host of daily practices – most notably, forms of leisure, such as *taranim*, that embody alternative visions.

The Church and *taranim*: the controlled production of a transnational communal culture

Born on the day of the assassination of President Anwar al-Sadat in 1981, Rasha grew up in a village in the Nile valley near the town of Mallawi, until her parents moved to 'Ain Shams in Cairo in the early 1990s. It took long years of work in Jordan, Iraq and the Gulf states for her father and uncles to acquire a little building in the Cairo suburbs, and they did not look back after leaving the harsh conditions of Upper Egypt to its thousand-and-one miseries. With a job in a chemist's, Rasha is financially independent. At twenty-six, she married Tamir, whose family had moved to the outskirts of the Egyptian capital at the same time as her parents. She is currently the mother of two children.

She regards herself as politically conservative, both in national terms and within her own community. She disagreed, for example, with the critics (increasingly numerous during the 2000s) of the policy pursued by patriarch Shenouda III and of his interventions in national political life – his intransigent opposition to divorce and the unconditional support he gave to the regime. Similarly, she has never shown any sympathy for the revolutionary movement that has thrown Egyptian society into turmoil since the winter of 2011, though she was glad to see the fall of the Mubarak clan.

As is true of most young Copts, her social activities and leisure mostly take place within the bosom of the Church. During his patriarchate (1971–2012), Shenouda III had actually undertaken two joint operations to centralise and expand the Church, mobilising the community to that end. He strove to oversee the workings of the clerical institution closely and extended the ecclesial space to the secular areas of the worshippers' lives. The world of the Coptic community became the main producer of meaning and values and was regarded by most of the faithful as a zone of refuge in a hostile national environment. Hence

Rasha learned English at the Coptic Orthodox patriarchate's language centre in the 'Abbasiyya district, acquiring the ability to carry on a fluent conversation. She pursued her enthusiasm for theology in courses offered by the Sunday school of one of the 'Ain Shams churches and currently teaches the rudiments of Bible history to the youngest congregants.

Her sole passion is, however, *taranim*. These praise songs, generally performed outside religious services, developed on the margins of liturgical music, the transcription of which had been the touchstone of the building of the community from the late nineteenth century onward, since that music enabled the primacy of a Coptic culture to be asserted which linked the days of the pharaohs to present-day Egypt. Drawing on liturgical music, without being constrained by the canonical straitjacket, the *taranim* also initially took their inspiration from the Protestant hymns that circulated from the nineteenth century onwards, from the times when Christian missions arrived in Egypt in large numbers. Currently, in terms of melody, harmony and instrumental backing, they also borrow from popular dialectal songs, such as *mawwāl*, but, above all, from Arabic light music and pop song.

Rasha likes to compare the different interpretations of her favourite songs and to learn the lyrics by heart. She picks them up quickly but wants to be sure that she can refer to them at any hour of the day or night. Each month, she stops at her local church to buy the latest collections of lyrics, which she purchases for a few Egyptian pounds. She sings them alone, though that does not mean that she is afraid to go in for public competitions and she has won several prizes at festivals organised by the churches. In 2009 she had great success singing a *tarnima* composed by Shenouda III, who wrote a large number of these songs.

The Church has been concerned for many years with controlling the production and modes of diffusion of these songs, anticipating and stimulating the desires of the faithful or following their innovations and managing them retrospectively. For example, some *taranim*, the oldest, which the priests regard as elements of the Church's heritage, are sometimes akin to the *madih* (hymn) and are hence incorporated into certain services. Others are taught in the Sunday schools. The bookshops of monasteries and churches are stocked high with collections of *taranim*, which sit alongside the icons and trinkets of all shapes and sizes, the patriarch's sermons and the volumes of lives of the saints. The anxious religious fervour that was stoked at the end of the Nasser era in the 1960s by the decline of the national ideal and the exacerbation of hostile feelings towards Christians did not only show itself in regular practices or extraordinary events

Taranim and videos

(from the Marian apparition at Zaytun in 1968 to the one in 2009 at Imbaba); it expressed itself in the mass production of religious artefacts. Produced and marketed by and for Copts, these artefacts gave rise to a host of others. Every life of a famous saint is the subject of publications in various formats, ranging from print to audio-visual media. In the same way, *taranim* have inspired the recent production of a plethora of videos.

New online religiosities

Like a large part of Coptic youth, both urban and rural, Rasha has downloaded tens of gigabytes of *taranim* videos to her computer and iPhone from YouTube and various Christian websites. She collects, classifies and comments on them on her Facebook page. Nothing irritated her so much as encountering references to a video she hadn't already discovered herself, so she had set up a system of alerts to tell her when new videos were being put online on a whole string of sites. But she constantly had to update the list and refine her search criteria – a herculean task. Abandoning such systematic listings to others, she now prefers to wander through the whole world's Coptic sites. In this way, she feels she can travel without leaving home; she chats and exchanges videos with co-religionists in Egypt and abroad. Preparing to make a video with her husband, she has already begun to choose strings of images from TV series or DVDs of films on the life of Christ and famous martyrs.

Whether amateur or professional, the makers of these videos ring the changes on the themes of martyrdom and redemption, following tried and tested symbolic models. From cinema and 'mainstream' TV series, they take narrative and visual schemas that are used worldwide, despite some local variants. Though there is nothing specifically Christian – or Coptic – about the form of these artefacts, the subjects and themes treated confer an undeniably Christian or Egyptian tenor to them.

Without claiming to be exhaustive, let us simply point out two types of narrative, the main characteristics of which appear in almost all these videos. A first type highlights persecution as a distinctive, founding feature of the Coptic community. In these scenarios, the imagery and *mise-en-scène* are akin to low-budget historical epics or other grand-scale 'archaizing' productions: images of Christ on the Cross in 'period' costume follow on from scenes of pitched battles and the commemorative telling of the martyrdom of some famous saint who had fallen into Roman, that is to say – generically and atemporally, and hence essentially – *enemy* hands. Let us also note the crucial influence of the American film *The Passion of the Christ* by Mel Gibson on the representation of Christ's martyrdom in a significant number of these videos, several of them incorporating shots and even sequences wholesale from the film that scandalised Europe.

In a second type of narrative, the individual relation with Christ is foregrounded. It is the event that initiates a radical turn in the life of an individual and signifies redemption. The ways in which Christ and his actions are depicted suggest an erotic dimension that seems at one with the properly physical and individual experience of this turn. The same tendency can be observed in many videos narrating a religious conversion to Christianity as spiritual and corporeal relief after a period of distress, doubt and physical pain. The story of Mary Magdalene, which is capable of representing the remission of sins and figuring desire (though through the Christ story and not a supposedly ideal image of the female body), becomes paradigmatic here. She was the subject of a TV series shown on Coptic satellite channels, many shots from which have been used in videos. In this kind of narration centred on personal redemption, the figure of Christ in period settings and costumes assumes the face of a lover – or the lover's face evokes the features of Christ. Admittedly, the eroticisation of the relationship to God – or to Christ – is a recurrent, longstanding feature of mystical literature. But these videos depict the ordinary individual, who claims neither sainthood nor the status of martyr.

Between the first and second of these narrative types, we can see two different eschatological models. While the community and Christianity have pride of place in the former, the latter fit with the narrative model of individual redemption of the 'born-again' Christians. This latter model betrays an individualisation of religious practices that is attested by other contemporary practices. And yet, the individualisation of religious experiences isn't synonymous with privatisation and doesn't imply a collapse of communal bonds. We are seeing, rather, an uncoupling of individualised religious practices from a community-belonging that defines itself increasingly in ethnic and transnational terms.

Alternative narratives and counter-behaviours

One evening, after an interminable day working at the chemist's in Qasr al-'Aini, Rasha's Protestant colleagues dragged her off to the evangelical church of Qasr al-Dubbara in central Cairo to listen to an American Pentecostal preacher who was visiting Egypt. His sermon was followed by a session of prayers and hymns. The crowd was in full voice and Rasha sang along with them. To her own amazement, she knew these honeyed lyrics by the Lebanese Maronite priest Mansur Labaky or those of the Egyptian Coptic singer Mahir Fayyiz, one of the most famous composers and performers of *taranim*. Her surprise became all the greater when she spotted neighbours of hers in the audience who, from a distance, made a sign to her that she understood only later: 'You go to the Protestants too!'

In these moments of communion, Rasha feels inexpressible joy, her voice mingling with a hundred others who respond to the singer's. She regularly goes to the – Pentecostal – Church of God at Shubra to take part in the meetings presided over by Mahir Fayyiz, whose music attracts Christian youth of all denominations. She has often climbed the Muqattam hill in the ragpickers' district in Cairo to listen to the preachings of Abuna (Father) Sam'an, a charismatic Coptic preacher. Despite the sometimes heterodox nature of the practices at the Muqattam church, Sam'an has managed not to offend either the Coptic Orthodox clerical hierarchy (to which he is answerable) or the local authorities. His presence there and his notoriety are based on his talents as a diplomat. Maintaining numerous contacts in Protestant, Catholic and also media circles, Sam'an has been careful not to upset the local political balances (supporting the official candidate of President Mubarak's National Democratic Party at every legislative election, that party enjoying the approval of the mother Church). This marginal space, which one can only reach on foot, currently siphons off Christians – and some Muslims – from the central districts and even from the wealthier suburbs to attend exorcism sessions and Abuna Sam'an's preaching.

Yet Rasha and her friends have no sense that they are being unfaithful by going there. They assert their attachment to Orthodoxy and their respect for Patriarch Shenouda III, even those of them – a minority – who took part in the revolutionary movement and clashed in public with him over that, for, though the *taranim* are likely to figure as part of explicit projects of protest against clerical authority, they are nonetheless part of Coptic – or, at least, Christian – cultural and religious history. As pre-eminently ambiguous objects, they combine, in various specific ways, with marginal or novel forms of piety, without necessarily deviating from the Orthodox path. Marginal religious practices have historically been integrated into the Church, or tolerated by it.

Indeed, the expression of religious fervour outside of the official places of worship and the frequenting of Protestant churches by Copts are not new phenomena. *Mawalid* (the celebration of the birth of saints), miracles and the cult of saints figure among the 'popular' practices the Church had encouraged under the patriarchate of Shenouda III. The activity of the Protestant missions, particularly notable from the nineteenth century onward, also played a crucial role in the successive transformations of the Coptic Church. Rivalry stimulated the modernisation plans promoted by the secular elites and subsequently by the Coptic clergy. Following a common pattern, the Church borrowed many elements from these competitors that were likely to pull worshippers into their own ambit, particularly in the area of religious education.

However, at present the charismatic and born-again currents have as a rival an institution which, under the reign of Shenouda III, has assumed international stature, is prosperous despite its internal splits and is structured by a hegemonic discourse embodied by the clerical hierarchy. The alternative vision conveyed by these new movements influenced by the charismatic churches seemingly challenges the founding credo and clerical leadership more dangerously than the state-recognised Egyptian protestant churches, with which the Coptic church had established a *modus vivendi* come what may, since the attraction exerted by these more recent currents seems contemporaneous with the increase in Coptic protest actions against patriarchal decisions and the public criticism of patriarch Shenouda III's allegiance to the Mubarak clan. Moreover, it does not simply affect Coptic worshippers, who are often already familiar with excursions into Protestant territory, but the members of the Coptic Orthodox clergy itself.

Many *taranim* – ambivalent objects – are invested with this alternative vision. They connect with the practices of those churches which, whether Coptic or Protestant, welcome the influences of the charismatic and born-again currents and invite Egyptian Christians to a religious experience that transcends the divisions between the Christian Churches. From Shubra to Qasr al-Dubbara, from Abuna Samʿan to the residents of Muqattam, similar narratives circulate, relating the overcoming of sin and the start of a new life following a personal encounter with Christ, an encounter synonymous with spiritual and physical deliverance.

However, the *taranim* lose their ambiguity as soon as they give voice to a project developed in explicit opposition to the Orthodox teaching of a piety guided by the idea of sacrifice, the model of martyrdom and the prospect of a collective redemption in the beyond. Thus Mahir Fayyiz's spiritual, political and aesthetic project calls into question the foundations of clerical theology and power. From his first steps in a musical career characterised by a rejection of the rules of canonical performance to his arrival as a charismatic personality, Fayyiz has connected the musical call for authenticity to the experience of a personal redemption in this life, foregrounding joy and spiritual victory. Drawing on a canonical liturgical corpus for the composition of his songs and sometimes calling for the use of 'authentic' instruments, he has asserted his attachment to a Coptic community anchored in the land of Egypt and has pitted one 'authenticity' against another – that favoured by the Church. He does, however, work in a cross-denominational, if not indeed inter-religious spirit. In this way, Mahir Fayyiz embodies the aspirations of a large part of Egyptian Christian youth, aspirations shared by many of their elders, as is attested by his success and the jubilant atmosphere that characterises the gatherings he presides over. Officiating regularly at the Pentecostal church at Shubra, Mahir Fayyiz is also the lead host on several interdenominational Protestant TV stations, such as SAT-7. Some months after the fall of the Mubarak clan, SAT-7 broadcast the desert retreat organised by Fayyiz which bore the name 'Reconquering/Saving the Earth' (*Da'wa al-fidaiyya li al-ard*). Accompanied by Nigerian and Ghanaian guests from the Global Apostolic and Prophetic Network (an African organisation with a mission to establish the presence of God in all spheres of society), Mahir Fayyiz and a group of several hundred Copts and Protestants gathered from 27 to 30 June 2011 for sessions of prayer, preaching and *taranim*. The fervour expressed during that event was stoked by the disappointment that ensued in the immediate aftermath of the beginnings of a revolution which, by publicly revealing the diversity of views and the divisions within Egyptian society, had contributed to a renewal of violence against Christians. While promoting individual and citizen engagement for national collective well-being, Fayyiz's project does not lay down any particular *political* posture, at least not in the narrow sense of the term. It brings an ethical vision into play, along with individualised spiritual practices.

Towards the integration of counter-behaviours and the charismatisation of the Coptic Church?

The strength of the Coptic Orthodox Church probably lies in its ability to absorb the diversity of practices and views, whether heteronomous or produced by its own expansion. The omnipresence of a host of charismatic preachers on the satellite channels and websites and in the ranks of the Coptic clergy, together with the mass marketing within the churches of collections of *taranim* and CDs and DVDs of their performance, suggest that the institution de facto recognises the existence of these aspirations on behalf of its followers, aspirations which, however deviant they may be, nonetheless stoke a sense of communal belonging.

It is too soon to say whether these leisure practices, expressive of new religiosities, will stimulate the large-scale institutional and ideological reform that a number of Coptic public figures are calling for. Although the new Patriarch, Tawadros II, enthroned in November 2012 after the death of Shenouda III, had initially given some signs of ecumenical openness, he has not undertaken the necessary overhaul of the clerical institution that would make it both inclusive of youth and the place for the plurality of Coptic voices to express themselves and engage in discussion and polemic.

Notes

1 Conversations with Séverine Gabry-Thienpont and Carolyn Ramzy have provided invaluable assistance in understanding this musical genre, and I thank them for their generosity.
2 Egypt's population is around 7 per cent Christian, more than 90 per cent of whom are affiliated to the Coptic Orthodox Church. Founded in the first century of the Christian era, that Church is independent and is led by a patriarch, appointed by drawing of lots from among three candidates selected by an electoral college. There are a host of other Catholic Christian denominations, following the Latin or Orthodox rite, and dozens of Protestant Churches. Some of these are the Egyptian offshoots of British – and later American – missionary activity and are recognised by the Egyptian state. In the last twenty years, various charismatic currents (not to speak of other religious movements, such as the Mormons or Jehovah's Witnesses) have grown in influence and visibility in Christian circles.

References

Armanios, Febe, 'The Coptic Charismatic Renewal in Egypt: Historical Roots and Recent Developments', Presentation given at the International Association of Coptic Studies Quadrennial Congress, Rome, 15–22 September 2012.
Du Roy, Gaëtan, 'Abûnâ Sam'ân and the "Evangelical Trend" within the Coptic Church', in Nelly Van Doorn-Harder, ed., *Reconsidering Coptic Studies* (Proceedings of the Conference *The Future of Coptic Studies: Theories, Methods, Topics*), Wake Forest University, Winston-Salem, 2015.
Du Roy, Gaëtan and Jamie Furniss, 'Sœur Emmanuelle et les chiffonniers. Partage de vie et développement, 1971–1982', in Caroline Sappia and Olivier Servais, eds, *Mission et engagement politique après 1945*, Karthala, Paris, 2010.
Gabry, Séverine, 'Processus et enjeux de la patrimonialisation de la musique copte', in Omnia Aboukorah and Jean-Gabriel Leturcq, eds, *Pratiques du Patrimoine en Égypte et au Soudan. Égypte/Monde arabe*, 3e série, 5–6, CEDEJ, Le Caire, 2009, pp. 132–153.

Taranim and videos

Guirguis, Laure, *Copts and the Security State: Violence, Coercion, and Sectarianism in Contemporary Egypt*, Stanford University Press, Stanford, CA, 2016.

Ibrahim, Vivian, *The Copts of Egypt. The Challenges of Modernisation and Identity*, I.B. Tauris, London, 2010.

Mayeur-Jaouen, Catherine, *Pèlerinages d'Égypte. Histoire de la piété copte et musulmane xve–xxe siècles*, Éditions de l'EHESS, Paris, 2005.

Ramzy, Carolyn, 'Repossessing the Land: Maher Fayez Negotiates Coptic Citizenry Through Charismatic Encounters and Songs', Paper given at the Tenth International Congress of Coptic Studies, Rome, September 2012.

19

'My identity is becoming clear like the sun'

Theatre in the Shiite schools of Lebanon

Catherine Le Thomas

The scene takes place in a classroom, where a teacher and three young girls, a veiled teenager and two much younger girls, are standing. The teacher accuses the fourteen-year-old girl of breaking the rules by wearing a hijab, but she refuses to take it off, claiming it is impossible for her to do so. The teacher then summons the school's 'higher court', 'in the name of secularism [*'almaniyya*] and democracy, freedom and justice'. Some adults arrive, handcuff the girl and place her behind bars in a courtroom with a scene that has been set in the meantime (with French flags, scales symbolising justice, the judge behind his bench and lawyers). The judge then reads to the girl, Zahra, the charge against her, namely an infraction 'of freedom and human rights'. The school's lawyer then begins his plea:

> Affiliation with the Muslim religion is antithetical to a secular system … Zahra Husayn is accused of a terrorist crime; she is a threat to civilization … Where is her hair? She is undoubtedly hiding a weapon underneath it. She is a symbol of terrorism. She must be expelled from school, and from any school.

This has not taken place in a real classroom but during a play performed by budding actors in a Shiite school in the al-Mustapha school network in the southern suburbs of Beirut. The establishment belongs to a cluster of institutions close to Hezbollah, the main Lebanese Shiite party. Written in 2004, the play satirises a law prohibiting wearing conspicuous religious symbols in public schools adopted in France in March of that year.

More than the message suggested, it is the context in which it is formulated that is interesting to observe. Over the past forty years, the Lebanese Shiite community has become politically structured, that is, a Shiite leadership and political institutions have been established alongside those of the other recognised

'My identity is becoming clear like the sun'

denominations in the country (Sunnis, Alawis, Maronites, Copts, Druze, etc.). It is in this context that social institutions and 'Shiite' schools have developed. Through them, the main partisan organisations in the community, Hezbollah and Amal, offer young Lebanese Shiites a wide range of leisure activities in scout camps (vacation camps focusing on nature and religious activities) as well as schools (Koran clubs, sports clubs, cultural or religious outings). Among these activities, theatre occupies a prominent place in schools from kindergarten to the baccalaureate. It is situated at the crossroads of religious, militant and community engagement, perceived by its promoters as a tool for socialisation and training as much – and perhaps even more than – as a means of creativity and expression.

'Hezbollah theatre'

The variety of theatre clubs in Shiite schools has resulted in a plurality of uses, sometimes serving divergent objectives. In schools associated with Hezbollah, whose three main networks (al-Mahdi, al-Imdad and al-Mustapha) contain about 25,000 students, the staging and dramatisation inherent in theatre are part of the growing visibility of Shiite religiosity in the public arena and its ideologisation since the 1980s. Theatre has become one of the key methods for socialising youth, permitted and even encouraged by religion as conceived by clerics close to Hezbollah. It plays an important part in activities favoured by young people (as recreational and educational extracurricular activities appear to be just as important as the classes themselves) and is part of a strategy thought out at the level of the party organisation. This is notably the case within the Association for Islamic Religious Education (*Jama`iyya al-ta`lim al-dini al-islami*, or JTDI), one of the main educational organisations linked to the party, which manages the network of al-Mustapha schools as well as the religious courses given in most Lebanese schools for young Shiites. Its informal leader and former president is none other than Naim Qasem, the number two man at Hezbollah.

Our focus here is on the theatrical practices of al-Mustapha schools, developed from the 1980s onwards in the suburbs of Beirut, in Southern Lebanon and in the Bekaa region, three predominantly Shiite but socially heterogeneous regions. They teach about 8,000 students in their six establishments and cater to a rather well-to-do clientele able to pay high tuition fees. The schools have a certain theatrical know-how, fostered by significant past experience. As such, they highlight the existence of 'Hezbollah theatre', which is itself evolving and is heir to an older Shiite religious theatre tradition.

The students attend as spectators or actively participate in various plays, the theme of which is often chosen according to current religious or political events, and which are performed on the major dates of the religious calendar or during ceremonies held throughout the school year. Although the teenagers rarely participate in writing the plays in which they perform, they may influence the staging during rehearsals, which take place over a period of about a month, in intensive sessions nearly every day. Actors for the troupe are usually recruited from the pool of students in each school's drama club. Some of the young adults may be employees of the school, others may be theatre students or even professional actors. Many of the plays feature multiple generations, although children and teens predominate. Friends and family are the main audience for the plays, but they may also be broadcast by the Hezbollah movement's media, notably the television channel al-Manar (schools in the competing, more secularised Shiite movement, Amal, are followed by the rival channel NBN).

Theatre is generally practised at the school level. While some JTDI schools educate boys and girls together in rural areas, the association runs enough schools in the Beirut area to separate the sexes. For instance, the al-Batul school in the al-Mustapha network, in the southern suburbs of Beirut, only teaches girls. About sixty of them of various ages take part in the local theatre club for two hours a week. These girls are joined by other students or actors from outside the school who participate more occasionally for ceremonies and special occasions.

Preparations for the big shows require a certain amount of organisation since the sound is recorded beforehand in a studio, and the actors do playback during performances. To explain their choice, supervisors point out the demands of sound and mastering the text, clearly a priority over spontaneity. Songs may also be composed to support the play's message. Overall, the al-Mustapha school plays are characterised by a high technical level, as well as accomplished sets and acting. The performances also reflect the material resources allocated to this pastime preferred by the party, since the average budget for a play ranges from 8,000 to 10,000 dollars.

There are about five people, mostly young adults, who write plays for al-Mustapha students on a regular basis. Among them is Hussein, a twenty-five-year-old Arabic teacher at JTDI, who also writes political comedies and sketches for television channels such as al-Manar and other more secular channels. Hussein has also written plays for the 'activities' section linked to Hezbollah's

'My identity is becoming clear like the sun'

youth branch, in which students close to the party perform. He likes to mix social criticism and political comedy and writes few works in the strictly religious arena. For example, he refrained from writing for Ashura, the commemoration of the martyrdom of Husayn, grandson of the Prophet, in Karbala, a classic theme of Shiite theatre that forbids satire. The plays he creates for the JTDI are nonetheless proofread by a cleric (sheikh) affiliated with the association, who checks their religious content and political and social stances for orthodoxy. The al-Manar channel subsequently broadcasts the plays it endorses, either in part or in their entirety. Majida, a colleague of Hussein's in her thirties, a graduate of religious studies and coordinator of artistic activities at al-Batul School, also writes for various institutions. In all, she has written about thirty plays on social and religious themes, including short plays for al-Manar. Majida advocates 'total theatre' (*masrah jamali*). In the Hezbollah movement, theatre is meant to be all-encompassing, as much in style and stage techniques as in subject matter. This kind of theatre respects neither unity of time nor of place, playing on the contrary on the back-and-forth movement and on analogies. It frequently mixes archival images on screen with the acting, and often interposes dialogued and sung parts. A certain tension exists, however, between the authors who favour satire and distraction, and sometimes laughs, and those who prefer to instruct and edify in a more serious fashion, more suited to religious commemorations. These inclinations themselves reflect the expectations and contradictions of audiences with varying degrees of piety.

From commemoration to mobilisation

Among the most common religious plays performed in schools is the ritual theatre related to Ashura, a Shiite tradition imported from Iran in the late nineteenth century and transposed here in a school setting. Religious theatre represents a kind of leisure activity rooted in older practices in Shiite villages. It expresses a shared culture while also informing it and putting it on stage and in words. As in most religious plays of the Hezbollah movement, it is not only a matter of evoking the battle of Karbala in 680, in which Imam Husayn perished, but of drawing an explicit analogy between past and present with pedagogical value. By taking the audience back to the founding moment of the community, the plays revive the group's religious identity in order to mobilise it. Most of the Ashura plays for children or teenagers also play on this relationship between the present and the past, to disseminate the meaning that Hezbollah attributes to

Imam Husayn's martyrdom. The plays often rely on an analogical motivation linked to a character in the drama, such as Husayn's daughter Ruqeyya, thereby aiming to create an emotional identification and a certain closeness between the young actors and the audience. It is less a matter of entertainment here than of learning and feeling.

For the plays' creators and actors, Ashura is intended to be more than a mere commemoration; it is pedagogy by example, concrete instruction about the idea of 'Islamic resistance' (*al-muqawama al-islamiyya*) as conceived by Hezbollah directed against Israel and placed under the auspices of Husayn. As a dramatic genre, it expresses a political, religious and military cause rooted in the experience of Lebanese Shiites, whose recent dynamics it reflects and underlines. This type of theatre does not appear to be specific to schools or to troupes composed of teenagers. It is widespread in several villages in the south. The politicisation of Shiite theatre, whether it is linked to Ashura, to the *taklif* ceremony (when nine-year-old girls begin wearing the hijab and attain the age of responsibility) or to an episode from the Koran, has led to a certain desacralisation of the subject matter, and even to its relative secularisation. Through these modifications, the religious episodes staged have indeed adapted to twenty-first-century audiences and their concerns in this life.

Other plays may be staged to celebrate a secular event rather than to commemorate a religious rite. Most of them, however, retain a more or less direct religious connection, even if at times it only serves as a medium for evoking social or political issues. A certain outspokenness may then be in the air. The play *Fil al-Malik* ('The King's Elephant'), performed in May 2006 for the inauguration of a theatre at the al-Mustapha school in Haret Hreik in the southern suburbs of Beirut, alludes to Sura 105 of the Koran, *al-Fil* (the elephant), evoking the fate reserved for the Abyssinians who attacked Mecca by unleashing a huge elephant on the city. A 'drama à clé', it also parodies the Lebanese political scene, mocking those who fear the king and his elephant, transparent symbols of the United States and Israel. After dramatising the villagers' disputes about how to deal with the elephant, news from the al-Manar channel is projected onto a screen. A larger-than-life journalist informs the audience that the resistance has averted the elephant peril; he follows up with other real-fake economic news, all favourable to Arab countries and unfavourable to certain Western powers, then announces 'the imminent liberation of Jerusalem by Islamic and Arab armies'. This burlesque news bulletin presented by a teenager from the school was filmed expressly in the Hezbollah TV news studio, which even seems to have trained the young man for the event. In this instance, school theatre has openly used party media outlets, co-opting them in a rather fantastical manner. This ironic nod at geopolitical power struggles clearly pleases the audience, which applauds wildly.

Some of the plays composed for JTDI students have even reached beyond the walls of the school to be performed for the entire community. A play entitled *Raji'in* ('They're Coming Back') was first staged in April 2007 in an al-Mustapha school. Depicting the war between Hezbollah and the Israeli army in July–August 2006, it became a success well beyond the school. This led to a tour of several months in about fifty Lebanese cities and villages in regions with a Shiite majority. The troupe was composed mainly of teenagers from al-Mustapha secondary schools. The different generations were won over by this school drama because it gave meaning to a recent and potentially traumatic experience, replaying it in the manner of a dramatic comedy and producing a kind of cathartic effect. Many other plays for young people have been staged in praise of Islamic resistance fighters, especially in the months following the 2006 war. Over and above their variety, they often display a cult of South Lebanon, of the martyrs killed in clashes with Israel and of Hezbollah leader Hassan Nasrallah. This form of theatre corresponds to a specific universe of meaning with its own codes, heroes and places of memory. As a result, it offers an alternative culture to that of other Lebanese groups, conveying a narrative centred on religious, militant and combat engagement.

Channelling individual aspirations

For the teenagers, being involved in theatre is as much about conforming to the group and its ethics as opposing the values of Hezbollah's adversaries. From their viewpoint, theatre can be seen as a space for self-realisation through integration into a political community. In the eyes of those in charge, it is above all a means of disciplining and controlling individuals within a collective dynamic. While the productions speak of individuals and their suffering, they encourage conformity more than questioning; if they evoke emancipation, it is far more collective than individual. This very well-rounded and comprehensive socialisation scheme relies on the complementarity of practices, as Naim Qasem underlined during a speech at a Mustapha school in 2006:

> If we provide our young people with playgrounds, theatres, friends, an Islamic school and ceremonies for Ashura and the month of Ramadan, an atmosphere

of resistance … Something remains from that atmosphere; the young people get something from it.

Furthermore, the values advocated by the JTDI prove to be opposed to the more secularised or politically antagonistic norms of other Lebanese denominational groups, which are themselves engaged in a dynamic of supervising their youth, as shown by the variety of denominational scouting and leisure groups.

Hezbollah movement playwrights strive to integrate young people's concerns into their plots, being aware of the tensions between integration into the group and individual aspirations, fostered by a certain prevailing secular culture that is more hedonistic and individualistic. Plays about the hijab, the behaviour of young girls and the place of women have crystallised these questions and addressed certain latent tensions within Shiite youth in an attempt to defuse them. The fact that many little girls are reluctant to wear the hijab and that many young girls are tempted to remove it is the subject of many plays performed at girls' schools.

The play *Huwiyya* ('Identity'), written by Majida and performed in 2008 in the al-Mustapha schools, explicitly evokes these tensions. It condemns the corrupt 'modern' hijab, contrasting it with the 'real' hijab, which includes not only the scarf but also a way of dressing, a kind of behaviour and values. On stage, some people have lost their identity cards. The point of this metaphor is to show that some young girls no longer know where they stand, between a globalised or 'Americanised' culture and values perceived as more specific to the Arab-Muslim world. The play criticises the behaviour of young girls who combine 'Western' values and hijab. The moral of the play asserts that the 'real' hijab is none other than a marker of identity, a philosophy of life linked to resistance, which makes it strong and conquering: 'my identity is becoming clear as the sun', proclaims an actress. To contrast the two kinds of hijab, the actors unravel at the same time a hijab decorated with an American flag and dollars, and another one representing Fatima, daughter of the prophet and wife of Ali, whom the Shiites consider their first imam. Religious morality and social propriety once again join political mobilisation in the name of the struggle 'for resistance and against imperialism'. *Huwiyya* was performed by nine-year-old girls and sixteen- and seventeen-year-old teenagers from high school; a professional actor was also recruited to play the role of a young man. However, the playwright points out the problem with the all-girl cast at al-Batul School. The male roles are played by actresses with beards or disguises (wearing a hijab), or by actors from outside the school. Since the al-Batul school does not teach the younger grades, there are no little boys who could act, nor hijab-free little girls who could perform various dances and freestyle movements, which are prohibited beyond the age of nine. Even if she plays along, Majida regrets this constraint which, although celebrated in the plays, limits staging options at the al-Batul girls' school.

From the models to their appropriation: continuity or generation gap?

Theatrical culture is part of the interface of competing models of society offered to the Shiite community and to Lebanese youth, as a favoured mode of artistic expression and an instrument of socialisation. Whatever its preferred tone – humour, pathos or tragedy – theatre seems most often rooted in the social and the contemporary, either directly or through historical analogy. In the case of JTDI-supported plays, this reflects a certain permeability of the boundaries between leisure, school, religious practices and activism. These leisure activities are (relatively) recent, but they promote conformity and communal exclusivity by being imposed from above as the dominant norm on the community level.

However, there is still a lot of crossover and borrowing between the main community organisations, if only through the work of youth and adults from different community institutions. Some smaller Shiite networks also offer their own theatrical style, sometimes stemming from the larger organisations, but often leaving young people more room for expression. In this regard, it is important to be aware of the potential gap between the models proposed and their reception by adolescents. The latter, who represent a 'second Hezbollah generation' born and raised in contact with the many institutions run or sponsored by the party, appear to be in step with its political options, but they may want to create their own culture in the future at odds with the militant patterns passed on, among others, through the school and extracurricular world. The relatively limited and restrictive nature of the entertainment offered in party circles seems to argue for such a development. Certain plays try to incorporate some of the more predominant codes of communication and consumption among Lebanese youth, to endorse or condemn them, in any case to harness them. Whether or not they take on the models proposed within the institutions, the youths from these schools recompose their signifiers and insert them into their own generational symbolic representations (fashions, musical tastes, sports or artistic references), which precludes considering these models in a fixed or unequivocal manner, and instead considers them through their interactions with other types of practices and cultural codes.

References

Bashshur, Munir, 'The Role of Education: A Mirror of a Fractured National Image', in Halim Barakat, ed., *Toward a Viable Lebanon*, Croom Helm, London, 1988, pp. 42–67.

Deeb, Lara, *An Enchanted Modern. Gender and Public Piety in Shi'i Lebanon*, Princeton University Press, Princeton, NJ, 2006.

Le Thomas, Catherine, *Les écoles chiites au Liban. Construction communautaire et mobilisation politique*, Presses de l'Ifpo/Karthala, Beirut/Paris, 2012.

Mervin, Sabrina, 'Le théâtre chiite au Liban, entre rituel et spectacle', in Nicolas Puig and Franck Mermier, eds, *Itinéraires esthétiques et scènes culturelles au Proche-Orient*, Presses de l'Ifpo, Beirut, 2007, pp. 57–75.

Shaery-Eisenlohr, Roschanack, *Shiite Lebanon. Transnational Religion and the Making of National Identities*, Columbia University Press, New York, 2008.

Part III
Constructing oneself

Introduction

Constructing oneself

Laurent Bonnefoy and Myriam Catusse

The weight of the past and inherited identities is not the only factor of creativity as the previous texts might suggest. Tensions are clearly manifested between individual aspirations and the group, but also between the pursuit of privacy and the need to express one's personality on the one hand and strong social constraints on the other. In this sense, it would be overly simplistic to observe leisure activities only through the prism of the group phenomena and mass cultures in which they are involved.

The following texts examine mechanisms of self-construction in the face of a variety of powerful constraints, whether familial and personal or political, economic and social. Although Arab societies do not appear to be specific in this regard, the third part of the book nevertheless highlights the difficulty of 'building the self', or more precisely the self-sufficient individual, in one's spare time in societies that remain marked by powerful social determinism, even though they are constantly changing. For that matter, nothing indicates that the years since the authors wrote these chapters have really changed the way social, state and family norms are exercised. The observations begin with a text underlining the frequent deficiency in providing a room of one's own, which, as various studies in Europe and in literature have shown, prefigures the appropriation of a space of their own by teenagers and becomes the quintessential place of distancing from the family within the home itself.[1]

This family unit, in the process of being recomposed in the Arab world where the nuclear family is still far from the norm, appears to be the favoured framework for learning codes and ways of being, as we saw previously. For some, it has turned into an alienating curse where imposed schedules, lack of privacy, violence, heavy secrets and the presence of a male third party for women continue to govern their leisure time and restrict the individual's ability to develop, not to mention the legal constraints imposed, in Saudi Arabia for instance, which up until 2019, prevented women (including the wealthiest) from travelling without permission from their male guardian.

Through a process of successive detachment from the group, self-development may involve an arduous struggle, literally for those who take up arms in the numerous conflicts that divide contemporary Arab societies, or in a more metaphorical way for those who face – sometimes physically – the kind of harassment to which many young women are subjected in large cities in the Arab world.

The awakening of the individual at the end of childhood and the affirmation of self-sufficient personalities on the way to becoming adults can be interpreted in the light of several practices analysed by the authors of this part. There are signs of a process of individualisation of practices, despite social obligations: for instance, the desire to have 'a room of one's own' in Egypt, the United Arab Emirates and Algeria; the desire expressed by some young girls in Cairo to become socially emancipated and to acquire the power to defend themselves physically in combat classes; or the tendency among young Yemenis to chew qat alone, although this activity is highly social and collective. Nevertheless, other chapters show through various activities how heavy the social constraints are: tourism abroad for young people from the wealthy Gulf monarchies, music in an Algerian organisation, the urban rambles of young Palestinians from the camps in Lebanon, the festive evenings of young people in Amman. Because they reveal internalised boundaries, the most harmless acts – singing, choosing a vacation spot, sitting on a café terrace – reveal the difficulty of freeing oneself from assigned identities and collective norms.

Some young people experience their 'free time', which is also an 'idle' time, as an at times insurmountable ordeal. Rather than being a period of building, youth is then seen as a time when one wastes away. Moreover, the theme of suicide is regularly associated with adolescence and youth. We may recall, in December 2010, Mohammed Bouazizi's desperate act of self-immolation in Sidi Bouzid, Tunisia, which, through a butterfly effect, sparked uprisings in the region. Far from being an isolated act, this suicide reveals on the contrary a proven phenomenon that is socially taboo, even religiously prohibited, and difficult to measure, but telling as to the troubles caused by the pivotal period of youth. Young people in the Arab world are no exception, as illustrated by the chapter analysing the suicide of a man from Kabylia as much as the terrible fate of LGBT activist from Egypt, Sarah Hegazi, who killed herself in 2020.

In the face of group constraints during this intermediary phase between childhood and the adult world, leisure time may in the end serve as an escape,

Introduction

a mechanism of individualisation and differentiation. In an increasingly urbanised context, where the virtual worlds of the Web keep expanding, the weakening of the fabric of support often plays an ambivalent role, fostering both destructive anomie and liberating emancipation. Such is the case for the powerfully told story of the unfortunate journey that some Moroccan women experience, led without quite realising it from rebellious and sexy teenage 'thrills' into a spiral of prostitution.

Note

1 Philippe Ariès and Georges Duby, ed., *Histoire de la vie privée. Tome IV. De la Révolution à la Grande Guerre*, Le Seuil, Paris, 2000.

20

'A room of one's own'

Young people in search of privacy

Anne-Marie Filaire

I am visiting Hadil, a young filmmaker in her thirties, at her home in Alexandria to photograph her bedroom. This meeting is part of a large-scale art project conducted over several years in the Arab world.

Hadil lives in her mother's house in the Ibrahimiyya district. We spend a long time talking on the balcony in the evening, looking out over an alleyway to a run-down building opposite, with a courtyard full of rubbish.

Her bedroom has a double bed; a wedding photo of her sister and brother-in-law hangs on the wall. Portrait shots of her mother when she was young (at the time of Nasser, after another revolution), with her hair uncovered (she now wears a veil), have been slid under the glass top of the desk, which is cluttered with a radio, medicines and an iron.

Hadil tells me that she is not sure if she will sleep here tonight because she has another room in El Mansheya and a third at her sister's house, near the port, as well as a studio flat down on the corniche near the Sporting Club. This nomadic lifestyle is not merely a sign of her family's wealth but offers a snapshot of the still uncertain status of having one's own bedroom in the Arab world.

Hadil has several rooms, but she says she is from nowhere because the rooms and beds described as 'hers' do not fully belong to her. Her real room is her body, which she takes with her.

It is common in Egypt, and elsewhere in the Arab world, to share a room. Girls share rooms with a sister or their grandmother, but sometimes also with their brothers, even during adolescence. The 'bedroom' (*bit*, from the Maghrebi Arabic, *bayt*, meaning 'house', and *ghurfa*, elsewhere) can also be just a room, the lounge, for example, in which when evening comes everyone lays down a mattress to sleep on, a room that is shared and used simply for rest. Having 'a room of one's own' is therefore quite unusual – partly because of a lack of space, especially in the cities, but also because the concept of private space for children and adolescents, or of a 'bedroom culture', both considered important steps towards gaining independence in much of the Western world, is not always seen as appropriate, or even recognised.

It is only with marriage that the bedroom becomes completely acceptable, and young men and women gain a degree of privacy and the opportunity to give their rooms a personal touch, decorate them and make them their own. Another young woman I went to see is Reham, a twenty-year-old student and committed feminist. She lives in Moharram Bek, a working-class district of Alexandria, with her family, who are originally from Upper Egypt. Reham and her younger sister Rana share a room. While we are chatting, we hear shouting outside and go onto the balcony to see what is happening. The street below is a happy hubbub of activity: preparations for a wedding are underway. A procession of furniture for the bride and groom passes beneath the windows. Their future bedroom bursts into the public space, on display for the whole neighbourhood, like a trophy.

The dynamics of carving out a private space before a young person's marriage are similar all over the Arab world. The degree of privacy, however, often depends on the wealth of the family. Sarah, a seventeen-year-old from Alexandria, who has travelled with her family, describes how adolescents personalise their space (and create a distance from their families). Her bedroom is incredibly untidy, with clothes and stuffed animals piled up everywhere. She shares it with four dogs, including two huge mastiffs standing guard. Sarah is proud of it and likes to provoke; she always says what she thinks and, she adds, kisses her male friends in the street. She lives alone with her mother, while her father lives in Cairo. She sees her room as her own space.

Yet the obstacles preventing young adults from creating their own private sphere are not merely financial. In 2007, I went to the United Arab Emirates, one of the richest countries in the world, to photograph the rooms of teenage girls. Despite having a permit from the Ministry of Culture and Knowledge Development, I faced some difficulties. Although the young Emirati girls I met agreed to have their rooms photographed, their parents were extremely reluctant, regardless of the age of their daughter or their social class.

Access to the girls' residence at the University of Sharjah allowed me to bypass families to gain entry to the private space I was looking for. The students, aged between fifteen and twenty-two, some of them married, were mostly from Saudi Arabia and the UAE, as well as from Qatar, Kuwait, Oman, Yemen, Chad, Palestine and Turkey. Their rooms in the residence were completely impersonal. Here, too, private space was constrained. Images in the rooms were

Constructing oneself

prohibited and adherence to this rule was strictly monitored: no posters of singers, no family photographs, nothing that might allow the students to express themselves. It was only on the outside of the doors that students could add a personal touch, but the personalisation of this space was merely a pretence. Flags and portraits of the emir, king or sultan of their home country, impersonal statements of allegiance and references to the Quran or other holy scriptures dominated. One student, no doubt braving certain prohibitions, issued a warning to the residence's staff: 'Don't come into my room. Tidying is pointless, and if something goes missing you'll be responsible.' Among these dozens of doors, there was just one that had a poster representing a female: a doll, a childlike image of a body before it takes on sexual characteristics.

The photographs of the student rooms in Sharjah were to be exhibited in Gaza in 2010. When the Israeli authorities refused to let me accompany the group, I decided to transform the exhibition into a workshop with teenage girls at the Al Qattan Child Centre in Gaza, to whom I handed over my work. Each girl, once told about the location and nature of my images, could then give free rein to her imagination by painting on the photos. Compared to the sparseness of the Emirati doors, a very different relationship with the body and femininity revealed itself in the Gaza paintings. Collages of pop stars, bright colours and expressive political messages signalled the dynamism and creativity of this society. In a context that was said to be controlled by the conservative ideology of Hamas, they displayed an astonishing capacity to express intimate feelings and appropriate a space despite the confinement that the Israeli blockade imposes on them.

When I continued my photographic project in Algeria in 2012, I rarely managed to get past the thresholds of apartments or buildings. The reinforced doors testified to an even stronger confinement which can be explained, among other things, by the years of civil war during the 1990s. Here, the privacy that my work was trying to show evaded me more than anywhere else.

In the Arab world, the 'right' to privacy within the home faces obstacles that are economic and political, handed down by tradition and linked to the history of each society. Nevertheless, teenagers all over the Arab world now seem to be creating their own private space. Of course, this still involves access to a 'room of one's own', full of symbolic meanings and promises of personalisation, but today young people's private sphere is more likely to be virtual. Privacy has shifted from the bedroom to the Internet. A teenager's home, life and intimate thoughts are all contained in their camera, mobile phone and computer – safely hidden behind a password.

References

Beaugrand, Claire, 'Sociabilités féminines en évolution: Les étudiantes omanaises à l'Université de Koweït', *Maghreb-Machrek*, 179, 2004: pp. 63–77.

Besse, Jean-Marc, 'Les marques du territoire', in Anne-Marie Filaire, ed., *Enfermement*, Tarabuste, Argenton-sur-Creuse, 2006.

Filaire, Anne-Marie, 'Chambres à part', in Anne-Marie Filaire, *Zone de sécurité temporaire*, Éditions Textuel/Mucem, Paris and Marseille, 2017.

Filaire, Anne-Marie, *Enfermement* (photographic film), 2007.

Filaire, Anne-Marie, 'Sanaa, 20 juillet 2005, une journée sans image', France Culture, *ACR*, 2006.

Glevarec, Hervé, *La culture de la chambre: Préadolescence et culture contemporaine dans l'espace familial*, Documentation française, Paris, 2009.

Woolf, Virginia, *A Room of One's Own*, Penguin, London, 2002.

21

A different way of being a young woman?

Self-defence in Cairo

Perrine Lachenal

A message is pinned to the door of a room: 'Self-defence for women, every Tuesday, 7:30 p.m.' Right now the room is empty; nobody has arrived yet. Strip lights flicker into life, bathing the space in a cold, white light. The floor is covered with slightly battered floorboards, the walls are white apart from one that is covered in mirrors. There is a piano in one corner; in another, chairs are piled up against the wall. An unpleasant smell lingers in the air, probably sweat. There are no windows; the only fresh air comes from the two air conditioners on the wall. The roar and rumble of Cairo's hellish traffic are impossible to ignore. And since the cultural centre of which it is a part was built right underneath the 15 May Bridge which straddles the Nile, the cars' vibrations can be felt, too. Time passes. The young women start arriving for the self-defence class, along with their teacher. Then someone sticks a notice on the door, in English and Arabic: 'Women only! *'al-saydat faqat'*.

Every Tuesday evening, the El Sawy Culture Wheel, a famous cultural centre in the Zamalek district of western Cairo, offers self-defence classes exclusively for young women. I have come as an observer to carry out fieldwork that will examine certain dynamics that are prevalent in Egyptian society today. What interests me is the context that has enabled this practice in Egypt and in this particular cultural centre and made it visible. Learning to defend themselves helps young women to formulate new ways of 'being a girl' that challenge conventional models of femininity. By listening to these young women who have come here to learn how to fight, or rather to fight back, I will explore what learning these combat skills means to them.

A different way of being a young woman?

A recent social practice

One day in 2011, a number of events and circumstances came together to make it possible for 'Women's self-defence' to appear on the programme of the Culture Wheel.

Sexual harassment

The first self-defence classes for women took place in Cairo in the 2000s and were confined largely to affluent areas. They were offered by martial arts and combat sports instructors – mostly men – who had spotted a new demand from women. Some NGOs involved in combatting violence against women also started organising one-day events to raise awareness, which included demonstrations of self-defence techniques. The number of courses on offer has increased steadily since then, but accurate data are not available since anyone can use the 'self-defence' label, which is not regulated by any institution or federation. Some courses are advertised on the Internet or in the press, but often women find out about classes through word of mouth or just by chance. Although the number of available courses is uncertain, the subject attracts more and more attention and is widely covered in the national or international press: there are endless reports, articles and interviews about self-defence training, often describing it as an unusual but sensible way for women to deal with sexual harassment.

The burning issue for women in the 2000s, which led to the development of women's self-defence in Egypt, was sexual harassment. In 2006, during the celebration of Eid al-Fitr, the holiday marking the end of Ramadan, men filling a whole street suddenly started assaulting the women present, attempting to grope them and pull off their veils. The scene was filmed, and the blogosphere took up the cause and sparked a debate. A nationwide inquiry was held to collect data. The results are indisputable: Egypt is 'sick', afflicted by the 'scourge' of *'tahrush al-jansi'*, 'sexual harassment'. Since then this term has been used more and more frequently by NGOs and in political, religious and media discourse at the local and international level. Projects targeting sexual harassment have multiplied in Cairo in recent years, ranging from attempts to bring in new legislation to helplines and debates. They aim to put these issues out in the open and encourage victims to speak out. In this context, self-defence classes seem to be a possible solution to mobilising – in the true sense of the term – women in the face of this 'scourge'.

Although the practice of women's self-defence immediately raises the issue of the relationship between the sexes, it is also important to look at the social context. The prices of classes and the neighbourhoods where they are held are good indicators: although there are a few initiatives planned in some working-class districts, self-defence courses are currently the preserve of young women from the middle and upper classes.

Gender boundaries, class boundaries

The El Sawy Culture Wheel is renowned for a wide range of events (theatre, music, workshops, festivals), all kinds of activities and the social space it offers to the young men and women who visit (including a café on the banks of the Nile with Internet access). It was created in 2003 by an Egyptian businessman and culture enthusiast, who still manages and finances it. Although it is located at the border of the affluent Zamalek neighbourhood, it is committed to making culture accessible to everyone and welcomes visitors from every class and background – admission prices to all the events and activities are kept very low. While encouraging certain kinds of 'alternative' practice (pro-revolution performances, metal concerts, etc.), the centre is also well regarded in some conservative circles, partly thanks to the ban on smoking and drinking and the tacit monitoring of relationships between young men and women. This reputation for 'moral standards' is probably one significant reason for the centre's popularity with young women. The self-defence class is not the only gender-segregated activity offered by the Culture Wheel. There are some women-only yoga classes and discussion groups as well.

Women's self-defence classes were first offered at the Culture Wheel in 2003, but despite their success, they also received a lot of criticism, as the teacher who led that class explained to me. She was told that it was simply not acceptable to encourage women to be 'violent'. In 2010, self-defence classes for women were offered again, and this time, because the debate about sexual harassment had become a public issue, they were met with more enthusiasm. The Culture Wheel now offers blocks of four ninety-minute sessions led by a woman called Anna. Very few women's self-defence courses in Cairo are taught by women, and this is in fact the only regular one for which this is the case. It is probably no coincidence that Anna is not Egyptian, but German. Aged thirty-two, she has lived in Cairo for six years and works as a foreign language teacher. Although

A different way of being a young woman?

she describes herself as a 'radical feminist', it was pure chance that led to her teaching women's self-defence, as she explains:

> It was in 2007, when everyone was talking about harassment. A lot of events were organised in Cairo including one at an organisation that I knew well. They were looking for someone to do a demonstration of self-defence for women. As I had done a bit of martial arts in Germany, I volunteered. It was the first time in my life, I had never thought about doing it before!

Following her intuition, Anna then put together a programme that she proposed to the Culture Wheel. The groups she teaches vary in size, from five to fifteen women, with ages ranging from eighteen to thirty; all the participants are, or were, in higher education, and nearly all of them are veiled. Anna gives the classes mostly in Arabic, apart from the odd moment when she speaks English.

Examining a social practice in a particular place involves 'big' and 'small' stories. The Egyptian revolution of 2011 and the turmoil that followed have created feelings of vulnerability and insecurity among the inhabitants of Cairo, which have had an effect on how women's self-defence is practised. Within a few months, many new classes, often at exorbitant prices, sprang up. Their sales strategy focused on women's safety. This critical period, during which tendencies that were already latent were intensifying, revealed deep-seated class divisions in Egyptian society, which had been less noticeable until then. Young Cairote women who attend self-defence classes seem to come from similar strata of society and experience their city and the world in comparable ways. By marking out specific urban spaces as reassuring or frightening, and describing the figure of the aggressor together, they create their own class narrative and show how fragile their shared identity has suddenly become after the revolution.

Challenging and reformulating 'femininity'

Dealing blows with knees, elbows and fists: the practice of female self-defence is all about the body. Enabling concrete learning – and 'unlearning' – it has a clearly transgressive dimension. Participants learn to use their bodies as weapons and thus embody a kind of femininity that is far from conventional. Mona, aged twenty-six, explains:

> My mother was not against me doing self-defence. She really likes the idea of me being able to defend myself, but she does not like what it involves. To her, girls

should be gentle and demure and she doesn't like the idea of me punching people. She is in favour of it in principle, but not in practice!

'Unlearning' to be a girl

The basic idea is simple: behaviours traditionally associated with women, such as gentleness or discretion, do a disservice to women by preventing them from defending themselves and thus contribute to putting them in danger. Girls and women therefore have to 'unlearn', as Anna puts it, this kind of behaviour: 'I don't want anything pretty, little, or nice. We are no longer girls here!'

Facial expressions, for example, require such practice. Anna tells her group that smiling is a 'dangerous' female reflex because it invites interaction: 'You smile all the time! I don't want smiles. A smile is an invitation. It's very important to maintain a closed expression.' Anna tirelessly repeats this warning. The other thing that she wants her class to unlearn – and she stresses this from the first session – is the voice. A woman's voice is her first 'weapon' that she should use in any situation that she wants to stop. Participants therefore spend a good part of each session learning how to raise their voices. It is important to avoid a high pitch. 'I want a strong voice', thunders Anna. The women form a circle for these vocal exercises, shouting one after the other, then all together. Anna encourages them, and the volume gradually increases. Then the women choose words to shout, each of them making a suggestion, and Anna rejects most of them. Too long! Too polite! The right words are those that clearly signify a refusal and cut short the exchange: *La!* (No!), *Khalas!* (Stop it!). Words that can attract the attention of people nearby are also important: *Shil idak!* (Keep your hands off me!), *Ihtaram nafsak!* (Respect yourself!). So are words that are scornful or humiliating: *Iba'id!* (Go away!), *Kalb!* (Dog!). These expressions will be repeated at the start of every class and accompany all the physical exercises.

Some participants use the opportunity of being in a women-only group to experiment with their clothing. Mona takes off her long skirt at the start of every session, revealing jogging trousers, which she hides whenever the door opens. Nawara is always fully veiled at first but takes her veil off after about half an hour and puts it on top of her bag. If she leaves the room for a moment during the break, she does not put her veil back but just pulls up the hood of her sweatshirt. Challenging boundaries – those of her forehead and her hair, those of the room – is a kind of training, she says, on her personal path towards abandoning the veil. A self-defence class is like a laboratory in which young women feel the need or the desire to try out other ways of being and other ways of presenting themselves to the outside world.

Fighting, hurting and getting hurt: bodies that learn and bodies that resist

Women learning self-defence tend to be very cautious during the first sessions, afraid they might hurt others or themselves. Anna tries to alleviate the fear of dealing or receiving a blow. Little by little, the movements and the blows become more forceful. Anna encourages the women to applaud every successful demonstration, to celebrate the moves that hit their target and to celebrate these young women who dare to hit back against attacks on their bodies. Being applauded also helps to mitigate any pain a woman may be suffering because of a clumsy move from a partner who is inexperienced or awkward – a scratch in the face, a headbutt in the mouth, an elbow in the stomach. The pain has a value because this is what the aggressor will feel in a real situation.

Learning combat techniques takes time and is often met with resistance. The young women taking the self-defence classes are not used to hitting people, and humour often helps them to accept these unconventional situations. Twenty-eight-year-old Mena comments: 'When I fight, I cannot take the smile off my face, I don't know why but I can't help it.' Fear triggers the same reaction: laughter, which distracts from the threatening gestures. Other strategies help to make violence more acceptable for the young women. Combat exercises in pairs are therefore usually followed by a tender gesture between the two partners: they hold hands, link arms, exchange a kiss or say sorry. These gestures serve to compensate for the aggression and to demonstrate, to themselves and others, that the transgression resulting from the fight is temporary.

The young women are learning ways to use their bodies – postures and movements – that are not found in traditional representations of femininity. The experience of being a girl, but differently, meets resistance at first and requires constant adjustments.

Having fun or changing the world?

The project of self-defence for women is a serious one – it is about violence against women – and must involve defiance and radical change – it's about

Constructing oneself

physical resistance. Do the classes reflect these aspects? How is the seriousness of the project expressed in the discourse and practices of the participants?

'Things have to change!': different participants, similar aims

> At the beginning of the year, I looked at the programme to see what I could sign up for. I really wanted to play the violin. And then I saw the ad for self-defence and thought: why not? (Fatma, aged twenty-four)

Most participants got involved in self-defence classes by chance. Few of them were specifically seeking a course like this. But once they have made the decision they seem to find it easy to integrate these classes into their lives, as if they had been predisposed to them.

Despite their differences, these young women share the same feeling of anger towards sexual harassment and the same desire for things to change. Their motivations fall into different categories. They may be religious, like in Sara's case:

> I think that God granted me a very high position as a woman. So why should I put up with this, when God himself raised me up?

They can be 'cultural', as in the case of Nawara:

> Egyptian girls are brought up to believe they should always be polite and respectful. When I was younger, even my mother used to tell me that I should always look down demurely, never make a fuss or cause trouble. But I've had enough of keeping my mouth shut.

Or they can be safety-related, like for Mona:

> Assaults can happen anywhere and anytime. I don't want to stop going out because I'm scared. Self-defence is a solution.

Despite these differences, the participants all share desires and aspirations that are not traditional for women. Lamia admits that she enjoys acting 'like a boy' and dreams of learning how to use a knife. Hoda likes complicated combat skills. Rasha loves skydiving. They present themselves as 'different', and they are outsiders to a certain extent. Sara says:

> I sometimes talk to my female friends about being a rebel, wanting independence – but not too often, because they think I'm from another planet!

A different way of being a young woman?

During the self-defence, the young women feel less alone and encourage each other. Omnia, for example, puts it like this:

> There aren't that many of us yet, so it is easy for people to say we're just outsiders. But there will be more and more of us and we'll get there! When all women start to react, things are going to change. We have to hang on in there till then!

Talking plays an important role in the self-defence course. In the gaps between exercises, or the start or finish of the session, the women chat with each other, sharing experiences and advice. Sometimes these discussions can go on for a long time, and the young women end up sitting in a circle on the floor. The teacher explains the function of these shared words, referring to feminist pedagogy:

> We must increase opportunities for women to talk to each other and recognise themselves in the discourse of the other. That is how the struggle will advance.

Dealing with aggression: between reality and fiction, seriousness and laughter

The combat techniques taught in self-defence classes aim to respond to real needs, and movements and situations are directly modelled on 'reality'. During each session, the participants are encouraged to talk about events – harassment, aggression – that they or their friends have experienced. The situations are then staged and the young women discuss how the victim should best react. Some women are therefore 'replaying' a traumatic situation they have experienced, and this can be uncomfortable for them.

The women are encouraged to be as realistic as possible, but these attempts are hampered by the absence of men. The body of the 'enemy', which is imagined as big and strong, is not present in these staged situations. As a result, the most physically imposing women usually take on the role of the aggressor, 'playing' the man. Anna concludes each session by encouraging the participants to train with men. 'Train at home, with your brother, your fiancé or your father', she insists. This 'immaterial' presence of men, evoked but absent, is often addressed with humour. The women imagine how they would hurt them, how they would call them every rude name that comes to their minds, '*hayawan*' (animals) or 'bastards'. But above all, they enjoy the fact that men's genitals make them particularly vulnerable. Sharing images of well-aimed kicks can offer a moment of amusement and relaxation.

Constructing oneself

In fact, attempts to stage assaults as realistically as possible usually lead to roars of laughter. Paradoxically, the more the group tries to make the aggression convincing, the funnier it gets. At this point, the session turns into role play or theatre. Participants might imagine being in a bus, created from six chairs, with an 'actress' at the steering wheel. Another young woman is hanging on to an imaginary handrail. While the teacher plays an elderly passenger trying to find a seat, the others reproduce the sounds of engines and honking horns. In another scene, which takes place in the street, the women play the roles of young male harassers, swaggering, ogling, making suggestive comments, whistling and heckling the girls that walk past.

Having fun in self-defence classes and wanting to change the world are not mutually exclusive, but there are boundaries that should not be overstepped. It can happen that some young women turn into 'bad examples' by not taking 'it' seriously. They risk turning the self-defence course into a joke, thus undermining its serious and radical aims. Anna takes great care to keep the discussion focused and to prevent it from descending into frivolity. Sometimes the women themselves address the issue at the end of the class, like Nawara:

> In our group, there are girls who giggle all the time. I don't know what they are looking for … And I am sure they all have cars and never get pestered by men! They come to this course to have a laugh, to wear fancy tops and look pretty. It's sickening!

Despite these occasional annoyances, the sessions usually have positive results: one participant now dares to hold her head high in the street, another has lectured a bus driver who got too close for comfort and another has gained self-confidence from knowing how and where to punch. Sometimes playfully, sometimes seriously, these young women are trying out new ways of behaving as women, new ways of being women. The Friday evening sessions at the Culture Wheel thus provide – even if only for a limited section of society – real and effective support for social change in a society which has undergone a rapid transformation, following the example of the revolutionary youth of 2011.

Of course, transformations like these are never straightforward. Some women find it hard to adapt to their new, combative roles, not only mentally but physically. Twenty-eight-year-old Rasha gives a powerful example of this in her account of what happened when she tried to join the demonstrations in the first days of the 2011 revolution:

A different way of being a young woman?

I had waited a long time for this revolution. I wanted to go and join the protests, but my brother didn't let me. He tried to prevent me from going out; he didn't want this revolution. That day, he hit me hard, and for a long time: he punched me in the mouth, and in the arms. It was the first time he ever laid a hand on me. The only way I would have had to stop him ... The only way to fight back, to really put him out of action, is that [a kick in the genitals]. I know how to do it, I learned it in our class, but of course I couldn't do it. It wouldn't be right – he's my brother!

By learning how to throw a punch, by having fun 'playing' men and by sharing their day-to-day anger, the young Egyptian women in this self-defence class are challenging some of the hierarchies and relationships of power that permeate the whole of Egyptian society.

References

Diab, Mohamed, ed., *Cairo 6, 7, 8* (film), Pyramide Distribution, 2010.
McCaughey, Martha, *Real Knockouts. The Physical Feminism of Women's Self-Defence*, New York University Press, New York, 1997.
Piquemal, Leslie, ed., 'New Gender-Related Struggles in Egypt since 2011', *Egypte monde arabe*, 13, 2015.
Rasha, Hassan Mohammed, *Clouds in Egypt's Sky*, ECWR, supervised by UNFPA.
Website of the El Sawy Culture Wheel: www.culturewheel.com

22

Chewing alone?

The transformations of qat consumption in Yemen

Marine Poirier

In the mid-1990s, the American sociologist Robert Putnam, drawing on his fellow citizens' increasing inclination to go bowling alone rather than in groups, analysed the decline of social capital in the United States, that is, what he interpreted as a decline in their ability to create cooperative and trusting relationships between individuals. Although his approach was widely criticised due to its restrictive definition of the concepts of social capital and civic participation, it nonetheless put its finger on certain dynamics of individualisation in group leisure practices, observable in varied contexts.

Rooted in long-standing social traditions, qat consumption became widespread in Yemen from the 1960s onwards, to the point of becoming a national 'institution'. Beyond the question of its disastrous health and economic effects, everyone agreed it enhanced social and political 'fluidity' and was a strong socialisation agent. For several decades, it has represented one of the country's markers for culture and identity, both in the city and the countryside, the North and South. The often-daily attendance of qat sessions (*maqyial* or *taghzina*; *tafrita* for women), during which the leaves of this light narcotic with euphoric effects are chewed for several hours on mattresses placed on the ground, constitutes in many ways a specifically Yemeni leisure activity, absent from other Arab societies.

This 'symbol of being Yemeni' acts as a powerful agent of socialisation and politicisation, especially among youth. The places where qat is consumed may also be seen as gateways to protests, since they are also where information is exchanged, opinions are formed and decisions are made. Qat sessions, which lead to many political interactions and deliberations and help to learn and practice public speaking, have contributed to the creation of an alternative public space, or even a (sub-)political space at 'ground level', in the figurative as well as the literal sense. Political decision-making has long been associated with group

Chewing alone?

consumption of qat, a practice that has steered Yemen's political vitality and the dynamism of its 'civil society'.

Chewing and tweeting?

During the 2000s, however, the deepening economic and social crisis disrupted traditional qat-related practices, particularly among youth. Due to underdeveloped cultural infrastructures and limited work opportunities (in 2011 unemployment affected between 40 and 50 per cent of eighteen to twenty-eight-year-olds), qat consumption was often experienced by young people as a way to 'kill time'. Whereas it used to signal a break or the completion of the working day, it seemed in the last decade to compensate for the absence of paid work, or even replace it. However, the euphoria caused by this soft amphetamine does not provide a lasting escape from the dire socio-economic realities. The effect is only ephemeral, and grand projects and dreams are usually followed by brutal disenchantment.

Furthermore, the routinisation of a daily life punctuated by the ingestion of qat results in Yemeni youth's increased dependence – first of all, financial and family dependence, as the share of the budget allocated to the drug increases to the detriment of food and housing, and simultaneously slows down the process of emancipation and self-sufficiency. In addition to its many physical consequences (anorexia, insomnia, sexual impotence, etc.), qat leads to psychological dependence, and above all to social dependence, as social relationships are mainly organised around its consumption. The generalisation of this practice, necessary to resist marginalisation and desocialisation, ultimately reinforces local youth's precariousness by keeping them in a sort of apathy and, more specifically, addiction.

At the same time, some youngsters have begun chewing alone. Particularly among students, there has been an individualisation of qat consumption during exam periods since studying is structured around the ingestion of the stimulant. A driver that helps them concentrate and stay awake for several hours at a time, qat is, for many students, at the heart of their university activity. Often idle, at times confronted with the increasingly anonymous nature of big cities, young people are changing their habits as their consumption takes on a new, less recreational and collective meaning. But by 'chewing alone' more and more frequently, like Americans 'bowling alone', are these young people normalising the drug, transforming it into a mere narcotic whose effects in terms of socialisation are dulled by the promise of a few hours of escape?

Moreover, widespread access to television and satellite channels, the spread of laptops and the growing use of online social networks have radically changed the political and social economy of qat. While qat sessions once favoured direct exchanges and communal exclusivity conducive to developing group solidarities, the importation of new technologies has theoretically favoured a withdrawal into oneself via one's screen. At least that is how some consumers have criticised the disruptive introduction of televisions, laptops and smartphones, especially by the new generations, into one of the main institutions of local sociability. The development of this individual and self-centred mode of consumption ostensibly cost qat parties their primary functions of networking and socialisation.

However, on closer examination, what is happening is less a weakening of traditional sociabilities or a depletion of social capital (in Putnam's sense of networks of cooperation between individuals) than a transformation of the types and forms of sociability, related to the potentialities of technological tools. First, they do not eliminate interactions nor even replace the musical or poetic 'traditions' of which qat sessions remain, to a large extent, the sounding board. Secondly, these technologies and new media, which occupy an increasingly central place in the *maqyial*, foster the development of diverse interactions via Twitter, Facebook and other chats, forums and blogs. The apparent individualisation of consumption must also be considered from the viewpoint of the progress of these 'online' exchanges which, far from destroying community feeling, have on the contrary reinforced it.

One of the most obvious illustrations of this transformation of the ways of 'being sociable' can be found in the revolutionary process initiated in early 2011. Led on the ground by Yemeni youth and student groups, it was characterised by the continuous occupation of public squares and the importation of qat consumption on the protest camps of Change Square (*sahat al-taghyir*) and Freedom Square (*sahat al-hurriyya*). The connection between traditional qat customs and this mode of protest action, manifested in the shift from the enclosed and segmented space of the *maqyial* to the street, helped keep up the numbers at sit-ins. It simultaneously facilitated the decompartmentalisation and reorganisation of militant social interactions. For this reason, the evolution of qat consumption practices more broadly reflects transformations in Yemeni society.

Since the war broke out in 2014, the multi-layered crises that have devastated Yemen have had little effect on qat's trade. Instead, it is often highlighted as the only sector that continues to function normally. Markets were never closed, nor were deliveries across the country. In the countryside south of Taez,

Chewing alone?

qat exploitation has expanded over that of cereals: with residents fleeing the city violence, the sudden explosion of land prices has favoured intensive culture, economically profitable albeit environmentally disastrous. While armed groups are using the plant to keep the fighters going, its ordinary consumption has grown steadily, despite rocketing prices (especially in the South because of depreciation) and growing surveillance of gatherings (especially in Houthi-controlled Sana'a). More than ever, the light euphoria and temporary distraction from daily miseries are welcome. Abroad, in the various countries where they have found refuge, Yemenis have had to (re)imagine other social activities and routines, like playing dominos in Cairo, drinking alcohol or, for those who afford it, consuming dried qat.

References

Carapico, Sheila, *Civil Society in Yemen. The Political Economy of Activism in Modern Arabia*, Cambridge University Press, Cambridge, 1998.
Destremau, Blandine, 'Le qat et la "narcotisation" de l'économie yéménite', *Revue du monde musulman et de la Méditerranée*, 55, 55–56, 1990: pp. 266–284.
Gatter, Peer, *Politics of Qat. The Role of a Drug in Ruling Yemen*, Reichert Verlag, Wiesbaden, 2012.
Lambert, Jean, 'Consommation de masse et tradition à Sanaa: vers une culture urbaine', in Gilbert Grandguillaume, Franck Mermier and Jean-François Troin, eds, *Sanaa hors les murs: Une ville arabe contemporaine*, CFEY-URBAMA, Tours, 1995, pp. 89–141.
Putnam, Robert D., 'Bowling Alone: America's Declining Social Capital', *Journal of Democracy*, 6, 1, 1995: pp. 65–78.
Varisco, Daniel Martin, 'On the Meaning of Chewing: The Significance of Qat (*Catha edulis*) in the Yemen Arab Republic', *International Journal of Middle East Studies*, 18, 1, 1986: pp. 1–13.
Wedeen, Lisa, *Peripheral Visions. Publics, Power and Performance in Yemen*, Chicago University Press, Chicago, IL, 2008.
Weir, Shelagh, *Qat in Yemen. Consumption and Social Change*, British Museum Publications, London, 1985.

23

Gulf holiday-goers in Europe

Five-star family favourites

Claire Beaugrand

> I on the contrary, as one who has had his fill of our customs, do not go looking for Gascons in Sicily – I have left enough of them at home. I look for Greeks, rather or Persians. I make their acquaintance and study them. That is what I devote myself to and work on.
>
> – Michel de Montaigne (*The Complete Essays*, 2004)

For most young people from wealthy families or the upper middle classes in the Gulf monarchies, Europe is not, contrary to the stereotype, a peculiar summer destination for individual eccentricities. While clichés portray young Gulf women on designer shopping binges or young men drinking to excess, chasing 'girls' and stocking up on luxury goods, most holidays prosaically reproduce the leisure practices and the behaviour practised in the Gulf countries during the rest of the year.

For these young people, holidays abroad are first and foremost a family affair (with certain variations depending on the family): they are spent in the company of parents, brothers and sisters (whether married or not), as well as grandparents, cousins, uncles and aunts – and families often bring domestic staff with them, such as the Filipina nanny or Egyptian driver. Moreover, going on holiday is seen as a necessity to escape the sweltering heat of the Gulf during the summer months. Young people are not necessarily consulted about the choice of destination and format of these trips – they simply go along with their families. In the past, Gulf merchant families often spent their holidays in Lebanon (in Beirut, then in Aley), favoured for its cultural and linguistic proximity and the pleasant summer climate, or in Britain, former colonial power, and the United States, security provider, with which the Gulf has weaved close political and economic links and where many of its elites were educated. In London, for example, royal families, princes and emirs have maintained the habit of sojourning on Park Lane, with the view of Hyde Park, while the upper middle class takes up residence in the luxury hotel chains of Mayfair. The middle class, following the trend, stays in hotels beyond Oxford Street, often on Edgware Road, nicknamed 'Arab Street', which is practical for those who struggle with English.

The preferred (although not exhaustive) list of European destinations, select locations reflecting the standard of living of the Gulf tourists, remains nowadays quite limited: Paris, London, Munich and Vienna, along with a handful of Alpine resorts – Geneva, Montreux, Zell-am-See (near Salzburg in Austria) – and a few upscale resorts on the Mediterranean, such as Marbella or Cannes. But returning time and again to the same place, where the family has a second home (or simply knows its way around), can become quite boring for young people, and for some from the wealthiest classes, even a stay in über-stylish Montreux, with its largely overlooked summer jazz festival, may just be a tedious chore.

The trips that offer young people more freedom and the opportunity to organise their stay to suit themselves are either honeymoons – allowing them to choose more original destinations, such as Italy – or holidays for lads, often a mix of brothers and friends. A jaunt with other young men, *shabab*, particularly to Asian countries or Morocco, does little to hide the real purpose of the trip; it is simply a more exotic and far-flung version of the weekends that young men from the Gulf in search of licentious entertainment spend in Manama or Dubai, 'in good company', at camps set up in the desert (*mukhayma*) or seaside chalets (*shaliyyat*, whose name is an interesting echo of Lake Geneva chalets). Places of sensual pleasure are no less accessible in the Gulf than elsewhere. Holidays abroad are tolerated for men, but they are almost unthinkable for groups of young (unmarried) women of the same age, unlike the 'girls' nights out' which are commonplace elsewhere.

Family holidays offer little in the way of discovery, adventure or rupture: tourist packages for hiking, themed sporting or cultural tours are often non-existent. Instead, holidays abroad tend to reproduce the leisure practices already present in the Gulf. The most popular places to visit are those that do not presuppose any familiarity with the 'legitimate culture' as defined by Bourdieu, let alone that of foreign countries. The Gulf citizens do not boast to possess such knowledge (or at least not yet, as some of the elite are increasingly taking an interest in fine arts, Islamic or otherwise, as well as in historical and architectural heritage). They often prefer to visit theme parks, particularly Disneyland Paris, attractions like London's Madame Tussaud's, impressive viewpoints such as the Eiffel Tower and the London Eye, and also the gardens and fountains of Hellbrunn

Constructing oneself

or the lakes and snow-covered peaks of Zell-am-See near Salzburg. Hunting, mainly falconry, on the Ukrainian steppes or in Scotland, is also a popular pastime among men from different generations – in particular royals, as is tracking bustards in the Syrian and Algerian deserts.

A road trip to Paris in a Ford Mustang

Leisure behaviours linked to consumption are thus reproduced in Europe where shopping in department stores is as popular as in the Gulf's malls. Europeans may consider these long shopping sessions excessive, even vulgar, and dismiss the 'Gulf Arabs' as 'nouveau riche', but for Gulf young people, shopping at a department store fulfils the same social function as it would in a mall in their home country: a place to stroll, socialise, watch others and assert one's self. Buying fashionable commodities is for them a sure sign of having spent a good holiday just as working up a tan is for Europeans; it also helps them stand out in the keen competition to outdo each other in style and elegance between individuals of the same sex, men and women alike. Consequently, Selfridges and Harrods in London, Galeries Lafayette in Paris, Globus in Geneva and Oberpollinger in Munich become little closed, familiar worlds for these Gulf holidaymakers. Wandering through the vast departments, they cross paths, exchange glances or greetings and identify people from the different Gulf states, but also sometimes keep their heads down and take care to avoid each other. The entire Gulf and its norms of behaviour are replicated in these luxury stores. Global brands (like Starbucks or Häagen-Dazs) work as familiar landmarks that do foster a sense of *entre soi* – also furthered by springing up in Western cities of well-known Gulf stores, such as the perfumery Arabian Oud, with shops on both the Champs-Élysées and Oxford Street. This logic of importing lifestyle and leisure activities to foreign settings reaches a peak when Gulf's gilded young bring their own sports cars with UAE, Qatari or Kuwaiti plates to cruise down Europe's most famous boulevards.

Contrary to the image of frivolity that is often attached to these youthful holidaymakers, the opportunities for them to express independent behaviour while abroad are relatively limited. Even for the new generations, the conformism displayed in the choice of holiday destinations, which can be explained by a classist reflex and a will to emulate elites leading to the concentration of fellow countrymen in the same location, reinforces the submission to established social norms. Most of the time, young people from wealthy Gulf families gravitate towards exactly the same places, in extremely demarcated leisure microcosms recommended, as good tips, by word of mouth before leaving home and where the same codes of behaviour will always be repeated. The commonly held Western idea that Gulf young people are getting away to cut loose and escape the social control that characterises the Gulf states, where everyone knows everyone else, must be seriously qualified, even if it proves accurate for other categories, such as married men or billionaire princes.

Although some young people may complain about the herd instinct of their relatives, this attitude marked by *entre soi* nevertheless seems reassuring when faced with Europeans who can be either servile or arrogant towards 'arrivistes' from the Gulf – it strengthens a sense of identity. Holidays are a time when strong tensions linked to otherness come to the fore. When exposed to wealthy and conservative milieux, young people, although better at languages than their parents, still reproduce the same behaviour of establishing personal relationships of trust with locals, hoteliers and neighbours in order to avoid the unpleasant surprises that can come with travel, particularly for those who come from the Gulf and are often reduced to their sole purchasing power. This is why young lads, even when they travel on their own, usually visit destinations chosen by their parents: in June 2012, for example, newspapers in Zell-am-See were filled with the news that twenty-five Kuwaitis were intending to drive to Paris in their Ford Mustangs, stopping off en route in Austria, at the resort where they had spent their holidays since childhood. Now that the younger generation is better travelled, more visible and better educated, it more proudly displays its values and identity, like the young Kuwaiti girl praying in the corner of the Globus lifts. The time-honoured culture of the European bourgeoisie is therefore countered by another social and value-based conservatism, both of which unite nevertheless in a class reflex largely shared by young holidaymakers for whom nothing less than five stars would ever do.

References

'Cars Registered in the Gulf Parked in the Streets of London', July 2010 (available at www
.youtube.com/watch?v=1U7_xCOolFo).
Le Renard, Amélie, 'The Ladies' Kingdom and Its Many Uses. A Shopping Mall in Riyadh for Women only', *Metropolitics*, 30 March 2011 (available at www.metropolitiques.eu/The
-Ladies-Kingdom-and-Its-Many.html).
Millionaire Boy Racers of London, Channel 4, January 2013 (available at www.dailymotion.com
/video/xwraoh).

Constructing oneself

Murphy, Carlyle, 'The Wild Card: Students Abroad', in *A Kingdom's Future. Saudi Arabia Through the Eyes of its Twentysomethings*, Wilson Center, Washington, DC, 2012, pp. 135–146.

Wagner, Anne-Catherine, 'The Role of Travel in the Education of the Elite', *Actes de la recherche en sciences sociales*, 170, 2007: pp. 58–65.

24

In SOS Bab-el-Oued

Rappers and rockers between integration and transgression

Layla Baamara

SOS Bab-el-Oued is a community organisation located in the working-class district of Algiers from which it takes its name. The neighbourhood is known for its jam-packed shops but is characterised above all by the riots in October 1988, by the mark of the Islamists who were particularly active during the 1990s and by the impact of the deadly floods in 2001. Poverty, violence and unemployment are also associated with this municipality, the most densely populated in the *wilaya* of Algiers (more than 55,000 inhabitants per square kilometre in 2008), a quarter of an hour's walk from the city centre. Located between two clothing stores across from a public garden, the association's premises are unmissable, the bright colours adorning the facade immediately attracting the eye. The equally colourful inside has walls covered with photographs of young people, portraits of Che Guevara and former president Houari Boumediene, the Declaration of the Rights of Man and of the Citizen of 1789 and press articles about the association. Young people of all ages – for whom artistic and cultural activities are not easily accessible in the Algerian capital – can take advantage of a fully equipped rehearsal room in the basement, a darkroom and film club equipment on the first floor, musical instruments, books and computers everywhere.

From anti-Islamist resistance to international funding

The association's origins are linked to the story of some of the neighbourhood's inhabitants in the context of the civil war in the 1990s. In reaction to their everyday life marked by fear, violence and death, Nacer Meghnine (born in 1961), who until then had taught military children during school holidays and was a turner the rest of the year, and his wife Djamila, a French teacher in a secondary school in Bab-el-Oued, felt the 'need to do something' to 'survive', along with some friends and neighbours in the area. Their personal histories, marked by the loss of loved ones and a politicised relationship with society, are not unrelated to what they describe as their mobilisation 'against the imposition of fundamentalist laws, to defend the republic', at the risk of appearing to certain detractors as defenders of the military authorities. Involved in networks of sociability mainly composed of artists and intellectuals (often close to the former Socialist Vanguard Party, heir to the Algerian Communist Party), they resolved to 'resist' in an informal way by continuing to organise parties for weddings and circumcisions or by refusing to comply with the new conservative standards of dress (headscarves for women, *qamis* for men, etc.).

Their 'secular' activism, in a context where they were largely in the minority, took a more concrete legal form with the creation in 1997 of an association which they initially named SOS-Culture Bab-el-Oued. They then received subsidies from the authorities, who saw it as a way to counter the Islamist currents that were particularly well established in Bab-el-Oued. Although ephemeral, this state support illustrates the complexity and ambivalence of the power struggle in which associations like SOS Bab-el-Oued were involved at the time. Since then, the association has operated with the help of foreign backers, through foreign aid programmes and international partnerships. Their meeting with members of Caritas and Secours Catholique was decisive at the time of the floods in the neighbourhood in 2001, resulting in a partnership that led to the financing of new premises.

The association's path is particularly clear in light of the post–civil war and post-9/11 context, which favoured the development of private and interstate initiatives aimed at promoting 'civil society' and, in so doing, at containing political Islamism. SOS Bab-el-Oued is emblematic of such organisations financed by international aid to countries in the region. As a member of the Algerian Concerted Multi-Stakeholder Program (CMSP or Joussour) initiated in 2007 and supported by the French Ministry of Foreign Affairs, the French Development Agency, the French Committee for International Solidarity and the Fondation de France, the association obtained funding to create a film club and present short films made by young people in Algeria and France. In the space of a few years, Nacer and Djamila, respectively president and vice-president, as well as Nacer's sister-in-law Fatiha, the treasurer, have become fully integrated into international cooperation and development aid networks, although this has not been without fuelling suspicions of 'collusion with the West'.

In SOS Bab-el-Oued

SOS Bab-el-Oued is typical of organisations which, because of their ability to offset a retreating government and to offer an alternative to 'Islamist' associations, are both encouraged by international actors and exploited by the authoritarian Algerian regime. The rarity of this type of organisation, particularly in the field of culture and leisure for young people, nevertheless gives it a certain singularity. Although the Ministry of Culture counts 335 cultural associations for the *wilaya* of Algiers and the Ministry of Youth and Sports mentions 170 community partners, in addition to its directly affiliated youth centres, the inhabitants point out the lack of spaces devoted to culture and youth in the capital. Most of these structures are not very visible, operate on a periodic basis and are often limited to hosting a few events per year.

In a neighbourhood where both institutional and community structures for young people are either non-existent or not highly functional, SOS Bab-el-Oued is an exception. Although its location in a working-class neighbourhood is highlighted, the association organises other activities outside Bab-el-Oued and the premises welcome people from other communes. The youngest (six to eighteen years old) are offered tutoring, manual activities (painting, sculpture, etc.) as well as cultural outings (museums, historical sites) and leisure activities (swimming). Older children can learn how to make films or photographs, write scripts, act and stage plays. Some of the young people decide to become more actively involved in the association by taking part in organising activities.

This chapter is devoted to those young people. From Bab-el-Oued or elsewhere, sons and daughters of workers or journalists, students, unemployed or in the workforce, they all landed in the same place, most often through friends already involved in the organisation. Those we met in May 2012 were mostly musicians. For several months, and sometimes several years, they spent their free time rehearsing and recording rock or rap songs, organising concerts and helping the younger children with their homework. This commitment goes hand in hand with an emotional attachment that pervades their often laudatory remarks about SOS Bab-el-Oued. Combined with on-site observation, studying these young musicians' communications has enabled us to identify their pathways, practices, and relationships with the organisation.

'I was full of violence and anger'

Bilal, Dounia, Hassan, Hanane, Nesrine, Iliès and Oussam all have in common their childhood and adolescence spent in working-class neighbourhoods,

Constructing oneself

in Bab-el-Oued or elsewhere, when the 'black decade' of the 1990s was in full swing. Whether they are from underprivileged social backgrounds or from the so-called 'middle' classes, their perceptions are marked by the material and moral harshness of their daily environment. The lack of space, financial means, leisure activities and family supervision seems to be at the origin of the 'hard times' that come up repeatedly in their comments. Those 'hard times', which in retrospect they believe to have suffered unjustly, have fuelled their criticism of the 'system' and are at the heart of their involvement in music and in the organisation.

Bilal (thirty), born in Bab-el-Oued, comes from a large family with whom he still lives in part today. The family lives in two rooms, with the father's salary as a manual worker the only source of income. 'That's why we spend so much time outdoors', he explains. Day and night, with his friends he squats on football fields, stairwells and public benches, and is involved in small-scale informal trade (selling cigarettes, in particular). As a child, he had trouble at school but left it primarily because he 'chose' football and joined the junior club of Mouloudia, one of the most popular teams in the capital. A teenager during the 1990s, Bilal is rather emotional when recalling this period during which he saw 'too many horrors, too much blood on the sidewalks, too many dead bodies, too many stray bullets'. The civil war, which put his football career on hold, 'marked him for life', fuelling his main question: 'Why?' The same question came up again when the director of his football club put him on the side-lines to place the son of 'somebody important'. Although he now claims to have an explanation for this injustice ('I was the poorest'), Bilal went through a difficult time after that humiliating exclusion:

> After that, I did some stupid things. I was full of violence and anger. I tried to leave three times, but it didn't work, so I realized that my life was here, and I had to cope.

Bilal's example shows the extent to which hardships experienced during childhood and adolescence have shaped representations that young people have of the society they live in. Not remaining a *hittist*[1] for his entire life and offering better living conditions to his future children are two of the main aspirations that Bilal thinks he can fulfil, in part with the help of rap and his investment in the association. For him, as for Oussam and Iliès, music was first and foremost an escape mechanism to express and externalise the anguish caused during their childhood by 'terror of the government and of the terrorists'. If, for Oussam

In SOS Bab-el-Oued

(twenty-six), 'all that is in the past', it is because he has found in rap a way to move forward and get a fresh start. At the age of thirteen, he began listening to French rap groups thanks to cassettes sent to him by his cousins, who had emigrated to France. With his older brother, he learned to understand lyrics by IAM and NTM:

> I liked their rebellious side. I was really inspired by their words about freedom. I lived in a working-class neighbourhood so I could relate to the lyrics. I found a way to express myself in rap, to talk about some things I didn't like here.

The lyrics by these rappers, also from working-class neighbourhoods, resonated with Bilal too, as proof that 'you can pull through despite the hardships'. It was through Oussam, a mere acquaintance from the neighbourhood at the time, that he learned to rap little by little. And his daily life was gradually transformed:

> It calmed me down. I learned French, writing, another way of life. I made new friends. I started to write my own texts. At night, when I went home, I would write until I fell asleep.

While rap was a way to express anger and hope, it was also a way of being, a state of mind. As sociologist and anthropologist Denis-Constant Martin, who has worked on rap in France, has pointed out, it is part of a 'process of identity configuration'. Young people, he explains, use music to 'negotiate their place in a society dominated by "old people"'; to do this, they invent new styles or genres and identify themselves through music with groups from elsewhere that they idealise in a context of protest. Through their passion for music, they can simultaneously contest the dominant order and become part of a new world.

Parental reactions help us to better understand the tension between these two transgressive and integrative aspects. Iliès, twenty-four, states:

> For my parents, the only way to be somebody is to have a degree. But even when I was allowed to have my guitar after getting my high school diploma, my father used to come and turn off the light at night and tell me he wasn't paying the electricity bill so I could play, but so that I would study!

Raised on the sounds that his 'music-loving' older brother and sister used to listen to, Iliès says he was 'frustrated not to have been allowed to play' and maintains that his 'story with music comes from that. My parents didn't want me to get side-tracked, but I did!' A jazz and rock fan, he learned to play the guitar, then the bass and drums by deciphering videos of musicians on the Internet.

Constructing oneself

He seems to have found a happy medium and, parallel to his computer studies, has created his own network, offering his services to bands for recordings and concerts to help pay for the instruments.

But there are still many difficulties. Along with his parents' disapproval and his own financial insecurity, there is the added pressure from the neighbourhood and the authorities, says Oussam:

> Here we are in the neighbourhood, watching the time go by, with the authorities pissing you off all the time, and you're afraid of screwing up … There's a lot of pressure. You go home, there's pressure, family fights … You go out, the cops keep frisking you all the time … You don't know what to do, you try to go out, but you need money for that … And you don't have any money … Your daily life is always the same. You could lose your confidence because there's nothing.

Oussam, Bilal and other friends formed a group in the mid-2000s, but they eventually 'gave up' because of all the difficulties in their daily lives.

'We're no longer all alone'

Faced with so many difficulties, our interviewees were extremely grateful towards the association. They often discovered SOS Bab-el-Oued at a time when they were going through particularly hard professional or personal times. With guidance from other young people who were already members, they were amazed and delighted at having a rehearsal space at their disposal and enjoying support in their creative endeavours. 'We finally found people who appreciated our art, our music', explains Oussam. 'Who appreciated us and provided equipment', adds Hassan, twenty-six:

> We've got basses, guitars, drums, and amplifiers here, everything you need, basically. Nacer understood that we needed equipment and he taught us how to take care of it and to use it well. It helps us show what we're capable of.

Use of the equipment is conditional, however. The young musicians must record at least five tracks to be able to use it for more than three months. As a manager and tour manager for the bands in his neighbourhood in the 1980s, Nacer has given them the benefit of his experience and connections in the professional music world. Often formed as a group before they discovered the association, the young artists can, for example, finalise their demos with the help of professional musicians he knows. Once the tracks have been recorded, Nacer helps them find their way in the world of producers, record companies, radio stations and also concert halls, cultural managers and journalists in order to make themselves known. Nacer acts as a go-between thanks to his network of personal acquaintances and contacts from the association's backers and partners. With the help of private organisations – the Diocesan House, the International Committee for the Development of Peoples – young groups can perform at events such as the Fête de la Musique. The most experienced, such as the rock groups Afrockaïne and Everest, who sing in Arabic and English, perform regularly and are featured in the press.

While SOS Bab-el-Oued serves as a professional springboard, there is another, more symbolic and emotional dimension in the relationship these young people have with the association. The case of Hassan is interesting in this regard. After a disappointing experience as a disc jockey, he was rather disillusioned with the professional music world, describing it as 'a rotten bourgeois milieu'. A musical career finally seemed possible after he came to the association's premises in 2008 and realised that 'you don't need money or connections to CEOs to make your way'. Hassan is now the artistic director of the association.

For Hassan, as well as for Bilal and Oussam, having no support from their families and no diplomas, they struggled to find stable jobs. The association has given them a second wind, enabling them to take up music again, which they had given up:

> Before, we rapped on our own, but we had no prospects, nobody who encouraged us. With SOS we found meaning in what we were doing. We picked up our pens and started writing again. We really feel like we're making progress now, given what's happening outside and how we live here in Bab-el-Oued. We needed that energy, the space to breathe a little. Now we can handle it.

Beyond its material and moral support ('You can call Uncle Nacer anytime, he'll come over and help you, whatever kind of problems you've got', confides Bilal), the association is an alternative space for social interaction where friendly relationships are forged in a close-knit environment. Meeting other musicians facing the same kind of difficulties is reassuring and encouraging. Their shared interest in music is the bond the young people gradually forge and sustain within the association, through musical experiences (rehearsals, concerts, recordings) and beyond. Everyone comes and goes, even when they are not on the rehearsal programme. While some of them already know each other, the space and

Constructing oneself

various activities offered (photo-video workshops, cultural outings, film club, etc.) foster new friendships. In this respect, Nacer is certainly concerned about 'his' young people's artistic careers, but his broader intention is to 'help them to blossom, feel good and support each other'. Most claim to have found a 'second family'. Dounia's case is more than just a metaphor. 'I met my husband, Ali, here', says the twenty-four-year-old. 'We met here, got engaged here, married here and our children will be born here too!' The 'parental' relationship that may develop between the association's founders and the young people somehow intensifies the family ties that connect the leaders themselves, perhaps indirectly fostering this close-knit culture and the personal and intimate relationships that are formed here.

One can understand the importance of the association's socialising role and the space for social interaction it embodies in the eyes of the young people we met in the light of their perceptions of community organisations. Most of them were somewhat apprehensive about SOS Bab-el-Oued at first. For instance, Iliès confided that he lacked 'trust', that for him 'it was an organisation like the others, which talked a lot' but didn't keep its promises. As for Dounia, she felt that 'organisations use people to make money' and remembers that she 'didn't believe in them'. Their first steps within the association changed these perceptions. It is easier to understand the enthusiasm they now express ('it's different here') given how highly disparaged the non-profit world is in Algeria.

Getting involved in a different way

This negative perception of associations is part of a broader, both disappointed and critical vision of 'politics'. Many young Algerians consider the situation to be 'stuck' and socio-economic difficulties to be worsening. Bilal's words are significant in this respect:

> I don't expect anything from politicians, they're all alike! We're in one of the richest countries in the region and we're living in poverty, that's not right! And some people are lining their pockets while millions are starving.

Despite this bitter observation, being involved in the association is a way for some young people to act in a different manner. In addition to personal development and prospects for artistic careers, those who get involved in the association have a desire to 'give' back. Considered 'associates' from the moment they decide to participate regularly in the association's activities, young people can choose to take a more active part in it by becoming 'members'. At first glance, these two levels are not easily distinguishable. Often 'associates' for a period of several months or even years, 'members' are involved in developing and supervising activity programmes. As the association's artistic director, Hassan supervises the work of young musicians. Dounia and Nesrine give theatre classes and tutor children.

For 'associates' as well as 'members', involvement in the world of established politics never seems to cross their minds. As the political scientist Mounia Bennani-Chraïbi points out, however, 'the mistrust that "politics" inspires tends to extend into an idealized projection about the work of community associations'. As commonly understood, the term 'politics' certainly sounds like a dirty word that should be avoided. But it would be wrong to deduce from that a widespread apolitical stance. The desire for 'things to change' is very clearly expressed, in words and in actions. 'Proud of leading this fight in [her] neighbourhood', Hanane thinks that 'more cultural organizations like SOS Bab-el-Oued should be created'.

Corresponding to an image of 'modernity', 'freedom' and 'dynamism' that appeals to international backers and that the Algerian public authorities are happy to project abroad, these young SOS Bab-el-Oued artists may of course appear to be a vector of legitimisation for a certain dominant system. However, beyond the discourse on politics, their practices also have a transgressive aspect. Playing rock, rap or heavy metal music, dyeing one's hair red, wearing dreadlocks or travelling the roads of Algeria with a theatre troupe are atypical practices, sometimes considered deviant. 'We have already received hate messages. Once we were called Satanists. But we're used to the intolerance', confides one of our interlocutors. While they have pursued their activities, the young people we met have nevertheless avoided taking a conflictual stance. This can be seen for instance in their desire to maintain 'good' relations with the neighbourhood's inhabitants: 'We avoid standing in mixed groups of boys and girls in front of the premises.' In the words of Denis-Constant Martin, it seems that the cultural and social practices of the young people we met are as much distinctive and transgressive as they are 'connective and integrative, because they strive more to acquire a place in society than to dismantle it'.

Note

1   See Chapter 2 by Loïc Le Pape in this volume, p. 33.

References

Bennani-Chraïbi, Mounia, 'Jeux de miroir de la "politization": Les acteurs associatifs de quartier à Casablanca', *Critique internationale*, 50, spring 2011: pp. 55–71.

Derras, Omar, *Le phénomène associatif en Algérie: État des lieux, participation sociale et vitalité associative*, Friedrich Ebert Stifung, Algiers, 2007.

Djelfaoui, Abderrahmane, *Bab-el-Oued. Ville ouverte*, Éditions Paris-Méditerranée, Paris, 1999.

Martin, Denis-Constant, '"Auprès de ma blonde ..." Musique et identité', *Revue française de science politique*, 62, 1, 2012: pp. 21–43.

Martin, Denis-Constant, 'Cherchez le peuple ... Culture, populaire et politique', *Critique internationale*, 7, 2000: pp. 169–183.

Miliani, Hadj, 'Culture planétaire et identités frontalières. À propos du rap en Algérie', *Cahiers d'études africaines*, 168, 2002: pp. 763–776.

Mouffok, Ghania, ed., *Apprendre à vivre ensemble*, Éditions Barzakh/CISP, Algiers, 2011.

25

Leaving the camp

The wanderings of young Palestinian refugees in Lebanon

Nicolas Puig

Dressed only in a pair of brightly coloured swim shorts, equipped nonetheless with a few accessories, his gaze drifting behind dark glasses and cell phone in hand, Nizar walks along the shore, carefully following the seam between sea and sand. On this summer Sunday, the crowded beach has turned into an arena of visibility, attitudes adjusting to flashing glances, although, at some point, the bodies inevitably drop the pose, growing languid and abandoning themselves to a beneficial torpor. Nizar pushes onto the stone pier at the end of which cargo ships come to moor and receive the tonnes of cement produced by the surrounding factories that whiten the landscape with their chalk-coloured waste. Then, turning back, he observes the people around him distractedly, looking out at the bay nestled between the cliffs and cement factories and meditating on the vague promise of European migration inspired by the blue horizon. He finally reaches the table where his two friends are standing and drops onto the plastic chair, sitting in the uncertain shade of a worn parasol. A few photos taken with their cell phones, which will regularly scroll in their Facebook feeds, chronicle this beautiful summer day beyond time, beyond the camp.

In the Palestinian camps in Lebanon, there is an appreciation for calm. On the one hand, life is difficult for the refugees. The war (1975–1990) has left its mark on people's minds, and refugees, mistrusted by the nationals, are subject to systematic discrimination. The fear of a permanent settlement that would alter the balance among communities in the country has led to significant restrictions on their social rights: limited access to the labour market, despite a relaxation of the law in 2010; inability to own property, etc. Furthermore, camp dwellers are regularly subjected to episodes of violence, the most recent of which led to the destruction of a large part of the Nahr al-Bared camp north of Tripoli in 2007. The routines established have therefore created a comforting 'cultural enclave',

Constructing oneself

were it not for the intense infighting that sometimes arises, especially in Ayn al-Helweh, the large camp in the city of Saida. The young people (*shabab*) exist in the camp's unusual social environment without seeking to disrupt its norms, either in their behaviour or appearance. Forms of entertainment are not fundamentally different from what can be found in poor neighbourhoods in cities around the world. Outside the home, where they rarely have a room of their own, young men meet in cafes to play cards and watch television (European football matches or the abundant political news from Arab countries) in arcades and cybercafes where the hopelessly slow connection doesn't stop them from spending hours on the Internet chatting, flirting, posting photos and links and commenting on each other's posts. Wedding celebrations, like political commemorations, provide choice opportunities for dancing, especially the *dabke*, a popular group dance with an electrified musical version known as *sha'abi* ('of the people'). But it's one thing to have fun in the rather boring routine of the camp, and another to occupy Lebanese spaces. For inhabitants of the camps, especially the younger generations, the latter offers a more interesting area of exploration where the entertainment, even when similar, is enhanced thanks to small shifts in atmosphere.

In small groups, from two to four or five, these young Palestinians roam Lebanese spaces, from the corniche to the city centres, travelling by private car or public transport, then on foot. They frequent venues on a more or less regular basis, helping to bolster their self-confidence. By examining leisure practices outside the two camps in North Lebanon, Nahr al-Bared and Beddawi, this chapter highlights their pedagogical properties as ways of learning about foreign social worlds and moments of experimenting autonomy in otherness. The outings away from the camp are an opportunity to frequent spheres that offer particular hooks to the contemporary world: modernity, consumerism, social and community diversity, but also landscapes and natural phenomena (winter outings to the mountains to touch the snow, seaside visits in summer). These spheres, or areas for play, are characterised by their recreational potential.

Urban civilities

Tripoli, a city of 200,000 inhabitants located 85 kilometres north of Beirut, offers a wide range of places for young Palestinians from the surrounding camps to explore. The central square of Tripoli, lined with cafes, and the port city of Al-Mina, which adjoins the northern capital, with its international restaurant chains and popular karaoke bars, are all fun stops along the way. The chic modern stores attract the more fashion-conscious who keep an eye on the latest trends, even though most of them could never afford a pair of pants that cost thirty or forty dollars, however well-cut and of a quality superior to the products from Syria sold in the camp. But the purpose of walking in public spaces in Lebanese cities is not to respond directly to consumer dictates. It corresponds first and foremost to the universal need for a change of scenery and atmosphere. In the refugee context, it offers people a break by thrusting them into an environment with social and community diversity, and general otherness in places and situations whose difference from everyday life in the camp lends them a discreetly exotic quality. So, one goes to take in the show of the city itself, to have a drink on the corniche in Tripoli or a cup of coffee in the town centre, mindful of the social scenes it offers, the encounters it sometimes affords or the surprising finds that one may make (for a pop singer in the camp, it could be to find a second-hand musical instrument store or to bump into a musician he/she knows and discuss future contracts together). The term serendipity perfectly captures how the city facilitates discovering new things or situations when looking for something else.

However, this ideal-type model needs some qualifying. A categorisation mindset resurfaces regularly, posing a challenge to this idea of universal hospitality in big cities, which assumes equal status for those who frequent them. Urban social interactions in Lebanon involve subtle games around the recognition of community and national attributes in the case of Palestinian refugees and international migrants. Often, the specific accent of the camp inhabitants raises questions, and the knowledge of their origins introduces varying degrees of tension, due to the stigmatisation which Palestinians are subject to from a part of the Lebanese population.

Access to public spaces in Lebanese cities is largely based on linguistic variables. As a result, wandering around urban areas involves a risk of awkward recognition. When alone, it is not uncommon for people to modify their accent or replace a word with another to 'facilitate conversation', ensure a smooth relationship and avoid embarrassment linked to the game – and issue – of being recognised. We know what it cost to be recognised as a member of the other side at a roadblock during the civil war in the 1970s and 1980s – a time when community-based kidnappings and murders were common.

In a group, people don't try to hide these identity-based and linguistic traits that lead to categorisation. They prefer to establish a relationship – spontaneously in fact – on mutually neutral ground, which is feasible in particular if one is a

Constructing oneself

consumer. To a café owner who asks about the origin of his seated customers – 'Welcome. Where are you from?' – the answer is simply: 'from the camp, Nahr al-Bared'. Consuming something allows them to redefine the situation, take on a universal role (a consumer like anyone else) and be defined by a classification that is independent of their assigned affiliation. This ultimately reflects an avoidance of identity assignment through a consumerist stance.

Social exchanges require exchanging civilities, thereby taking on a pedagogical aspect as a kind of apprenticeship in the city nearby, in preparation for other encounters in distant cities (in Europe, in the Gulf, in Australia). Most young people envision a future involving migration and 'travelling', *safar*. This notion plays an important role in the camp dwellers' imaginations. It expresses the complex connections between the local and elsewhere, the near and the far, which bind the camp to its doubles formed by an imposing diaspora, a significant part of which lives in Scandinavia. Travel is a generic category, close to experience, which includes all the variations of transnational movement. A source of tension in collective and individual life, it has become a social issue and has been appropriated as a narrative item, thereby becoming the subject of debates and controversies, on the dignity or indignity of clandestine migration for instance. The perspective of travelling promotes a state of waiting interrupted by outings in the city during which one can perfect one's knowledge of urban civilities.

In a more structural way, exploring spaces outside the camp provides a framework for self-empowerment through leaving places of attachment (and childhood), in other words, spaces of proximity, the home and the camp, and envisioning a future in a foreign environment where one must be capable of finding one's place. The anthropology of adolescence emphasises the importance of a 'probationary space for experimentation' embodied by places of co-presence in which one may experiment with different relational and social modes with others. The young refugees' use of space undoubtedly stems from this phenomenon of self-construction and self-validation through acquiring loose ties with strangers in external spaces characteristic of adolescence. But the phenomenon can be extended to the whole of this season of life, a transitional time that opens between adolescence and the move towards leaving the family home, with a view to 'opening a house' (*fatah bayt*) according to the current expression, i.e. founding a family and settling in a home of one's own. This formula for self-empowerment by leaving the camp is one of the few available to its young inhabitants, who express their feeling of suffocating due to remaining 'prisoners of the camp' during periods of confinement. The latter occur regularly, for instance whenever there are clashes between the two antagonistic neighbourhoods in Tripoli, Jabal Mohsen and Bab al-Tabbeneh – the first is home to an Alawite population close to the Syrian regime of Assad, the second to Sunnis who oppose that regime – thereby prohibiting entry into the city. Their insatiable desire for moving around then results in long aimless walks and roaming up and down the camp, smoking cigarette after cigarette.

Maritime pleasures

A trip to the seaside, like a summer without war, helps to highlight how the refugees can make playful use of the surrounding space. Chekka Beach is located about ten kilometres south of Tripoli, and many Palestinians from the camps at Baddawi and Bared, respectively about fifteen and thirty kilometres away, escape there regularly during the summer season.

Lebanon, known equally for its political instability and its inhabitants' dynamism, has more than two hundred kilometres of coastline along the Mediterranean. It is also home to between 250,000 and 270,000 Palestinian refugees according to the latest estimates. And, like the Lebanese, they are not averse to seaside pleasures. On Sunday mornings, fishermen from the Nahr al-Bared camp can be seen on the seafront, at a place called 'the Corniche' (al-Kurnish), fishing rods in hand and eyes staring out to sea, exchanging light-hearted remarks about their gear, for example, or more serious ones about the unbearably slow pace of rebuilding the camp. The younger ones aspire to other pleasures and, as soon as they can afford it, they go to Chekka Beach for a few hours. Among the places they frequent, the beach holds special appeal, due to its periodic nature. For the rest of the year, they will remember the day – or ideally the few days – that will have been the highlight of the summer season. Several years later, when some of these young people have succeeded in gaining a foothold in Europe or Australia, posting photos of maritime moments captioned with nostalgic comments about those beautiful days in a bygone era helps to maintain a link with the camp and their friends.

Apart from their political status and restrictions on their social rights, there is little to separate refugees from the Lebanese working classes, especially with regard to spending a day at the seaside. Young and not-so-young residents of Nahr al-Bared head for the beach, which is private most of the time and costs between two and three euros to enter. For that price, they can sit under a parasol on plain chairs around a plastic table. Clothes and identity papers are left in a

Constructing oneself

cabana shared by several people. Comfortably positioned, they are ready to enjoy their observation post. Chekka Beach, embraced by the *shabab* of Nahr al-Bared, is located in a small Christian region about ten kilometres south of Tripoli, while far-off Jounieh, not easily accessible due to the prices charged and the distance, is often referred to as the local Saint-Tropez or, if you prefer, the seaside Mecca.

Chekka attracts young people from the camps because they find it rather exotic, especially due to the social diversity that reigns there. The atmosphere contrasts with the more conservative one inside the camps. The area's beach attendants sell alcohol, a feature which undeniably heightens its appeal. Customers can have a few beers, such as the local Almaza, or much stronger imported drinks, especially those made with vodka. The presence of young women, sometimes in bathing suits, also contributes to the allure of the place, known for the possibilities it affords to meet new people. One of the tried and tested techniques consists in exchanging glances and then, as one is leaving, scribbling one's cell phone number on a piece of paper discreetly placed in the coveted young woman's belongings.

The beach temporarily offers an opportunity to change worlds and slip into a more playful environment. It provides a break in the daily routine that gives one a chance to 'see people'. In this arena of visibility, everyone finds something pleasant to do to pass the time, while observing others and putting oneself in view. The physical manifestations of self-exposure, duly photographed by friends, are initially validated by peers based on a gendered logic, according to which men show themselves first to men (and women to women) to experiment with their physicality (both perception by others and sensations of their body) in displays that blend self-promotion, humour and self-mockery. Working on one's appearance, including taking care of one's body and striving for elegance – portraits and self-portraits in advantageous situations and outfits are very common on Facebook walls – can be read as an effort towards personal growth. This contrasts a manifestation of subjective autonomy with how the camps are managed by humanitarian organisations that reduce human life to the mere satisfaction of basic needs.

Private activities that are forbidden in the camp may be displayed on the beach and in certain places in the city (in the car on the coastal road, in the city's natural wastelands, etc.). Young men meet there on occasion to drink alcohol. While the older men can drink at home, where they are the 'master', it is disrespectful for a young man to drink in front of his parents. Some of them get drunk at the beach, taking advantage of the free sale of alcohol, which is not tolerated in the camp for moral reasons. This trait is shared by all the Palestinian camps in Lebanon, so drinking establishments are relegated outside their borders, even if they are often in close proximity. It is important to drink discreetly, without being noticed. In the words of Emmanuel Buisson, this attitude reflects a 'morality of visibility' that is more relevant in this context for analysing the drinker's ethic than the 'morality of guilt'. Sensitivity to social conventions is a sufficient motive for compartmentalising one's existence, and so one uses spaces outside the camp to indulge in practices that are condemned within its borders. This is the case for the beach, but also for many other places, such as vacant lots or the seashore along the maritime road, where friends can drink a few beers in the shelter of their cars.

Jaunts, tourism, migration

> I'm not going as a tourist. My first thought is how to survive. How can I think about leisure when I don't even have enough to live on? I have no money; I'm totally destitute. How can I go out if I have no money to spend or to feed myself? That's why we want to leave. People who leave and travel to work abroad for two or three years can afford to come back for a visit every year. […] They come here as tourists, then they go back home, although they are originally from here.

In this interview excerpt, Samir explains that his failed attempt to migrate to Europe was not a response to any desire to go touring but rather to the need to seek a better life. A tourist is someone who has gone to build his life elsewhere and can afford the luxury of returning to his former home base to do nothing. Such is the case for the Palestinians from the diaspora living in Europe or America who take up residence in the camp during summer vacations. This kind of relationship to places seems very distant and somewhat incongruous, achievable for those who have found their place in the world but quite out of reach for Palestinian refugees in Lebanon. The situation is different regarding walking or strolling, known as *kandura*, which is the only option within their grasp and is quite popular and widespread. Its success is due in particular to the fact that it reflects a personal action of taking charge of one's own time frame in a context where control of one's space and time is uncertain.

While going out for food or drink, for example, is an undeniable motivation for getting out of the camp, mobility constitutes a form of leisure that offers its own temporality. It helps circumvent phases during which time seems to take a more solid form, occupied only by smoking, where the cigarette is like an hourglass ticking away in boredom.

With no car and no other means of transportation, walking is the only way to satisfy the need for locomotion, with a pack of cigarettes in one's pocket. The walk is essential to spatial practices and continues after emigrating. Abdallah used to walk through the silent camp of Nahr al-Bared at night to keep his anguish at bay after the violence he had endured. He has continued his modest odysseys in the outskirts of Odense, Denmark's third largest city, where he settled recently. Permanently out of the camp now, he will be eligible to come back to visit, as a 'tourist', once he has official papers. Until that day, still a little far off, walking continues to offer him apparent control over his own space-time on more modest outings.

References

Breviglieri, Marc, 'Ouvrir le monde en personne. Une anthropologie des adolescences', in Marc Breviglieri and Vincenzo Cicchelli, eds, *Adolescences méditerranéennes, l'espace public à petit pas*, L'Harmattan, coll. Débats jeunesses, Paris, 2007, pp. 19–59.

Buisson-Fenet, Emmanuel, 'Ivresse et rapport à l'occidentalisation au Maghreb. Bars et débits de boissons à Tunis', *Égypte monde arabe*, 30–31, 1997: pp. 303–320.

Chaaban, Jad, Hala Ghattas, Rima Habib, Sari Hanafi, Nadine Sahyoun, Nisreen Salti, Karin Seyfert and Nadia Naamani, *Socio-Economic Survey of Palestinian Refugees in Lebanon*, report published by the American University of Beirut (AUB) and the United Nations Relief and Works Agency for Palestine Refugees in the Near East (UNRWA), 2011 (available at www.unrwa.org).

Joseph, Isaac, 'Reprendre la rue', in *La ville sans qualités*, Éditions de l'Aube, coll. Société, Paris, 1998.

26

'Rainbow Street'

The diversity, compartmentalisation and assertion of youth in Amman (Jordan)

Cyril Roussel

Jordan is a young country, independent only since 1946. Jordan's cities also give the impression of newness, their nascent historical centres contrasting with the vast residential areas that surround them. Home to nearly half of the country's six million inhabitants, the capital city of Amman looks at first glance like a sprawl of square buildings as far as the eye can see, with no real shared focus for its inhabitants. Apart from its ancient settlement, making it one of the oldest continuously inhabited sites in the Middle East, the city's development dates to the time of the British Mandate (1920–1948) when it was chosen as the capital of the territory, to the detriment of Salt, closer to Palestine. Although it languished for a long time, Jordan's capital was an early recipient of refugee flows, compounded by rural exodus and the city's natural growth. The refugees were Palestinian on several occasions, Iraqi since 2003 and, since 2012, Syrian. For a long time, Amman remained in the shadow of other cities in the region, such as Beirut, known for their commercial activities, flourishing bourgeoisie and entertainment venues that attracted the elites of the Arab world and the nouveau riche from the Gulf.

Although Amman is the young capital of a new country, is it a city for young people? Despite its reputation as a dull town, the city has gradually turned into an increasingly attractive hub. Today, it is characterised by a configuration that is dual, with working-class neighbourhoods to the east and affluent neighbourhoods to the west, and 'multipolar zed', with each neighbourhood having its own commercial, business and recreational spaces. Over half of its population is under twenty years old. Leisure activities have gradually expanded, offering among other things more venues for outings and entertainment spread out in a rather random way in the upscale western part of the conurbation. Built on former undeveloped areas, the new neighbourhoods of Shmeysani (1980s),

Constructing oneself

Sweifieh (late 1980s to early 1990s) and Abdun (late 1990s) have become attractive hubs for the cosmopolitan and privileged youth of the Jordanian capital. Consumerism exploded as shopping malls modelled on those in the Gulf states were developed in the western part of the city. Amusement arcades, coffee shops and fast-food restaurants attracted young Jordanians and non-Jordanians to the capital. Over a dozen of these shopping malls have opened since the 1990s. This sprinkling of leisure facilities in various parts of Amman reinforces the city's multi-hub nature.

A notable exception to the development of these consumer-leisure venues in increasingly outlying neighbourhoods is a central residential area from the 1940s and 1950s, which has been renovated into a friendly and attractive space: the eastern part of Jabal Amman Hill, known as 'Rainbow Street'. The area is often presented as Amman's 'bohemian' spot due to its exhibition venues for local artists, a cinema, restaurants and 'trendy' cafes. It remains a place where young men and women, street musicians, connoisseurs of fine cars, families out for a walk, young football fans and hookah smokers meet – in short, a special place to observe the different young people who live in Amman but do not necessarily meet.

A football evening on Rainbow Street

Rainbow Street overlooks Amman's old town and its little marketplace. When shops in the lower city close, establishments on Jabal Amman Hill, and especially those on Rainbow Street, the backbone of the neighbourhood, start to come alive. It is a narrow street with one-way traffic, and not very long either. Young people like it because it is lined with oriental restaurants and snack bars offering falafels, oriental pizzas, *mana'ish* on a *saj* – a curved metal plate placed on a gas fire – and all kinds of Syrian and European culinary specialties. Rainbow Street attracts people of all socio-economic backgrounds, each one consuming according to their means, because it allows them to stroll among friends and to sit on a bench while contemplating the lower city and listening to young musicians play guitar in the small squares.

During the day, the street doesn't stand out from Amman's other 'fashionable' shopping areas. But on football match nights, the street comes alive with a special fervour. The street vendors selling pennants and flags in the colours of Jordanian youth's two favourite clubs – Real Madrid and FC Barcelona – can all be found here.[1] Hookah bars fill up more than two hours before the game kicks off, as the most ardent fans want to make sure they get a good seat – just in front of the screen! The staunchest fans meet in two characteristic establishments on the street, two adjoining cafés that share the same sidewalk. Tables at the two establishments are just next to each other and their giant screens hang back-to-back on the same wall. One hosts the pro-Barcelona crowd while the other welcomes the pro-Madrid fans. The atmosphere between the two groups is overexcited, at times electric, a bit provocative but never aggressive. Once the game has begun, the two groups switch to a duel where each one taunts the other in reaction to their favourite team's moves and dexterity. The confrontation between the two groups of young people is indirect; it is the sound level that informs us which team has the advantage, temporarily or conclusively. The young men stand in a cluster on the sidewalk, so as not to disturb the flow of traffic on the road, very close by.

The cars are also part of it. Some are decorated or covered with the favourite team's flag. They crawl along, stopping in turn wherever the crowd is thronging. Acting as if they all knew each other already, the discussion starts about the score of the match or about predictions. Further back, other drivers honk their horns. Traffic resumes in fits and starts at a snail's pace, then pauses anew before starting up again in an endless merry-go-round. The fate of the match ultimately determines who will occupy the street for the rest of the evening. The 'defeated' will have no choice but to leave while waiting to take their revenge.

Showing off, standing out, getting noticed

When it is not football factions symbolically dividing the space, evenings on Rainbow Street, especially on Thursday nights – because they precede the weekend – are the scene of another, more touching kind of confrontation. In small clusters, teenagers position themselves along the road to observe the traffic. Sitting, leaning on their elbows, or resting against parked vehicles, they watch the endless procession of other young people, who are older and especially richer, showing off at the wheel of their German or American cars. For the drivers, the most important thing, apart from the make and model of the vehicle, is to drive with the music blasting and the windows down. For the more brazen, parading with a young girl in the passenger seat – or even several! – gives them a great deal of prestige. Some of the teenage pedestrians film or take pictures, cell phone in one hand, cigarette in the other.

Constructing oneself

Rainbow Street is above all a place to be seen to show that one is both different and privileged – to show others that you are not from the same world. Most of the young people who watch the processions of beautiful cars are young Jordanians from the distant suburbs. Some of them are probably from Zarqa, famous for being a Salafist stronghold and the hometown of one of the leaders of Al-Qaeda in Iraq, Abu Mus'ab al-Zarqawi, killed by an American bomber at the age of thirty-nine in 2006. The young Jordanians are sometimes joined by young people of Palestinian origin, most of whom live in the Wahdad or Jabal Hussein refugee camps.

But the segmentation is also gendered. The small groups of young men also observe the groups of young women who dare to parade down Rainbow Street. For these girls, there is no question of stopping in the street and doing as the boys do; they're just passing by, under the male gaze. Sometimes they rush into a restaurant or a bar. But most of the time, they are content to cross the street from one side to the other. Strictly speaking, the street is not a place where the two sexes meet, contrary to the university which has undoubtedly remained the main place for mixing between genders. Rainbow Street is above all a place to parade in order to be noticed, but also, to stand out! In general, on the feminine side, outfits are rather light and casual, without ever being provocative. Amman is not Beirut! Closer to what one can observe in Damascus or Tehran, this part of Amman offers a chance to escape from the country's rather conservative social norms without completely transgressing them. Young girls, usually dressed in jeans and T-shirts, and often wearing a light scarf over their hair, are particularly fond of taking this route or coming here to have tea and smoke a hookah. They demonstrate their self-confidence as rather modern, trendy girls. They may nonetheless be perceived as less respectable by some of the young men who frequent the street.

At nightfall, Rainbow Street turns into a place for asserting privilege and differences, a place where it is appropriate to show others a facet or image of oneself, but without ever revealing oneself.

Leisure time, a break for middle-class girls

It is Thursday, late afternoon. A group of young women are walking down Rainbow Street and catch the eye of some boys sitting on a bench. The boys immediately start to talk louder, tossing out a few remarks and jokes in the girls' direction, hoping to catch their attention. The girls walk past without really looking and whisper a few words to each other, laughing. They might go to the ice cream shop or stop for some juice. But they probably won't do anything other than walk, holding each other's hands. While it's early enough for these students to still be out with their girlfriends, they won't go home late because they have a reputation to maintain. In any case, their brothers and cousins go out in the same neighbourhoods, so conventions are respected. Tomorrow is Friday, the weekly day off devoted to family. For now, they talk about love and their dreams. They compare the look of the boys on the bench, preferring the guitarist's hairstyle to that of his classmate who was playing with his cell phone while eyeing them out of the corner of his eye. One of them texts her cousin to tell her about their adventure.

Observing this scene, one can't help imagining the fate of these young women who clearly come from modest socio-economic backgrounds. According to the statistics about Jordanian society, these young girls will probably be married before the age of twenty-five and will have their first child within a year. Their future seems mapped out from childhood. After going to a girls' school, they attend university for a few years. Sometimes they break off their studies to get married. This youthful period is also the moment when they have the most free time in their lives. As young adults, they can choose activities according to their tastes and are now mature enough to venture out of the family circle.

The range of leisure activities is relatively limited, however. In terms of sports, the most attractive discipline is probably taekwondo, in which Jordan is well-placed internationally, and young women attend the numerous halls in the city assiduously. There are also aerobics and dance classes, and recently, due to a global trend, Zumba, a highly rhythmic athletic dance. Others prefer artistic disciplines (drawing, painting, music) or language courses. But most of their free time is spent with friends. The girls go out a lot with their friends – from the neighbourhood, from college or school. They invite each other to their homes. They go shopping or for walks in the few pedestrian areas of Amman. They also watch a great deal of television and spend a considerable amount of time on Facebook. Sometimes the young women join (women's) clubs that organise outings to the Dead Sea or the countryside.

A period of relative freedom, the years at university are also when the most interaction occurs between genders. Boys and girls mix and talk to each other in the cafeteria during breaks. Behind the banter, however, there is always the idea of a possible marriage. There is no question of going out for coffee together unless the relationship is on a serious track. The only real times for mingling are when the extended family gets together, and cousins can see each other.

Constructing oneself

But here again, the relationships forged then are not free of hidden matrimonial agendas. Later, once they are married and have families, these girls will certainly still visit one another and continue to 'cross paths' on Facebook, but a little less often since they must look after the house. Possibilities for leisure activities outside the family framework will become almost non-existent. In retrospect, the time when they were studying will seem like an interlude in their well-ordered life.

Amman's affluent youth: international leisure activities

Still on Rainbow Street, two very well-dressed young women wearing high-heeled boots and carrying brand-name leather handbags walk out of the British Council. They are taking classes to improve their English. They will probably go to the United States or England in a year or two, and before they do, they need to take language tests to confirm their enrolment at university. They haven't come to Rainbow Street to walk around or hang out with their friends. The neighbourhood is a bit too working-class and too crowded. While some trendy cafes and restaurants have opened here in the past few years, their favourite neighbourhood is Abdun, where they will go in the evening to eat at an upscale restaurant and hang out at a popular bar. During the week, they also go to Taj Mall, a huge shopping mall opened in 2012 with the chicest boutiques in the capital. Afterwards, they'll have tea at Paul's and nibble on French pastries, dropping the bags of clothes and shoes they have just bought by their chairs. They'll talk about their girlfriend who has just returned from a weekend in London.

These young women come from the aristocratic or bourgeois Jordanian elite, or from the Palestinian upper middle class. At this social level, national distinction is not so important. They have received a highly Westernised education and a lifestyle to go with it. Going out is no longer necessarily gender-related since their social milieu allows young men and women to date. Marriage is not an end in itself either. Although it is rare for a woman not to marry, she will do so later, sometimes after a period spent abroad to pursue her studies or acquire a professional specialisation. Until then, they have abundant leisure activities. They are enrolled in the most luxurious (mixed) gyms in Amman. They study music with a private teacher, go to the movies and go out a lot in the few trendy areas of the city. But Amman is too small for them. These young women dream of elsewhere.

'Rainbow Street'

The search for external role models to identify with remains strong in Jordanian society. This can be seen in a thousand details, by observing the young people from all social classes who cross paths on Rainbow Street. In the context of globalisation, Jordan offers few models to enhance these young people's self-esteem. As a result, they are tempted to turn to representations and idols imported from abroad. This is especially true since the government seems terrified of the models emerging elsewhere in the Arab world, whether revolutionary, free-market or Islamist. The apparent depoliticisation of young people has been reinforced by a Jordanian state looking more towards a future involving a consumerist Western model or the hedonistic and conservative Gulf model, rather than that of its immediate neighbours, Lebanon, Syria and Palestine, too politicised to be stable. Nonetheless, the innocuous aspect of these leisure activities cannot conceal that it is a society in great turmoil, but in which the political ferment is partly stifled by a particularly tense regional context.

Note

1 Regarding 'long-distance fans' in Palestine, see Chapter 9 by Abaher El Sakka in this volume, p. 93.

References

Ababsa, Myriam, *Atlas of Jordan. History, Territories and Society*, Presses de l'Ifpo, Beirut, 2013.
Ababsa, Myriam and Rami Daher, eds, *Cities, Urban Practices and Nation Building in Jordan*. Les Cahiers de l'Ifpo, no. 6, Presses de l'Ifpo, Beirut, 2011.
Bocco, Riccardo and Géraldine Chatelard, eds, *Jordanie. Le royaume frontière*, Éditions Autrement, coll. Monde, no. 128, Paris, 2001.
Hannoyer, Jean and Seteney Shami, eds, *Amman. Ville et société*, Cermoc, Beirut, 1996.

27

Brahim

Autopsy of a suicide in Kabylia

Kamel Chachoua

Around 2 p.m. early in the month of July 2012, on the fiftieth anniversary of Algeria's independence, Yousef, a young man in his thirties returning from the weekly market, nears the last turn on his way back home to the village of Taza, in Upper Kabylia. Assailed by the sun screeching as loud as the cicadas, dripping with sweat, Yousef decides to leave the trail to cross a deserted but shady field of olive trees to get home faster. At the bottom of the ravine, he gags at a nauseating smell, which he first thinks is that of a decaying animal. Since 1992, when Algeria sank into the 'black decade' that pitted the military in power against its Islamist adversaries, high mountain altitudes as well as riverbeds, and even outlying fields, have been abandoned by the population who left them 'to the terrorists and wild boars'. To escape the smell, Yousef covers his face with his arm, lowers his head and runs towards the Agouni water source that serves as a fountain for the Ath Ahmed lineage, who live on a small peripheral plateau inside the village of Taza. Suddenly, the body of a tall, dark man like the trunk of an olive tree looms in front of him in the middle of the path. Blinded and bent over from the stench, Yousef almost bumps into the hanged man. Terrified, he runs on to the village.

In the mosque, where a few young people are playing scrabble and dominoes on the shiny tiles of a room that serves as a meeting place for the village assembly (the *djama'a*), Yousef, looking despondent, shouts to them, 'A man hanged himself at the Agouni spring, you must go there!' The three or four adults and the few young men present wonder whether to go or to call the gendarmes or firemen first. The 1990s, marked by terrorist violence, have made people vigilant about public and anonymous deaths.

A few moments later, a handful of villagers take the direction indicated by Yousef, who refuses to accompany them. The young people also prefer to let the 'old men' go. They fear that the suicide may be linked to a crime, a murder or terrorism. 'In any case, we're just going to see, we won't touch anything', says one of the men as they're heading off. 'We'll just alert the fire brigade.' 'If it's a suicide, we won't take him down', confirms another.

On-site, in front of the silhouette of the young man hanging there with thick blond hair, a man stammers a verse from the Koran: 'There is no God but God, Mohammed is his prophet.' But Islam condemns suicide and denies burial to those who commit it. Belkacem, bringing up the rear, says quietly: 'He's not from our country, he's a foreigner [...] He's black! He has blond hair. By God, it's a mystery ... How is that possible?' 'No, he changed colour', someone answers: 'He's been here for several days.'

'The German'

Back in the village, the 'old men' describe the man to the young people who stayed behind: 'Maybe he's a foreigner', 'Maybe he's from the next village.' Among the young people, Kamel, an apprentice gendarme nearly twenty-two years old, is seized with fear. He slips off hastily in the direction of his family home. His older brother, Brahim, twenty-six years old, has been missing for over two days now. Arriving just before the firemen, one of the young people says: 'Oh, it's the German!' 'Yes, of course, it's Brahim!', confirms another. Brahim, the most handsome boy in the village of Taza. His blond hair and blue eyes had earned him the nickname 'the German'.

The firemen are familiar with suicides in general and especially hangings in this district of Upper Kabylia, which has broken the record for voluntary deaths for nearly twenty years. They arrive dressed in white, gloved and masked like beekeepers. One of them climbs the tree, cuts the rope and Brahim collapses heavily on the ground. Another fireman pulls a tarpaulin over him, zips it and takes him to the truck 'for an autopsy'. That evening, the body is brought back to the village where the young people have hastily dug a grave. They bury him late in the evening with no ritual, no sobbing and no wake.

Brahim, the 'German', had graduated from the University of Tizi-Ouzou two years earlier as a civil engineer. After college he moved to Oran, the capital of western Algeria, to live with his maternal uncle, a former officer in the Algerian army, who owned several businesses. Brahim went looking for a job, probably trying to find a way to avoid, or delay, his military service. Waiting 'to see' what he could find, he returned to the village over summer vacation. This was when the young people of Taza, who hadn't seen him for a long time, noticed that Brahim had gone 'weird', 'got carried away easily' and 'thought others were making fun of him'. In short, he seemed to be convinced that they thought he was a 'madman'.

Brahim belonged to the Algerian youth of the 2000s, which came after those who had actively experienced the 1990s. Young people in the 1990s had supplied many contingents to the various political parties in the Algerian Islamist and democratic opposition that emerged from the 'October 5, 1988' movement, which had led to the establishment of a multi-party system after nearly thirty years of hegemonic domination by the single party, the National Liberation Front (FLN). Educated during the period of terrorism that followed political liberalisation and the interruption of the electoral process in 1992, the new generation of the 2000s tended to focus on personal success and self-fulfilment. Of course, some spoke out and didn't hesitate to protest openly, such as during the Kabyle black spring of 2001, triggered by the death of a young man in a police station in Kabylia. But while their elders joined opposition political parties clandestinely or, in a few cases, sacrificed themselves for a cause in suicide attacks, the youth of the 2000s protested by demonstrating, striking or, more silently, 'fleeing' to Europe or – the ultimate act of turning violence experienced against oneself – committing suicide.

The state, which knew very little about these 'young people', has since learned about them and grasped their potential for harm and violence 'thanks' to terrorism – a fear on the part of the authorities that was further rekindled by the Arab revolts of 2011. That fear explains the vast policy of assistance and financial support 'for youth' in the 2000s, which took no account of economic and political considerations but seemed directed above all at maintaining social peace. This policy did not prevent a proliferation of sporadic and localised protest movements throughout the last decade or demands invariably presented by the authorities as riots to be silenced by the carrot or the stick.

'You know, mom, I'm going to hang myself'

So it was on 2 July 2012 that Brahim committed suicide. On that day, like every summer, the young people in the village of Taza, sitting on a cement bench inside the vast mosque, sheltered from the sun and close to the *djama'a*, are indulging in their favourite pastimes – dominoes for the less educated, scrabble for the more 'refined'. Brahim doesn't take part in the games; his reputation as a young man 'going crazy' relegates him to the status of a mere spectator.

Brahim

Around noon, at lunchtime, the place empties and only livens up again later, when everyone returns from their family home to give their parents a little rest, whether they like it or not.

Like them, Brahim goes off at midday. But he doesn't come back in the afternoon. After finishing his lunch, he goes – by pure chance or in a determined gesture? – to take a rope from the small storeroom at the back of the courtyard where his mother stores her tools and her supplies of wood and hay. At this hour, his mother has already found refuge in a nap, a moment of rest and dozing, but above all a private time to brood over her sorrows and worries and to take a break from reality. Still, as she will remember later, she heard Brahim say to her: 'You know, mom, I'm going to hang myself.' But she thought he was only 'joking'. Brahim goes to the spring, which the Ath Ahmed are the only beneficiaries of. There he chooses a forked branch of an olive tree to which he ties the rope and hangs himself.

The month of Ramadan fell in the middle of summer vacation that year. Several families were rushing to celebrate weddings before the fasting month began. Due to the multiple celebrations happening during this time, Fazia, Brahim's mother, isn't too worried and doesn't sound the alarm, thinking that her son is taking part in the village festivities. On those first warm nights that signal the beginning of vacation, the young people are all outside, on the roadsides, in cafés and on the village square where they stay up until the first light of dawn. The women, young and old, gather in the courtyards of their houses, the girls on the balconies and terraces.

As for Brahim's father, Mokrane, who has been severely handicapped since he was hit by a car on the highway, he has been living at home for almost four years. From time to time, he ventures into one of the two cemeteries in the village. He can be seen with his bony face, vacant body, and lowered eyes, walking with difficulty, alone, along the path. This image contrasts with another one from the 1970s, when Mokrane the 'madman', about thirty years old then, would suddenly appear in the village square, brandishing a long knife or an axe. The villagers pretended to ignore his madness so as not to provoke him. Seeing him from afar, the men would go the other way, the women would seek refuge in any house and the children would run off and bolt through the first open door. But Mokrane's 'madness' was also a show, a human-interest story and bit of entertainment, especially for the women who would observe him through the keyhole or the shutters.

Periodically, Mokrane went through more acute crises. He would knock on the door of a house, start cussing in public and shouting insults, keeping the women from going out, the men from leaving and the children from getting around for a few days. During these fits of 'madness', two or three men would take charge of him, due to their family kinship or public authority. They would drive him back to his house on the edge of the village, lock him up at home and let him wander around the area bordering the Ath Ahmed's block and the cemetery where his father's grave was.

The curse

Very little is known about Mokrane's childhood; we only know that he had been depressed and violent since adolescence. His mother died prematurely, it was said, while he was still an infant. His father, Menad, remarried and had three more children. When the war of liberation broke out in November 1954, Mokrane was about ten years old. It was his father, reputed to be 'turbulent', who brought the war to the village of Taza.

Menad was indeed among the very first men from the village to advocate for the FLN, in early 1955. He oversaw collecting contributions from several surrounding villages. A man from a neighbouring village, who refused to pay, denounced Menad to the municipal authorities. The next day, a group of French soldiers from the Tamazirt barracks surrounded the Ath Ahmed block of houses. One of the officers, who was about to question him in the courtyard of the house, was mortally wounded by Menad, who fled into the steep olive field that he knew by heart – the same field where his grandson Brahim committed suicide fifty-eight years later.

During the war, the reprisals on the household were violent and caused a stir in the community. A helicopter landed in the village, which had never even seen an automobile. Soldiers rounded up men between the ages of fifteen and sixty and took them to barracks. Only women, children and a few elderly men remained in Taza. Young people from a neighbouring village had to volunteer to come and dig the four graves to bury Menad's brothers, who had been executed by the French soldiers. During the many searches that followed, Menad's niece Salima, 'a beautiful seventeen-year-old girl with blue eyes', was repeatedly raped by the same soldiers until she committed suicide. Menad was finally killed after being reported by a teenager close to the family, during another sweep in 1958. After that date, the village was evacuated, and the entire population regrouped in another village on the plain until 1962.

Brahim

After independence, Mokrane lived alone in an empty house. The house where his father had been executed was temporarily 'handed over' to a family that resettled from a neighbouring hamlet and, ten years later, became Mokrane's in-laws. The 'arranged' marriage between Fazia, a poor orphan who had lost both her father and mother and was a 'foreigner' in the village, and Mokrane, also an orphan and 'crazy', was subdued and rather low-profile.

A year later, their first son, Brahim, was born. Mokrane seemed to have 'healed a bit'. He went once or twice a week to the village square, sitting silently on the low cement wall. He seemed to be entertained by listening to the others, staring down at his feet. Then he would go back home alone, satisfied at having accomplished his duty of being publicly present at the *djama'a*. Around 1978, Mokrane emigrated to Libya for a year or two. He was believed to be cured. The whole village, especially the young people and the women, whispered that the marriage had been salutary.

While Mokrane seemed to have recovered, it was his two half-brothers, Kader and Akli, sons of Menad and his second wife, who were struck by the curse. The former went through a spectacular depression. As for the latter, he experienced a rapid decline. Life seemed to smile on Akli, a 'tar worker', when he returned from a period of emigration to France. In the days following his return, he was even admired. He smelled nice, was well-dressed and, it was said, changed twice a day like a bride. Akli had long curly hair, wore colourful, close-fitting clothes, a sparkling bracelet on his wrist, two rings, a shiny chain around his neck, a large watch and a wide leather belt. 'All he was missing were earrings', recalled an old woman. For the first two months, Akli's presence was valued and even sought after for the stories he told about France. However, his influence diminished little by little and melted away as quickly as his savings. He sold his 'jewels' one by one, parted with his French clothes and ended up in pants with holes in them. He became undesirable at the grocer's and young people were wary of pulling out their packs of cigarettes in front of him.

For one villager, Brahim's extended family, his paternal uncles, in particular, were struck by a mysterious evil:

> Of all the four children of Menad, that valiant martyr, only Tahar has escaped madness ... By God, I don't understand a thing, yet they get a pension like all the sons of martyrs, they get a building grant, they're given priority for everything, they have a license for a café, and they've all been exempted from the draft ... Mokrane, their eldest half-brother, they say he's been mad since birth. Akli, the eldest from the second marriage, isn't crazy but he's wild and a delinquent. He left for France in the late 1960s as a young man [...], then he came back

empty-handed and started acting like someone from the projects here in the village. He became the number one drunkard, and he's also crude, provocative, and violent. But in that family, I feel like it's a curse or something, because even when they do well in school and behave well, they end up getting sick.

According to a local story, the curse that affects this family is rooted in the history of Taza. Brahim killed himself near the Agouni spring, of which the Ath Ahmed lineage was the sole beneficiary. Now, some inhabitants in the village think the spring water is the source – for magical or chemical reasons depending on who's speaking – of the curse that has struck the Ath Ahmed 'forever'.

'Arab' rebellions and 'Muslim' suicide

It is difficult to find an explanation for 'the German's' suicide. Even more so because Taza had already experienced other equally 'unexplained' hangings. If some see Brahim's unfortunate act as 'madness' or a 'curse', others evoke, even laconically, his discontent about his social status as the main cause of his action. In any case, it seems difficult to attribute Brahim's act to a single cause.

As commonly understood in the village, it was not the 'temporary' unemployment of this young engineer who had just graduated from university, nor a probable conflict or emotional unease with his parents, that 'killed' Brahim on its own. He was the pride and joy of the family due to his academic success. As for Brahim's mental health, it doesn't seem to be a determining factor, or at least not sufficient, to explain his suicide. Certainly, the young people in the village suspected 'the beginning of a depression' but no one saw in it such a deadly 'madness'. Finally, from a sociological point of view, it is risky to consider the war and its consequences as an unequivocal explanation for the mental disturbance of his father, Mokrane, who due to the curse would have 'contaminated' his son Brahim. The villagers from Mokrane's generation, who had experienced the war's consequences just as intensely, have for the most part avoided mental degeneration (it should be recalled that, at independence, any stigma resulting from the war was considered emblematic and, as such, was the object of official recognition and financial compensation).

The social sciences, like the common understanding in the Maghreb and in the Arab world in general, seemed to discover the 'civil' suicide (as opposed to a suicide bombing) of young people with the open-air immolation of young Mohammed Bouazizi on 17 December 2010, in a town in Tunisia – a gesture that the whole world analysed in retrospect as a political suicide linked to the massive unemployment and the contempt that young people suffered from the dictator Zine al-Abidine Ben Ali's corrupt and nepotistic regime. It is for this reason that the rumour mill, locally and nationally at first, then internationally, mistakenly accredited Mohammed Bouazizi with a university degree and wrongly accused a policewoman of having slapped him.

In fact, since Tunisia's independence in 1956 more than thirty years before the arrival of Ben Ali to power in 1987, it was the country that provided the largest contingent of suicide to the statistics of voluntary deaths in the Maghreb and the Arab world. One could say this was the price that Tunisian society paid for its policy of modernising public life, which disrupted Tunisian society's traditional points of reference. The two elements in the story, the diploma and the slap (both disproven), express the link established in local understanding between suicide and two phenomena: the dishonour inflicted by the slap from a woman on the one hand, and unemployment and political injustice on the other. Mohammed Bouazizi was neither a graduate nor unemployed, and he was not slapped by a policewoman. If one focuses on finding a single cause, his suicide ultimately remains 'unexplained', like Brahim's.

References

Ahmad, Majdi and Mohammad Abdallah, *Al-ittijah nahwa al-intihar wa ilaqatuhu bi-shakhsiyya* (The tendency to commit suicide and its relationship to the personality), Dar al-ma'rifa, Alexandria, 2008.

Chachoua, Kamel, 'Genre, suicides et sexualité(s) en Algérie', *Revue internationale de sociologie*, 20, 2, 2010: pp. 301–321.

Chachoua, Kamel, 'Le suicide en Algérie', in Henri Bresc and Christiane Veauvy, eds, *Religion et politique en Méditerranée*, Bouchène, Paris, 2007, pp. 387–412.

Motassem-Mimouni, Badra, *Tentatives de suicides et suicides des jeunes à Oran*, Éditions du CRASC, Algiers, 2011.

Moussaoui, Abderrahmane, 'Pertes et fracas, une décennie algérienne meurtrière', *NAQD, Revue d'études et de critiques sociales*, 18, autumn/winter, 2003: pp. 133–149.

Taieb, Yousef, *Le suicide. Ce tragique destin*, El Amel, Tizi-Ouzou, 2004.

28

'Bnat lycée dayrin sexy'

From fun to sex work in Tangier (Morocco)

Mériam Cheikh

In the 2000s, Cheb Rayan, the famous singer of 'Raï Love' from Tangier, released a track entitled '*Bnat lycée*' ('The Schoolgirls'). In his judgemental lyrics, he criticised the behaviour of young *lycée* schoolgirls (aged fifteen to eighteen), whom he accused of 'having sex' ('*dayrin sexy*'). Instead of studying and behaving like good girls, he stated, they used the school as a place for meeting and 'debauchery'. His song was in tune with the urban rumours that filled the public imagination and the Moroccan Web 2.0. For a decade, young women in school uniforms (in Morocco, schoolgirls in elementary, middle and high school wear pink or white uniforms and boys wear blue or white uniforms) were 'under the microscope', as expressed in the title of an article in the French-speaking weekly *Maroc Hebdo* in 2007. Since the status of pupils allows for a certain freedom of movement, schoolgirls could contribute to the depravity that characterises current urban Morocco. He criticised them for having questionable morals, for going out with boys and for hanging around outside the school gates for longer than is reasonable. They were also accused of following strangers who approached them and of getting into cars with men.

This image of the schoolgirl resonated with the accounts that young sex workers can tell about their adolescence and their schooling. These women give an important place to the themes of self-discovery and fun in their stories, in a departure from a sociological discourse that only highlights poverty, deprivation, violence, ignorance, rape or incest to describe their situation. The telling of these 'wild nights' or '*tkehkih*' in Moroccan allows us to see these young girls for who they are, i.e. youths, adolescents and girls, but also reveals the processes at play when engaging in romantic relationships in which men's financial help matters. In these accounts, occasional prostitution or entry into sex work starts in the context of leisure activities. Even if 'youth', 'adolescence' and 'fun' seem to go together, it is rare that we talk about these terms when we broach the subject of monetised sexuality in general and sex work in Morocco more specifically. However, it is by looking at these phenomena together that we can understand the complexities of the journey of a youth caught between expectations of marriage and migration that are hard to come by, a sense of humiliation triggered by the experience of working in key sectors of unskilled female work (industry, cleaning), and committing to a career of sex worker. Rather than the lives of sex workers, it will therefore be more a question of difficult or sometimes compromised entries into adult life.

In the account that follows, that of Hayat, born in 1989, we will discover the daily life of a young working-class woman, subverting the norms of modesty and overtly displaying a desire to have fun. We will also see how, as they discover the opposite sex, young women learn how to make money despite the risk of being brutally assigned to a sexual identity and gradually committing themselves to a career of sex work as soon as the need to care for themselves becomes more pressing and as the traditional channels for female fulfilment – notably, marriage – become more scarce.

Wild teenage nights

It was an ordinary afternoon, as I had often spent with the youngest of the girls that I met in the course of my research and with whom I shared a large part of my daily life. On that day in June 2007, Hayat telephoned me and proposed that we go to the beach. About an hour later, she collected me from the apartment that I shared with her former school friends. It was almost 3 p.m. At the foot of the building, Hayat was waiting for me in a sports car that was double parked. Her boyfriend, two years older than her – they had been together on and off for several years – was at the wheel and a friend was in the passenger seat. I joined her in the back seat, and we left in the direction of the Atlantic coast, about ten kilometres from Tangier. Hayat told me about her week, her voice covered by the deafening music. These last few days, she had returned to school. She had tried to catch up as much as possible in her studies in order to be able to revise. In several days, the first baccalaureate exams were going to take place. Although she had spent all of the last year outside the school, she seemed confident. At nineteen years old, she considered the 'bac' as her last chance to get a decent job. Her father, a primary school teacher in a small country school, had told her that if she got it, he would take care of getting her into the teacher training college: 'He's got connections', she told me. Her boyfriend listened to her carefully, despite him looking stoned and having bloodshot eyes that suggested that he was somewhere else. In a slow and mocking tone, he asked her: 'You, a teacher! That's a good one!' Hayat believed that she could do it. 'What do you know about school, you idiot!' He replied that he had been there longer than she had. Then, she turned to me and asked eagerly how she could answer the exam questions. I was taken aback because we have never talked about her studies. She had already stopped listening to me. Her boyfriend, in response to her teasing, took one hand off the wheel and reached over to smack her. They had a playfight, which tested the young man's driving skills as he was no longer looking at the road. Hayat giggled. Still on the road, we forgot school and had fun squabbling. The wheels rolled, the sun shone down and, when we arrived, carried along by the carefreeness of the moment, we looked for a spot on the beach away from the path where we could kill time until the evening. The long afternoon was punctuated with joking, swimming, music played on mobile phones, playfighting and verbal sparring. The group swelled when other young girls and boys joined us and thinned out when couples retreated to more secluded spots.

The school of entertainment

Officially, Hayat had been 'schooled'. But this does not reflect the reality of her daily life. During the day, she joined her female friends and boys in cafés, on the beach or in neighbourhood *golfazurs*, games rooms (often billiards) which remained open until late at night in Tangier. The boys were schoolmates, neighbourhood friends or young people they met in the places they spend time in. The most sought-after are cafés where smoking hashish is allowed. The history of hashish in the Tangier region explains its free consumption in certain cafés in the city, usually in the 'medina' (the old part of the city). These are often old and essentially male cafés, but girls can be accepted as long as a man accompanies them or introduces them to the place. Between joints and games (*parchis*), the atmosphere is good-natured. At night, the girls go out dancing, flirting and having fun. In nightclubs, which play Western music, they are sometimes offered gifts and a small amount of cash. Hayat's teenage outings have left her with memories that still make her laugh out loud when she recounts them a few years later:

> Once when I was with Salima, we had to join some guys in Tangier. We met them, they were nice and they invited us out. We didn't have any money and we didn't want to do the 'we have no money' thing. So, we stole a hen from Salima's

parents and came to town with it to sell it. It was so embarrassing! We had the hen in a bag. I remember it well: we went up the boulevard and, near the *Place des Paresseux*, there were some good-looking guys [*bogosses* from French *beau gosses*] in a 4x4 who were hitting on us. We started doing our thing. That day, we thought we had it all: we had the latest hairstyle [and] the latest *djellabas*. We swayed our hips and pretended to snub them. In reality, we were dying to get into their car, we had forgotten who was waiting for us in the evening. Anyway, suddenly the hen tried to get out of the bag, flapping her wings all over the place. How embarrassing! The guys fled. I bet even today they must talk about the '*jebliate*' [country girls] who showed off.

Before being a young girl engaged in the intimate economy, i.e. in intimate relationships where money and love overlap, Hayat was a schoolgirl who liked to enjoy herself. As a teenager, she was even a 'troublemaker' for her family and school. Of all the girls I see and have lived with, she is the last one who still clings to her schooling. She and my housemates met on the school benches. It was at this time that they were introduced to the small, guilty pleasures of adolescence: the first cigarettes, the first dates with boys outside school, the first trips to discos, the first joints and so on. When Hayat visited us at the apartment, the girls liked to reminisce about those first experiences. Hayat recounted:

> I really liked school, but I preferred to spend my time out of school [...]. I hung out in the street, with the boys [*drari*] in the games rooms. Sometimes I didn't go to school for days. I told the teacher that I had to stay home to help my mother with the housework. My mother didn't know anything about my day, so I could tell her that the teacher changed the time or that he was not there. The teachers didn't care if I wasn't there. It was better for them, they'd rather not see me. I didn't do anything in class except have a laugh. It was worse before when Salima and the others [i.e. my housemates] were there. Our attitude [*aqliya*] before was not the same as it is today. [...] We didn't use our brains at the time, they were always spinning out of control, we'd put them back in place and they'd run away again.

Hayat thus adopted a negative attitude towards school which inevitably put her on the path of academic failure. Her socialisation occurred during the time she played truant. Far from the classroom, Hayat wanted to mix with boys, which was allowed on school benches but was considered suspicious outside the school walls. By leaving her home every day to go to her classes, she avoided the control of her family and schools – and was able to be around other young students, both boys and girls. Paradoxically, schooling played a crucial role in Hayat's life. This is proved by the ties that she continues to have with my housemates. It was with them that she learned to socialise with boys, to develop friendships with them or more intimate relationships. Socialisation within or around the school is all the stronger because these young girls have spent an average of ten years of their lives there. In working-class urban areas, where families are made more vulnerable by their daily financial struggles, it is clearly a defining space for the construction of their adolescent individuality.

Unfortunate journey: when amusement becomes alienating

In May 2008, I found Hayat and the apartment that I had temporarily left. Having left school without getting her 'bac', she now lived in our shabby apartment squeezed together with young girls with precarious employment – casual workers, occasional sex workers or both at the same time. Hayat added her own trajectory alongside the others, moving seamlessly from school to this collective household of young and poor urban single women. When we gather in the evenings in front of the TV, she sometimes speaks to me again about her school years.

> You were out having fun, having a good time. I didn't feel like I was devalued [*naqsa*]. I was just like everybody else. When we went out with guys, we thought we were at the other side of the world. I could smoke, take out my pack of cigarettes. I was only going to Azilah [forty kilometres from Tangier] and I felt like I had gone a long way away. We'd arrive, we'd get the cigarettes out, we'd think we were in Europe. We would say: it's fine, we're far away, no one knows us here. It was as if we had taken the boat and left here [laughs]. Today, we have a lot of hang-ups. I have hang-ups about everything, about my body, everything. I'm afraid of everything. Last time, at the beach, with Nadira, we kept changing places because we wanted to avoid being next to groups of boys. Even the lifeguard looked at us and laughed and said, 'What's the matter with you? Are you lost?' We didn't even dare to put on our bathing suits, even though no one was bothering us, everyone was minding their own business.

Her self-mocking tale, however, shows remorse about her adolescence. This is contained in the term '*zigha*', which she frequently uses when she talks about recreational behaviours that often flirt with the conventional boundaries of female behaviour. Difficult to translate, *zigha* designates the irrepressible desire for fun and discovery that draws us away from rationality, from self-control, and makes us, as Hayat says, 'stray from the path'. She tried to explain to me:

Zigha, zigha … you don't know what it is! How am I going to explain it? It's when you're unsettled, when you absolutely have to do something. You have to go out to the nightclub, you have to go out and have fun, you have to have a good time. You start smoking, you try drugs, you laugh with the boys, you spend time with them […]. I needed to go out [*zanqa*]. Once I was outside, I felt good. I needed to get out, to get in cars, drink, smoke … I had to try everything. I had to try all that, we didn't know how to give thanks to God or do our studies and all that, no.

When put into the context of a present lived in fear and an uncertain future, these adolescent 'wild times' become, in retrospect, what 'messes up' (*tkarfast b-had l-hbal*) the trajectories. Certainly, these moments opened up the experience of 'modern' individuality. But, in view of the present situation, it cannot be acknowledged as such. These outings 'mess up' because they make young girls into bad girls, street girls (*bent ez-zanqa*) as opposed to house girls (*bent ad-dar*).

Hayat became a street girl because she made youthful urban pleasures a means of earning a livelihood. By going out to have fun, receiving gifts and being paid for her outings by the boys, she became a woman who could take charge of her life because the men supported her. She complied with this gender-specific arrangement, which eventually took over. While 'fun' in adolescence holds the promise of individual fulfilment, it turns into an alienating form of entertainment as one enters adulthood.

First relationships: made fragile by money

Hayat slid into sex work at the end of her adolescence. There were almost no marriage offers (let alone from 'good parties') and there was little paid work for a young girl with no professional qualifications or experience. For Hayat, the alternative was to take a risk by investing in stable relationships with boys in order to realise her goal of marriage. This conforms to a traditional model of gender roles, in which economic inequality between men and women means that women are dependent on men – with the difference that this type of relationship takes place outside of marriage.

After leaving school, Hayat moved into a small studio with her boyfriend for a few months. In the spring of 2008, the daily routines and his family's refusal to see him married at such a young age precipitated a painful breakup. Hayat then began a relationship with another man who supported her. Without leaving our flatshare, which she continued to pay to make sure she had a place to fall back on in case of problems, she spent long months confined in his house, without

Constructing oneself

being able to go out. The jealousy of her boyfriend reinforced her belief that this relationship would lead to marriage. However, when we met again in 2009, he had left her for someone else. Her roommates were relieved that she had not got married before them and commented upon the break-up in these terms:

> He used her. She played at being his wife and she ended up on the streets. She cooked for him and washed his clothes. Now she'll understand how to deal with men: treat them like dogs!

Not only did this event shake Hayat's feelings and hopes, but it also weakened her financial situation. From now on, she had to rely only on herself. At the time of the break-up, her true vulnerability came to the surface.

Hayat was driven into relationships that offered her the prospect of respectable social status. She had a series of other relationships that did not last but created a momentum that propelled her into 'the going out'. In Moroccan, going out (*tan khrej*) encompasses all kinds of acts that contravene female morality (going out on the street, going out to have fun, going out with a boy). Over time, it came to mean prostitution. It is in the realm of entertainment that Hayat expanded her knowledge. It is also in this space that she gradually assumed a reputation as a girl who goes out or as a 'whore', especially when money became uppermost.

> [My last boyfriend], he didn't promise to marry me, but I was hoping, I was thinking, you never know. I stayed with him in his apartment. Every night he took me out, we got all dressed up and went to restaurants, he gave me everything I needed. I was fine, I didn't have to look for work. But then we had a row. Little by little, he didn't come home and I found myself all alone, shut in and with no money at all. I had to get by, go out and make some money. I joined Salima and the others and stayed to live with them. They encouraged me to go out […]. The boys, they keep on giving you things, giving you things. They even give you money. And you get used to that system and then you need a boy who can give you things.

The search for fun doesn't stop the girls from hoping that their first love will be 'serious' (*l-ma'qul*). Although it began as hedonistic, 'going out' gradually evolves into a less casual and more 'professional' affair. As intimate relationships become sources of income, what seemed to be a process of subjectification and emancipation evolves into a process of social alienation, through dependence upon the wealth of men and practical necessity. Little by little, these young girls drift towards the 'forced' adoption of a transgressive lifestyle that endangers their respectability, their health and their safety. Their experiences are tragic in the sense that the girls have a dual sense of belonging while having fun but it then melts away in unsuccessful intimate relationships.

Getting out of it?

Having been 'schooled', Hayat becomes an unemployed woman seeking marriage and respectable adult status. In her search, she uses the means available to her: her experience of fun and relationships with men. She and my roommates are regular visitors to one of the biggest nightclubs in Tangier. Nearly every night, they find themselves on the dance floor and share the same groups of male acquaintances just like when they were teenagers, flirt with clients together and experience the same ordeals of sexuality outside marriage (arrests, detention and charges).

In the last two years, Hayat has changed tremendously. She has gained a lot of weight, her face is marked and the dark circles around her eyes are constant. She hardly sleeps at all and spends her nights outside. She dances on the dance floor, waiting for a client to suggest they spent the night together. By the time she gets back in the morning, she has little time to recover. She tells me that she plans to leave the nightclub, while touching the intimate parts of her body and repeating, 'I hate myself, I'm ugly. I am only a pair of breasts.' In scarcely a year, the nightclub has turned her into a fully-fledged sex worker. In the past, she was able to escape this reductive identity because she had her own career. Today, the controlling way that the nightclub manager manages her nights prevents her from defining herself differently:

> If you don't come one night, you're not allowed in. If you don't follow the dress code, you're not allowed in. Every night, you must wear a particular colour. On Wednesdays, it's orange; it's red on Tuesdays and Thursdays its always more dressed up. If you don't respect that, you're stuck because they won't let you in anymore. For example, if you miss days, they won't allow you in or then they'll make you pay 200 dirhams. They treat you like their employee even though you don't have any contract with them. If you miss nights, they will ask you for an explanation.

The illicit management of girls who come to the disco to engage in prostitution is a powerful mechanism shaping the sex worker. Hayat is not wrong. She sees clearly that frequenting this place takes away her means of resistance. The injunction to be there every night places the girl at the heart of the nightclub, no longer as a girl who is having fun and thus can meet a boy with whom she

Constructing oneself

can create a life outside of the nightclub scene, but as a girl who is part of the furniture of the place and identifiable by a colour code like the rest of the staff (waiters, bouncers and cleaners). Hayat dreads this possibility of being identified because it reminds her of the degradation of her condition: from being a young girl having fun in this same nightclub, she has become a sex worker put to work for an employer who does not even pay her. The bouncers stationed at the entry have the task of discreetly reminding them of an informal rule: they cannot leave with a client at the beginning of the night and must entertain and make the men drink, or else they will be refused entry the next time.

The girls carry out their business on their own but their activities benefit the nightclub and feed small parasitic middlemen – bouncers, taxi drivers, police and hoteliers – who make extra money thanks to the girls: the client generally pays more than the girls receive. Hayat, like the other girls, thus became a nighttime professional:

> [Before], all I used to think about was going out, having fun [*ntkahkah*] with the boys. Life was simple. We were crazy. Now I'm fed up with the one who tells you to come here, stand like this, turn around like this, or the other one who snatches your breasts and the other one who tells you: 'Now it's my friend's turn.' The other day, I saw Zoubida again. It's been a long time since I heard anything about her. I saw her at the foot of a building. When she saw me from a distance, she was ashamed and pretended that she hadn't recognised me. She was ashamed because she was acting like a street whore. You know, the ones that get made fun of because they go off with the boys whoever they are. The dirty ones, the sick ones. Imagine Zoubida, the one we were having fun with, we were going to Marrakech for the weekend. She turned her head, she didn't want me to see her. The street frightens me. When I try to keep a boyfriend, I can't because I need money and I have to go out every night.

Hayat found it all the more difficult to secure a stable and serious relationship because the way she viewed money within a relationship had now changed. In order not to frighten potential husbands, she had to refuse any money offered to her and seek it elsewhere. She tried to retrain and had unsuccessful attempts at factory work. Each time, she was sent back towards 'going out', from which is increasingly difficult to escape. Hayat was already in too deep. You could see this on her body and her face:

> I went to the wiring factory for work, some girls told me that they were hiring at the moment. We were in a queue and they made us stand there for two hours. Afterwards, each took turns in front of a girl who would say whether or not you

went in for the [job] interview. When I was in front of her, she didn't even look at me, she just said, 'Next.' I had my CV with me and I was qualified because I had the education level that they asked for. And she didn't even look up. I didn't get it. That day, I hated myself. The other day, my cousin challenged me: 'Don't bother, we all know what you're doing, you should go home to your mother.' I hate myself! I hate myself!

In leaving childhood, one ends one's adolescence and waits for the fulfilment of hopes for marriage, the only way out for young girls dreading submission to menial female work, the embodiment of poverty, and giving up social mobility. 'Going out' is, in the beginning, the way out of indignity, confusion and uncertainty. 'Going out' for entertainment provides compensation. It provides pleasure for oneself as well as purchasing power. But it struggles to be what young girls wish it to be: an interim while they wait to become adults. When marriage offers and decent jobs become scarce, the sex work trap tightens. That's how Hayat entered the entertainment and sex industry. Self-affirmation as an individual ideal, or, in the case of a disaffiliated young woman, the compensation of her social indignity through recreation, is transformed into a life of pain marked by the difficulty of freeing oneself from one's condition.

References

Ayouch, Nabil, *Much Loved*, 2015 (film).
Cheikh, Mériam, *Les filles qui sortent. Jeunesse, sexualité et prostitution au Maroc*, Éditions de l'Université de Bruxelles, Brussels, 2020.
Derkaoui, Mustapha, *Casablanca by Night*, Art 7, 2003 (film).
Kilani, Leïla, *Sur la planche*, Aurora Films, 2011 (film).

Part IV

Speaking out

Introduction

Speaking out

Laurent Bonnefoy and Myriam Catusse

The fourth part of the book looks at the relationship between Arab youth's leisure time and the act of speaking out and being engaged, whether ephemeral like the insurrectionary and revolutionary events in 2011 or more established over the long term. Until recently, any interest in movements in the region was generally articulated around two main ideas, a result of the repression carried out by authoritarian regimes in the Arab world until the 2011 uprisings. The first was that Arab societies, and their youth in particular, were politically passive, subjugated by regimes that wielded the carrot and stick or more subtle forms of domination, or were discouraged by the exorbitant cost of protest action in such contexts (from one country to another, there have been countless numbers of missing persons, political prisoners, people tortured, exiled or subjected to various modes of oppression). The second idea described the political field in a binary way, contrasting ageing regimes heir to nationalist ideologies with Islamist or identity-based movements that have significant dissident potential.

While these two assertions are unquestionably based on major trends that characterise Arab societies, they may, however, have overlooked a string of other, more complex relationships to public affairs. Inspired among others by the work of the American political scientist James C. Scott, who highlighted understated and unexpected forms of peaceful resistance led by farmers in Southeast Asia in the face of agrarian reform,[1] many of the young researchers working on the Arab world for the last few years have availed themselves of this insight. In their research, they have detected masked protests and even the beginnings of new political practices, breaking with previous militant generations (often socialised at university around socialist, Arabist or Islamist slogans) and frequently structured around local causes. The texts in this last part are an extension of this highly stimulating line of inquiry which, also due to the apparent failure of the revolutionary uprisings of 2011, remains a very relevant way of understanding the diversity of the ways of speaking out.

The forms of entertainment described in the following texts flirt with various types of politicisation. This means giving a voice to young people who have long been confined to a world of silence or exile ('exit', to use the well-known category invented by Albert Hirschman[2]). But we are not exploring professional activists strictly speaking here or activities that may be carried out within the framework of partisan enlistment. Rather, the ten chapters that follow observe how social relations are loudly reinvented, including in the virtual world and in the face of various forms of censorship, how viewpoints are expressed, but also how the boundaries of public action and private happiness are redrawn through playful (re)creative and often altruistic activities.

In previous parts of the book, we have seen how singular subcultures have already developed. Some of them are reserved for personal fulfilment, contemplation or hedonistic pleasures and are removed from any political activity. Others, without being explicitly formulated as a public commitment, are more inclined to be linked to partisan dynamics or to betray a vision of society: Sufi or Salafist practices, nostalgic rambles in left-wing bars or Shiite theatre blur the boundaries between recreation and activism. Among the multitude of practices that we could have observed in this last part, three more distinctive angles seemed to us to be the most telling.

First, we wanted to explore how new technologies, and in particular the Internet, are used. Highlighted around the figure of the 'cyber-dissident', they may appear to be a virtual grassroots mobilisation, heralding the advent of practices that are as 'playful' as they are 'democratic' and 'participatory'. The more realistic analyses developed in this part of the book allow us to get a closer look at these young Web activists and to show how an apparently 'apolitical' struggle against censorship and repression has shifted in Tunisia, Syria and to a lesser extent Saudi Arabia, into more explicit power games.

We then wanted to call to mind how revolutionary moments can influence free time and leisure activities, shown through two contrasting examples. One chapter looks at how young Libyan *thuwwar* (revolutionaries), returning from combat, extended their military exploits and kept alive their collective experience on the front in their daily meetings in a café in the city centre. Another text looks at the growing 'political' awareness among some young Sunni Bahrainis used to a consumerist life. Giving up their usual leisure activities momentarily, they decided to commit themselves to 'defending their homeland' against movements perceived as a threat to their community.

Introduction

Finally, the book ends with a series of chapters devoted to activist art. As speaking out is often severely restricted in the Arab world, art can be used to thwart prohibitions, raise public awareness and touch people. Describing the emergence of new languages and forms of dissidence, the last five chapters of the book address these practices of (re)creative resistance and artistic innovation. The texts show the street art that has developed in a remarkable way in Yemen (or in Egypt); depict Palestinian art as a way to transcend colonial domination; and listen to those 'angry'[3] musicians who, in Beirut, Casablanca or Alexandria, orchestrate the words of protest in lyrics and melodies.

Notes

1 James Scott, *Domination and the Arts of Resistance*, Yale University Press, New Haven, CT, 1990.
2 Albert O. Hirschman, *Exit, Voice, and Loyalty. Responses to Decline in Firms, Organizations, and States,* Harvard University Press, Cambridge, MA, 1970.
3 Christophe Traïni, *La musique en colère*, Presses de Science Po, Paris, 2008.

29

'A bad day for Ammar'

When Tunisian bloggers took on Internet censorship

Romain Lecomte

An old, balding civil servant, bespectacled, frustrated, devoid of charisma and with no social life, often equipped with a pair of scissors: this was how many imagined 'Ammar', a character invented by Tunisian Internet users to personify Internet censorship in the era of Ben Ali. Ammar was symbolic of the link forged on the Tunisian web throughout the 2000s between leisure and politics: as well as being entertaining and an inexhaustible source of jokes, he was also an expression of discontent with regard to the repeated attacks on freedom of the Tunisian Internet, the freedom to express an opinion about public affairs but also simply how to spend one's free time. Operation *Nhar 3la 3ammar* ('Bad Day for Ammar' in *arabizi*[1]) was launched in May 2010 by Tunisian bloggers in order to organise demonstrations abroad and especially in Tunis against Internet censorship in Tunisia and is particularly interesting in this respect. Barely six months before the revolution, it was led by actors who, although they did not cling to the portrayal of 'symbols' and 'leaders' in the media, would play an important role during the revolutionary uprising, by updating their (cyber) activist networks and their methods of protesting. This was a new project in the history of Tunisian cyberactivism, taking a 'virtual' protest out into the streets, which illustrated two types of connection between leisure and politics that have existed throughout the history of Tunisian Internet usage. First of all, it shows how a digital space that was initially adopted by (predominantly young) individuals to occupy their free time, entertain themselves, maintain and create social bonds and build and affirm their identities finds itself politicised in large part in response to blanket censorship. Secondly, in terms of the forms of political expression and collective action that flow from it, it reflects the integration of characteristics of leisure: humour, entertainment and informality. The leaders of this operation chose the path of using entertainment to encourage ordinary Tunisian Internet users to get involved in activism. In addition to the playful and amusing character of Ammar, this mobilisation was characterised by three major features: transparency, legalism and 'apoliticism'.

Not enamoured with Ammar: from leisure to protest

Although the development of the Tunisian Internet had been promoted by the Ben Ali regime, it feared that this technology would be 'misused' against it and implemented a very strict control on its use, of which censorship constituted an essential aspect. Based upon sophisticated 'made in democracy' technology (exported from the US, in particular), this essentially consisted of blocking access to an entire website or even a profile on a 'social network' platform such as Facebook or Twitter. Instead of blocked pages, the censors hypocritically presented Internet users in Tunisia with an 'error 404' page (like Ammar, this was a good source of jokes), indicating a technical problem. Far from being limited only to cyber-dissidents and opposition activists, this censorship was a steamroller that spared few spaces adopted by 'ordinary' Tunisian Internet users, for whom the web was above all a completely harmless means of relaxing and sharing. Unless they used circumvention tools, Internet users could not, for example, watch the latest video of their favourite pop singer on YouTube or DailyMotion, or even share their personal photos on Flickr, which were all banned websites. Personal blogs primarily centred on the private lives or personal passions of their authors were also '404ized'. Far from stifling criticism online, this increasingly suffocating censorship, on the contrary, pushed an increasing number of initially uncommitted Internet users to express their dissatisfaction, not only individually but also collectively. As a common enemy, Ammar inadvertently helped to pierce through the partition between the minority of 'cyberdissidents' in search of political change and the majority of Tunisian 'ordinary' Internet users in search of entertainment and self-expression.

It was in this context that an umpteenth wave of censorship led to yet another wave of protest in April and May 2010. A 'virtual demonstration' was launched first: *Sayeb Sala7 (ya 3ammar)* – '(Ammar) Get off my back' – an online photo gallery fed over a number of days by Tunisians addressing Ammar by displaying funny anti-censorship slogans. But above all, in the wake of *Sayeb Sala7*, a handful of more ambitious bloggers announced 'real demonstrations for virtual freedom' at the beginning of May in foreign cities and especially in Tunis, in front of the Ministry of Communication Technologies. Were Tunisian Internet users about to take to the street?

Speaking out

The hard core of *Nhar 3la 3ammar*, formed during the first week of May, was composed of a little more than a dozen young Tunisian adults (the oldest was thirty-five years old and the vast majority were between the ages of twenty and thirty), educated and urban (they lived in Greater Tunis and in major European or American cities). Only a minority grew up in an activist family environment (where parents and sometimes other family members were or had previously spoken out against the current regime). Some of them, especially those who lived abroad, were already known as 'cyberactivists'. Others were much less well known, such as the two young men who would become the main figures of the mobilisation in Tunis: Yassine Ayari (a twenty-seven-year-old computer engineer) and Slim Amamou (a thirty-two-year-old computer scientist). The group relied largely on a mailing list (Google group) to coordinate and develop the mobilisation campaign. Despite the repressive environment, this mailing list, which includes standard Arabic, Tunisian dialect and French, was made public in the name of an ideal of transparency and openness: participation required an application for membership approved by votes of its members, but anyone, from the ordinary individual to the 'cop', could consult it.

The focus of the *Nhar 3la 3ammar* protagonists' concerns quickly became the implementation of the Tunis demonstration, relegating the demonstrations abroad planned in front of the Tunisian consulates in Paris, Montreal, New York and Bonn to the rank of 'supporters'. Opting for a legalistic approach, the group intended to file a formal declaration of assembly with the Tunisian authorities in order to receive a formal legal acknowledgement in due course. Since the law required that this 'declaration [be] signed by at least two people', the first difficulty bloggers faced was finding at least two citizens in Tunisia willing to sign such a document, and therefore to expose themselves particularly to the 'joys' of engaging in protest in Tunisia. It was agreed by the group of *Nhar 3la 3ammar* that these signatories, beyond their legal responsibility, became the two main public figures of the mobilisation, in particular by providing detailed information to Internet users about the administrative procedures in order to legalise the demonstration. For the group, it was therefore essential that these signatories be 'apolitical', independent of any activist structure. After a few days of discussions and doubts, Yassine Ayari and Slim Amamou were finally the only two confirmed signatories, joined about ten days later by Lina Ben Mhenni (a twenty-seven-year-old assistant professor at the university). These two computer scientists did not know each other but developed a strong personal bond and become the real heads of *Nhar 3la 3ammar*.

'A bad day for Ammar'

'Vaseline is necessary' ☺

This quest for non-politicised representatives (legal as well as public) was in fact part of the 'apolitical' interpretative frame (in the sense given by the sociologist David Snow) that the group was trying to give to the 22 May gathering throughout the three weeks of its preparation. The tone was declared on the Facebook page dedicated to the event:

> The demonstration is independent of any political party or association.
> It will be peaceful. PS: Please do not bring back flags or music that could give a political or religious meaning to the demonstration.

On their blogs and other personal web spaces, certain members of the group presented the demonstration as 'apolitical' in a more explicit way. As reflected in their conversations on the mailing list, for example, this public distancing from any 'political' connotation refers not only to a profound disavowal by these young Tunisians who are not 'party members' with regard to the approaches to organisation and action of the traditional Tunisian opposition but also, inextricably, to tactical considerations (taking into account authoritarian coercion) and strategic considerations (mobilising a large number of 'ordinary' Internet users). Without being able to go into detail about the different meanings and issues of this avowed 'apoliticism' that has been proclaimed throughout the history of Internet protest in Tunisia, let us focus in particular on its tactical dimension.

With regard to power, this 'apoliticism' aimed to reduce the costs of engagement (repression and other forms of harassment), especially for those living in Tunisia. Focusing criticism solely on censoring the Internet without openly denouncing those responsible, it avoided implying a radical questioning of power. Inextricably, this caution aimed to 'reassure' the ordinary Internet user who would have liked to take part in the Tunis demonstration. Ammar was a very convenient target in this regard: this fictional character had a humorous and entertaining dimension, making it possible to avoid clearly pointing out the real people in charge. While Ammar is symbolic of the connection between 'leisure' and 'politics' on the Tunisian Internet, this connection was also favoured by the repressive environment in which it took place. Throughout the last decade, Tunisian Internet users have refined what political scientist James C. Scott calls the 'arts of political dissimulation', insinuating criticism in public but anonymously or 'disguising' this criticism. This art of concealment, recognised among peers, often had a playful dimension: a game with the authorities (sorry, with Ammar!). Many Internet users had become experts in the use of language codes (particularly to avoid keywords that they assumed were integrated into surveillance software), allusions, metaphors and other euphemisms to escape the vigilance of the very zealous Ammar, but also in the use of anonymisation software to reduce the risks of being unmasked or simply accessing censored spaces. 'As you can see, we keep reading you!', they sometimes liked to indicate to their censored companions, like thumbing their nose at Ammar. The game was not without risk and *Nhar 3la 3ammar* led its protagonists to redouble their caution with its particularly bold project (to take to the streets).

-Z-, an anonymous cartoonist blogger (a thirty-something Parisian architect) who used to mock the most senior state officials on his blog, for example, faced this tactical 'apoliticism' of *Nhar 3la 3ammar*'s bloggers, after having proposed a poster for the demonstration to them on the mailing list. On this poster is a close-up of Ben Ali, sitting in front of a computer with the censor's scissors in his hand, surprised by a rush of citizens coming out of the screen celebrating. A much smaller Ammar, dressed in a purple suit (the president's favourite colour), is already running away. For the bloggers of *Nhar 3la 3ammar*, this poster is 'out of line' for directly targeting the central political power: it certainly takes into account the 'celebratory' side of the gathering, essential to them, but it neglects the 'apolitical' side. Faced with this rejection, -Z- mixes disappointment and understanding:

> Yesterday's discussion summarized the paradox of this demonstration, which in my opinion is intrinsically political but which we are obliged to depoliticize, even give it an air of celebration (the celebration at Ammar's expense) so that in Tunis no one gets punished. (19 May 2010 on the mailing list)

Responding to -Z-, Azyz Amami confirmed the tactical considerations that are the driving force in the group, concluding with a little note of humour:

> Regarding its intrinsically political nature, we are obliged by the logic of stages, to go through the denunciation of the act of censorship itself. [...] even if we haven't touched the system so far, we haven't talked about repression, freedoms or anything, it's still difficult ... Vaseline is necessary :-)

Entertain in order to mobilise

Nhar 3la 3ammar's bloggers wanted the 22 May action to be perceived as 'apolitical', but also as 'light' and even 'celebratory' ('as if it were a party', wrote one of them). *Nhar 3la 3ammar* could also be translated as the French expression '(faire) la fête à Ammar' (to party at Ammar's expense). 'We didn't want to shock, we wanted to make the action something cool, to reassure and to make people want to do it', said Amira Yahyaoui, a Tunisian blogger in Paris who was the first to launch this idea of 'real demonstrations'. Humour and entertainment ran throughout the entire mobilisation campaign.

The organisers of *Nhar 3la 3ammar* sought and were sought by some Tunisian and foreign media, but the campaign was mainly deployed on 'social media' (blogs, Facebook, Twitter, etc.). It was fed by various texts, sounds and images proposed by the central actors of the mobilisation, but also by other Internet users, the bloggers of *Nhar 3la 3ammar* having called on all Internet users to make their contribution. Images, in particular, occupied a central place and further blurred the line between political expression and entertainment. As a result, many Internet users rewrote and remixed media content, which was characteristic of what researcher Henry Jenkins calls the 'culture of convergence' between old and new media. In particular, reclaiming content from the great classics of cinema, they rewrote their subtitles, worked on montages of different films, altered certain scenes, etc. For instance, a video modifies a scene from the film *Gladiator* (Ridley Scott, 2000): in the subtitles, the valiant hero no longer calls for the release of all prisoners, but the reopening of all Tunisian websites. Another, less tragic, reappropriates a cult scene from the first *Star Wars* (George Lucas, 1977). The author of the video, after recalling that 'Star Wars was shot in Tunisia', modifies the holographic message delivered by the famous robot R2-D2: the message '404 not found' replaces the call for help sent by Princess Leia to Obi-Wan Kenobi. Other film classics (*V for Vendetta* [James McTeigue, 2006], *The Matrix* [Lilly and Lana Wachowski, 1999], *The Exorcist* [Friedkin, 1973], etc.) are thus diverted from their original meaning to denounce the censorship of the Tunisian Internet and support the demonstration of 22 May.

The series of short videos produced by the two signatories of the rally declaration document was another variation of this connection between entertainment and political expression and was faithful to the 'spirit' defended by the actors of *Nhar 3la 3ammar*, humour and entertainment on the one hand and legalism and transparency on the other. In these videos, which appeared as episodes of a thriller series, Slim and Yassine report on their adventures, those of two 'ordinary' citizens striving to obtain a receipt for a 'pacifist' and 'apolitical' rally declaration. Filming themselves in various places, from the Ministry of Interior to Slim's home, the two heroes express themselves in Tunisian dialect and in a familiar way, sometimes with vulgarity, demonstrating humour,

Speaking out

recalling personal desires such as smoking a cigarette or drinking a beer (this will provoke criticism from more 'conservative' Internet users). Creating a 'buzz', these videos were part of a framework for collective action that was likely to interest non-politicised Internet users, but also a stage where these two leaders affirm their personalities in public, revealing their sense of humour, their boldness, their personal habits and tastes. They combined very subjective and informal remarks with detailed explanations of their administrative procedures and the obstacles they encountered, thus demonstrating the difficulties of organising an independent gathering in Tunisia in accordance with the law.

Until the evening of 21 May, the outcome of this adventure remained uncertain: what would happen to its heroes? Would it be possible to legalise the Tunis demonstration? If not, would it still take place?

From the 'demonstration' to the 'white t-shirts'

Throughout this original and entertaining mobilisation campaign, thousands of Tunisian Internet users expressed their interest and sympathy for *Nhar 3la 3ammar*. Having said that, other factors came into play as well as uncertainties about whether support previously shown on the Internet in a risk-free way would be translated into action on the Tunisian street on 22 May. Having never been able to obtain a written acknowledgement from the authorities for the legal rally declaration (which was finally sent by registered mail because it could not be delivered by hand) and sticking to their legalistic approach, Slim and Yassine prepared to make a video on 21 May to announce the cancellation of the Tunis 'demonstration' on the web. However, they did not have time: at the end of the morning, they were taken to two separate police stations and interrogated for about twelve hours. Released in the evening, at the request of their 'kidnappers', the two computer scientists each announced the cancellation of the rally.

The next day, small demonstrations took place in Paris and elsewhere abroad, but in the end, none took place in front of the ministry in Tunis. Another action was deployed, much softer, which consisted of 'going to Habib Bourguiba Avenue in white t-shirts and shirts, walking around and simply sitting in its cafés as a symbolic support for the principle of denouncing censorship'. The call for this 'Plan B' had in fact already been launched three days earlier by other bloggers (in consultation with *Nhar 3la 3ammar*): it was an alternative for citizens who could not or did not dare to demonstrate on 22 May. Despite the weakly subversive nature of this action and the limited number of participants (a few dozen people spread over different times – between 3 p.m. and 7:30 p.m. – and in space – on several terraces), those dressed in white were dispersed that day by the police officers crisscrossing the central avenue of the capital.

Nhar 3la 3ammar therefore illustrated the limits of the politicisation of young urban and educated Internet users under the Ben Ali regime. The unprecedented project of taking 'virtual' protests to the streets only half materialised, in a modest and weak form of protest. By using the 'arts of political concealment', more and more young 'non-party' Internet users engaged in implicit criticism in public, but they avoided questioning and openly denouncing the root causes of this censorship. This being the case, the *Nhar 3la 3ammar* operation aroused the interest of many Tunisian citizens on the web, who followed and encouraged preparations for the demonstration. It demonstrated in detail and in an original and attractive way the impossibility of legally organising an independent demonstration in Tunisia on a domestic political issue. It was perceived by some as the beginning of a new era in which 'virtual' and 'physical' public spaces became more connected.

From *Nhar 3la 3ammar* to the revolution: the role of 'bridge-blogger'

After Ben Ali's departure on 14 January 2011 bathed in the media euphoria of the myth of 'revolution 2.0', some of the social actors studied and various commentators retrospectively presented *Nhar 3la 3ammar* as an essential step 'towards the revolution'. In many cases, the vague accounts of this mobilisation even omitted the fact that the Tunis demonstration did not take place in the end. Before the revolution, however, no one perceived this mobilisation as a sign of a major uprising to come in the short or medium term. On the contrary, its initiators tried to present *Nhar 3la 3ammar* as an action without political significance. Internet access was only available to a small part of the inhabitants in the impoverished regions of the country's interior, particularly those of Sidi Bouzid, the cradle of the revolution, and Kasserine, where the large number of 'martyrs' had a shocking effect in 2011. Various statistics reveal a glaring digital divide in Tunisia: according to surveys of Tunisian households by the National Institute of Statistics, for example, in 2010 only 7.7 per cent of households in the Centre-West region (where Sidi Bouzid and Kasserine are located) had one or more members using the Internet (at home or abroad), compared to 26.3 per cent in Greater Tunis.

Speaking out

Although they did not herald or bring about the 2010–2011 winter uprising, many 'non-party' Internet users, including those of *Nhar 3la 3ammar*, nevertheless played an important role as 'media activists' during this period of insurrection, accompanying the uprising by sharing, relaying information and accelerating its dissemination. In this crisis situation, their involvement has evolved. Having engaged in dissent and questioned the legitimacy of the regime, many of them have played the role of 'bridge-bloggers', to use the expression of digital media specialist Ethan Zuckerman, that is, as a bridge between the proliferation of scattered information on 'social media' (especially Facebook) and foreign media. Indeed, while the online public spaces invested by these bloggers and other committed Internet users had only a limited direct reach in the poorly connected regions of the country's interior, journalists from major Arabic-language satellite channels popular in Tunisia, such as Al Jazeera and France 24 in Arabic, drew a significant part of their information, including images, from these 'bridge-bloggers'.

The engagement of these Internet users took on a new dimension at the end of December 2010, but it did not come out of the blue: before, during and after the May 2010 affair, *Nhar 3la 3ammar*'s bloggers, in particular, had developed an identity, know-how and cyberactivist links on the online public space that nourished and reinforced the effectiveness of their 'revolutionary' commitment. In addition, some had already established connections with foreign journalists in the past. At the time of the revolution, as a sign of the perceived subversive nature of their commitment, the central actors of *Nhar 3la 3ammar*, Azyz Amami and Slim Amamou, were both arrested on 6 January, to be released a week later on the eve of Ben Ali's departure. Lina Ben Mhenni, for whom the *Nhar 3la 3ammar* adventure was also decisive in consolidating her commitment, very quickly shared and commented on the news and images scattered on the web in Arabic, French and English after the self-immolation of the young Mohammed Bouazizi. A few days before the dictator's fall, she even went inside the country as a 'fixer' for foreign journalists and brought back photos and testimonies. Most of *Nhar 3la 3ammar*'s other protagonists, in Tunisia and abroad, also quickly relayed information from the insurgent regions. It is in fact partly because of this privileged connection between these urban and educated bloggers and foreign media that they were so quick to perceive them as the engines of the revolution, calling them 'icons', 'symbols' or 'muses' of the revolution.

Without being able to dwell on the paths of the social actors of *Nhar 3la 3ammar* after 14 January 2011, let us conclude by stressing that they have been significantly and completely affected and disrupted by the 'revolution'. They have been elevated to the rank of heroes, sought out by the Tunisian and foreign media, but also by political parties and high-ranking political representatives. A few have held positions of responsibility in political bodies, usually without remaining there. Several have co-founded associations in Tunisia in favour of democratic transition, sometimes by abandoning or temporarily putting their former professional activities on hold. Those residing abroad have either resettled in Tunisia or come there much more regularly, often for activist purposes.

Note

1 See Chapter 4 by Yves Gonzalez-Quijano in this work, p. 53.

References

Benford, Robert D. and David A. Snow, 'Ideology, Frame Resonance, and Participant Mobilization', *International Social Movement Research*, 1, 1988: pp. 197–217.
Jenkins, Henry, *Convergence Culture. Where Old and New Media Collide*, New York University Press, New York, 2006.
Lecomte, Romain, 'Au-delà du mythe d'une révolution Facebook. Le rôle des médias sociaux dans la protestation en Tunisie', in Amin Allal and Thomas Pierret, eds, *Au cœur des révoltes arabes. Devenir révolutionnaires*, Armand Colin, Paris, 2013.
Lecomte, Romain, 'Révolution tunisienne et Internet: Le rôle des médias sociaux', *L'Année du Maghreb 2011*, CNRS Éditions, Paris, 2011, pp. 389–418.
Nhar 3la 3ammar. www.facebook.com/nhar3la3amma
Scott, James C., *La domination et les arts de résistance. Fragments du discours subalterne*, Amsterdam, Paris, 2009 [1990].
Zuckerman, Ethan, 'Meet the Bridgebloggers', *Public Choice*, 134, 2008: pp. 47–65.

30

A new social world?

Young Syrian activists and online social networks

Enrico De Angelis

Khater Dawa has quickly become one of the emblematic singers of the Syrian revolution. In 2011, when his songs first appeared on the Internet, he was a twenty-three-year-old unknown. His music blends traditional melodies with jazz, rock and even reggae rhythms. His lyrics are sometimes original, sometimes drawn from the repertoire of popular songs. Khater, who has been living in Cairo since 2010, sings in support of the revolution in Syria and holds concerts in several Arab countries, during which the public never fails to wave the three-starred flag of independence introduced in 1946, which has been readopted to symbolise the revolution against Bashar al-Assad's regime.

Khater owes his popularity less to live concerts than to his YouTube videos. Most of them are recordings of his stage performances, but a new, more commercial and more Western kind of video, produced by a design agency based in Egypt, has also helped to spread his fame.

In one of these videos, Khater appears in a short sketch with Ahmad and Mohammed Malas, two brothers in their thirties who are also 'artists of the revolution', as many Syrians call them. This amateur film, shot on a hand-held camera, resembles an American 'crossover', an episode of a television series which features characters from another season or series. The Malas brothers ask Khater to sing some of their favourite songs. The video ends with Khater insulting Bashar al-Assad, in an imitation of the Malas brothers' *Fashet khaleq* ('we've had enough') sketches, also broadcast on social media.

Like Khater, the Malas brothers know how to use new technologies to market themselves. In November 2011 they gave their voices to the characters of the finger-puppet show *Topgoon* by Masasit Mati, episodes of which were also shown on YouTube. Forced to leave Syria and seek refuge in Cairo in October 2011, the Malas brothers radically changed their working method. Theatrical performances that once were their main means of expression have been largely

A new social world?

replaced by short and medium-length videos. But it is these amateur sketches – filmed independently with their own digital camera – that have made them famous among young Syrians. The fact that the sketches are so short makes them extremely easy to broadcast and discuss on Facebook and YouTube.

In mid-October 2011, the revolutionary song '*Irhal Irhal Ya Bashar*' ('Leave, Leave, Bashar') was played at full volume without any warning in various public and ministerial buildings across Damascus. The music came from carefully concealed radio cassette players. Those responsible were militants from *Ayyam al-Hurriyya* ('Freedom Days'), a group calling for acts of civil disobedience: in October 2011, for example, they dyed the Fountains of Damascus and the Barada River red in memory of the martyrs of the revolution. Neither a movement nor an organisation, *Ayyam al-Hurriyya* is a loose network of activists who share the same objective: to overthrow the regime through non-violent resistance. Founded in October 2011, when Damascus and Aleppo were still on the fringes of the uprising, *Ayyam al-Hurriyya* carried out spectacular actions to make people in both cities aware of the revolution.

Ayyam al-Hurriyya has a solid base in Syria but is also present all over the world. Its activists do not lay claim to a particular ideology: although many of them might define themselves as liberals, their ranks also include Islamists. Digital platforms have been their fundamental tools for launching and coordinating new activities involving a variety of groups. Mutasem Abou al-Shamat, a Dubai-based activist from the Non-Violence Movement which is part of the initiative, confirmed that it would have been extremely difficult to set up such a campaign without the Internet.

When Rima Dali, a hitherto unknown independent activist, and other militants succeeded in holding a placard saying 'Stop the killing' in front of the Syrian parliament for several minutes on 8 April 2012, they were aware that their gesture, seen live by only a handful of passersby, would be shared thousands of times on the Web.

Khater, the Malas brothers, Mutasem, Rima and many others are typical of a new generation that is seeking to radically transform modes of social interaction, political action and the creation and consumption of cultural products. They are part of a dispersed but interconnected network, which aims to establish a parallel social fabric that offers an alternative to traditional family and community relations. These young people are not the only part of the network, but they undoubtedly represent its core and vanguard.

This chapter aims to explore some of these practices, focusing in particular on young people, whether activists or sympathisers in the struggle against the regime, who call for 'non-violent action'. Welcoming a variety of political positions and different levels of activism and participation, this group is not easy to define. The distinguishing lines between those who live in Syria and those who act from the outside are less clear-cut than they may seem, not only because digital media have facilitated constant communication between the two, but also because militants move frequently between Syria and other countries. Workshops, conferences and visits allow young people to meet up quite often and strengthen their ties. Despite the fluid, indeterminate nature of these groups, they are quite distinct from other political and social milieux, such as armed opposition groups, supporters of the regime and activists delivering an explicitly Islamist discourse.

Before the uprising

Osama al-Samman, aged twenty-six, is part of the '17 April' youth movement that takes its name from the day on which Syria gained independence from the French in 1946. At the beginning of 2011, when Syria saw uprisings against Ben Ali and Mubarak, Osama, like many other young people, rarely watched television. He preferred to follow the actions of his Egyptian and Tunisian counterparts online and interact directly with them. It was thanks to this experience that he and other young people decided to found '17 April', which seeks to encourage political mobilisation in Syria. Like other movements, '17 April' immediately saw social networks as an ideal base for discussing and organising the first protest movements.

Until then, online political activism in Syria was almost non-existent. Facebook was used mainly as a window into the world, to form new friendships and stay in touch with friends and relatives abroad. Like other platforms, such as YouTube and Blogspot, it had been censored since November 2007, under the official pretext of 'preventing Israeli infiltration among Syrian youth'. Although this obviously slowed down navigation speeds, widespread recourse to proxy programmes allowed Syrians to bypass the ban and continue surfing the web.

The regime also closely monitored any attempts to form communities of bloggers like those that had emerged in Egypt, and persecuted net activists with extreme violence. Yet the authorities, aware that Internet use could be curbed but never stopped completely, allowed certain new spaces to emerge, which played the role of 'safety valves'. Dozens of news websites sprung up in 2004,

A new social world?

including *SyriaNews*, *ChamPress* and *DPress*. The phenomenon of online journalism was hailed as a minor revolution in the national mediascape. It was news sites like these – much more so than Facebook and blogs – that provided the first platforms for online resistance and helped negotiate new spaces for debate with the regime.

The Arab uprisings of 2011 unexpectedly disrupted this situation and profoundly changed new media use in Syria, so that it began to resemble practices in Egypt or Tunisia. On 6 February 2011, the regime suddenly lifted the ban on Facebook, Blogspot and YouTube. This may have been a clumsy attempt to demonstrate willingness to introduce reforms and to appease the young activists. But this measure, coupled with the political ferment that was spreading across the country, had an unexpected effect. According to the *Social Media Report* published by the Dubai School of Government, more than 200,000 people in Syria joined Facebook between January and April 2011.

Groups of friends and shared practices

At a time when many young Syrians, encouraged by the Arab uprisings, decided to act, they had only two resources at their disposal: their social capital of friends and acquaintances and the Web. As Bill Wasik, a senior editor of *Wired* magazine, has explained, social networks are extremely effective at bringing out what he defines as 'mega-undergrounds': groups of people who share the same ideas and passions but for whatever reason have been isolated from one another.

In the 'kingdom of silence', as many Syrians call their country, young people are politically isolated: constant surveillance by the security services makes it impossible to hold meetings or discussions in public. Offering the most direct and safe way of connecting with like-minded people, Web 2.0 culture thus encourages the emergence of a 'mega-underground' of dissent. According to new media expert Clay Shirky, new technologies help activists to 'organise without organisations' by reducing the economic and human costs of planning collective action. The only thing that is needed to organise a demonstration, at least in theory, is a computer and an Internet connection.

Towards the end of January 2011, web pages in solidarity with the Egyptians, Tunisians and Libyans began to appear. On 2 February, a small gathering in support of the Egyptian revolution in Bab Touma in central Damascus was dispersed by the police. At the same time, a number of young people were beginning to meet in small groups to discuss the possibility of mobilising against the regime. Initially, these were people who already knew each other and were linked by a certain degree of mutual trust. Facebook then became an essential daily tool: secret pages enabled discussions that were hidden from the regime and brought in more people via acquaintance networks. These groups were led largely by young city dwellers, especially Damascenes. Most of them were university students or graduates working in the cultural sector, such as journalists, artists or intellectuals. Establishing new groupings within civil society, they were inspired by the opposition movements repressed during the Damascus Spring, which had begun in 2000,[1] and the Damascus Declaration of 2005.[2] Although some came from families known for their political commitment and had parents or relatives in prison, most were motivated by the uprisings in neighbouring countries. The vast majority of those who mobilised during this first period did so independently, outside existing organisations.

It was also in early 2011 that the Internet was first used openly as a way of mobilising resistance, modelled on the strategies of Egyptian activists. Facebook pages were used to call on people to gather in front of the parliament in Damascus on 4 February for a 'day of anger' against the regime. But the demonstration was a failure. Too afraid to sign up to open pages, many activists hid behind anonymity. On the day of the demonstration, the streets around the parliament building were guarded by the security services, which were known for their brutality. Sensing the danger, the few activists who did turn up pretended to be customers of fruit and vegetable stalls. Some were nevertheless arrested.

They learned much from this first failure. Syria was not Egypt; it still lacked a sufficiently organised structure and online reach to be used as an effective means of mobilisation. Young activists therefore mainly used the Internet as a tool for aggregation and interaction via secret groups and public pages, sometimes using their real names, sometimes pseudonyms. These small groups gradually grew into new political movements: 17 April, the Non-Violence Movement, Jasmine Youth and the Movement of Consciousness. Apart from 17 April, founded in January 2011, most of the larger groups only emerged at a second stage, several months after the protests began. Rather than being organised or hierarchical movements, they were mostly interconnected networks of individuals who united to support a particular campaign.

What initially appeared to be a fragmented umbrella organisation composed of isolated groups gradually became an increasingly joined-up social environment in which more and more people got to know each other through collaborations or joint projects, demonstrations or in some cases experiences shared in prison. Transcending different time zones and locations, Web 2.0 ensured

A new social world?

continuity in these relationships and thus helped to densify the network. Inside Syria, social networks brought together young activists from different regions isolated from each other by government forces. They became even more strategic for the many activists forced to leave their country. Thanks to this new virtual mobility, young people could connect, sometimes even in person, at lectures, workshops and other initiatives in several countries. Coordination between each of these activities was based on constant online communication. Initiatives such as *Ayyam al-Hurriyya*, which in December 2011 mobilised public service employees and traders to protest against the regime with a 'strike for dignity', as well as news agencies inviting citizens to document events and campaigns against violence and for the release of political prisoners, are just some examples of the many collective enterprises made possible by virtual social networks. The revolutionary graffiti that now covers the walls of many Syrian cities is testimony to the gradual shift from virtual to real-life activities: groups of artists, often settled abroad, took it upon themselves to prepare drawings – drawn either on paper and scanned or created with graphics software – which could then be assembled by secret Facebook groups, so that activists living in Syria could download and print them. Armed with cut-outs of these drawings and spray paint, activists put them up on walls, photographed them and then uploaded them on the Web.

Before being political, this interactive world was an unprecedented social experiment that enabled thousands of young people to freely exchange their views and enjoy a daily life in which, as Mutasem Abou al-Shamat confirms, 'new relationships were born, intense friendships came into being, people fell in love and even got married'. Through the interweaving of these two dimensions, political and social, new identities emerged that were not based on preconceived ideologies, as coordination centred on shared projects or personal acquaintances. Yet the absence of an 'ideology' did not mean an absence of tension: the choice of strategies to be adopted, the relationship between the armed struggle and civil disobedience or between different ethnic or denominational communities inevitably resulted in intense debate.

From a culture of silence to a 'remix culture'

In the first episode of the satirical programme *'Anza wa lau taret* ('It's a sheep, even if it flies'), the female presenter stages an imaginary dialogue with the Hezbollah leader Hassan Nasrallah, the Lebanese ally of Bashar al-Assad's regime. At a demonstration filmed by the Lebanese channel Al-Manar and playing on a screen next to the presenter, Nasrallah asks: 'Where are the Syrian people? Tell us and we will stand with you.' The presenter, who is wearing a mask to conceal her identity, replies: 'Hello, *here we are*, masked. I'll give you our address so you can be sure to find us.'

'Anza wa lau taret has been airing since July 2011, only on YouTube, and no one knows the identity of the mysterious presenter, who is said to live in Aleppo. According to one of her friends, even her mother does not suspect her to be the one behind the mask. The producers of the programme live in the country but do not want to reveal their identities.

Devised with very limited means by previously unknown young people, *'Anza wa lau taret* is part of a rich cultural production which is primarily circulated online. Re-appropriating an active role, both social and political, these young people adopt new ways of consuming and producing cultural content. Perhaps for the first time, they try to listen to each other, look at each other, read each other's comments and, most importantly, talk to each other. From this emerges a new cultural environment focused primarily on the Web. It is an environment that is clearly in opposition to that of the professional media, which is viewed with suspicion by many young people. Many activists complain about the behaviour of journalists. They are particularly critical of Al Jazeera, which they accuse of bias and of giving too much air time to certain stakeholders. Ultimately, many young people consider Web 2.0 to be the only space in which an independent voice can express itself. According to the thirty-six-year-old caricaturist Juan Zero:

> I spend 80 per cent of my time on Facebook. Not only because of my drawings, but because I want to see what people are writing, to find out about the latest news and communicate with everyone. My point of view as a caricaturist must reflect that of the people. As I no longer live in Syria, I want to gather information from everyone. And I don't depend on news, from Al-Jazeera or any other channels.

Juan Zero, like Khater Dawa and the Malas brothers, is part of a new generation of content producers. Even before the revolution, he published caricatures on Facebook. His official page now has tens of thousands of followers.

Some of these content producers have gained considerable visibility. But sometimes it is difficult to make a clear distinction between the producers and the consumers of content. They all share the widespread desire to have a presence and express themselves in whatever way they can. Facebook statuses are perhaps the most obvious example: they constitute a space through which

A new social world?

young people (and others) can present and share ideas and experiences every day. Unlike elsewhere, this is not a trivial pastime, but a means of expression respected as such, used by many Syrians as if it were a new literary genre.

But Facebook is only the most visible part of an explosion of different forms of expression and creativity that are part of everyday life for many Syrians. The Web broadcasts a continuous stream of images of protesters exhibiting placards bearing ideas and slogans – photographs of graffiti and murals, drawings and paintings, music videos and performance events.

Sometimes several individuals collaborate on a single project, using email, Skype and Facebook. The artists may never meet in person and for reasons of security only know each other by their virtual names. Once the project is completed, everyone goes back to their own activities. The *Shakhabit* group, part of a *Ayyam al-Hurriyya* initiative, is a good example: its creative team produces videos exploring young people's ideas in civil movements and their hopes for a post-revolutionary Syria. The videos show a hand creating very simple drawings on a blank piece of paper, accompanied by a female voiceover, hence the name *Shakhabit*, 'doodles': drawings that, for their authors, represent a potential reality, although one yet to be realised. A Damascus-based director edits the voices, graphics, animations and drawings produced by other artists. Although most of the group's members knew each other before the revolution, their work is now carried out entirely via Skype and Google. The cultural environment in which these young Syrians are immersed corresponds to what the legal expert Lawrence Lessig calls the 'remix culture', a culture in which citing, mixing and re-contextualising pre-existing content becomes an increasingly common practice.

For many young people, this 'remix culture' represents an effective weapon in their fight against more powerful competing narratives based on fear, community division and civil war. It is a culture that, at first glance, wants to express 'being young' in contrast with the older generations. Syrians have thus moved directly from a culture of silence to practices largely inspired by digital technologies, thus creating an open cultural environment which enables them to produce and exchange content, but most importantly to transform it, discuss it and redefine it, in a continuous game of quotations and references. Young people are trying to construct different narrative paths and meanings that lay the foundations for an acceptable future. Mutasem Abou al-Shamat thinks it is no coincidence that many political groups have shifted their strategy away from the struggle against the regime towards debates about their visions of a post-revolutionary Syria. As *Shakhabit* describes itself on its Facebook page: '*Shakhabit*

Speaking out

is simply a pen that creates, on scattered pages, a vision and a dream about to be realised.'

Notes

1. A period of intense political activity in which intellectuals and other oppositionists came together to demand greater political pluralism.
2. A declaration launched by the writer Michel Kilo and signed by more than 250 intellectuals and protesters demanding 'peaceful and gradual' reforms towards political pluralism.

References

De Angelis, Enrico, 'The State of Disarray of a Networked Revolution: The Syrian Uprising's Information Environment', *Sociologica*, 3, 2011 (available at www.sociologica.mulino.it).

Gonzalez-Quijano, Yves and Christophe Varin, eds, *La société de l'information au Proche-Orient. Internet au Liban et en Syrie*, CEMAM Université Saint Joseph, Beirut, 2007.

Lessig, Lawrence, *Remix. Making Art and Commerce Thrive in the Hybrid Economy*, Penguin Books, New York, 2008.

Shirky, Clay, *Here Comes Everybody. The Power of Organizing without Organizations*, Penguin Books, New York, 2008.

Video for the song 'Mufti Suria' by Khater Dawa: www.youtube.com/watch?v=BzhLRB2moH8

YouTube channel of *'Anza wa lau taret*: www.youtube.com/user/3nzehWalo6aret

YouTube channel of *Ayyam al-Hurriyya* with videos by *Shakhabit*: www.youtube.com/user/FreedomDaysSyria

YouTube channel of *Masasit Mati – Topgoon*: www.youtube.com/user/MasasitMati

31

Stand up

Saudi youth take the floor ... on YouTube!

Yves Gonzalez-Quijano

Ninety million videos were being viewed every day on YouTube in Saudi Arabia in the early 2010s: the absence of cinemas (up until 2018) partly explained the record figure which placed this country of just under thirty million inhabitants in third place worldwide in terms of audience on this online video platform – behind the United States and Brazil with about 300 and 200 million inhabitants respectively. This figure is a good indicator of the importance of the transformations brought about by the meteoric development of the Arab Internet. A little more than a decade after the authorities opened it to the public, just around the turn of the millennium, nearly one in two Saudis watched videos on YouTube on a daily basis, and four out of five logged into the site at least once a week. For almost all Saudis, online video viewing had thus become a daily ritual for the youngest age groups that make up the overwhelming majority of social media users (70 per cent of their users in the Arab world are aged between fifteen and thirty).

Such a growing demand naturally generated an expanding supply for the local public. A survey conducted in October 2012 by the Middle East edition of *Forbes Magazine* showed that, of the twenty-five most widely viewed Arab programmes on the world's leading video-sharing site, seventeen were Saudi Arabian productions. A surprising illustration of the negative effects that can come with the globalisation of digital information flows is the appearance of anachronistic censorship. Wahhabi Islam in fact subjects the diffusion of images in public spaces – whether in cinemas or just on billboards in the streets – to exceptionally strict regulations, or even simply bans them altogether. For example, advertisers are advised to conceal the eyes of the people shown.

Behind the 'digital miracle' there has been the boom since 2010 of one particular genre, American-style stand-up comedy – in other words, monologues, in principle sharp and funny, concerning local, social and inevitably somewhat

Speaking out

political news. The indisputable star in this respect was Bader Saleh whose show, *Eish Elly* ('What did he say?'), attracted more than 400,000 subscribers and added up to nearly 100 million viewings at the end of 2012! Among the Internet celebrities who appeared from 2010 onwards, there was Muhammad Bazeed with his series *A Quarter to Nine* (the daily viewing peak on the Internet, and formerly the most popular time for watching TV) and Omar Hussein and his series *3al6ayer* ('As it comes!'). All these newcomers, who were barely twenty years old when they started, undoubtedly brought young people into Saudi social media. But they still did not overcome the gender barrier. While the viewers were undoubtedly mixed, as can be seen from comments left on the sites or in the shows' advertising campaigns, which routinely include female faces, women remained largely absent from the local material offered on YouTube.

Saudi-style stand-up comedies never pretended to revolutionise society. On the contrary, alongside series which, like *Fallimha*,[1] claim to be educational, even the most critical productions proposed nothing more than shaking up society a little, mocking its most blatant faults. But like the episodes of the TV series *Tash ma Tash* – which means something like 'Hit or miss!' – that was an unfailing success from the start of the 1990s onwards (and in recent years has been directly available on smartphones), humour offers precisely a way to address just about all the problems of society. AIDS, social injustice, the situation of immigrants, gender relations, corruption and even sometimes almost direct allusions to the ruling family of the country all became subjects that were 'lightly' tackled by Saudi showmen on YouTube. Like this, they could do so without causing any great stir, unlike other interventions, more directly political, on social networks.

Despite a few scandals, political, religious or civic (insults, libel, etc.), the reactions of the authorities have been limited and penalties light. The threat of much harsher censorship, however, remains very real, especially in view of the 'Internet law' adopted at the end of 2012, which would pave the way for an all-out crackdown in the form of long prison sentences and heavy fines. For a while, a degree of tolerance has allowed all talents to express themselves, especially since the possibilities offered by the digital age are immense. No real technical knowledge is required to broadcast on YouTube, nor very much money. In some cases, the limited costs are covered by sponsorship from local firms, usually ones specialising in IT or high tech, only too happy to find cheap advertising.

Technically speaking, the products have offered a merry mix of all the models and other visual and sound resources that the World Wide Web can provide, all carefully adapted to the local context. With a preference for American formats, still unchallenged leaders in the genre, people 'cut and paste', 'sample' or

Stand up

'remix', more or less in local Arabic, which itself is more or less transcribed in *Arabizi*. Adopted by Arabic-speaking users to communicate more easily using the keyboards of the technology that now surrounds them, *Arabizi*, the Arabic chat alphabet, uses the Latin alphabet and adds a few digits to render specific Arabic letters. It has remained widely used by young Arabs for some years. Contrary to a century and a half of reforms that vainly tried to impose 'from above' a unified practice of language, in particular written, to the population, this linguistic code, which rapidly became common – with some variations – to the new generations of the entire region, as well as of the diaspora, is one of the most spectacular expressions of the dynamics of this new 'digital Arabness' that is forged 'from below' through the social networks of the Internet.

After two or three years of experimentation by those who were among the first to showcase their creations, there are now signs of professionalisation. In order to give more visibility to their videos, companies like Sa7i have launched dedicated platforms that also produce 'real' mini-series. Ramadan 2012, for example, saw the broadcast of the *Blood Price Bazaar* (*Bazar al-diyya*), a very short film that mocks the abuse – thanks to social media by the way! – by some unscrupulous victims of claims for compensation for physical injuries according to the rules of Muslim tradition. The web plainly became a niche for productions by imaginative and somewhat offbeat young entrepreneurs. For example, there was Uturn, which brought together a good number of young Saudi stars of the Internet, and Telfaz 11, an online video broadcasting platform that summarised its activities by the 'C3' motto standing for Creative Culture Catalysts.

Even if these were not financially very profitable operations – although initial investments remained minimal – productions for the Web rapidly became a critical success. But this did not stop the emergence of certain vague ideas about 'reappropriation', a frequent phenomenon with productions initiated in more or less alternative sectors of society (as with rap, graffiti, etc.). Videos consequently started including commercials, and their stars became regular guests on TV shows, especially during the evenings of Ramadan. However, even 'commodified' as widely distributed products, they were still different from other material available on the vast market of local consumption. Shaped by the Internet universe, they retain their 'values', their spirit and their traditions, notably the absence of hierarchy and convention, mockery and irony, and a culture that is *glocal* (the combination of global and local, adapting world markets to local needs). Far beyond the social networks of YouTube, Saudi videos thus created echoes on a social and political scene that was reconfigured by the 2011 uprisings in the region.

Speaking out

In the 'Kingdom of Man', with a gerontocracy trying feebly to preserve the values of the past, the 'breakthrough', almost in the literal sense of the word, achieved by local youth through the cracks of the Web, and their search to show they exist and can escape from consumer passivity – this was already a revolution.

Note

1 www.youtube.com/user/Fallimha

References

Gonzalez-Quijano, Yves, *Arabités numériques. Le printemps du Web arabe*, Sindbad, Paris, 2012.
Ménoret, Pascal, 'Le feuilleton qui bouscule la société saoudienne', *Le Monde diplomatique*, September 2004 (available at www.monde-diplomatique.fr).

To view some of the material shown on YouTube mentioned here see: www.youtube.com/user/EyshElly; www.youtube.com/user/3al6aye; www.youtube.com/user/s7ch; www.youtube.com/user/UTURNentertainment

32

The café in Jadu

A place for 'revolutionary' emancipation in Libya

Arthur Quesnay

Among the first to rise up in rebellion in 2011, the residents of the town of Jadu, a small rural community in the Djebel Nafusa region of north-western Libya, discovered new forms of sociability and leisure early on. Those had only become possible after the Muammar Gaddafi regime's forces were expelled in February 2011. For many, the desire to reconquer a public space, closed down by forty-two years of dictatorship, was a driving force of the mobilisation. The popular uprising that began in early 2011 was indeed far from limited to political and military confrontation. Moving freely, expressing oneself and getting together peacefully to carry out playful activities in dedicated spaces are themselves acts of rebellion and now set the tempo of everyday life for the liberated population. The war was also perceived as a means of social emancipation for young combatants. For them, the ideal of an egalitarian and fraternal revolution, irrespective of class, age or qualifications, was a shared reference throughout the war. As one veteran of Jadu declared, 'we were all *thuwwar* [revolutionaries], there were no differences between us'. However, as the combatants were gradually demobilised and the difficult political transition began in Tripoli, the tumult of the revolutionary moment also faded, much to the regret of those who had taken up arms. In this context, specific spaces for leisure started to become memorials of a sort, places where the 'revolutionary spirit' was prolonged through meetings between former revolutionary combatants. The memory of armed struggle persisted here and so did the spirit of the revolution. In fact, although there was virtually no fighting on the ground in the town, Jadu was heavily shelled and the highly mobilised populace played a central role in the struggle. Elsewhere in Libya, Jadu fighters were renowned for their feats. These young people, all civilians and between fifteen and thirty-five years of age, took part in all the battles. They helped to liberate Jebel Nafusa, taking part in the capture of the coastal towns of the north. Once Tripoli fell, the *kata'ib* (brigades) of Jadu left to fight in the last bastions of Gaddafi, Sirte and Ben Walid. Though the war was visibly over, the *thuwwar* of Jadu remained mobilised, a year after the death of Gaddafi, watching over a vast territory stretching many tens of thousands of square kilometres around their own area. For them, the 'revolutionary moment' was not over and the future remained full of uncertainty. 'There are so many good reasons to continue to meet in the evening at the Jadu café, to relish a space of hard-won freedom', confided one young militiaman who had returned from duty.

Thus, far from the turmoil of battle and political struggles, the Jadu Café in the middle of town had become a central space of sociability for the *shabab* (young people). It was a place of leisure that retained, frozen in time, the atmosphere of what had been a moment of revolution – an ideal spot to slip into the world of the young Libyan revolutionaries in the midst of questioning their future and a political process which they had sometimes based on armed struggle and which now seemed to elude them.

This evening Barcelona was playing against Real Madrid, a football match not to be missed. It did not matter much who won, it was just an excuse for the *shabab* who were turning up one by one in the Jadu Café. Inside, the decor was simple: a bar with a huge Italian coffee machine, a pool table and a television surrounded by scattered chairs. As elsewhere in Libya, alcohol was banned from public space – self-censorship to show 'respect', as a young man at the bar explained:

We're the children of the revolution. We did it and there is no way we will discredit ourselves by drinking alcohol or getting drunk and fighting each other.

On the walls of the café hung banners with the names of the main *kata'ib* who had organised themselves locally to overthrow the Gaddafi regime by force. 'These are the colours of my brigade', pointed out a young man in the café, 'the *katiba* of the martyrs of Jadu. It had a few dozen fighters'. Beside the banners, there were several portraits of armed teenagers dressed in scraps of ill-fitting military uniforms. These were the photos of the 'martyrs' of the town, fallen in battle.

A café transformed by war

Since the war, it is striking to see how much the atmosphere in the city has changed. The experience of war has left its mark, but it is above all the liveliness of the streets that is astonishing. Some *thuwwar* I met in the café explained:

Before, people wouldn't have dared meet in such large numbers in town, even for a football match. Only when the regime's forces had evacuated the town did we

The café in Jadu

gather spontaneously in the main square, to talk, to keep up with the news ... But it was cold out there and that is how the café became our meeting place. [...] So we renamed it the 'Jadu Café'.

A waiter recalled evenings during the war:

There was no electricity and no football match on TV. So between two cups of coffee, we played our own games in the square outside. The most famous teams [of young people in the city] were those who continued to play even when the city was being shelled.

A player from one of the teams added:

You have to imagine that under Gaddafi, we did nothing in public, didn't even take a stroll in our free time. So playing football under the bombs was our way of showing Gaddafi that we were not afraid of him. It meant a lot to spend time together, freely. [...] We were prepared to risk our lives, just for the sheer pleasure of playing with our friends!

In the café, the atmosphere was sometimes tense. The 'young men' were almost all fighters just back from a mission or getting ready to return, to guard the Algerian border or the main roads, perhaps to act as police in other towns. Although the war was over, the pictures of the martyrs hanging on the walls reminded us all of the price some had paid to obtain this space of freedom. The brutality of the experience had taken its toll. Sharing life together in the café became more central, more crucial, as one fighter emphasised:

Coming to watch the match on TV is just an excuse. I have a bigger TV at home! But after all we have lived and suffered together, we need to get together and do things that are not military.

So the café has become a place where combatants can express their group identity. The idea of going out for a coffee has changed dramatically for them. 'Before, downtown was reserved for the police and tourists who came to visit the museum nearby', explained a waiter. The café was considered a place for outsiders, not somewhere that belonged to the people who live here. The same server continued:

Now it is the place of the young revolutionaries. They were quite shocked by the fighting and they can't forget what they experienced. For them it's hard to turn the page. So they come here, kill time, watch TV, play football and snooker. Like our customers, our café has been transformed by the conflict.

The café is also neutral ground where the social origin of combatants and how they earn their livings is of little importance. It offers emancipation for young people, outside the control of their families in a world of their own which they have created. Though they came from different backgrounds, and may just be 'colleagues' or brothers-in-arms, no one here speaks about their social origins. Those with the most impressive combat records are still called by their *noms de guerre*. Despite his young age, the commander of a *katiba* was always being offered drinks; people would get up and give him their seats. No one wanted to detach themselves from the rest of society in what was a model of community integration, but nonetheless, in the café the main source of authority among the customers was their reputation from the revolutionary past.

> I was nothing before the revolution, a simple peasant […]. I don't want to go back to that life. Being here with the 'brothers' of my unit is something unique that I can't find anywhere else, not even within my own family.

Keeping busy between one mission and the next, continuing to share a social status as a 'revolutionary' and trying to relive all the intensity of feelings born during the war – the new leisure activities we see here are full of meaning. They also show the learning process of a new life, where once the crisis is over, individuals try gradually to return to a civilian situation in which group memories are still an essential feature. In this context, the few leisure opportunities to be found in the café were more than ever a means of transition for these young militiamen.

References

Facebook page of a brigade from Jadu: www.facebook.com/kateebattwarjado.
Quesnay, Arthur, 'L'insurrection libyenne: Un mouvement révolutionnaire décentralisé', in Amin Allal and Thomas Pierret, eds, *Au coeur des révoltes arabes. Devenir révolutionnaires*, Armand Colin, Paris, 2013.
Quesnay, Arthur, 'Renégocier l'espace politique libyen du local au national', *NORIA*, 1 October 2012 (available at www.noria-research.com).
Revolutionary speeches from Jadu, March 2011: www.tamazgha.fr/Tawalt-n-igrewliwen-n-Jadu-di.html
Vandewalle, Dirk J., *A History of Modern Libya*, Cambridge University Press, Cambridge, 2006.

33

From consumerism to political engagement

Young Sunnis in Bahrain react in 'defence of their country' (2011–2012)

Claire Beaugrand

Stereotypes in the West and the Arab world often depict the younger generations of the six Gulf monarchies as gilded and idle. The high standards of living in the Gulf, deriving from the rentier economy, have shaped cultural practices dominated by unbridled consumerism. The leisure culture of the Gulf's young people appears quite specific – in the sense that it is based on a mixture of idleness and entertainment – and at the same time largely banal in terms of socialisation and consumption patterns, widely shared in an increasingly global context. The general impression remains nevertheless that Gulf youth does not care much about politics.

The events that shook Bahrain in 2011, in the wake of the Tunisian and Egyptian revolutions, call for a more nuanced picture. The smallest of the Gulf countries, with 600,000 nationals (out of a total population of 1.3 million inhabitants), is torn by socio-economic and communal tensions which, in the context of the Arab Spring crisis, generated new forms of political engagement among young people. The Al-Khalifa monarchy is overwhelmingly backed by a Sunni minority, the group from which it also stems and which it co-opts economically and politically in return for its support. Meanwhile, the Shiites, said to make up two-thirds of the country's national population, feel marginalised and stigmatised. This sectarian divide forms the background against which the wave of protest in February 2011 erupted. The protest started in response to a call posted on Facebook by a group, hitherto unknown, called Young People of the Revolution of February 14, a reference to the day when the King proclaimed the new Constitution in 2002 – just a year after the Bahrainis voted in a referendum on a new National Action Charter, thought to be a reform road map. The King had promised in the Charter to commit the country to a path

Speaking out

of reform and pluralism but the achievements and the Constitution itself were far below expectations.

The slogans that the protesters chanted on the symbolic roundabout of the Pearl in the centre of the capital Manama were at first quite varied. One of them, characterised by its non-sectarian message 'neither Shiite nor Sunni, just Bahraini', was intended to prevent an over-schematic reading of the uprising that would delegitimise broad political aspirations by equating them with community demands. Following the death of the first protesters and the resulting radicalisation of the movement, the rulers embarked on a massive crackdown (which would claim the lives of at least thirty-five people) and declared a state of emergency in mid-March 2011, when troops of the Gulf Cooperation Council (GCC) crossed the causeway from Saudi Arabia to help out the national army.

The radical and violent turn taken by the events both terrified and awakened part of the youth, stemming from pro-government Sunni backgrounds encouraging it to overcome its political lethargy. When it became obvious that the rally on the Pearl Roundabout was not a Sunday festival but a real political event that threatened to shake up the political system, most Sunni youths were stunned. Some of them feared that their future could be confiscated by a predominantly Shiite opposition that they did not identify with, and felt that they were being turned into the victims and the hostages of a conflict that was not theirs in the first place, so they showed responsiveness to the regime's call to mobilise 'in defence of the country'. Yet while the government welcomed this engagement, which boosted its popularity, it was careful to keep it within certain limits, lest the 'politicisation' of Sunni youth ultimately force it to open the political field.

From entertainment to political engagement: the test of the uprising

In their leisure activities, the youth of the Bahraini middle and upper classes could easily be mistaken for the young men and women of other Gulf states. Keen users of the Internet and cutting-edge technology (phones, tablets, computers), the youngsters are concerned about their virtual image as well as their real one. They usually aspire to own designer clothes and the latest cars and enjoy motor racing – an elite sport whose symbol is the Sakhir Formula 1 circuit, the first racing circuit in the Arab world that opened in 2004 in Bahrain.[1] They spend their time in multiplex cinemas watching the same blockbusters as any other youngster in the Gulf and throughout the rest of the world. They meet in the same global chains of restaurants and cafés, like Costa and Starbucks. They stroll leisurely past the shop windows, in groups of girls or boys, watching each other through the shopping malls, but rarely mixing. Free time is shared between the pleasures of consumer society and family sociability.

Self-conscious though Bahrain is due to its size, the weakness of its natural resources and its position as the poor relation of the Gulf Cooperation Council, the upper-class Bahraini youth are, for the most part, just as ambitious as their counterparts from the richer countries of the Gulf. Impatient to succeed, they dream of reaching positions of responsibility and prestige. Because these young people know that oil production in their country is a thing of the past, the most educated of them have spent much of their time taking management courses or, sometimes in addition to their paid work, setting up small businesses with the financial support of *Tamkeen*, the training fund for Bahrainis which has a dedicated programme for young entrepreneurs.

But young people from lower classes, almost exclusively Shiites, have long abandoned such dreams. They believe that their careers will hit a glass ceiling due to the mistrust that the government and the Sunni elites feel towards their community. Historically, the economic and social frustration of the Shiites has encouraged their strong politicisation, unlike the Sunnis, who are generally more satisfied with their lot and their financial situation and imbued with a tradition of loyalty. This became obvious between 1994 and 1998 when young people living on the outskirts, known as 'the villages', took to the streets in protest against their economic circumstances, in particular the high levels of unemployment, clashing relentlessly with the police for four years. This frustration continued to grow during the 2000s decade and the Shiite political movements split over the tactics to adopt to express this frustration. The *al-wifaq* 'political association' (the term is used because 'parties' do not officially exist in Bahrain) opted for cautious cooperation with the regime in 2006, while other more radical and youth-oriented organisations chose to adopt civil disobedience, often working in tandem with human rights organisations, like the Bahrain Centre for Human Rights. Such acute political consciousness and sense of oppression were of course not shared by all Shiite youth, but this narrative was precisely the target of the Sunni response and retaliation triggered by the shock that the 2011 crisis brought about.

Before February 2011, free time had, for these young Sunnis, very little political content: public affairs in their community were mainly seen, for the more senior, as a matter of networks and connections with the royal family more than conviction. Politics, for them, were the prerogative of the notables of the existing Sunni 'political associations'. The two main such organisations, one linked to the Muslim Brotherhood, the other to the Salafis, had little appeal for the youth and served primarily to keep the Shiites at bay. When the February 2011 crisis started, Sunni politicians, because they lacked much popularity, felt compelled to create a completely new movement to bring together, through a call to protest on 21 February 2011, all Sunni tendencies in a single anti-opposition front, the Gathering of National Unity (*tajammu' al wahda al wataniyya*, often called simply *al-tajammu'*).

From the outset, the Gathering (*al-tajammu'*) presented itself as a source of renewal and reform unfettered by the cumbersome legacy of the existing movements. Its leaders aimed to bring in as many supporters as possible, particularly young people seeking political regeneration who, apart from the few active Salafis and Muslim Brothers, had largely neglected public affairs.

At the climax of the crisis, the idea circulated among part of the Sunni youth that while they were immersed in their dreams of professional success and consumerist recreation, most Shiite youth were getting organised to denounce the discrimination that they felt they were suffering from and hatching plans for reform and change.

In response, some Sunnis felt that it was time to abandon their apathetic lifestyle and engage in politicised activities. For example, in the summer of 2011, when violence had just started to wane after the state of emergency had been lifted, some young Sunnis decided to give up their summer holidays. 'I am not even going away this year, so that I can protect my country', said Muna, an upper-class woman in her thirties.

In 2001, faced with young protesters from Shiite areas who were now mobilised and seemed comparatively experienced, many youngsters from Sunni backgrounds expressed their fears: the fear of being outdone, of missing a historic moment, of allowing the future of their country to slip away from them. So they decided to take over, using all the tools of political activism available to them: Twitter, transformed into a battlefield, mass mobilisation, which was suitable for creating slogans, and an international presence using a certain standardised discourse on democracy, representation, human rights and the question of minorities.

Some of them tried to 'revamp the image' of Bahrain, which they claimed had been damaged by unfair media coverage in the wake of the 2011 uprising. Annoyed at being portrayed as being on the side of oppressors, these new militants also took care of shaping their own image. 'The Bahrain of rebellious and violent young people who stir up sectarian hatred is not ours', explained some of them (mostly from quite wealthy Sunni backgrounds) who volunteered to join the Discover Bahrain programme, launched in January 2012. Independent in theory although adopting a line very much in tune with the interests of the regime (it was founded by the Good Word Society, an NGO sponsored by the Prime Minister's grandson), this programme sought to 'rejuvenate' the image of the island and defend its international reputation by inserting the country into the networks of globalised youth. With the help of young volunteers, its mission was to promote the country abroad, highlighting its ancient civilisation, its hospitality, its tolerance and its liberal, business-friendly tradition. Modelled on the Young Leaders' programmes which bring selected young people from all over the world to the United States, 'high calibre' thirty-somethings 'of different professions', originating from twenty-five countries as diverse as Estonia, the United States or Turkey, were invited to discover the charms of the island, its culture, its customs and its modernity. They could then, based on this visit, spread an alternative vision of Bahrain, differing from that conveyed by the media which allegedly concentrated on the crisis and the sectarian issue.

In parallel, new human rights organisations emerged, seeking to compete with existing organisations seen as mostly Shiite or sensitive to Shiite grievances or rights violations which had until then dominated the field. Created in March 2012 'in reaction to human rights activists with a political agenda', the Manama Human Rights Centre's motto was, according to a press release issued by the official news agency, to 'understand, learn, teach' and 'raise awareness on human rights issues'. Its members tried to adopt good practices, drawing attention to the dysfunctions of the judicial system and the Bahraini media.

The limits of political engagement, circumscribed again to a leisure practice

These committed young Sunnis did not only express their opposition to the Shiite rebellion. They also challenged the incumbent Sunni political class. Although they had been won over by appeals to patriotism, the young activists who took part in the Sunni counter-mobilisation movement in February 2011 also blamed the government and its political supporters for allowing protest and violence to spread. Because it wanted to renew Sunni politics, seen as too subservient to a government perceived as corrupt, this surge of political activism partially replacing leisure activities ran up against a double barrier: first, the persistence of habits which soon led to a return to entertainment less serious in its implications, and second, the tighter control on politics imposed by a regime which was not prepared to let young people follow an independent path, even when they were on the same side.

In the wake of the 2011 uprising, dozens of political newcomers devoted their free time to political activities. Even if they did not develop a clear programme, the new activists found in these political activities a meaningful way to occupy their spare time and to counteract the anti-government activism of young Shiites. Yet they had not yet learned how to fully master mobilisation techniques and they struggled, in the long run, to find a concrete meaning in political activity, while shying away from entering into professional politics.

The new Sunni political association, *al-tajammu'*, certainly seduced new activists with its sheer novelty. The *tajammu'* emancipation from the Islamist old guard from which it sprang (and which eventually withdrew its support despite having played a key role in its creation), offered young activists some symbolic rewards by allowing them to gain positions of political responsibility. This new structure also provided newcomers in politics with new opportunities to socialise, reinforcing their sense of belonging, beyond their usual social circles. In July 2012, in the head office of the *tajammu'*, young people from different backgrounds – doctors, students in design or management – prepared a buffet in a festive atmosphere to celebrate the victory of their friends in the election of the new central committee that saw the young generation take on decision-making roles.

These young people formed a small nucleus with shared values, coming from the wealthy Sunni class and some of the merchant families. They were proposing a new form of politics that was neither radically 'revolutionary' nor automatically subordinate to power. Though their objectives and room for manoeuvre were still uncertain, their new engagement had also come to fill a gap, after the parenthesis of their studies (quite often abroad for this social category), between family sociability and professional circles where young people are often embedded in rigid hierarchical relationships. From then on, this sudden surge of political activism seemed to reveal a coherent and planned commitment to principles and ideas as much as a quest for alternative spaces of socialisation that seemed all the more exciting as they emerged at a time perceived as exceptional. The political project and the ensuing concrete results were as important as the feeling of having lived together during this historic period of intense political upheaval, of being able to recall it collectively, through the key moments of the mobilisation, with a form of personal pride, despite the unfinished and in many respects frustrating character of the whole political journey.

From consumerism to political engagement

The engagement of Sunni youth, via *al-tajammu'*, had indeed rapidly led to clashes with other more loyalist young people perceived as representing political organisations supported by the government. At the turn of the year 2011–2012 a new Sunni movement emerged, called the *Sahwat al-Fatih* (Awakening of *al-Fatih*). A radical offshoot of the *tajammu'*, it was often said to be funded by the 'hawks' of the royal family. Following an outbidding logic, the rather nebulous members of *Sahwat al-Fatih* meant to use street pressure and stay away from getting institutionalised. They adopted a political line very close to that of the regime by supporting the restoration of order and rejecting any dialogue with the opposition or foreign interference. This movement, after having conducted a few campaigns in support of the hard line held by some members of the ruling family hostile to any form of compromise, was itself eventually disavowed by the government, which did not want to be outflanked by Islamist groups, leaving behind a number of embittered young activists.

In sum, all these young Sunnis, who in 2011 had found a reason to engage politically for the first time in various movements, experienced, a year later, the obstacles and limits laid by the existing regime, happy to confine them eventually to the role of useful stooges and, once the worst of the crisis had passed, to send them back to their apolitical futile activities.

Note

1 With the exception of the Aïn Diab circuit, south of Casablanca, that hosted a race of the 1958 F1 season.

References

Al-Hasan, Hasan Tariq, 'Sectarianism Meets the Arab Spring: TGONU, a Broad-Based Sunni Movement Emerges in Bahrain', *Arabian Humanities*, 4, 2015 (available at https://journals.openedition.org/cy/2807).
Discover Bahrain, Facebook page: www.facebook.com/discoverbh
'Discover Bahrain 2012 – A Journey from Delmun, Tylos, Arados, Awal to Bahrain', January 2012: www.youtube.com/watch?v=hNPgrfpiXbU
Gengler, Justin, *Group Conflict and Political Mobilization in Bahrain and the Arab Gulf. Rethinking the Rentier State*, Indiana University Press, Bloomington, IN, 2015.
Mathiesen, Toby, *Sectarian Gulf. Bahrain, Saudi Arabia, and the Arab Spring That Wasn't*, Stanford University Press, Stanford, CA, 2014.

34

When walls speak

Revolutionary street art in Yemen

Anahi Alviso-Marino

In early 2011, in Sana'a, as in other large cities of Yemen, contentious mobilisations calling for the departure of President Ali Abdallah Saleh quickly took the form of permanent occupations of public space. Sit-ins and revolutionary camps/squares were established, some of which lasted until April 2013, well beyond Saleh's formal resignation in February 2012. Located in front of the new University of Sana'a, Change Square (*sahat al-taghyir*) became one of such political, social and cultural laboratories occupied among others by artists who settled in the tents and whose creative practices picked up new visibility in the heart of the uprising.

Street art, which its protagonists define as the use of various artistic techniques on and in public space without prior authorisation, fed on the Yemeni revolutionary context and contributed to visually translating political demands much like photography or painting. Each of these artistic practices was nevertheless more or less subject to experimentation. For example, while painting and photography seemed to conform primarily to the expectations of foreign media and audiences, graffiti, stencils or wall painting, techniques specific to street art, were immediately displayed as a means of artistic and political transgression, contravening the aesthetic that hitherto prevailed in Yemen. Through this, they participated in civil disobedience by prolonging not only the spatial but also the visual occupation of streets and walls. Gradually, contentious street art transformed the walls of Sana'a into a centre of interest that mixed playful, artistic and political practices. A turning point for this transformation took place in March 2012 at the crossroads of Zubayri and Da'iri streets in Sana'a, when following the initiative of a young artist named Murad Subay, painters, amateurs and ordinary citizens joined the project of painting the walls of their streets. In this chapter I will explore how walls came to speak, telling stories that intersect leisure, artistic professionalisation and political commitment.

When walls speak

An aesthetic and political turnaround

When revolutionaries erected the first tents on the streets in February 2011, painters and photographers under thirty were among the first *mu'tasimin* ('sit-inners') on Change Square in Sana'a. Despite being much slower to reach the Internet than for example digital photography was, painting soon emerged as a means to formulate and spread political demands, giving them a unique artistic dimension. Artworks thus appeared displayed on walls and inside the tents where painting workshops were organised, as well as exhibitions of paintings, photographs, posters and caricatures.

The art of painting is not new in Yemen. Since the 1930s, the discipline has gradually established itself, notably in Aden, then in Taez and Sana'a, in a market dominated by the state and influenced by foreign demand. The young painters who began to exhibit their work in the 2000s and who participated in the contentious mobilisations of 2011 were heirs to this history and to the aesthetics that accompany it. In the wake of the first Yemeni painters, they echoed an art of Orientalist aesthetics (privileging the exoticism of scenes of life, landscapes and portraits of women) that their predecessors had adapted and adopted to present an art meant to be Yemeni. While trying to become independent from a state that relatively retreated from the cultural field after the unification of 1990, visual artists have managed to enter the worlds of production, sales, exhibitions and diffusion adapted to Western tastes in order to earn a living through their art. This influenced their work and distanced it to a certain extent from political subjects directly related to the ideology of the state. Dynamics like these that shaped the work of older artists were reinvented by young painters who began to exhibit their work in the 2000s. The creation at this time of a new group of artists marked a partial break with Orientalist aesthetics. Their work was influenced by abstract art and surrealism but also by political criticism concealed enough to avoid censorship or repression.

Embedded in this larger history and searching for novel subjects and aesthetics, a section of this group of young artists embarked on the project of transforming their country in early 2011. Among them were artists who had a somewhat marginal status in the artistic community. This position meant, for instance, that in spite of having rather regular contact with foreigners living in Yemen, they had rarely been invited to exhibit in European cultural centres or received any support from the few government institutions devoted to art. However, this position also translated to the possibility to distance themselves from dominant aesthetics.

Speaking out

The new political lessons learned beneath the tents of Change Square in Sana'a were at first confined to that physical space and took some time to go beyond it. The street art project launched by Murad Subay in March 2012 provided a catalyst. By shaking up dominant aesthetics and getting media attention, he aimed to spread his work throughout the city, beyond the space specifically occupied by the contentious mobilisations in Change Square. Street art was not totally unknown in other urban landscapes across Yemen, but it had never been presented as what it was, 'unauthorised art in public space'. In the past, graffiti, stencils or free writing on the walls had been used in religious variations, endlessly stating that 'God is great' or that 'there is no god but God', or covering the walls with the slogans of political parties and, more recently, to 'tag' names written in Latin characters. But the revolutionary context swung Murad towards a more abstract project linked to experiences of non-violent civil disobedience. The 2011 protests certainly unleashed energy and creativity affecting Murad's project as well as other street art creations: the walls around Change Square were then covered with graffiti demanding 'Go!' (*irhal*) in Arabic and English, or, with a nod to Facebook, reproduced tabs with 'Yemeni revolution' on them with an arrow ready to give the 'OK' to the option 'delete Ali Abdallah Saleh'. But this spontaneous appropriation of the walls appeared as a variation and extension of the slogans and political project that had been assembled beneath the tents of the Square. Murad's street art project, launched by an open call on his Facebook page, came to diversify the simple reproduction of existing slogans. While retaining a kind of political practice born and performed in the streets, he let art find its own independent path.

Murad Subay's call: 'colour the walls of your street!'

A student in English philology at the University of Sana'a, Murad Subay, born in 1987, was a self-taught painter. Without being part of the usual circles of Yemeni painters under thirty who regularly exhibit, he worked in parallel with these artistic networks. Born into a family of modest means (his father is a building worker in Saudi Arabia), he was raised by his mother in her village, and then in the city, and was greatly influenced by two of his older brothers. Both threw themselves into the arts at the end of their teens: one took up writing and poetry, the other photography. In Murad's case, having only published in 2012 images of some of his abstract canvases in cultural journals such as the prestigious Omani quarterly *Nizwa*, he found with his project of bringing art onto the streets a way to gain visibility for his work while experimenting with a rather novel form of artistic expression that allowed him to place his practice somewhere between leisure, political engagement and a means to professionalise his position.

When a few dozen young people decided to set up camp outside the university in mid-February 2011, Murad joined them. He immediately volunteered to monitor the entrances to the newly occupied space to ensure the sit-in remained peaceful. It was through this form of civil disobedience that he found a new way of taking political action which would very soon have repercussions for his work as an artist. His home was not far from the sit-in and he spent his days, and many of his nights, on Change Square. While he mainly worked in abstract art, using acrylic on canvas, he also discovered – mainly through the Internet – the techniques of graffiti, stencil, photo collage and mural painting.

Without ever exhibiting his work, because he didn't feel ready yet, but encouraged by all the connections that he had forged on the Square, he decided to launch an open call on Facebook, asking people to come and 'colour the walls of your street' (*lawun jidar shari'ak*). When he started painting on the walls of Sana'a in March 2012, he did it by reproducing his own creations that had formerly been confined to canvases. White silhouettes of hands on a black background or cube-shaped faces fitting together like pieces of a jigsaw puzzle started appearing on walls, all accompanied by Murad's easily readable signature and the date of creation as it accustomed on canvases. Gradually, his paintings became public and accessible works of art, furthermore inspiring other artists who also followed his example.

The project ended up being a success on several levels. With his ideas taken up by a growing number of painters and ordinary citizens, he attracted considerable media coverage. Very soon, the vast canvases provided by street walls helped him pursue new aesthetic experiments while spreading a transgressive way of making art in public space in Yemen. Furthermore, this visual occupation of space and walls as well as the location of the project made it possible to connect artistic expression with political commitment. Not only was the reappropriation of space a practice learnt at the heart of the sit-in, but the choice of painting walls could also never be politically neutral: on Facebook, Murad's open call was an invitation to paint on the walls at a street crossroads where fighting had taken place in 2011 between the Special Forces of Saleh's government and those claiming to represent the 'army of the revolution'. It was the walls of these streets that painting would redefine, without erasing the bullet holes so that they would not be forgotten. As Murad explained, the aim was to bring hope in an environment shaped by violence and political struggle but also to embellish the city, to colour its walls that bore the stigma of 'sickening/disgusting' (*qadhara*) politics.

Alone at first, he was soon joined by passers-by and other citizens, painters or not. A great many abstract images thus filled the walls of Sana'a. Among them were giant faces drawn in straight lines or lists of ancient Yemeni names written in the South Arabian alphabet used in antiquity. Beside these images, others carried a very clear message of political and social criticism, such as that of a child setting fire to a weapon or a drawing accompanied by words in English: 'I don't have a job'. This project, which Murad defined as apolitical, was certainly a long way from institutional and partisan politics but also anchored a participative practice of social and political critique in the streets. This 'politics from below', in the public space, was accompanied by an artistic change. It stirred the curiosity of passers-by, caught their eyes, and led to a new way of observing public space. From the start, Murad Subay had signed the walls in the same way that he signed his paintings, an element that distinguished him from European, North and South American street art where anonymity is almost essential because of the illegality of the practice. In times of revolutionary uprising, that precaution was useless. By signing his works, Murad symbolically changed the scope of this practice in Yemen while at the same time making a name for himself. The media, by providing important coverage on Yemeni and foreign television and press, gave visibility to these walls and to Murad Subay's individual role and signature, in this project. But despite his growing recognition, Murad continued to refuse any commercialisation of his art.

'Someone has to take the first step'

In the summer of 2012, Murad gradually started mixing the paints, brushes and sprays that he bought with his own money or with the help of those who supported his initiative (his family and friends) with photo collages, another technique widely used in street art and unknown until then in Yemen. If the walls in Murad's first project were not politically neutral, the images he pasted in this second initiative were even less so: they were photographs taken by his older brother, Jameel Subay, full of social and political criticism. Some of these images had already been used in various publications and exhibitions to question poverty, social exclusion or war and the fact that these critical issues were often diverted by international issues, turning Yemeni attention to other causes such as support for Palestine. The walls of the city, rethought by Murad's street art project, had since his first intervention in public space become more visible and could thus offer Jameel Subay's photographs the perfect medium in which to return to these images and make them more visible than ever in the eyes of Yemenis. Among the images 'borrowed' from Jameel, there was one of a street sweeper (identified in Yemen with the social group of the *akhdam* –literally meaning servant, of African origin) cleaning the streets of the capital. Murad had chosen to express his solidarity with them because they were currently on strike. Another image depicted a man holding a bouquet of aloe flowers (*kadhi*) and was pasted onto a wall of the Police College following a bomb attack there. He wanted to 'offer a gift to the souls of the dead, just as flowers are offered at funerals'.

This project introduced Murad Subay to a whole range of artistic disciplines and to the various ways of finding and using street art. It also brought him closer to increasingly political subjects. Such was also the case with his next project, in September 2012, in which he used stencils. Conceived, as he put it, as a 'campaign', launched once again through Facebook, and entitled 'The Walls Remember Their Faces' (*al-judran tatadhakar wajuhahum*), this project reproduced the faces of political activists, writers, journalists, party members and sometimes people without any political involvement whom the authorities were suspected of having kidnapped or killed under the Saleh regime. In his stencils, the image of the disappeared person's face was accompanied by a text in Arabic and English, giving the name of the person alongside the quote 'enforced disappearance' and the date on which this happened. Well aware of the political impact these images would have and of the risks he ran, he had decided to go ahead because 'someone must take the first step'. He did not sign these stencils and at the beginning of the campaign, always made them very early in the morning when the risk of being seen was minimal. But he still gave interviews on TV during which he was quite open about the project. This newly acquired visibility, which he accessed during his first campaign, gave him certain symbolic resources such as public recognition and popular support, placing his approach within an artistic continuity and practice that was becoming more and more critical. Although these activities did not generate enough money to live on, they offered some rewards, and the chance to contribute to the cause he supported. One welcome result was that the Minister of Human Rights took up the issue, opened a register of 'disappearances' and announced the creation of a committee to deal with the problem of missing persons. Popular participation also helped to revive memories and to retrace biographies, in some cases even crucially helping to find some missing people who were still alive.

Speaking out

Murad Subay's idea of making street art ended up spreading not only throughout the capital but also to other cities like Taez, Ibb or Aden. Painters, writers, activists or ordinary passers-by coloured walls or copied stencils, making art visible and accessible to everyone, and also leaving powerful political images behind them.

In the city, out of the market

Murad Subay's campaigns revealed new forms of artistic and political engagement among young Yemenis. In a revolutionary context, facing urgency and necessity, leisure became political and art became a form of political participation and commitment. Visual art in Yemen was adapted and transformed. The difficulty of having access to the market and to professional recognition faced by young artists who, like Murad, did not belong to the networks of institutionalised artists, partly explains the rupture caused by the reappropriation of street walls and their use as canvases and exhibition venues. Murad did not make a living from his art before these campaigns, and that remained the case after he first gained recognition. His declared ambition to 'change society' through art was used to shrug aside financial questions: by putting his work voluntarily on the walls of the city and therefore outside the market, he retained the independence that remained necessary if he wanted to create committed art on his own terms. First used to reproduce his own paintings while also promoting and supporting the talents and creativity of other artists and non-artists alike, the walls chosen by Murad gradually became places for self-expression, empowerment and the assertion of artistic as well as political identities. This choice, of places and skills, to make art public and free, revealed an approach that did not necessarily seek to be marketable. This aspect, which was originally at the heart of street art and is now a subject of debate and controversy worldwide, was largely bypassed in the case of Murad. However, in a country where even the most renowned painters are far from being able to live exclusively from their art, making art without expecting any financial remuneration is part of the process for most visual artists and especially the youngest of them. In this sense, Murad's approach was no different from that in its artistic and generational context. It was a new form of expression that signified a rupture at the aesthetic and disciplinary level and showed that other ways to make art, exhibit it and express oneself were possible.

References

AFP, 'Yémen: des graffitis pour oublier la politique', 3 April 2012 (available at https://www.youtube.com/watch?v=DW_tqFtxuy8).

Alviso-Marino, Anahi, 'Making Stories Visible. A Yemeni Art History', in Anthony Downey, ed., *Future Imperfect. Cultural Institutions and Contemporary Art Practices in the Middle East*, Sternberg Press, Berlin, 2016, pp. 98–106.

Alviso-Marino, Anahi, 'The Politics of Street Art in Yemen (2012–2017)', *Communication and the Public*, 2, 2, 2017: pp. 120–135.

Subay, Murad, https://muradsubay.com

Wender, Jessie, 'Postcards from Yemen: Words of Eyes', *The New Yorker*, 21 April 2011 (available at https://www.newyorker.com/culture/photo-booth/postcards-from-yemen-words-of-eyes).

Wiacek, Benjamin, 'The Walls Remember' (available at https://muradsubay.com/2013/03/09/0024/).

35

Art under occupation

The Young Artist of the Year (Palestine)

Marion Slitine

In Gaza, on 16 February 2013,[1] entering the home of the artist Salman Nawati is like stepping into a different world, from the violence of Gaza under the blockade to a haven of peace. As if to fill a void, Salman has covered the walls with his sketches and paintings. There is a power cut this evening, but life goes on and art is everywhere. Since finishing high school, Salman, aged twenty-five at the time of writing, has only had one idea in his head: 'to be an artist'. At an early age, Salman began swapping his pocket money for paints during Eid al-Fitr, a Muslim holiday on which children receive gifts of toys and clothes. When he decided to study art at the al-Aqsa University, he went against his father, a sheikh, and his entire family who, from a modest background of low-level civil servants, had little interest in art. But his perseverance paid off: he received a special award for his degree and now exhibits abroad.

As for many other young Palestinians of his generation, being an artist is much more for Salman than a mere pastime to stave off boredom: in Gaza, where artistic activity is not the preserve of the wealthy classes, art has become a 'necessity', a 'means of survival' or even a means of resistance in an extremely tense situation. At a time of political disillusionment, after the failure of the first Oslo Accords of 1993, Salman questions the 'artist's ability to change the world'.

The Young Artist of the Year Award

Like Salman Nawati, a finalist in 2010, dozens participate every two years in one of the flagship events of the Palestinian art scene, the Young Artist of the Year Award – YAYA for those in the know – organised since 2000 by the philanthropic family-run Qattan Foundation, one of the few institutions promoting culture in Palestine. Founded in London in 1993 by Abdel Muhsin Al-Qattan – who was once linked to the Palestine Liberation Organisation (PLO) and made his fortune in construction with the Kuwait-based Al-Hani Construction and Trading Company – the charity has an average annual budget of more than $2 million and employs some seventy people in London, Ramallah and Gaza. It has been active in Palestine since 1998 thanks to funds provided by Al-Qattan's company and some foreign donors (including the Ford Foundation, the European Union, the Embassy of the Netherlands and the Swedish International Development Agency). The foundation has indeed almost acquired a monopoly in the support of cultural projects in Palestine, something which has an impact on the development of the whole artistic landscape today.

Offering resources to rather precarious Palestinian artistic infrastructures, the YAYA has become an unmissable event in the cultural calendar. Within a decade, this prize has made a name for itself both with artists and the public. Open to any artist between twenty-two and thirty, the YAYA is targeted at all young Palestinians from 'historical Palestine and its diaspora', regardless of their place of residence. It offers artists from the West Bank as well as from Gaza, Jerusalem, Haifa, London or Berlin a public platform where they can come together to compete for a visual art award that is unique in the region. The jury chosen by the Qattan Foundation – artists, art professionals and well-known curators, both Palestinian and international – selects about ten candidates every year. Each finalist receives $1,000 for the creation of a new work, and after six months the jury chooses the winner.

Since 2012, the Qattan Foundation, together with six other private Palestinian cultural bodies, has organised the Qalandiya International Festival, which culminates in the award of the YAYA prize. This biennial – which takes its name from one of the most famous symbols of the Israeli military occupation, the Qalandiya checkpoint separating Jerusalem from the rest of the West Bank through which thousands of Palestinians pass every day – offers a fortnight of cultural events in several towns and villages in the Palestinian territories, from Gaza to Ramallah, via Jerusalem and Hebron, and beyond, from Nazareth to Amman. At the first festival, on 1 November 2012, Dirar Kalash, a Palestinian musician and multimedia artist 'of 1948' (born in Israel), presented a work created especially for the launch party of YAYA 2012: *Sawt mustaskhar (Petrified Voice)*. The title has a special significance for this artist, born in 1982, who uses his partial deafness to create sound improvisations. Kalash's spectral sound performance accompanied by projections of historical footage of Palestinian camps did not fail to move those that experienced it at YAYA's launch party, which took place in a beautiful crumbling Ottoman house in the heart of the village of Qalandiya (West Bank). The two-week-long 'artistic marathon' then took visitors on a journey through the West Bank to discover equally disturbing works by the finalists of the competition.

From hobby to profession

The YAYA is a rare opportunity for Palestinian artists to produce work outside the many constraints they normally face: the obvious political problems, a cultural scene mainly confined to Ramallah, and the fact that the support they receive from the private sector and a handful of international organisations is very limited. Mirna Bamieh, a twenty-nine-year-old visual artist from Jerusalem who currently lives on the other side of the wall, in Ramallah, explains what this has meant to her:

> I had been following the YAYA since its first year, hoping for one thing and one thing only, to be able to exhibit there one day. It was among the first important barometers in the visual arts in the West Bank. I watched the finalists with admiration, particularly at that time, when I saw art as a hobby and not as a way of life, a career, as is the case today.

Mirna Bamieh took part in the competition three times before winning third prize in 2012. Despite her first two failures, or perhaps because of them, her participation in the YAYA has been a catalyst. Like all the other finalists, she benefited from the advice of the Qattan Foundation's knowledgeable curators throughout the creation of her work. They helped her to mature her 'concept', to consider her work's spatial qualities and its relationship with the viewer. When she first took part in the YAYA, art was just a hobby she pursued in her spare time from her psychology studies at Birzeit University near Ramallah, one of the largest universities in the West Bank. The rivalry stimulated by this competition eventually encouraged her to turn her hobby into a 'way of life': in 2010, she decided to train at the Israeli Bezalel Academy of Arts and Design. Mirna is now well established in the art world, with more and more exhibitions and residencies abroad (Poland, Britain and India) and invitations to curate artistic events (Istanbul and Dubai).

For the finalists living in – and often confined to – Palestine, the prize offers an opportunity to look outwards. Thanks to the international network developed by the foundation, supported by a jury almost half of whom come from overseas, the finalists from the West Bank or Gaza often find their paths opening up well beyond Palestine. In 2008, the Qattan Foundation also opened a large art gallery, the Mosaic Rooms, in the heart of London. A selection of work by the finalists is exhibited there every time the YAYA is held. This first experience of international exposure frequently leads to exhibitions or residencies abroad, as Salman Nawati discovered after his first experimental video *Torsion … in the Neck of Time!*

> After the YAYA, I had a residency in Germany and then, shortly afterwards, another in France, in Aix (at 'Labofictions' for Marseille-Provence 2013), thanks to the film that was shown at The Mosaic Rooms. It was the first time they had held an exhibition by a Palestinian in Aix and the first time I'd left Gaza. It was an incredible opportunity.

Subsequently, the Qattan Foundation asked Salman to sell his video for $8,600: 'It was totally surreal for me! I would even have accepted $200!'

For young artists of the diaspora, perhaps the most important thing they gain from the prize is not just local recognition but also the chance to reconnect with their 'community' of origin, as the most recent prize-winner, Jumana Manna, explains. Born in New Jersey in 1987, a graduate of art schools in Israel, Norway and the US, he currently lives in Berlin:

> As I don't live in Palestine anymore, [...] it's a great opportunity to make a work of art in Palestine, for a Palestinian audience, knowing that there are very few exhibition spaces in the country. The YAYA has a wide audience and has given me recognition in my community.

Looking back at the first prize-winners, it is clear that yesterday's new Palestinian talents are today's internationally renowned artists: Raeda Saadeh, who took home the first prize in 2000, has seen her work acquired by the Victoria and Albert Museum in London; Ahlam Shibli, a finalist in the same year, exhibited at the Jeu de Paume in Paris in May 2013; photographs by Steve Sabella – a finalist in 2002 – have recently been acquired by the British Museum in London. By formalising and internationalising the artist's status, the prestigious YAYA thus also plays a role in the transition of art from hobby to profession. Sometimes this may happen a little too fast, though, and this can hamper the artist's personal and professional development.

Defying the occupation, braving the borders

Although the prize opens up many new horizons for young Palestinians, it cannot distract from the harsh reality of the occupation – quite the contrary. Omar Al-Qattan, chairman of the foundation's board, explains:

Speaking out

Because of the political and military situation, the prize has become increasingly important, as opportunities for these young people to meet are diminishing every year because of the wall, because of checkpoints and the closure of Gaza ... For us, it remains a very valuable platform for bringing people together, even if most artists from Gaza are unable to set foot in the West Bank anymore. Only once, in 2000, in the first year of the prize, did they manage to come.

How can you organise an art competition under occupation? Sometimes the Internet can be used to circumvent travel restrictions. For the 2012 prize, the YAYA curators set up an interactive blog intended to promote exchange between artists. The finalists were asked a different question every month, which provided an opportunity to create a platform for exchanging ideas, a kind of virtual incubator.

On the night of the 2012 awards ceremony in Ramallah, a giant screen on which the names of the lucky winners would be revealed was hung in front of the stage: participants who lived in Gaza would attend the evening, alongside their West Bank colleagues, live by video link. This proximity would let participants forget – for that night at least – that none of them had been able to leave Gaza, not because of the eighty kilometres separating them from Ramallah, but because of the Israeli embargo, which requires Gaza inhabitants to have authorisation to leave from the Israeli authorities, which is rarely granted. Just for a moment, it seemed as if the borders had been removed. But then the connection was interrupted and the picture vanished; the political reality of colonial domination returned. Gaza would not see live coverage of the judges' verdict.

The artist Abdallah Alruzzi had a similar experience. A graduate of Gaza's al-Aqsa University in his thirties, he would have liked to present his work, for which he won second prize in 2010, in Ramallah: 'I was supposed to attend the opening of the exhibition, an exit permit had been requested, but it was refused without reason.' Like many others, Abdallah dreams of one day visiting the other part of his country, the West Bank. This territorial and political fragmentation has damaging consequences for Palestine's cultural landscape. Abdallah adds:

It was my dream to get to know the artists and cultural institutions of the West Bank. We try to collaborate with them, but the only possible communication is by phone or online. It's not enough. [...] What is important about the YAYA is that it connects the art of Gaza with that of the West Bank. Through the prize, Gaza remains present.

Art under occupation

In 2010, viewers in Ramallah, rather than seeing the artist, had to content themselves with just a video of what was an extremely sophisticated installation, *The Germ*. Created in an old abandoned water tank that supplied Israeli settlers in Gaza before their unilateral withdrawal in 2005, Abdallah's hallucinatory and anguished work temporarily transformed the huge space into an art gallery, recreating a giant germ, a symbol of suffering and a bitter criticism of the occupation.

Outside virtual space, workaround strategies bear witness to the resilience of Palestinian society. Omar Al-Qattan says he has never cancelled the competition, even during some of the most volatile moments in the conflict's history. The simple fact of continuing with an event that, on the face of it, may not seem like a priority at a particular moment can represent an act of resistance.

Opening the competition to 'anyone from historical Palestine and its diaspora' is a way to show contempt for borders not recognised by international law. In 2008, the organisers even went one step further, extending entry to artists from the Golan Heights. This Syrian territory, occupied by Israel since 1967, was annexed in 1981. The inclusion of artists from the Golan Heights, a veritable hotbed of talent, had an obvious political dimension. For these young people, the competition became an opportunity to connect with Palestinian artists who in a sense share the same 'cause', as the thirty-something artist Shada Safadi from Majdal Shams on the Israel–Syria border explains:

> For me and the artists of the occupied Syrian Golan, participation was crucial because we live under the same form of occupation as the Palestinians. We are isolated from our nation, Syria, and from Palestine. The prize is important for building relationships with Palestinian artists and institutions.

A number of politically targeted strategies have been used by the organisers and artists in an attempt to overcome fragmentation. A new regional map is being drawn up through art, one that seeks to rebuild a common identity among young people from Gaza, Ramallah, Jerusalem and the Golan Heights.

Other words, other ideas: an avant-garde generation

Over the years, and despite the tense political context, the prize has given visibility to young Palestinian artists and played a part in their emergence as a new generation, distinct from that of their parents. The young artists of the YAYA each express, in their own way, the socio-political reality that surrounds them by using a new, more conceptual and avant-garde language. In 2000, Jerusalem-based Raeda Saadeh recreated the apartment of a newlywed couple and staged a series of symbols that condemned arranged marriage; in 2010, Majd Abdel Hamid, Ramallah-based at that time, constructed a model of the Dome of the Rock, the emblem of Palestine, using painkillers and antidepressants, thus combining social, political and religious criticism. Ironic installations like these, allusive but effective, give visual expression to social criticism. Performance art, too, is becoming increasingly popular with the new generation of artists. On the opening day of YAYA 2012, for example, Dirar Kalash combined a *tableau vivant* with musical improvisation and video art. Many of the finalists attach particular importance to interaction with the viewer. With new forms of expression that are conceptual and interactive, young artists are differentiating themselves from the practices of the pioneering generation of Palestinian modern art, who mostly used traditional media (painting and sculpture), thus sanctioning the hierarchical relationship between the artists and their audience.

Is all this an authentic expression of the aspirations of the young artists or does the Qattan Foundation simply conform to the prevailing trend in international contemporary art? It is an important question, especially as the artist's statement constitutes the largest part of the final score awarded by the YAYA jury. Most of the artists I spoke to admitted that this was the first time in their lives that they had written a statement or created an installation. In a decade of the prize's history, the use of 'new media' (installation, video art and performance) has clearly increased: from 2004 onwards, traditional disciplines (painting, photography and sculpture) have gradually given way to installations – which are very popular in contemporary art everywhere. In 2010, all of the finalists' works were installations. The practices of these young artists tend to conform to the requirements of international contemporary art, just like contemporary Arab art as a whole, whose popularity in the last ten years is not so different from a certain kind of nostalgia for orientalism.

The finalists do not only use new practices and forms of expression, but they also approach local and regional socio-political realities in ways that distinguish them from the older generation. In fresh, provocative language, they question notions of identity, commitment, norms and borders, while being part of a more global landscape.

The Palestinian flag, the olive tree, the Dome of the Rock, the Key of Jerusalem or Palestinian embroidery were elements of the symbolist and nationalistic iconography of earlier Palestinian artists, such as Sliman Mansour,

Art under occupation

Nabil Anani or Ismail Shammout. These images have been replaced by more original, personal and conceptual elements aimed at denouncing the same reality. Even though the occupation remains a central theme, young artists often approach it indirectly. One such example is the poetic and participatory installation *Sea Package* by Ayed Arafah (born in 1983), which won the third prize in 2010. Suspended from the ceiling, a big plastic bag filled with water hangs over a large square of fine sand. Using plastic bags and bottles – an integral part of the installation – Ayed, a Palestinian from the West Bank, asked friends to send him water from the sea that he himself was not allowed to visit.

The video installation *Gazawood* by two young twins from Gaza, Arab and Tarzan (Ahmed and Mohamed Abu Nasser, born in 1988), which took first prize in 2010 puts a twist on classic Hollywood movie posters by replacing the titles with the names of different Israeli military campaigns in Gaza. *Grapes of Wrath* (the bombardment of southern Lebanon in April 1996), *Summer Rain* (a ground and air attack on Lebanon in 2006), *Wrath of God* (a secret operation in 1972 following the assassination of Israelis at the Olympic Games in Munich) and *Pillar of Cloud* (the Israeli military operation in November 2012) were among the classics of Gaza's *cinéma réalité*. The installation consisted of a video and a series of posters for films that do not exist, with the artists in various guises pictured as the films' stars, and the IDF (Israel Defence Forces) credited as the lead producer, with Israeli Prime Minister as writer and director. Combining specific elements from the local context with wider references, they turn art into satire and alienation into their playground. Arab and Tarzan were selected at the Cannes Film Festival in 2013 for their film *Condom Lead* – a reference to the name given to the Israeli offensive against Gaza, 'Cast Lead' during the winter of 2008–2009 – which echoes their prize-winning *Gazawood* in a number of ways.

At a time of political turmoil in the region, many YAYA artists have taken on the role of 'witness to an era'. The 2012 YAYA was particularly marked by the theme of the Arab Spring. Majd Abdel Hamid, for example, invited eight women from the West Bank village of Salfit to weave a Pop Art portrait of Mohammed Bouazizi, the young man who set himself on fire on 17 December 2010 in Sidi Bouzid and became the symbol of the Tunisian revolution. In her installation *Promises*, Shada Safadi, who won the third prize in 2012, took viewers on a journey past threatening silhouettes of men and children, the outlines of which were engraved on life-sized plexiglass plates. Using a subtle play of light and shadow, the thirty-year-old artist from the Golan Heights referred directly to the deaths caused by the war in Syria. Like other artists from her region, Shada refused Israeli nationality and, after graduating from high school, began studying art in Syria, 'her country', while vowing that once she had graduated she would never set foot there again. For now, her nationality remains 'undefined', as stated by her only travel document.

Being an artist in Palestine today: hobby, identity and survival

Although the YAYA – whose transnational vocation and political ambition are evident – formalises the status of 'young artist', and even 'manufactures' the artists of tomorrow in a context that leaves this art scene largely fragmented, we should not overlook the fact that it also catapults these young artists into an institutional, globalised and commercial circuit.

For young artists from Jerusalem, Ramallah, Gaza, Israel, the Golan Heights and the diaspora, the YAYA speeds up the transition from art as hobby to art as profession. Despite profound socio-economic disparities – the artists from the West Bank and Jerusalem come from relatively wealthy backgrounds (their parents are doctors, lawyers and businessmen), while those from Gaza are usually middle-class (the offspring of teachers, civil servants and shopkeepers) and, for the most part, also have a job on the side – it is possible to sketch out the common features of contemporary Palestinian art. Although the current scene is far from homogeneous, we can observe a move away from a committed and nationalistic art in the service of the 'cause' to an art which, without having lost its political aspirations, is more intimate and more 'universal' (in the words of the artists).

For Jumana Manna, the winner of the 2012 prize, art is a way of questioning her identity, which, as we have already seen, was forged on several continents. A former swimming champion, she decided at the age of seventeen to leave the pool for the palette. 'Art', she explains, 'gave me the tools to create my own territory, to breathe more freely and feel more at home in my own skin'. For the Franco-Palestinian artist Hani Amra, selected in 2008 for his photographs *Talamussat* (*Indiscretions*), art has been a means of survival. Born in Martinique in 1981, he grew up in Paris and remembers arriving in Jerusalem during the First Intifada, at the age of nine:

> I ended up here in a no man's land, a bit like nowhere. I think it was this feeling that pushed me towards art because I needed a way out, somewhere I could breathe and escape the harsh reality in which I found myself.

Art under occupation

Although his participation in the YAYA helped Hani to obtain a residency in Italy, he then took on a position as a press officer at the Consulate General of France in Jerusalem, while pursuing his art in parallel. This apparent lack of professionalisation once again raises questions about the purpose and relevance of premature media exposure of emerging artists and their work in progress.

Note

1 This chapter was written in 2013, based on an ethnographic study in the frame of a PhD started the same year. The data collected corresponds to the period from September 2011 to mid-2013.

References

Al-Qattan, Omar, *Diary of an Art Competition under Curfew*, Sindibad Films-Qattan Foundation, London, 2002.
Boullata, Kamal, *Palestinian Art*, Saqi Books, London, 2009.
Gray, Nicola, 'How to Make Things Made for Looking That Actually Work: Meanderings on Curatorial and Artistic Responsibility', in *Brief Encounters. The Young Artist of the Year Award 2010*, Qattan Foundation, Ramallah, 2012.
Halaby, Samia, *Liberation Art of Palestine. Palestinian Painting and Drawing of the Second Half of the 20th Century*, H.T.T.B. Publications, New York, 2003.
Makhoul, Bashir and Gordon Hon, *The Origins of Palestinian Art*, Liverpool University Press, Liverpool, 2013.
Preoccupying Zones. The Young Artist of the Year Award 2004, Qattan Foundation, Ramallah, 2004.
Qattan Foundation official website: www.qattanfoundation.org
Slitine, Marion, 'Contemporary Art from a City at War: The Case of Gaza (Palestine)', *Cities, the International Journal of Urban Policy and Planning*, 77, 2018: pp. 49–59.

36

'The instinct of rap'

Palestinian rap, political contents and artistic explorations

Nicolas Puig

In Gaza, Ramallah and Nablus, and in Lebanon, Jordan, Israeli towns and East Jerusalem, for the past decade, rap bands and singers have grown out of the fertile soil of the new Palestinian generations. By combining entertainment with the ethics of protest, rap songs have become a powerful means to broadcast political and social messages that translate in artistic terms the contemporary experience of a segment of the Palestinian youth, and of young Araby in general.

Dam are often seen as the pioneering band of Palestinian rap. They acquired a reputation in the early 2000s, initially among small local audiences who tended to be quite cosmopolitan, and also among political activists. The band's three musicians and singers originate from the Israeli city of Lod, which has a large Palestinian population. Their lyrics denounce the living conditions of Palestinians in Israel, who are regarded as second-class citizens (*'Born Here'*), as well as the occupation and colonisation in the Territories. Their *song 'Min al-irhabi?'* ('Who Is the Terrorist?') is the most popular Palestinian rap song in the world, thanks to YouTube. In the Arab world, one of the first rap bands to emerge was MBS (Le Micro Brise le Silence) in Algeria in the early 1990s. After listening to this rap sung in Algerian dialect, the Naffar brothers of Dam decided to substitute Arabic for English in their songs, the language by which this music had first been known in Palestine and the Middle East.

While it still remains relatively restricted in Palestinian societies compared to pan-Arab songs and local commercial music, rap was taken up in the refugee camps, in Palestinian towns and by members of the diaspora in the United States and Europe (for example by Shadia Mansour, who was born in London). It became a tool for social and political criticism, bringing freedom through creativity.

'The instinct of rap'

Hip-hop bands and rappers enjoy an international media audience that for the moment goes beyond their local influence. The political dimension of this music, which media observers may think is effective in spreading the word within Palestinian society as well as on a global level, is regularly questioned by certain local moral entrepreneurs. These latter, who are not only religious figures, condemn – whether in Gaza or the Palestinian camps of Lebanon – a movement suspected of Western corruption, or of inauthenticity at the very least, and of immorality from a religious perspective. So far there has been no Islamic rap in Palestine, even though it is spreading in other parts of the Arab world, for example in Tunisia.

However, whenever they get the chance, rappers are careful to distinguish themselves from more dubious forms of rap, in particular those related to American gangsta rap and the images it spreads (naked young women, luxury cars, drug use, etc.). On the contrary, they promote a militant form of rap and stress its ability to re-politicise young generations disenchanted after decades of struggle and renew the essential current of Palestinian political song ('The nationalist song is over. Ok, now we sing samples', claimed Katibeh Khamseh from the Burj al-Barajneh camp in Beirut). The choice of colloquial language, the language of the streets, that is to say, Palestinian Arabic in all its regional variations, emphasises this ambition.

For young Palestinians, the global music of rap is seen as a means to acquire an independent identity, a new form of self-expression. Inseparably linked to this existential dimension, it offers a platform for attacking everyday problems and for the promotion of the 'cause'. In the latter, of course, the rappers are directly following the tradition of political songs. But by building political connections indirectly rather than simply endorsing militant mass mobilisations, they are individualising political engagement and thus exposing themselves to criticism from members of political parties and organisations who are anxious to respect traditional forms of activism and the cultures that go with them, especially in the refugee camps where their influence is very strong. Moreover, the rap musicians do not hesitate to apply their critical intelligence to various problems in Palestinian society, for example, 'crimes of honour', most of which are in fact crimes perpetrated against women in the name of family honour ('If I Could Go Back in Time' by Dam), cronyism in the camps ('Associations' by Katibeh Khamseh) or racism in host societies ('Blue Identity Card' by a group of rappers from Ayn al-Héloueh in Lebanon, referring to the colour of the refugee ID cards in that country).

Speaking out

From local to national ... and the galaxy!

By multiplying references to local contexts, the contents of rap highlight the balances between the identities of town, neighbourhood or camp, between the national insofar as it touches on music production (the lost homeland relocated in cultural productions among refugees or the denunciation of occupation in the Territories) and the international. This last dimension offers new meanings for the universalisation of the Palestinian cause linked to the values conveyed by rap, at least as understood by Palestinian rappers. As music that carries the revolt of the oppressed, rap is especially suitable for summarising the situation and demanding justice for the Palestinians, who have become global symbols of the dispossession of rights by unjust political authorities. This is why Palestinians have 'the rap instinct' ('*Amru*' by Katibeh Khamseh) and some of them 'find their way in rap' (Gaza Team) with which they can find a peaceful way to express their rebellion (Palestinian Rapperz, on their Myspace site). Thus, rap is the framework for a renewal of nationalism through a new contextualisation of the Palestinian cause. It allows a way of thinking in artistic terms about the transposition of the category of armed struggle into that of civil resistance, the shift from the image of the fighter to that of the oppressed. The refugee camp no longer appears as the place where combatants of the Palestinian revolution shelter, but as a ghetto, a marginalised urban zone ('Welcome to the Camps' by Katibeh Khamseh). Out of this, unimagined forms of solidarity become possible, like those making connections between the struggle of Palestinian refugees and that of Australian aboriginals, between immigrants in France and people living in the black ghettoes of North America. As a result, Katibeh Khamseh's rappers present themselves as spokespersons for the victims of oppression all over the world. In the end, the dispossession and injustice they suffer from leave them one last resort: the galaxy! This is what the various artistic projects suggest, somewhere between mockery and disenchantment, when they take the cosmos as a subject, as in the video of Larissa Sansour, 'A Space Exodus' (2009), a project of the 'Palestinian Space Agency' (2011) and a song from Dam, 'We Danced on the Moon' (2012).

The way rap music is composed expresses visible connections to disjointed and heterogeneous cultural worlds, in particular as the majority of rappers do not just download 'second-hand samples' to rap on them. Indeed, the sound loops are made, among other things, by sampling a selection of different music, including Eastern, Western and more rarely Asian and African, and Palestinian creations from different periods. In addition to fresh compositions obtained with specialised

'The instinct of rap'

software, political and poetic speech as well as music or dialogues taken from films are also borrowed. This material is mixed in compositions with inserts from everyday sounds: Boikutt, one of the founders of Ramallah Underground, presents himself on his Myspace page as a sound designer who creates musical loops by mixing samples, field recordings and sounds generated by electronics.

For some years now, the paths of the most creative musicians have been changing towards attempts at professionalisation by inventing new artistic careers. Amru (whose stage name is Osloob, 'style'), co-founder of the group Katibeh Khamseh ('Battalion Five', but *katibeh* also contains the root 'ka-ta-ba' which describes the action of writing), defines himself as a composer of samples. Alongside his rap activity, he has increasingly taken on projects with local and foreign musicians who visit him in his studio (he has never left Lebanon) to offer purely instrumental pieces exploring new areas of electronic music. Boikutt is one of the founding members of a travelling project called '*Tashweesh*' ('Interferences'), which interweaves music, photos and videos in a single performance. Dam have also moved towards more diversified musical forms and have tried to find an ethical commercial path by selling their last CD directly on their website, without intermediaries. These developments follow the approach of Kamilya Jubran, the singer in the emblematic group of Palestinian political music Sabreen ('Jerusalem'), who has embarked on avant-garde musical experiments since moving to Switzerland in the 2000s. And so rap continues its slow progress among young Palestinians, while composers explore musical universes that are not so directly political. With experiments in poetry chanted on sound loops (Abdel Rahman Jassim, on compositions by his brother, Osloob), rap and electro come together to create music moves between styles that can be both narrative (the tale, news stories, realist fiction, denunciation, poetic declamation) and musical. This electro-rap musical current remains Palestinian and sees itself as Palestinian. Ultimately, the game of referencing that is inherent to this form of composition fertilises the music with many different influences that are as much Western as they are Eastern, but it also integrates it, if only through metonymy – to quote a part to depict the whole – into Palestinian cultural history.

References

Boikutt: Myspace (up until 2011): www.myspace.com/boikutt; Soundcloud: https://soundcloud.com/boikutt
Dam: www.damrap.com
Gaza Team: www.gazateam.com

Interferences: http://tashweesh.com

Khamseh, Katibeh, *Ahla fik bil-mukhayamat* (*Welcome to the Camp*), Incognito, Beirut, 2008.

Khamseh, Katibeh, *At-Tariq wahid marsum* (*The Road Is Drawn*), auto-production, Beirut, 2011.

Khamseh, Katibeh: YouTube: www.youtube.com/user/osloob20; Soundcloud: https://soundcloud.com/katibe-5

Palestinian Rapperz: www.myspace.com/palrapperz

Puig, Nicolas, '"*Bienvenue dans les camps!*" L'émergence d'un rap palestinien au Liban: Une nouvelle chanson sociale et politique', in Nicolas Puig and Franck Mermier, eds, *Itinéraires esthétiques et scènes culturelles au Proche-Orient*, Presses de l'Ifpo, Beirut, 2007, pp. 147–171 (available at http://ifpo.revues.org/554).

Puig, Nicolas, 'La cause du rap. Engagements d'un compositeur palestinien au Liban', *Cahiers d'ethnomusicologie, Société française d'ethnomusicologie*, 25, 2012: pp. 93–109.

37

Rocking in Morocco

The new urban scene in Casablanca

Dominique Caubet and Catherine Miller

The Tunisian and Egyptian revolutions in the spring of 2011 brought to the foreground some social actors who had hardly been known until then by either the general public or the Western media: young musicians of the alternative scene (hip-hop, rock or fusion). El General in Tunisia, as well as Karim Adel Eissa, Ramy Essam, Amir Eid, Nour Ayman Nour and a few others in Egypt, presented themselves or, more often, were presented as the standard bearers of youth in revolt. These young artists were not born with the movements of 2011. Most of them emerged in the mid-2000s, more or less from the underground, depending on the country and the context. This new craze raises the difficult and ambiguous question of where this alternative music fits in the societies concerned. The fashions of the moment, the different media and above all the Internet make these artists seem like social phenomena, probably over-hyped by the media compared with their real impact. But no one can deny that these young musicians, along with many other artists or ordinary citizens, are also voices of social change. The profiles of Moroccan rockers, particularly those in the urban region stretching from Casablanca to Rabat, and their relationship with other alternative musical trends (hip-hop, fusion) are good examples to help us understand the capacities for mobilisation and self-expression of these new musical movements. They also show how difficult it is for them to put down lasting roots given their fragility, even their weakness, in the face of powerful networks of social and political control. To outline the complexity and ambivalence of this underground movement, it will help if we briefly trace the history of rock in Casablanca.

Speaking out

Prehistory: the 1960s, go west! Go north!

For the sixteen-year-old rockers whom we met at concerts in Casablanca in June 2012, the period prior to the 1990s is seen as almost prehistory. Very few of them knew the older Moroccan bands, including those of the 1990s, and most discovered rock music eclectically, via Michael Jackson or other big international stars. Rock, however, has a relatively long history in Morocco, starting with groups that appeared in the 1960s, especially in Casablanca. But most of them had more of an 'international' career, and they were not perceived as specifically Moroccan. Vigon, born and raised in the medina of Rabat, began playing at the American base in Kenitra before moving to France in 1960, where he formed a group called Les Lemons and recorded for Barclay and Atlantic Records in the United States. Coming mainly from the Atlantic coast, these precursors did not leave any notable 'successors' behind them in the 1970s and 1980s. Rock music, as a musical culture, remained alive, although with a low profile, in the Moroccan audio-visual landscape, mainly through radio shows of the French-speaking Rabat Chaîne Inter (a branch of Radio Télévision Marocaine, RTM), in particular, *Boogie* and *RockLine* (from 6 to 8 p.m.) produced by Alifi Hafid (who was inspired by the *Nocturnes* programme hosted by Georges Lang of RTL in France), or the nightly jazz-rock show *Pop Sessions* (from 11 p.m. to 1 a.m.) by Saïd Fouad that helped a whole generation discover American music and jazz.

The emergence of rockers: Casa underground scene (1992–2003)

It was at the beginning of the 1990s that a revival of the Casablanca rock scene began, partly linked to the country's political changes (the gradual transition out of the so-called 'years of lead') and the simultaneous opening up of the Moroccan media field. The creation of the TV channel 2M (encrypted on the model of the French Canal+ and pay-per-view from 1989 to 1997, then taken over by the Moroccan state to become open access) and the arrival of satellite dishes and televisions (MTV, M6, VIVA, etc.) in the early 1990s allowed Moroccan viewers to have access to new music shows. Among the Moroccan TV and radio hosts who participated in this broadcasting of Western rock culture, Anis Hajjam was particularly important, presenting RTM shows such as *Ça bouge à la télé* in 1986 followed by 2M with shows like *Hit International*, *Megamix*, *Music Box* or *Rock Space* in the 1990s. He represents an element of continuity, having hosted a daily francophone programme devoted to rock on Radio 2M (*Feeling* from 8 to 10 p.m.) from 2003 to 2016. On the satellite channels of the 1990s, *Headbanger's Ball*, on MTV every Sunday evening, helped a whole new generation discover hard rock, in particular metal. In an interview for *Volume!* magazine, Amine Hamma, one of the rockers of that generation, explained:

> From 1993 onwards, the influence of MTV was crucial for discovering death metal. I am thinking in particular of the shocks we experienced when we encountered bands such as Obituary, Carcass, Entombed, Morbid Angel, Death or Cannibal Corpse.

Between 1992 and 1998, the rock scene in Casablanca remained very informal and seemed to mainly reach students in high school or in university. Since there were no places devoted to urban culture, musicians and fans got together in little 'spots' (beaches, small squares, discreet corners between the villas, private garages or cafés) in middle-class and well-to-do neighbourhoods near the city centre, like the Bourgogne and CIL districts. They would meet there to chat, learn to play the guitar, exchange musical riffs, listen to tapes, and sometimes start setting up bands. Young musicians like Amine Hamma, Tarik Lahjili, Yassine Souhair, Nabil Andaloussi and Saïd Guemha started the first Moroccan metal band, Immortal Spirit, and began to give their first concerts in private rented venues (like the Bab el-Bahr hall in the medina, mostly used for weddings, that rapidly became the mythical hall for the first rock-metal concerts in Casablanca) or in some exclusive private schools like the Jabr school, the Spanish school Juan Ramon Jimenez or the French Lycée Lyautey. These latter served as 'incubators' for the young musicians. Two of the bands from that time, formed by students at Lyautey (Seven Sins) and the Spanish school (KDB), played a catalysing role and attracted young people from more working-class backgrounds. These young rockers played covers of Anglo-Saxon bands, and did not seek (yet) to sound 'Moroccan'. However, their concerts attracted a bigger and wilder young audience. Amine Hamma recalled the growing number of metal fans in 2008:

> There were people who followed us all the time, wherever we played. They were always there and, they'd go crazy, shouting and screaming. That was in 1997. Then we met other bands. Carpe Diem was created in the meantime; we met one another the following year in El-Jabr, the second time they had that festival, and once again the fans wrecked the place. Every time we played there'd be pogoing and moshing, it would all ignite. It was a real mess!

From these first places, a whole network of relationships was gradually being put in place. It materialised in 1999 with an event that marked the beginning of a slightly more structured alternative scene: the creation by Hicham Bahou and Mohamed 'Momo' Merhari of the first 'Young Musicians Springboard' in the premises of the Fédération des Oeuvres Laïques (FOL), with links with the French Federation of the same name, in the Gauthier district in Casablanca. The Springboard would become the Boulevard des Jeunes Musiciens in 2000 and L'Boulevard in 2006.

Through the Association culturelle et artistique laïque (ACAL), the FOL provided a hall with 400 seats where groups could rehearse and organise concerts from 1998 onwards. It became the dedicated cultural centre of the Casablanca alternative scene and a meeting place for rock musicians but also for fusion and hip-hop bands. All the big names of the 'urban' scene of the 2000s (Barry, Hoba-Hoba Spirit, Darga and Haoussa) socialised at one time or another at the FOL and L'Boulevard. New rock bands appeared: Total Eclypse (1998), Nekros, Orient (1999), Killer Zone, Keops, Dust'N'Bones (2000), Barry and the Survivors (2001) and Reborn (2002). Several 'unforgettable' hard rock and metal concerts were organised at the FOL. The room was packed, overflowing into the streets, and these events are now remembered as the 'great moment' of Moroccan rock. But until 2003, the alternative music scene still remained relatively underground, known only to amateurs and a few specialised journalists like Amale Samie, nicknamed 'Tonton', a journalist at Maroc Hebdo who would become a tutelary figure for rockers, one of the first to highlight the political and social dimensions of this music.

Often presented by their detractors as *'oulad la Mission'* ('children of the mission', students of the French Lycée), and thus associated with the French-speaking Moroccan elite whose loyalty to so-called 'Moroccan identity' could be doubted, the rockers of the 1990s and early 2000 were in fact of mixed origins. Those who came from wealthy families were the first to get the expensive music equipment (electric guitars, amps, drum kits) and to have access to places (garages) necessary for rehearsals, or to have a car. They would help launch the movement by lending their equipment and sharing their premises with young musicians from less privileged backgrounds attending state schools like Amine Hamma, Tarik Lahjili and Yassine Souhair. The two main unifiers of this scene, Hicham and Momo, do not belong to the Moroccan elite. Momo Merhari's father was a studio manager at the FOL, so the young Momo grew up in a working-class but francophone milieu and had privileged access to the association's hall.

Witnesses at that time insisted on the need to use what was known as 'Système D', basically being resourceful, that allowed musicians and fans to follow rock'n'roll codes. They would buy cheap t-shirts from famous international bands in the popular Derb Ghellef or flea markets. They would photocopy and distribute hard rock fanzines that only existed for a few issues and would organise concerts and festivals on a volunteer basis, designing their own posters. This resourceful spirit, driven by a strong desire to transform the Moroccan cultural scene, has remained one of the hallmarks of L'Boulevard's organisers, despite a decline in the underground and expanding media coverage. Now in their thirties or forties, rockers of the 1990s have taken different paths: some have given up music for economic, family or religious reasons (though many still go to the major rock concerts organised by L'Boulevard); others have become actors in the Moroccan music scene. This is notably the case of Tarik Lahjili, who is now the musical artistic director of the Sigma production company, or Saïd Guemha who returned to Morocco in 2010, after some time in the United States, to become the 'agent' of one of the most famous rock-fusion bands of the 2000s, Hoba Hoba Spirit.

The turning point of 2003

According to all observers of this cultural scene, 2003 represented *the* turning point in the media, political and cultural spheres. Starting with a dramatic trial, followed by an even more shocking series of bomb attacks and the first big festival in a rugby stadium in 'Casa', that year marked the gradual move away from the underground. It highlighted the media success of part of this alternative scene that rapidly became a business card for the urban culture of new, dynamic Morocco.

It all started with a rock concert held at the FOL on 25 January 2003, which attracted a large audience that once again overflowed into the street. Following a press campaign and pressure from Islamist groups demanding that the concert be banned, fourteen young people, members of bands or fans of metal, along with the owner of the café L'Égyptien (one of the rockers' usual meeting places), were arrested on 16 February 2003. They were questioned and then taken to court under Article 220 of the penal code, which punishes anyone undermining the Muslim faith, and Articles 59 and 60 of the press code, which penalise the possession and distribution of immoral musical material. They were initially sentenced to prison for periods between one month and one year, after the prosecution had compared their activities to those of satanic sects – which echoed the decisions in a similar trial in Cairo in 1997.

But unlike Cairo in 1997, the 2003 Casablanca trial triggered a major mobilisation in Morocco that united musicians, various organisations, symbolic figures like the former political prisoner Abraham Serfaty, and Moroccan journalists who spread the story locally and internationally. A petition launched on the Web and hosted by the weekly magazine *TelQuel* was signed by tens of thousands of people. A sit-in held on 12 March outside the *wilaya* (prefecture of Casablanca) to demand their release brought together more than five thousand people. Finally, all the musicians were acquitted.

This trial had a double impact. On the one hand, although its leaders had always avoided representing a defined political current, the mobilisation had helped to turn the groups around L'Boulevard into the symbol of the 'secular movement' against the 'Islamic movement' that had won parliamentary elections in 2002. On the other hand, it was from this trial onwards that many alternative groups started feeling the need to highlight their 'Moroccanness', or even their piety. Musicians were no longer content to cover imported cultural productions but now sought to express sensibilities and concerns that were 'authentically local'. Continuing to sing in English or French was seen more and more as evidence of a lack of 'Moroccan' identity. The use of *Darija* (Moroccan Arabic) became the sign of an ability to express the hopes and demands of the street (*zzenqa*). But while rap and fusion bands had now largely adopted *Darija*, this was much less the case for rockers, who preferred English – which would also contribute to their marginalisation.

Two months later, on 16 May 2003, fourteen young Islamist suicide bombers blew themselves up in seven places in Casablanca, killing forty-five people, almost all of them Moroccan. These attacks caused a great shock wave and there were demonstrations throughout the country. Some of those who had taken to the streets during the trial of February 2003 did not fail to point out that it was not the rockers who represented a danger to Moroccan society but rather Islamist extremists – an argument that seemed to be endorsed at the highest levels of the state. Indeed, the Royal Palace gave several signs of backing the new urban scene. However, this did not prevent tensions between L'Boulevard, the Ministry of Culture and the Casablanca police authorities.

This new context could be seen in developments following the trial. L'Boulevard left the hall of the FOL to organise its own festival (30 May–1 June 2003) at the Olympic Club of Casablanca (COC) rugby stadium, gathering between 5,000 and 10,000 people per night. At the Young Musicians

Springboard, the title of 'Best Newcomer of the Year' was awarded to Reborn, a band of which three of its four members had been imprisoned. In the following years, the Festival L'Boulevard became one of the largest independent festivals in Africa, attracting nearly 120,000 spectators over four days in 2005–2006. And yet the organising committee was deprived of permanent premises from 2005 after tensions arose with the FOL.[1] It thus always had to negotiate permission at the last minute, and received no public funding, while constantly facing a host of financial problems because of its dependence on private sponsors.

2004–2008: hopes and illusions of the *Nayda* movement

After the big mobilisations of 2003, a wave of optimism spread for some years in the urban cultural milieu. People had the feeling that a new cultural movement was blossoming, one of a kind that Morocco had not known for many years. Some compared it to the Spanish *Movida* of the 1980s. In 2007, this movement, which encompassed artistic and creative sectors (music, fashion, design, graphics, video, photo, press, voluntary groups, etc.) was labelled *Nayda*, literally 'it rises, it's moving, it rocks!', in 2007. For the most politicised or committed, whose views were widely expressed in the French-language weeklies *TelQuel* and *Le Journal Hebdomadaire* and *Nishane* (partly written in *Darija*), the movement was not only about making music but also about asserting a plural identity, breaking certain taboos and supporting freedom of thought and the right to difference, democracy and the creation of a new public space. For the less politicised, it was mainly about self-expression and – why not? – about making a name for yourself and trying to earn a living through your talents.

Presented as a citizens' initiative by the 'young', namely the generation of twenty-five to thirty-five-year-olds, like those of L'Boulevard, this cultural movement benefited from a favourable political context. From 2002 onwards, reforms of television and radio led to the creation of ten new private radio stations in 2006–2007, some of which, like Hit Radio, helped to popularise young urban music groups. Music festivals were being held all over the country, offering a few opportunities for these young musicians. The new urban scene thus gained more visibility. Generation Mawazine, created in 2006 as part of the Mawazine Festival (the largest festival in Morocco, considered *the* royal festival that has attracted considerable private sponsorship since 2008) adopted the same principle as the Tremplin (competitive sessions open to young bands), but with much larger financial means. Soon, just about every festival in the country wanted to have its own 'young' scene. TV shows like *Ajyal* or *Korsa* on 2M, *100% Chabab* (*100% Young*) on the public channel Al-Aoula, as well as many radio stations, regularly invited the most famous groups of the new scene, mainly rappers who became celebrities like Don Bigg (of Casablanca), Casa Crew group (Casablanca), H-Kayne (Meknes), Muslim (Tangier), Fez City Clan (Fez), Fnaire (Marrakech), etc.[2]

This favourable context encouraged many young people to create their own bands (rap, fusion, rock) or to launch other kinds of artistic activity. Each different scene brought its own kind of audience: 'rastas' for world music, with their dreadlocks and colourful clothes, the hip-hop style for rap, with baggies and baseball caps, the metalheads, all in black, and, the most spectacular, punks with their multi-coloured Mohawks for rock concerts. For the punks, the 'look' is often perfected on the spot because it is not accepted everywhere, to say the least! But there are no watertight partitions between each style; the public and the musicians mix with each other on the same stages, in the same places, only too happy to enjoy these little spaces of freedom.

Since they do not require much equipment or money, and there is not even any need to learn an instrument, rap and hip-hop culture have developed rapidly in many Moroccan towns, including among young people from poor working-class areas. Rappers produced texts in *Darija* that were at first very socially engaged, reinventing the language and style of Moroccan songs. As the numbers of rappers increased they soon split into different types, from the most anti-establishment to the most patriotic – not without a bit of opportunism now and then, trying to win over the authorities, the media and festival organisers. Like American stars, some young people dreamt of making their fortunes through music.

Rockers remained a minority and less known to the public, especially metalheads and punks, considered too outrageous. Only two groups mixing rap and rock, and chanting texts in an elaborate version of *Darija* (or mixing Arabic and French), have had any significant success with the media and the public. Hoba Hoba Spirit is supported by the weekly *TelQuel* – in which one of the band's members, Reda Allali, has a column – which reviewed their lyrics and their first albums. Their concerts always attracted a large audience, as did those of the group Haoussa, created in 2002 by Khalid Moukdar. He benefited from the unconditional support of L'Boulevard, which has become a major player in the recognition of urban music groups via national and international partnerships. Apart from the 'Tremplins de L'Boulevard', the younger metal and punk rock bands (sixteen to twenty-five years old in 2012) only performed in more private venues, such as the French Institute of Rabat or the Villa des Arts, also located in the Moroccan capital. A punk movement appeared in Rabat-Salé, and the group ZWM (Zla9 Wella Moot – Skate or Die – which made its debut in 2004), from the Youssoufia district, won the first prize at Tremplin 2006, again with anti-establishment and comic lyrics in *Darija*. Despite poor visibility, bands were forming all over the country (Lazywall in Tangier, Wanted and Raining Madness in Tetouan, Sakadoya in Settat, Noisea in Azemmour, Vicious Vision, LooNope and Despotism in Casablanca, etc.).

Most of these young musicians came from the small middle class of Rabat and Casablanca, and many knew they were playing rock for their own enjoyment and not to make a living. Some sang in English, others in *Darija*. Few developed any real political discourse. Most just wanted to express themselves and to dress as they wished. All of them shared the taste for a 'rocker' look, especially with t-shirts from metal bands. As Mehdi Metallica, one of the oldest metal fans in Morocco, whose body was covered with tattoos back in 2008, explained in an interview in L'Boulevard's magazine, *L'Kounache*: 'Of course, there's always stigmatisation and resistance from people. They are omnipresent but we don't care, it is just one of our constraints. The fact is that we are always there, our music is like any other music, we don't force anyone to listen, we just want to be accepted as we are.'

For a long time, Moroccan rockers rarely seemed to listen to one another. Their references remained famous international bands like Iron Maiden, Black Sabbath or Sepultura. Concerts in L'Boulevard by foreign bands such as Gojira, Moonspell, Sepultura or Arch Enemy were experienced as exceptional moments, pulling in the rock tribe from all over the country, whatever their age. It was at big concerts like these that teenage fans might get the chance to meet their elders, who were forty years older than them.

Since 2011: disappointments and ambiguities

The media visibility of this new urban scene masks the fragility of the *Nayda* movement which, between economic realities and political manipulation, soon showed its limits despite the opening of some new and important venues that tried to perpetuate urban culture (such as the former Casablanca slaughterhouses converted into a culture factory in 2009, organised by a collective of associations). But festivals, whatever form they take, do not in themselves constitute a cultural policy and do not create a cultural economy. In 2008, during the Mawazine festival, prize money in the form of a substantial check, donated by the king of Morocco, was awarded to four bands from the new scene, a gesture interpreted as an extremely ambiguous political sign: giving support to these young bands who had a hard time making a living from their music, but in the form of a royal gift with all that could lead to in terms of dependency and cooptation. The new urban scene badly needed places to rehearse and plan, permanent spaces where musicians could work every day, and not just locations for ephemeral events. Very few musicians managed to make a living from their work and many started dropping out in their thirties. L'Boulevard continued to act as an incubator for young musicians but always in unpredictable conditions. At the end of 2008, Omar Balafrej, the director of Technopark, a pioneer in the high-tech sector of information and communication technologies (1,500 young employees in 2012, in a huge concrete and glass building in the Californie district, far from the city centre), offered L'Boulevard the empty space in the basement, giving birth to the Boultek. Donations from private sponsors and a royal gift in 2009 helped finance the construction of rehearsal rooms, recording studios and offices, which allowed L'Boulevard to set up long-term training schemes so that bands could develop and professionalise. But new funds were lacking and since 2009 L'Boulevard has had difficulty organising its annual musical meetings (Tremplin and Boulevard). 2012 saw the cancellation of six major festivals for lack of money. There were editions of L'Boulevard from 2013 to 2015 and in 2017–2018. However, the Boultek venue has allowed young bands to rehearse and concerts have been organised regularly by young associations that have gradually taken over (Metall'Os and Block 10). Since 2014, new places have opened in Casablanca (L'Uzine in Aïn Sbaâ and Les Etoiles in Sidi Moumen) that provide theatre and dance classes and other activities, and where groups can rehearse.

Since the early 2000s, the new scene in Morocco has seemed livelier and more creative than in most other Arab countries. It certainly owes this to its artists and its activists, who gave themselves body and soul to make it come alive, but also to a pragmatic political choice which has allowed these bands to have a media presence that some see as over-inflated. So there has been some ambiguity and some contradictions, and these were highlighted in 2011. Apart from the singer Khansa Batma, the rapper Koman and the group Hoba Hoba Spirit, few well-known artists publicly gave support to the 'February 20' protest movement.[3] On the contrary, several icons of the new scene appeared on government video clips to encourage viewers to vote in support of King Mohammed VI in the referendum on the reform of the constitution. Many others in recent years have taken similar positions, using particularly patriotic songs or clips, especially around the cause of the Moroccan Sahara.

In early September 2011, a young rapper and supporter of the 'February 20' movement called L'Haqed (The Enraged) who came from the working-class neighbourhood of El Oulfa, was arrested on a false charge of assault. He remained in custody for four months, was released and then arrested again at the end of March 2012 and sentenced to one year in prison two months later for allegedly 'insulting a public official in the performance of his duties' on the basis of a video deemed offensive and posted anonymously on Facebook – a video he denied making. A support group was created and, via Facebook, it mobilised part of the French-speaking and Arabic-speaking press – *TelQuel*, *al-ahdath al-maghribiyya*, *akhbar al-yom*, *lakom.com*, etc. The website *mamfakinch.com*, born out of the 'February 20' movement, also spread the message. But the mobilisation bore little resemblance to that of 2003, and very few artists of the new scene publicly defended the rapper. He went on hunger strike to protest against the conditions in which he was being held; in December 2012 he received the 'Integrity Award' of the Transparency Morocco NGO. In 2015 after a concert in Europe, he fled to Belgium where he was granted political asylum and where he has been living since.

Even if the new scene still has an audience, it is far from being supported by any popular surge in interest, and there has been no response to the expectations once held in certain intellectual and journalistic circles. The idea of a *Nayda* movement has even been disputed by those who were most enthusiastic about it in the 2000s. The term itself seems stale, over-used in advertising and taken over by the ruling elites. Young artists, for their part, defend themselves, asserting that it is not their task to take clear political stances or join particular movements. For them, the very fact of trying to exist and to create as artists is already commitment enough. Although some new youth associations, such as Metall'Os for rock and Block 10 for rap, have tried to revive the earlier philosophy by combining concerts and debates in monthly meetings at the Boultek, many 'new artists' have abandoned any idea of social engagement and dream only of success.

Whether free or not, concerts by young Moroccan artists never attract as much audience as the Moroccan stars of popular music (*sha'abi*) that is played in festivals, such as Najat Atabou, Stati or Daoudi. The most popular 'youth' groups, such as Fnaire (from Marrakech), H-Kayne (Meknes) or Mazagan (El-Jadida), whose members are well into their thirties, drew the most from the Moroccan popular repertoire. The rockers at the origin of this supposed movement tend to stay on the fringes, but even so, have been partly co-opted by the system. It is hard to imagine anything more paradoxical and ironic than the sight of 'metal evenings' organised in Rabat in the hushed and chic surroundings of the Villa des Arts, which is run by the ONA Group (a holding company partly owned by the royal family), with a small audience of polite young people, mostly college students, trying to pogo in this sanitised venue where concerts obediently finish at 11 p.m.! Of all the forms of contemporary urban music, it is rock, especially in its metal and punk versions, that keeps its bad reputation and has the most difficulty becoming a 'native' genre that would enable it to have a better reception. In 2007 in an interview in the magazine *Volume!*, Amine Hamma, who started playing music ten years earlier at the age of sixteen, looked back:

> When we embraced the metal culture, we didn't approach it as Moroccans, but rather as young people. There is a certain rebellion that comes with adolescence, a way of wanting to be 'against everything', a refusal of all the obligations and 'correct' social behaviour to which we were subjected. Musically, it was very different from traditional Moroccan music, in terms of the instruments as well as the tunes. On the other hand, at the rhythmic level, metal music is comparable to folklore, and maybe even to the music of Gnawas or Issawa groups. […] In the end, the dark and occult side of metal is not so strange for us, even if musically we have only made a few connections between local music and what the media have offered us. Metal music doesn't speak to everyone but in this world anyone can become a fan of metal or can hate it, as they choose.

Notes

1. The FOL association decided to stand apart from L'Boulevard following the fourteen musicians' trial.
2. See the film *Casanayda!* (2007).
3. The 'February 20' movement was launched on Facebook following the Tunisian revolution of 2010–2011. Organising several marches in the cities of the kingdom throughout the winter and spring of 2011, its initiators urged the Moroccan people to follow in the wake traced by the Tunisians and the Egyptians to demand the democratisation of the Moroccan regime and more social justice and to denounce rampant corruption.

References

Boubia, Amina, 'Les nouvelles formes de production du politique dans le monde arabe à l'exemple des festivals de musique au Maroc: Culture et politique en contexte autoritaire', PhD thesis, Institut d'Etudes Politiques (IEP), Paris, 2014.

Casanayda! by Dominique Caubet, directed by Farida Benlyazid and Abderrahim Mettour, Sigma Technologies, Casablanca, 2007. Trailer: www.youtube.com/watch?v=ZhOFBKRH0M4

Caubet, Dominique, 'DIY in Morocco from the Mid 90s to 2015: Back to the Roots?', in Paula Guerra and Tânia Moreira, eds, *Keep It Simple, Make It Fast! An Approach to Underground Music Scenes (KISMIF, Volume 2)*, Facultade de Letra, Porto, 2016, pp. 249–256.

Caubet, Dominique, '"Nayda" and Its Venues in Morocco: Starting Underground and Going Public', in H. Hanru, T. Raspail and A. Damani, eds, *The Spectacle and the Everyday. 'Elsewhere', Biennale de Lyon 2009*, Les presses du réel, Dijon, 2009, pp. 221–228.

Caubet, Dominique and Amine Hamma, *Jil Lklam, les poètes urbains*, Senso Unico & Éditions du Sirocco, Casablanca, 2017.

Dima Punk (Once a Punk) by Dominique Caubet, Lardux Films, Pan Production and 2M TV, France-Maroc, 2019. Trailer: https://vimeo.com/331407336

Hamma, Amine, 'De l'Internationale-metal au conflit sociétal local: La scène de Casablanca', *Volume! La revue des musiques populaires*, 5, 2, 2007: pp. 153–178 (available at https://journals.openedition.org/volume/550).

Levine, Mark, *Heavy Metal Islam. Rock, Resistance and the Struggle for the Soul of Islam*, Three Rivers Press, New York, 2008.

Samie, Amale, 'Métal Intifada', *Maroc Hebdo*, 8 December 2000 (available at https://www.maghress.com/fr/marochebdo/44325).

Special Issue 'Avant nous les autres', *L'Kounache*, Le Boulevard, Casablanca, 2008.

38

Alexandrians in fusion

Trajectories of Egyptian musicians from alternative milieux to the revolution

Youssef El Chazli

Alexandria, 30 June 2012, 8 p.m.: on a narrow street in the central district of Mahatit El Raml, beneath the signs of two shoe shops whose owners pass the time sitting on the pavement listening to Farid el-Atrash, the Syrian-Egyptian star of the 1950s, stands a wide metal door on which someone has painted a young woman wearing a *keffiyeh* (Palestinian headscarf) and riding on a black swan. This unusual entrance hides from prying eyes a place that has become a centre of the 'alternative' art scene in Alexandria: El Cabina (The Cabin). It is alternative, firstly, because it breaks with the canons of mainstream culture (whether institutional or popular) of the 1990s, particularly with the Egyptian pop music that is known throughout the Arab world, and, secondly, because this space supports a whole way of life, ranging from clothing to hairstyles, from tastes in music and films to political opinions, from a relation to religiosity (rather than religion itself) to an original and constructed relationship to 'Alexandrianity'.

El Cabina is defined on its website as 'a new artistic space in Alexandria dedicated to experimentation [...] for young local artists, musicians and writers'. Financially and administratively, El Cabina depends on the Gudran (meaning 'walls') Association for Art and Development which manages different projects and similar spaces in the city and draws its funding from donations from international organisations (for example, the Ford Foundation or various cultural cooperation services of Western embassies).[1]

Once they pass through the metal door, happy throngs of young people jostle their way through the cigarette smoke and overwhelming humidity of Alexandrian summers. A passageway leads to stairs going down to the music venue, which also serves as a recording studio, set up in an underground room to insulate the noise. Upstairs, there is a small library. On that day, the narrow courtyard leading from one room to another has been rearranged. Spotlights have been placed high up, along with two large and brand-new speakers. A small stage is welcoming Khyam Allami, an Iraqi *oud* (lute) player, and Ayman Mabrouk, an Egyptian percussionist.

A few El Cabina regulars are sitting at the only table, shabby and rickety, near the entrance. Three *birams* (terracotta dishes traditionally used to bake rice) are overflowing with cigarette ends. High white walls dotted with photographs support a ceiling crisscrossed by long blue pipes. One metre away on a display stand, there are copies of the album *Resonance/Dissonance* by Khyam Allami, a large pile of the newspaper *al-'Assima 2 (Capital 2)*, and a few brochures listing upcoming cultural events at El Cabina. *Al-'Assima 2* is an independent newspaper that presents itself as the first independent Alexandrian weekly of 'popular journalism'. Its name (the second capital and not the second city) is in itself evocative of its stance towards the actual capital, Cairo. Its two double sheets contain many political articles, in a tone clearly 'revolutionary' and anti-militarist. On the second page, the cultural agenda lists the different activities of the week. In the following pages, 'national' news (in other words, from Cairo) remains absent. Readers will mostly find coverage of protest activities (sit-ins, demonstrations, strikes) in and around Alexandria. At the end of the newspaper, a history section narrates the stories of notable Alexandrians (in this issue, an actress of the 1940s and 1950s) or praises a particular place (here, the Sayed Darwish Theatre).

The concert begins. The music is not easy listening: the rhythmic constructions are complex and the pace slow. The audience listens attentively, without moving or dancing. Some people choose to stay near the front door to discuss the music. The audience is mixed, although there are more men than women. Many share similar styles: long hair, unkempt beards, hipster glasses, t-shirts with the logos of music bands, etc. A few young women can also be seen, conspicuously accompanied by their younger brothers. In a corner, dressed very soberly, a young man with the moustache-less beard of Salafis listens to the plaintive melodies of the *oud* with his eyes half-closed.

All these things add to the strangeness of the place. A few years ago it would have been unimaginable, as I remark to Karam, a musical all-rounder and one of the managers of El Cabina. He nods. The concert goes on and, shortly before the end, the young man tells me that the evening will certainly continue afterwards with a small group of friends: the people who run El Cabina, their entourage, the musicians and a few expats. Where will they go? There isn't really a lot of choice: most of the people at the concert meet almost every day, in the same few places. There is the Spit Fire, a little bar with an entrance hard to spot from the street; inside, the walls are plastered with memorabilia and posters from another age, along with beer mats and graffiti. And there are the Greek Clubs, in particular, the one which was seen by these groups as the most 'underground', and therefore the favourite, but which was demolished in the summer of 2012, as well as Al Tugareyya, a large café overlooking the Corniche, a popular place to drink tea or smoke shisha in an amazing interior that seems to have frozen back in the 1970s. Apart from these few places, all located in the city centre stretching from Mahatit El-Raml to Manshiyyeh, private flats are the favourite choice, offering privacy and freedom from social pressure.

A nearby flat belonging to one of the young men is eventually selected. This huge, two-storey flat opens onto a roof offering a magnificent view over the bay of Alexandria, with the Citadel of Qaitbay, built on the site of the famous Lighthouse, one of the Seven Wonders of the World, clearly visible. The size and location of the flat indicates the social status of its occupant. Cultural associations funded by international donations soon created a relatively lucrative niche for many artists and intellectuals who had been marginalised by official national institutions. Although it is quite typical of the city centre in its size and layout, the flat escapes the somewhat kitsch style of standard Egyptian interior design. Books, musical instruments, fabrics, paintings and photographs are spread all over the floors, walls and shelves in intentional disorder. The party goes on into the early hours, divided between musical jams (incredibly precise, complex and slow) and debates on all sorts of subjects.

These scenes are quite surprising to me. When I left Alexandria in 2005, this milieu, to which I belonged as a novice musician, simply did not exist. Not yet. Some local bands played covers of metal and hard rock and gave performances at the Library of Alexandria or at the end-of-year parties of some high schools (such as at St Mark's College in Alexandria). But no sense of belonging to a community or a political identity had ever emerged from those gatherings. The transformation I now witnessed could be felt most strongly in Alexandria, but it was visible elsewhere, notably in the capital, and beyond the paths of individuals it was dependent on more global social, economic and political transformations.

The 'Alexandrian revival'

It has been widely accepted in research on contemporary Egypt that the decade between 2000 and 2010 witnessed a number of 'openings', of which economic liberalisation (begun in the 1990s) and political liberalisation were representative. The decade was marked by certain key moments: constitutional reforms (2005), elections (2000, 2005, 2010), the proliferation of 'independent' media and the rise of protest movements. 2004 saw the spread of movements demanding the democratisation of the government such as Kifaya ('enough'), as well as widespread protests by workers, like the ones in the town of El Mahalla that started in 2006. The decade put an end to the lull of the 1990s.

In cultural circles, transformations were also felt. New institutions appeared and stirred the stagnant waters of artistic production. This was the case, for example, with the grand inauguration of the new Biblioteca Alexandrina (Library of Alexandria) in 2002, a mammoth project sponsored by UNESCO. The 'Bibalex' – as it was called – was one of the few places that provided high-quality halls for live performances, and a market for underground music rapidly grew up around it by organising various festivals, mainly in the summer. In the same way, the Al-Sawy Cultural Centre which opened in Cairo in 2003 quickly became a central landmark for new bands, before later becoming a relatively mainstream venue for cultural and intellectual entertainment.

These new places were rapidly taken over by more or less homogeneous social groups. Coming from the upper middle classes, the petite and grand bourgeoisie, they mainly represented an age group that had not known the major events that shaped the previous generation: the wars with Israel (or colonisation for those further in the past). Private language schools in the two main cities of the country, Cairo and Alexandria, followed by private universities and fee-paying sections of public universities, such as the French Department of legal studies in Cairo, were the privileged paths of these young people. While initially these places tended to be male-only, co-education gradually became more and more common, reaching a peak after the revolution of 2011.

A number of music groups emerged from these circles and took part in a variety of activities. They were particularly interested in Western music (metal, rock), and by the middle of the decade, some metal bands had acquired local reputations through their covers of songs by groups like Metallica or Megadeth. These bands slowly began to compose their own original music, immersed in the dark and angst-ridden worlds of metal (heavy, black, speed, death, etc.). Nonetheless, these mixes of genres remained fairly marginal in musical circles. There were very few connections with 'classical' musicians, especially professional musicians from less privileged social backgrounds who had mastered traditional genres of oriental music. The 'Western' music scene thus appeared as merely a passing hobby, of interest only to a fraction of the population, and consequently reproduced a class division where the equipment used (guitars, amplifiers, etc.) were bigger marks of distinction than the more traditional ones linked to the field of music as a whole (virtuosity, grasp of musical theory, technique, musical culture, etc.).

But with the proliferation of groups and festivals, a diversification of repertoires became apparent. It stemmed either from reflections by musicians on the meaning of their work or simply from a wish to stand out in this burgeoning microcosm. These imported musical genres were hybridised and merged. The archetype of all these experiments was the band Eftekasat, who created an impressive synthesis of jazz and oriental music in an album entitled 'Mouled Sidi el Latini'. And this trend was not only found in Egypt. It could be seen in various Arab countries and very often these musicians and groups formed transnational, interactive networks.

These new cultural dynamics were accompanied by a renewed interest in filmmaking in Alexandria. In fact, the city had never really disappeared from the screen: for the citizens of Cairo, it had always played the role of a seaside resort. But two films in particular, both made in 2010, focused on Alexandria itself, either to document its new energy or to distil the Alexandrian myth of underground magic. The first, *Messages of the Sea*, directed by filmmaker Daoud Abdel Sayed,[2] is an ode to an Alexandria in which the harshness of the world seems to dissipate in the face of the slowness and lightness of the city. The usual images of Alexandria (the sea, the fishermen, etc.) are mixed with a more subterranean and nocturnal city, that of bars and seedy cabarets. The other film, *Microphone*, the second feature film directed by Ahmad Abdallah, a young editor and filmmaker born in 1978, is even more striking. It tells the story of Khaled, an Alexandrian who returns home after many years in the United States. He discovers the city's new underground art scene and wants to set up a festival that would bring together the city's thirty or so underground music groups. The film has a central quality: apart from the leading roles and the main storyline, the film uses real musicians, real artists and real institutions. Thus, we can see Khaled trying to support the work of these alternative cultures through his work in the Gudran Foundation, to which El Cabina belongs.

The film *Microphone* was released in cinemas in the middle of January 2011, a time of great tension in Egypt. The parliamentary elections of November 2010 had been marred by ballot-rigging and an attack on a church in Alexandria had killed around twenty people. In the wake of the flight of the corrupt Tunisian President Ben Ali, many activists prepared protest actions for the day of 25 January, officially labelled 'Police Holiday', and renamed for the occasion 'Day of Anger'. 25 January arrived and, eighteen days later, President Mubarak resigned.

Karam: from the Lasallian Brothers to Guns N' Roses

During these eighteen days of revolution (25 January to 11 February 2011), the mobilisation of the Alexandrians is remarkable. The city is among the first places to witness deaths from state repression, but it is also one of the first places 'liberated' from police control on 28 January. Before midnight, almost every police station has been burnt down by demonstrators. The huge governorate building on Fouad Avenue is also reduced to ashes. On the following days, massive demonstrations are organised, as in Cairo, on Tuesday and Friday. On some days, there are almost as many demonstrators in Alexandria as in Cairo (while the population of Cairo is more than ten million greater). Several groups start a camp, like the one on Tahrir Square in Cairo, and are repeatedly attacked by armed men. In between these rampages, the atmosphere is almost festive. Slogans are chanted, people cheer, drums play, revolutionary songs are sung, but also, and especially, traditional Alexandrian songs.

Among the thousands of participants, a few dozen display an unusual look. These young people from artistic and cultural backgrounds (in their own words), with ponytails and all kinds of bracelets, are right in the heart of the uprising. Later on, especially on 11 and 12 February, they get together on the Corniche or in the very popular café Al Tugareyya to play mixtures of oriental and jazz music under the amused eyes of passers-by. Some of them have spent most of the eighteen days in the street, sometimes sleeping on the spot on a piece of cardboard. They have participated in the camp but also in the clashes with the police. Karam is one of them. Equipped with a semi-professional digital recorder, he has documented the events. As well as joining in himself, he has tried to keep an audio record of these tumultuous days; a record that he hopes he could later reuse in musical projects. His commitment is there, on the frontier between experiments in sound and political participation.

Karam is twenty-five years old. With a massive helmet protecting his head and neck, this long-haired Alexandrian attracts the half-amused, half-surprised gaze of his fellow citizens every time he crosses the city on his bike, trailing behind him a bandana attached to the bottom of his rucksack which flaps around every time he hits a pothole. His path is original in its radicalness but it is also shared by a number of inhabitants of the Alexandrian alternative galaxy.

Speaking out

Coming from a family of the petite bourgeoisie (his father is a computer engineer), he has spent his childhood in the well-to-do neighbourhood of Saba Pacha. His parents are well-educated, speak foreign languages and have travelled in Europe and elsewhere. Leisure activities have a significant place in a family which has a particular interest in music (his older sister took flute lessons at the conservatory for many years). This taste for music in general, and for the world of Western music of the 1960s and 1970s in particular, was passed on to Karam when he was still very young. Thus from infancy, he was exposed to the trippy harmonies of Pink Floyd and to the little bluesy riffs of Dire Straits, bands that were usually only discovered by most members of the alternative scene when they got immersed in music in their teens.

Karam was educated from preschool to the end of secondary school in the Collège Saint Mark in Alexandria, established by the Lasallian Brothers.[3] This is an all-boys school with a slight majority of Muslim students like him, although he himself had a Christian grandmother. The school's strong identity is cultivated through a number of rituals such as special annual events, pride in the institution's history, etc. Discipline is rigorous and the students have to wear school uniforms and ties. The school also offers all kinds of activities, from sports to theatre to scouting, as well as charitable or religious work. As a child, Karam played a bit of piano, which seemed to him a tedious obligation, and played basketball. Not very enthusiastic about these activities chosen by his family, he first joined the Marine Scouts (whose discipline was very strict and often violent), and then decided to join the Valiant Hearts, another group of scouts but more communal, social and playful. He was a team member of this group for some years before becoming head of the different 'legions', from the youngest to the oldest.

At the beginning of the 2000s, Karam sported all the looks of a good student, with short hair, glasses, sweaters and smart trousers. His musical tastes, however, were quite different from those of his classmates who usually alternated between Egyptian and Western pop. Among Karam's preferred tastes were the wild harmonies and nasal voice of Guns N' Roses whose enigmatic guitarist Slash, shirtless, with leather trousers and a top hat, amazed the teenager. At the end of 2003, he got an acoustic guitar and patiently began learning. Little by little, moving on from jam sessions in the dilapidated hall of St Mark's College to the new rehearsal studios that were then spreading in Alexandria, he began taking part in performances in the first places where it was possible to play in public, between 2005 and 2006. He took part in the first metal concert at Bibalex where eight young bands performed.

Alexandrians in fusion

Concerts multiplied, and as with emerging music scenes elsewhere, a microcosm began to take shape. This alternative scene soon found its favourite venues. First, there was the Shakespeare café in the upmarket Rushdy district or, for a very short time, the Crossroads on Fouad Avenue. This latter, a small café, attracted many people during its short existence, which lasted only a few months. Two amplifiers (bass and guitar), along with drums, were set up at the entrance. Photographs of the big names of American rock and grunge plastered the walls. The café's fridge was covered in graffiti by the regulars (including Karam), and customers could grab a drink from it as if they were at home. However, the experiment soon collapsed, because of a lack of finance, said some; because of pressure from the police, said others.

An anarchist spirit

Between 2005 and 2010, Karam dived into music as a way to withdraw and isolate himself from a social environment that he found too restrictive. A great fan of experimental music and progressive rock, he was interested in music theory and the foundations of jazz, as well as in guitar technique. By playing in several bands with different musical orientations, he began to mingle with musicians playing oriental classical music. It was undoubtedly his involvement in a band called Station that had the biggest impact on him. Station, which defined itself as an 'Alexandrian' band, brought together musicians from various backgrounds (traditional oriental music, rock and jazz) and this gave it a very distinctive fusion sound. The band's experimental and progressive tastes could also be seen in the concerts they arranged based on the model of the concept album. Each performance was one 'station', a distance travelled. The group also reinvented tradition through their inclusion of traditional elements, such as the participation of a whirling dervish at concerts, and covers of pieces by Sayyed Darwich (an Alexandrian singer and composer considered one of the fathers of Egyptian music) as well as compositions of *mawawil* (traditional songs).

Throughout this time, Karam conceived of music as a way of escaping. Withdrawing into his own community in the alternative microcosm allowed for a more emancipatory life, freed from the moral constraints of the surrounding. Although he believed that music should play a role and reach a wider public, he was largely uninterested in politics in the strict sense.

It was in April 2008 that Karam first took part in a collective action defined by its organisers as 'political'. He joined an online event, launched by Cairo activists, calling for a day of anger throughout Egypt in solidarity with a workers' strike in the city of Mahalla planned for 6 April. He joined the rally with friends but had to quickly leave in the face of police intimidation. He did not take part in mobilisations again until June 2010, when Alexandria and the rest of the country saw a wave of protests in response to the murder in custody of a young Alexandrian by two non-commissioned officers. This case prompted the creation of the famous Facebook page 'We Are All Khaled Said', named after this 'police martyr'. Early in 2011, after returning from a trip with his band at the oasis of Siwa, Karam took to the streets again following the bomb attack on the Coptic Church of the Two Saints in a popular area of Alexandria. He rushed to a printer and made some t-shirts with motifs of national unity – a (Christian) cross and a (Muslim) crescent – under which the inscription 'mourning' was printed in English. He attended all the actions of solidarity with the victims in the days that followed, always wearing this t-shirt. A few weeks later, on Tuesday 25 January 2011 (now known as the first day of the Egyptian Revolution), like many other Alexandrians he made his way to join the protests at the Ibrahim Mosque in the city centre. Immersed in this collective experience, after his relatively solitary and confined path until then, something awoke in him. He had been dazzled by the power of the uprising and ever since that day he joined in all the protests.

In the wake of the revolution, alternative art circles in Alexandria expanded rapidly even though they were still a relatively isolated microcosm. On New Year's Eve, 31 December 2012, between 150 and 200 people gathered at El Cabina. Barely thirty people had turned up at the same event the year before. The existence of so many artists who took part in revolutionary activities, as well as revolutionaries who took part in art, helped to build bridges between the worlds of alternative art and radical politics. At the same time, revolutionary themes could easily be found in artworks along with a will to break religious or political taboos.

The political positions of these circles went from the centre to the far left, which included communists, Trotskyists and libertarians. It was notable that more and more people in the current climate identified themselves in opposition to Islamist currents. This tendency could be seen in the trajectory of Karam, and that of many others, who expressed an antireligious view of society and a strong interest in the libertarian and anarchist philosophical galaxy. In his music too, Karam, by going beyond the usual forms of commercial music, by exploring music theory and experimenting with sound, sought to break away from musical dogma and create a genuinely revolutionary sound, in other words, one that rejected the established order.

Post-script

In 2021, little remains of the people, spaces and events described here. El Cabina closed in 2016, many of the artists and cultural workers chose to move to Cairo or leave Egypt altogether, and the general effervescence of post-revolutionary years appears as a distant memory. Karam exemplifies that trend, as he has moved to Europe to pursue his artistic career and doesn't engage in politics anymore. The global crackdown on political spaces since 2013 has also been visible in cultural and artistic spheres. Access to foreign funding has become scarce and security agencies monitor closely all forms of public activities. Nevertheless, the invisible afterlives of this effervescent moment are many. Youths who hung out in these milieux have reinvented new spaces, notably on social media, and have explored new artistic and political avenues. While they may not be as visible, nothing tells us they aren't there.

Notes

1 While Gudran remains relatively independent, its dependence on foreign funding highlights two trends: on the one hand, a professionalisation in the relationship with international donors, visible in the use of English as the language of communication and the incorporation, conscious or not, of specific norms making interactions with international partners easier; on the other hand, the existence of a political resistance displayed by some art groups who refuse to accept money coming from abroad (and especially from 'the West') and thus positioning themselves in a dual situation of radical criticism and meagre material resources. This observation holds true for many of the cases considered throughout this book.
2 Born in 1946, Daoud Abdel Sayed is the godfather of the whole new generation of independent cinema and a leader of New Realism, known for his films dissecting the social problems of Egyptians, such as *El Kit Kat* (1992).
3 The Catholic establishment belongs to the lineage of St Jean-Baptiste de La Salle who founded a religious institute for the education of children in Reims (France) in the seventeenth century.

References

Abdallah, Ahmad, *Microphone* (film), Rotana Cinema, 2010.
Battesti, Vincent and François Ireton, eds, *L'Égypte au présent. Inventaire d'une société avant révolution*, Sindbad, Paris, 2011.
El Chazli, Youssef and Chayma Hassabo, 'Socio-histoire d'un processus révolutionnaire. Analyse de la "configuration contestataire" égyptienne (2003–2011)', in Amin Allal and Thomas Pierret, eds, *Au cœur des révoltes arabes. Devenir révolutionnaires*, Armand Colin, Recherches, Paris, 2013.
Ilbert, Robert and Ilios Yannakakis, *Alexandrie 1860–1960*, Autrement, Paris, 1992.
Mini Mobile Concerts, Ramez Ashraf: http://minimobileconcert.tumblr.com

Index

Abu Dhabi 43–52
Aden 78, 84, 87, 301, 306
alcohol 28, 94, 112–120, 152, 211, 232, 250, 290
Aleppo 70, 74–75, 277
Alexandria 2, 194–195, 336–345
Algeria 5, 12, 33–42, 101, 103, 121–127, 214–215, 217–226
Algiers 33–34, 217–226
Allouache, M. 36
Arab Spring 2, 8, 77, 91, 201, 289, 293, 303, 315
armed conflict 3, 81, 211, 278, 289–292
army 6, 128, 243, 294, 303
arts
 visual 300–307, 308–318

Baghdad 3, 128–132
Bahrain 293–299
Bedouin 23–24, 28–29, 145
Beirut 112–120, 180–188, 212, 228, 235, 319
Ben Mhenni, L. 1, 268
Bennani-Chraïbi, M. 7
Bey, M. 35, 37
bookshops 81, 112, 128–132, 172
boredom 6, 8, 24, 35–38, 97, 104, 234, 308
Bouazizi, M. 1, 248–249, 274, 315
Bourdieu, P. xv, 9, 122, 213
buyat 57–66

Cairo 3, 63, 101, 103, 170–179, 195, 198–207
car (vehicle) 22–32, 36, 40, 43–45, 48, 99, 125, 131, 137, 214, 234

Casablanca 151, 157, 323–335
Christianity 3, 133, 137, 170–179, 344
cinema 23, 36, 132, 159, 173, 217, 271, 276, 315, 340, 345
coffee shop 43–52, 139–149, 289–292
consumerism 9, 64, 112, 115, 236, 293

Dakhla 150–159
Damascus 238, 277, 279, 280, 283
dance 9, 187, 239, 257, 332
 dabke 160–169
Davis, M. 28
Debray, R. xv
drugs 23, 28, 37, 40, 153, 208–211, 319
Dubai 277, 310

education 10
 primary and secondary school 23–25, 35, 50, 54, 88, 110, 122, 125–126, 164, 180–189, 217, 250, 325
 religious 122, 172
 university 43–47, 57–60, 68, 71–74, 78–81, 94, 103, 113, 134, 144, 195, 209, 238, 248, 263, 280, 300, 303, 308, 310
Egypt 10, 55, 104, 165, 170–179, 194–195, 198–207, 276, 323, 336–345
Europe 212–216, 244, 254, 308, 333, 342, 345
expatriates
 in the Gulf 45, 49–50, 78, 84, 212

family 133–138, 150–159, 171, 182, 191, 195, 212–216
fashion 10, 26, 51, 64–66, 112, 214, 229, 236, 240, 293, 329

Index

Fellag 33–34
fertility 4

Gafsa 88–92
Gaza 93, 99, 142, 147, 162, 196, 313, 315, 319
gender xv, 5, 8, 20–21, 36, 44, 47, 50–51, 57–66, 91–92, 143, 161, 163, 200, 250–261
Ghonim, W. 1

Haifa 139–149
harassment
  sexual 192, 199–200, 204
harraga 33, 36, 38, 40
Hezbollah 115, 116, 180–189, 281
hittist 33–42
homosexuality 23, 29, 61, 116, 142, 192

Internet
  arabizi 19, 266, 287
  mobilisation 266–275, 276–285
  social media 51, 53–56, 58, 131, 173, 210, 227, 232, 267, 271, 274, 277, 279, 285–288
Iraq 6, 10, 70, 77, 128–132, 171, 238, 337
Islam 3, 7, 9, 11, 31, 37, 63, 68–72, 83, 98, 128, 180–189, 243, 285
Islamism xv, 24, 37, 68, 81, 84, 217–219, 241, 242, 244, 263, 278, 298, 327–328, 344
Israel 4, 99, 103, 116–117, 139–149, 165, 185, 309, 311, 313, 315, 318, 339
Istanbul 2, 310

Jeddah 25, 26, 27
Jerusalem 94, 160, 165, 184, 309–310, 318, 321
Jordan 55, 103, 133–138, 161, 165, 166, 171, 235–241, 318
joyriding 22–32
Judaism 4, 139–141

Kabylia 122–125, 242–249
Karman, T. 1
kasra 28–29
al-Khatib, H. 2
Kuwait 57, 59, 63, 78, 214, 215, 309

Lebanon 45, 53–56, 112–120, 180–189, 227–234, 315, 318, 321
left movements 84, 87, 89, 98, 113, 116–119, 131, 134, 218, 263, 344

Libya 247, 289–292
literature 5, 70, 117, 123, 130, 174

al-Mahdi, A. M. 1
Manama 213, 293–299
marriage 5–6, 38, 46, 48, 61, 121, 137, 153, 195, 239, 247, 251, 255, 257, 314
martial arts 126, 198–207, 239
Mauss, M. 93
migration 3, 154–157, 227, 230, 233, 235, 244
Morocco 41, 73, 150–152, 154–155, 250–261, 323–335
music 115, 182, 217, 222, 251, 276, 283, 318
  rap 318–322
  religious 73, 170–179
  rock 323–335, 336–345
  traditional 160, 334, 339, 341
Muslim Brotherhood 23, 26, 67, 71, 75, 80, 81, 104, 116, 293–299

Oman 14, 195
Oran 40, 243

Palestine 155, 93–100, 305, 308–317
  diaspora 230, 313, 318
  identity 139–149, 160–169, 318–323
  Ramallah 93, 143, 160, 309–312, 321
  refugees 160–161, 227–234
poetry 29, 117, 123, 130–131, 168, 302, 321
police 24, 26, 28, 88, 119, 131, 139, 144, 151, 244, 272, 279, 291, 295, 305, 328, 340–341, 344
political mobilisations 8, 12, 88, 100, 113, 118, 293–299, 300, 328, 336–346
privacy 47, 157, 163, 191, 194–197
Putnam, R. 208, 210

qat 208–211
Qatar 4, 95, 101, 195, 282

radio 40, 162, 223, 329
Ramallah 93, 95, 99, 142, 160–169, 309–316, 321
Riyadh 20, 22–32, 57–66, 87

Said, K. 171, 344
Salafism 19, 23, 38, 74, 77–87, 110, 296, 337
Sana'a 211, 300, 302

Index

Saudi Arabia 5, 22–32, 53, 57–66, 72, 78, 82, 101, 191, 195, 285–288, 294, 302
Sayad, A. 122
Scott, J. C. 263
scouting 10, 144, 181, 186, 342
sexuality 54, 60, 90, 112, 152, 250–261
Sidi Bouzid 1, 273, 315
sports 8, 82, 94, 101, 125, 219, 239, 342
    football 7, 57, 64, 83, 86, 20, 93–100, 101–106, 125–126, 153, 157, 165, 220, 228, 236, 290–291
    kite-surfing 152
    self-defence
    see also martial arts
subculture 21, 36, 44, 58, 82–87
Sufism 67–76, 85
suicide 38, 41, 192, 242–249, 328
Syria 2, 47, 56, 67–76, 117, 162, 214, 229, 231, 235, 241, 276–284, 313, 315

tafhit see joyriding
Tangier 250–259, 331
taranim see music, religious
telephone 48, 53, 56, 102, 196, 227, 232, 237, 312

television 36, 46, 53–56, 59, 83, 101–106, 135, 137, 152, 155, 160, 163, 173, 177, 182, 184, 210, 228, 239, 254, 276, 278, 286, 291, 304, 324, 329
theatre 112, 141, 180–188, 200, 206, 225, 332
Thompson, E. P. 28
tourism xiv, 9, 48, 141, 154, 213, 233, 291
tribes 4, 23, 29, 121, 124, 133, 135, 150
Tunis 101, 266–275
Tunisia 10, 88–92, 248, 264, 266–275, 323

unemployment 5, 6, 24, 34–35, 89, 110, 154, 166, 209, 217, 248–249, 295
United States 6, 31, 59, 110, 128, 184, 208, 212, 233, 240, 285, 320, 324, 340

violence xv, 35, 77, 79, 92, 95, 125, 128, 140, 148, 177, 199, 219, 234, 242, 278, 308

Western Sahara 150–159
working class 92, 217–221, 231, 235, 240, 251, 254, 325–326, 330, 333

Yemen 3, 4, 10, 77–87, 208–221, 300–307

Milton Keynes UK
Ingram Content Group UK Ltd.
UKHW011305010324
438760UK00005B/40